AF753545

Studies in Development Economics and Policy
General Editor: **Anthony Shorrocks**

UNU WORLD INSTITUTE FOR DEVELOPMENT ECONOMICS RESEARCH (UNU-WIDER) was established by the United Nations University as its first research and training centre and started work in Helsinki, Finland, in 1985. The purpose of the Institute is to undertake applied research and policy analysis on structural changes affecting the developing and transitional economies, to provide a forum for the advocacy of policies leading to robust, equitable and environmentally sustainable growth, and to promote capacity strengthening and training in the field of economic and social policy-making. Its work is carried out by staff researchers and visiting scholars in Helsinki and through networks of collaborating scholars and institutions around the world.

UNU World Institute for Development Economics Research (UNU-WIDER), Katajanokanlaituri 6B, FIN-00160 Helsinki, Finland

Titles include:

Tony Addison, Henrik Hansen and Finn Tarp *(editors)*
DEBT RELIEF FOR POOR COUNTRIES

Tony Addison and Alan Roe *(editors)*
FISCAL POLICY FOR DEVELOPMENT
Poverty, Reconstruction and Growth

George G. Borjas and Jeff Crisp *(editors)*
POVERTY, INTERNATIONAL MIGRATION AND ASYLUM

Ricardo Ffrench-Davis and Stephany Griffith-Jones *(editors)*
FROM CAPITAL SURGES TO DROUGHT
Seeking Stability for Emerging Economies

David Fielding *(editor)*
MACROECONOMIC POLICY IN THE FRANC ZONE

Basudeb Guha-Khasnobis *(editor)*
THE WTO, DEVELOPING COUNTRIES AND THE DOHA DEVELOPMENT AGENDA
Prospects and Challenges for Trade-led Growth

Basudeb Guha-Khasnobis, Shabd S. Acharya and Benjamin Davis *(editors)*
FOOD INSECURITY, VULNERABILITY AND HUMAN RIGHTS FAILURE

Basudeb Guha-Khasnobis and Ravi Kanbur *(editors)*
INFORMAL LABOUR MARKETS AND DEVELOPMENT

Aiguo Lu and Manuel F. Montes *(editors)*
POVERTY, INCOME DISTRIBUTION AND WELL-BEING IN ASIA DURING THE TRANSITION

George Mavrotas and Anthony Shorrocks *(editors)*
ADVANCING DEVELOPMENT
Core Themes in Global Economics

Mark McGillivray *(editor)*
HUMAN WELL-BEING
Concept and Measurement

Mark McGillivray *(editor)*
INEQUALITY, POVERTY AND WELL-BEING

Robert J. McIntyre and Bruno Dallago *(editors)*
SMALL AND MEDIUM ENTERPRISES IN TRANSITIONAL ECONOMIES

Vladimir Mikhalev *(editor)*
INEQUALITY AND SOCIAL STRUCTURE DURING THE TRANSITION

E. Wayne Nafziger and Raimo Väyrynen *(editors)*
THE PREVENTION OF HUMANITARIAN EMERGENCIES

Machiko Nissanke and Erik Thorbecke *(editors)*
THE IMPACT OF GLOBALIZATION ON THE WORLD'S POOR
Transmission Mechanisms

Matthew Odedokun *(editor)*
EXTERNAL FINANCE FOR PRIVATE SECTOR DEVELOPMENT
Appraisals and Issues

Laixiang Sun *(editor)*
OWNERSHIP AND GOVERNANCE OF ENTERPRISES
Recent Innovative Developments

Guanghua Wan *(editor)*
UNDERSTANDING INEQUALITY AND POVERTY IN CHINA
Methods and Applications

UNU-WIDER *(editors)*
WIDER PERSPECTIVES ON GLOBAL DEVELOPMENT

Studies in Development Economics and Policy Series Standing Order
ISBN 978-0-333-96424-8 (hardback)
ISBN 978-0-230-20041-8 (paperback)

(*outside North America only*)

You can receive future titles in this series as they are published by placing a standing order. Please contact your bookseller or, in case of difficulty, write to us at the address below with your name and address, the title of the series and the ISBN quoted above.

Customer Services Department, Macmillan Distribution Ltd, Houndmills, Basingstoke, Hampshire RG21 6XS, England

---

Understanding Inequality and Poverty in China

Methods and Applications

Edited by

Guanghua Wan

palgrave
macmillan

in association with the World Institute for Development Economics Research of the United Nations University (UNU-WIDER)

© United Nations University 2008

All rights reserved. No reproduction, copy or transmission of this publication may be made without written permission.

No paragraph of this publication may be reproduced, copied or transmitted save with written permission or in accordance with the provisions of the Copyright, Designs and Patents Act 1988, or under the terms of any licence permitting limited copying issued by the Copyright Licensing Agency, 90 Tottenham Court Road, London W1T 4LP.

Any person who does any unauthorized act in relation to this publication may be liable to criminal prosecution and civil claims for damages.

The authors have asserted their rights to be identified as the authors of this work in accordance with the Copyright, Designs and Patents Act 1988.

First published 2008 by
PALGRAVE MACMILLAN
Houndmills, Basingstoke, Hampshire RG21 6XS and
175 Fifth Avenue, New York, N.Y. 10010
Companies and representatives throughout the world

PALGRAVE MACMILLAN is the global academic imprint of the Palgrave Macmillan division of St. Martin's Press, LLC and of Palgrave Macmillan Ltd. Macmillan® is a registered trademark in the United States, United Kingdom and other countries. Palgrave is a registered trademark in the European Union and other countries.

ISBN-13: 978-0-230-53804-7
ISBN-10: 0-230-53804-5

This book is printed on paper suitable for recycling and made from fully managed and sustained forest sources. Logging, pulping and manufacturing processes are expected to conform to the environmental regulations of the country of origin.

A catalogue record for this book is available from the British Library.

A catalog record for this book is available from the Library of Congress.

10 9 8 7 6 5 4 3 2 1
17 16 15 14 13 12 11 10 09 08

Printed and bound in Great Britain by CPI Antony Rowe,
Chippenham and Eastbourne

Contents

List of Figures

List of Tables

Preface

Introduction

The issues regarding inequality and poverty in China are of concern not only to stakeholders inside China, but also to other national governments and international organizations. On one hand, accurate assessment of poverty and inequality trends and patterns in the most populous country on earth is central to understanding changes in worldwide inequality and poverty; however, this assessment alters significantly dependent on whether China is included or excluded. In the same context, China's future performance is crucial to the achievement of the Millennium Development Goals of the United Nations at the global level. On the other hand, policy makers in China are increasingly concerned about the regional divide and the urban–rural gap, which could undermine social and political stability, and adversely affect long-term economic growth in China. As a matter of fact, rising inequality and emerging poverty have contributed to sluggish domestic demand and over-production, generating pressures on China's exports and causing many trade-related disputes. As a consequence, the Chinese government has recently launched a nationwide campaign – Building a Harmonious Society – targeting deteriorating income distribution and poverty, particularly the regional income disparities and the urban–rural gap.

Since the 1980s, the coastal areas have experienced phenomenal growth while the inland has lagged behind. Meanwhile, the urban biases that existed before the reform era seem to have become more serious. Interpersonal inequality has risen as well, largely driven by growing returns to skills and education. Earlier research on poverty in China is sketchy, and that on inequality is mostly focused on the measurement of regional inequality. This has been followed by inequality decompositions, aiming at gauging the broad compositions of regional inequality. More recently, attention has turned to analyzing inequality at the disaggregated levels of counties, villages, households – and even individuals. These research efforts, aided by the wider availability of household survey data, certainly help enrich our understanding of poverty and the increasing trend in inequality in China. However, there continues to be a lack of analytical work on sources or causes, consequences and policy measures regarding inequality and poverty in China. Speculations are abundant; many attribute the rising inequality to globalization, policy biases, decentralization and different endowments of geographical or other resources. However, few of these assertions have been substantiated by empirical evidence. Certainly, little is known about the relative importance of these potentially relevant contributing factors.

It is against this background that in 2004 the World Institute for Development Economics Research of the United Nations University (UNU-WIDER) launched the project on Poverty and Inequality in China. The project, directed by myself, aims at providing a more complete account of the inequality and poverty issues in China, including measurement, causes, consequences and policy implications. Two international conferences were held under the auspices of this project: one in Beijing in April 2005 (co-hosted by the Institute of Population and Labour Economics, Chinese Academy of Social Sciences) and the other at UNU-WIDER in Helsinki in August 2005. Some 40 papers written in English were selected from over 300 submissions and were presented at these conferences. This volume is part of the research outcomes arising from the two-year UNU-WIDER project.

The Outline to 'Understanding Inequality and Poverty in China'

This volume begins with a chapter by Wan, Lu and Chen, focusing on sources of regional inequality in China. Since traditional decomposition techniques cannot incorporate control variables, the corresponding research results are usually contaminated. For example, not all income gaps between city and country residents are due to the urban–rural divide in China; there are differences in human capital and other characteristics between these two population subgroups. Similarly, regional inequality is determined by a number of variables in addition to location. Consequently, Wan, Lu and Chen develop a new regression-based inequality decomposition methodology and then provide a complete accounting of China's regional inequality for the period 1987–2001, with a special emphasis on the contribution of globalization. A striking finding is that globalization, as represented by trade and FDI variables, is one of the most influential factors causing fast rises in regional inequality in China. Uneven distributions of domestic capital, FDI and trade account for almost 50 per cent of the total regional inequality. These findings imply a need for the development of sound financial systems, particularly capital markets, in rural China. The authors also appeal for policy initiatives to bring more benefits of globalization to the interior regions. In passing, it is noted that the role of location is found to have declined over time.

While the first chapter focuses on inter-province disparities, the other dimension of spatial inequality – the urban–rural gap – is taken up by Sicular, Yue, Gustafsson and Li in Chapter 2. Their major contributions include a better measure of income, consideration of migrants and empirically decomposing the urban–rural gaps using a modified Oaxaca –Blinder framework. By including housing-related income and employing better regional price deflators, they find that the urban–rural gap makes a smaller contribution to overall regional inequality. As expected, the incorporation of the migrant population leads to a narrower urban–rural gap. Regarding components of the urban–rural gap, they find that differences in the endowments of household characteristics comprise approximately half of the gap, with the remaining half being due to differences in the returns to these endowments. The contribution of location is found to have declined from 1995 to 2002, which accords well with the finding of Chapter 1.

Over 60 per cent of China's population resides in the rural areas and inequality across rural regions is more severe than the urban counterpart. It is in this context that the subsequent two chapters on regional inequality in rural China take on significance. The contribution by Liang explores the relationship between financial development and inequality in rural China. Alternative theories concerning the finance–inequality nexus are examined using provincial data over the period 1991–2000 and by applying the generalized method of moment (GMM) estimation technique. The chapter concludes with a negative and linear relationship, implying that financial development had led to reductions in income inequality in post-reform rural China. Therefore, one way to abate inequality in rural China is to strengthen the rural financial systems. Interestingly, the same policy recommendation is reached in Chapter 4 by Wan, who uncovered the fact that physical capital represents the second largest contributor, next to location, to regional inequality in rural China. Unlike location, however, the contribution of capital had been on the rise since the mid-1980s. Accordingly, Wan appeals for more attention to be given to capital accumulation at the household level in the poor regions, although infrastructure investment in inland regions seems necessary as well. Capital accumulation requires development of formal financial markets and access to credit for poor households in rural China. Another finding by Wan is that schooling or human capital has been gaining importance as a determinant of regional inequality.

On the subject of human capital, Chapter 5 by Xing attempts to explain how education exerts impact on inequality. Specifically, he examines the differences in the endowments of human capital and in returns to education among private, state-owned and collective-owned enterprises. Consistent with other research results, Xing finds that returns to education in China have increased over time, particularly in the private sector. On the other hand, the education level is the highest in state-owned enterprises, followed by the large collective-owned enterprises, although their wages are low compared to the private counterparts. Clearly, job security and, perhaps, social status associated with different ownerships are important in determining job choices. In terms of the urban–rural divide, education levels are higher in the urban areas in all sectors, except for the small collective-owned enterprises. However, returns to education do not differ significantly between urban and rural China.

While Xing focuses on education, the chapter by Li and Zhu addresses the other major component of human capital: health. Rather than analyzing health inequality or determinants of health, Chapter 6 assesses the impacts of rising income inequality on health in China. It is noted that little has appeared in the literature, which investigates the various consequences of high inequality. This is rather surprising given the many publicized media reports of incidences that are not unrelated to inequality; such as graduate or school prostitutes working on a part-time basis, murder cases out of envy in schools and universities, and emerging migrant crimes in cities. Using a fairly large dataset, Li and Zhu find that – irrespective of health indicators used, self-reported status, or physical measures – inequality at the local level is found to exert a detrimental impact on individual health in China. Interestingly, inequality is found to contribute to smoking and drinking, which not only affects the health of individuals but may also lead to socioeconomic problems at the family or community level. Another finding is that income is positively related to health. Since health is a component of human capital, such a finding is indicative of the simultaneous relationship between health and income and income inequality.

Given the rising inequality and its serious consequences, what can be done? One of the major policy tools is the social welfare system. Since the late 1980s, China's welfare reforms were directly aimed at reducing the social benefits of those employed in public institutions, state-owned or collective-owned enterprises. In Chapter 7, Gao provides empirical evidence on the determinants of these benefits and their impact on income inequality in urban China. It is demonstrated that total urban social benefits were targeted at the bottom income deciles in both 1988 and 2002. The top income decile in 1988 also gained, mainly from housing benefits. Cash transfers were negatively associated with pre-tax pre-transfer income distribution in both years, while important in-kind benefits – namely, health and food in 1988 and education in 2002 – were positively related to pre-tax pre-transfer income. In terms of population groups, the elderly and the educated gained more, while larger households gained little from the provision of social benefits. The working poor (the near-bottom income groups) have not only fared poorly in market competition but have also been left behind with respect to social benefits. Residents in the central and western regions received less social benefits of all types than those in the eastern regions. Overall, Gao shows that social benefits played a significant role in reducing income inequality in urban China as social benefits, particularly cash transfers, were targeted more towards the bottom segments of the income distribution in 2002 than in 1988. However, these were not sufficient to close the rising income gaps driven by other forces. As a result, post-transfer post-tax income inequality was still greater in 2002 than in 1988.

The last two chapters deal with the issue of poverty in China. Meng, Gregory and Wan explore the role of regional inequality in affecting urban poverty and poverty determinants during the 1986–2000 period. They decompose the difference in the probability of being poor over time and attribute the difference to three sets of factors: the demographic structure of households, human capital stock and regional effects. As expected, large families or families with few members in the labour force suffered greater increases in poverty. Better educated households are less inclined to fall below the poverty line and, everything else remaining the same, households in less affluent regions are more likely to be poor. These findings corroborate well with those of the preceding chapter by Gao.

Zhang and Wan, in the final chapter, propose a new poverty decomposition framework under which a change in poverty can be attributed to two components. The so-called pro-poor growth component is a weighted average of the absolute income changes of the originally poor: income changes of the initially non-poor do not affect this component. Therefore, it represents the absolute gains to the poor. On the other hand, the downward mobility component measures changes in the income ranking positions of those who are poor in the terminal period. It reflects changes in the composition of the poor over time and is always non-negative. This component will be nil if, and only if, all of the initially non-poor stay out of poverty and no changes occur to the ranking positions of the initially poor in the terminal period. Applied to a Chinese dataset, the empirical results indicate that the rise in intensity of urban poverty in 1988–92 is attributable to adverse distributional changes, which in turn are caused by negative income growth and large downward mobility among the poorest urban residents. Conversely, the sustained decline in the intensity of rural poverty is primarily a result of income growth that has a pro-poor pattern.

Some caveats

There are a number of issues that deserve particular mention. First, given the size of China's territory, it is almost inevitable that price levels differ across locations. This requires deflation of observations measured in monetary terms. Most chapters in this book use such deflated data. Others do not, either due to unavailability of deflators or because it deemed unnecessary. Second, discrepancies exist in grouping provinces into regional belts. This arises from the absence of unified official classification. The provinces in question involve Guangxi and Inner Mongolia. Guangxi is a coastal region, thus some studies classify Guangxi as being in eastern China. However, it is located along the south rather than the east coast and is a relatively poor region. As a consequence, some researchers place Guangxi into the central or even western belt. By the similar token, Inner Mongolia is often classified as being in the western belt due to its low per capita income, while others treat it as a central region because it is located in central China. Finally, the large amount of internal migration poses a problem for poverty and inequality research. While Chapter 2 in this book takes migration into consideration, this proves impossible for other research as relevant data are not available.

The above caveats are certainly worth future research efforts. Nevertheless, their presence is unlikely to change the major findings, conclusions or policy implications contained in this book.

GUANGHUA WAN
Senior Research Fellow and Project Director
UNU-WIDER

Acknowledgements

In March 2007, the *Review of Income and Wealth* (series 53, number 1) comprised a special issue on 'Inequality and Poverty in China', and included the original versions of three chapters from this volume: Chapter 1, 'Globalization and Regional Inequality in China: Evidence from within China', by Guanghua Wan, Ming Lu and Zhao Chen; Chapter 2, 'The Urban–Rural Gap and Income Inequality in China', by Terry Sicular, Yue Ximing, Björn Gustafsson and Shi Li; and Chapter 8, 'China Urban Poverty and its Contributing Factors, 1986–2000', by Xin Meng, Robert Gregory and Guanghua Wan). UNU-WIDER and the authors kindly acknowledge the *Review of Income and Wealth*, the International Association for Research in Income and Wealth, and Blackwell Publishing for permission to include revised versions (in light of this volume's referees' comments) of these papers.

Chapter 6 is a revised version of the paper that was published in the *Journal of Comparative Economics* ('Income, Income Inequality, and Health: Evidence from China', by Hongbin Li and Yi Zhu, volume 34, number 4, December 2006: 668–93), symposium articles on 'Analysing the Socioeconomic Consequences of Rising Inequality in China', guest edited by Guanghua Wan and Xiaobo Zhang. UNU-WIDER and the authors kindly acknowledge the *Journal of Comparative Economics*, the Association of Comparative Economic Studies and Elsevier Inc.

Special thanks are due to John Bonin, Bart van Ark and Stephan Klasen for their ongoing support of research from UNU-WIDER and facilitating its publication.

Guanghua Wan thanks several anonymous referees for their detailed and timely reports, which were invaluable in shaping the book. Adam Swallow, Lorraine Telfer-Taivainen and Barbara Fagerman of UNU-WIDER provided assistance and support, for which the editor is grateful. Special acknowledgement is made to Janis Vehmaan-Kreula of UNU-WIDER who, as Project Assistant, provided tremendous help in running the China project.

UNU-WIDER gratefully acknowledges the financial contributions to the research programme by the governments of Denmark (Royal Ministry of Foreign Affairs), Finland (Ministry for Foreign Affairs), Norway (Royal Ministry of Foreign Affairs), Sweden (Swedish International Development Cooperation Agency – Sida) and the United Kingdom (Department for International Development – DfID).

Notes on Contributors

Zhao Chen is Associate Professor of Economics at the China Centre for Economic Studies (CCES), Fudan University, China, and Director of the Fudan Institute for Industrial Development Studies. He holds a PhD in Economics from Fudan University. His research interests include: urban and rural development, economic transition, and economics of information and organization. He also has co-authored publications on regional development and income distribution.

Qin Gao is Assistant Professor at Fordham University Graduate School of Social Service. Gao holds a PhD in Social Policy and Policy Analysis from Columbia University. Gao's research examines social policy trends, structures, outcomes for families, and impacts on poverty and inequality in China and the United States.

Robert Gregory is Professor Emeritus in the Research School of Social Sciences at the Australian National University. He has an interest in labour markets in China but primarily writes on Australian labour markets and policy. His current major project focuses on the rapid growth of the welfare state in Australia, with a particular emphasis on women with dependent children.

Björn Gustafsson is Professor in the Department of Social Work at Göteborg University. His research covers empirical studies on poverty, social assistance, the distribution of economic wellbeing, and the welfare state, as well as the economics of immigration. Since the mid-1990s, one of his research interests has been poverty and the distribution of income in China.

Hongbin Li is Associate Professor in the Department of Economics at the Chinese University of Hong Kong. Li received a PhD in economics from Stanford University in 2001. Li's research interests include labour, development, economic transition and the Chinese economy.

Shi Li is a Professor of Economics at the School of Economics and Business, and Director of the Center for Income Inequality and Poverty Studies at Beijing Normal University; he is also Professor of Economics at the Graduate School of the Chinese Academy of Social Sciences. His current studies focus on income and wealth distribution, poverty, wage inequality, unemployment and re-employment, migration and the returns to education in China. He has published widely in scholarly journals.

Zhicheng Liang is a PhD candidate at CERDI, CNRS, University of Auvergne (Université d'Auvergne), France. His major research fields include: market-oriented reforms in transitional countries, sources of economic growth, income distribution, finance and monetary economics, decentralization, industrial localization and regional disparities.

Ming Lu is Associate Professor of Economics at Fudan University, China, and Director of the Centre for China Development and Policy Studies. He is also research fellow of the Employment and Social Security Research Centre (ESSRC), and the China Centre for Economic Studies (CCES), Fudan University. He has a PhD in Economics from Fudan University. His recent research includes work on social economics and the labour market, inequality and economic development.

Xin Meng is Professor of Economics at the Research School of Pacific and Asian Studies at the Australian National University. She writes extensively on labour market reforms and income distribution in China. Her other research interests include the influence of institutions and culture on gender discrimination, economic assimilation of immigrants in developed countries, and the economic implications of major catastrophes.

Terry Sicular is Professor of Economics at the University of Western Ontario. She is a specialist on the Chinese economy. Her recent research addresses topics such as China's market reforms, rural labour and employment, capital flight and inequality. She has published widely in scholarly journals and has served as a consultant to international donor organizations.

Guanghua Wan is Senior Research Fellow and Project Director at the World Institute for Development Economics Research (UNU-WIDER). Previously he taught econometrics and development economics at the University of New England and the University of Sydney. Honorary professor of several leading universities in China and a prolific researcher with over 50 analytical papers in reputable refereed journals, Wan is a pioneer in developing regression-based decomposition techniques for inequality and poverty accounting.

Chunbing Xing is Assistant Professor of Economics at the School of Economics and Business Administration, Beijing Normal University, and holds a PhD from Peking University. His primary fields of interest are labour economics, applied econometrics and China's economy.

Ximing Yue is Professor of Economics at the Renmin University of China. He has done extensive research on convergence in prefectural income in Japan and national income in China, and on income distribution and rural poverty in China. Local public finance in China is one of his current research interests.

Yin Zhang is a lecturer in economics at the School of Social Science, University of Dundee, Scotland. Her research interests include applied macroeconomics, economic development and Asian economies.

Yi Zhu is a PhD candidate in the Department of Economics at Michigan State University. Having graduated from the Fudan University (1999) and the Chinese University of Hong Kong (2004), Zhu has research interests in labour economics and development economics.

List of Abbreviations

ABC	Agricultural Bank of China
ADBC	Agricultural Development Bank of China
BOC	Bank of China
CCB	China Construction Bank
CCP	Chinese Communist Party
CEESY	*China Education Expenditure Statistical Yearbook*
CHIP	China Household Income Project
CHNS	China's Household Nutrition Survey
CNY	Chinese *yuan*
CPI	consumer price index
ECEC	early childhood education and care
FDI	foreign direct investment
GDP	gross domestic product
GMM	generalized method of moments methodology
ICBC	Industrial and Commercial Bank of China
LCEs	large collective enterprises
NBS	National Bureau of Statistics (of China)
OLS	ordinary least squares
PBC	People's Bank of China
PRI	private sector enterprises
RCCs	rural credit cooperatives
RCFs	rural cooperative foundations
RRR	relative risk ratio
SCEs	small collective enterprises
SOEs	state-owned enterprises
SSB	State Statistical Bureau of China
TVEs	township and village enterprises

1

Globalization and Regional Income Inequality: Empirical evidence from within China

Guanghua Wan, Ming Lu and Zhao Chen

> 'The debate over globalization is lively, often passionate, and has sometimes been violent.'
>
> (Stanley Fischer 2003:2)

Introduction

How globalization affects inequality is subject to heated debate (Fischer 2003:5). Stiglitz (1998) and Hurrell and Woods (2000), among others, argue that globalization leads to increases in inequality because trade increases differentials in returns to education and skills, globalization marginalizes certain groups of people or geographic regions, and liberalization is not complemented by development of adequate institutions and governance. This view is supported by evidence from China and some transitional economies that are experiencing significant increases in inequality after their having opened up to the outside world (Birdsall 1999; Mazur 2000). In developed countries, rising inequalities are being attributed to trade growth or international specialization as well (Atkinson 2001). To the contrary, Ben-David (1993) and Srinivasan and Bhagwati (1999) conclude that globalization helps to reduce inequality. This is also supported by evidence from a number of countries where inequality decreased when they liberalized their economies (Wade 2001). In between these two opposing views, Lindert and Williamson (2001) and Sala-i-Martin (2002a, 2002b) find that a significant globalization–inequality relationship does not exist. Krugman and Venables (1995:859) deduce a U-shaped pattern between inequality and trade.

A number of factors can explain these mixed findings. First, inequality is measured differently, not only by employing alternative indices.

While some consider inequality among individuals, others focus on inequality between countries. Some explore inequality of one country or a group of countries; others discuss global inequality. Second, there exist differences in the analytical techniques. Most studies use cross-country regressions; however, some simply rely on partial correlations between inequality and globalization defined in various ways.[1] Correlation analysis cannot control for other causal variables, and cross-country regressions may produce different results when different control variables or different model specifications are used. Finally, sample coverage (selection of countries and time periods) differs from study to study.

This chapter contributes to the literature by examining the impact of globalization on regional income inequality in China. Focusing on China requires little justification, especially given China's importance in determining the global inequality trend. In addition, it can help alleviate the heterogeneity and data comparability problems often encountered in cross-country studies (Srinivasan and Bhagwati 1999; Atkinson and Brandolini 2001). To enhance the robustness of our empirical results, we first characterize the underlying income generating process using the flexible Box–Cox model, and then quantify the impact of globalization under all conventional measures of inequality. In decomposing total inequality into components associated with relevant determinants, the Shapley value framework of Shorrocks (1999) is combined with the estimated income generating function. The Shapley methodology is based on the cooperative game theory, and has been recently used by Wan (2004) and Kolenikov and Shorrocks (2005).

To elaborate further, in this chapter we seek to answer two questions: how globalization and regional income inequality are related in China; how much globalization contributes to regional inequality in China. The first question has received some attention. Kanbur and Zhang (2005) obtain a positive relationship between openness (measured by effective tariff rate and the trade/GDP ratio) and interregional inequality. Xing and Zhang (2004) find the same using FDI as a measure of globalization. However, Wei and Wu (2003) conclude with a negative relationship between urban–rural disparity and the trade/GDP ratio. With respect to the second question, little has been published with the exception of Zhang and Zhang (2003), who estimate a labour productivity (GDP/labour ratio) function and decompose inequality (measured by the log variance) in labour productivity into a number of components, including those associated with openness. The log variance measure, however, violates the crucial principle of transfers and the GDP/labour ratio does not necessarily relate to personal income in China (Lin and Liu 2003). Bourguignon and Morrisson (2002) appeal for the use of income rather than GDP data in analyzing inequality.

The remainder of this chapter is organized as follows: the next section presents a background description of China's journey to globalization. We go on to specify and estimate functions that generate income, and discuss inequality decomposition results. Finally, we close the chapter by exploring policy implications.

China's journey to globalization and regional inequality

As an active participant of the third globalization process, China is fast integrating into the world economy at a pace as remarkable as her economic growth. After over 20 years of opening up, China has become the largest recipient of foreign direct investment (FDI) and the fifth largest trader in the world since 2002.

Growing international trade

Before 1979, international trade was under the supervision of central government, which controlled more than 90 per cent of trade by monopolizing the imports and exports of over 3000 kinds of commodities. These commodities can be classified into two categories: government-controlled goods (where both the value and volume of trade were strictly controlled) and government guideline goods (where only the value of trade was controlled). In 1985, the number of goods comprising these categories was cut to about 100 each. By 1991, almost all exports were deregulated, with only 15 per cent controlled by specially appointed trading companies. Imports have also been deregulated. The proportion of government-controlled imports in the total import volume was reduced from 40 per cent in 1985 to 18.5 per cent in 1991. By 1994, almost all control of imports and exports was abolished, with a few exceptions where extremely important goods were traded by especially appointed trading companies.

In pre-reform China, tariffs were high and represented the only form of protection. When China initiated significant trade reforms in 1992, the rates of tariff remained high, averaging 44.05 per cent. Since 1992, China has cut its tariff rates substantially every year. The average tariff rate fell to 17.1 per cent in 1998 (Yin 1998:126). On the other hand, non-tariff barriers were introduced in the early 1980s. Subsequently, an increasing number of goods were placed under licensed trading and quota controls. In 1992, some 25 per cent of imports and 15 per cent of exports were managed under licences. However, the scope of licence and quota management has been narrowed down since 1992. By 1997, only 384 categories of imports – a mere 5 per cent of the total – were managed under quota and licences (Yin 1998:129).

Both exports and imports have experienced remarkable growth. The growth trend was maintained, even during the Asian financial crisis in the late 1990s. In 1978, China ranked 32nd in the world in terms of international trade. The ranking improved to 15th in 1989, 10th in 1997 and 6th in 2001. The ratio of international trade to GDP also rose from 9.85 per cent in 1978 to as high as 42.78 per cent in 2001. In 2002, total trade exceeded US$600 billion, representing more than 50 per cent of China's GDP.[2] This places China as the 5th largest trader in the world. In passing, it is noted that export of manufactured goods has accounted for an increasingly large share since the mid-1980s, while the corresponding import has declined, albeit at a slow rate. Clearly, China has been industrializing and is becoming a major exporter of manufactured commodities.

Increasing cross-border capital flows

In 1979, three Special Economic Zones (SEZs) were set up in Guangdong in order to attract FDI.[3] However, not until 1984 did FDI start to pour in. In the same year, fourteen coastal cities were designated as Open Cities and ten Economic and Technology Development Zones (ETDZs) were established. Since that time, increasingly more SEZs, Open Cities and ETDZs have been developed to attract FDI and technology transfer, and to enhance exports. The second wave of FDI inflow occurred in 1992, when Deng Xiaoping made his well-known tour of South China.

For many years, China was the largest recipient of FDI among developing countries, and the second largest in the world since 1993, next to the United States. In 2002, China attracted US$52.743 billion of FDI and led the world for FDI. The ratio of FDI to GDP was as high as approximately 4 per cent in 2001. Meanwhile, a large amount in foreign loans has been utilized in various areas of development.[4] Also, China has seen an impressive growth of capital outflows in recent years, owing to the rapid growth of domestic enterprises. China's investment abroad nearly tripled from US$2562.49 million in 1997 to US$6885.398 million in 2001.

Further opening up after WTO accession

Since becoming a member of the WTO in 2002, China has taken several steps to promote globalization. On 1 January 2002, China cut import tariffs for more than 5000 goods. The average tariff rate was reduced to 12 per cent from 15.3 per cent in 2001. The rate for manufacturing goods was reduced from 14.7 per cent to 11.3 per cent, while that for agricultural goods (except aquatic products) from 18.8 per cent to 15.8 per cent. At the same time, China abolished quota and licence arrangements for grains, wool, cotton, chemical fertilizers and so on. In addition, China modified or abolished those laws and regulations inconsistent with WTO rules. New laws on anti-dumping and anti-subsidy have been implemented since 1 January 2002.

At about the time of China's entry into the WTO, China issued new laws and regulations concerning service trade, covering legal service, telecommunications, financial institutions, insurance, audio and video products, tourism and so on. Laws regarding the entry of foreign sales companies and joint ventures on the stock exchange were being drawn up. Also, measures were taken to ensure compliance with rules of the WTO on intellectual property, foreign investment and information transmission.

Globalization and regional inequality

Clearly, China, as a whole, has gone a long way in globalizing. However, there exist significant differences in the pace and extent of globalization across regions. This is particularly true when China is divided into three areas: the east, the central region and the west. Figures 1.1 and 1.2 plot the ratios of regional per capita FDI and the regional openness index to the national averages (selected years). It is clear that east China attracts much more FDI and trade than the central region and the west, although convergences appear to have taken place within each area. This pattern also applies to other variables such as income, capital and extent of privatization. Therefore, disparity in globalization is largely an inter-area issue and including area dummies in the income generating functions for later consideration is justified.

Such differences in globalization may arise through a number of mechanisms and are expected to affect regional inequality. First, some regions have location advantages and thus can better exploit benefits of trade (close to ports, Hong Kong, Macau, Russia and Vietnam). Second, some regions possess more family ties to overseas investors and thus attract more FDI and associated spill over effects. Third, some regions are endowed with more or better resources (infrastructure, human capital, market potential) and thus can better attract FDI and develop trade. Finally, local culture, customs and traditions differ from region to region. These non-economic factors are embedded in the leadership styles of the regional and local governments, thus making regional economies more, or less, receptive to foreign capital and technologies. All the above differences lead to different paces of globalization in different regions,

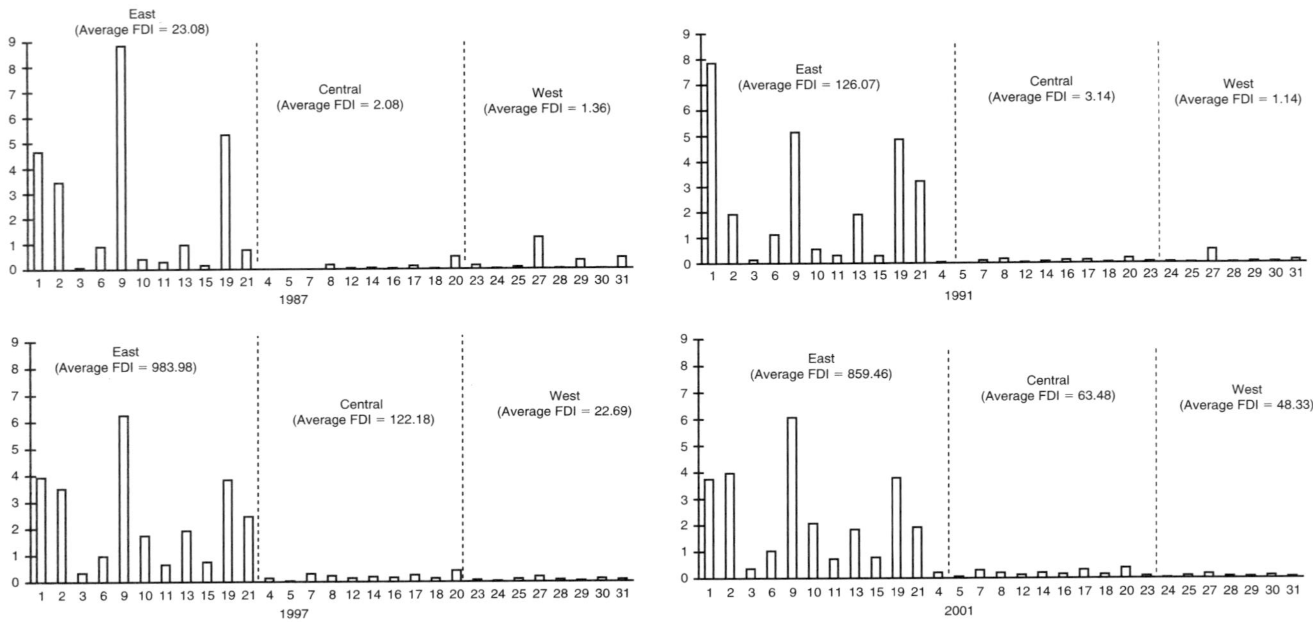

Figure 1.1 Ratio of regional per capita FDI to the national average
Notes: Eastern: 1 = Beijing, 2 = Tianjin, 3 = Hebei, 6 = Liaoning, 9 = Shanghai, 10 = Jiangsu, 11 = Zhejiang, 13 = Fujian, 15 = Shandong, 19 = Guangdong, 21 = Hainan; Central: 4 = Shanxi, 5 = Inner Mongolia, 7 = Jilin, 8 = Heilongjiang, 12 = Anhui, 14 = Jiangxi, 16 = Henan, 17 = Hubei, 18 = Hunan; 20 = Guangxi; Western: 23 = Sichuan, 24 = Guizhou, 25 = Yunnan, 27 = Shaanxi, 28 = Gansu, 29 = Qinghai, 30 = Ningxia, 31 = Xinjiang.

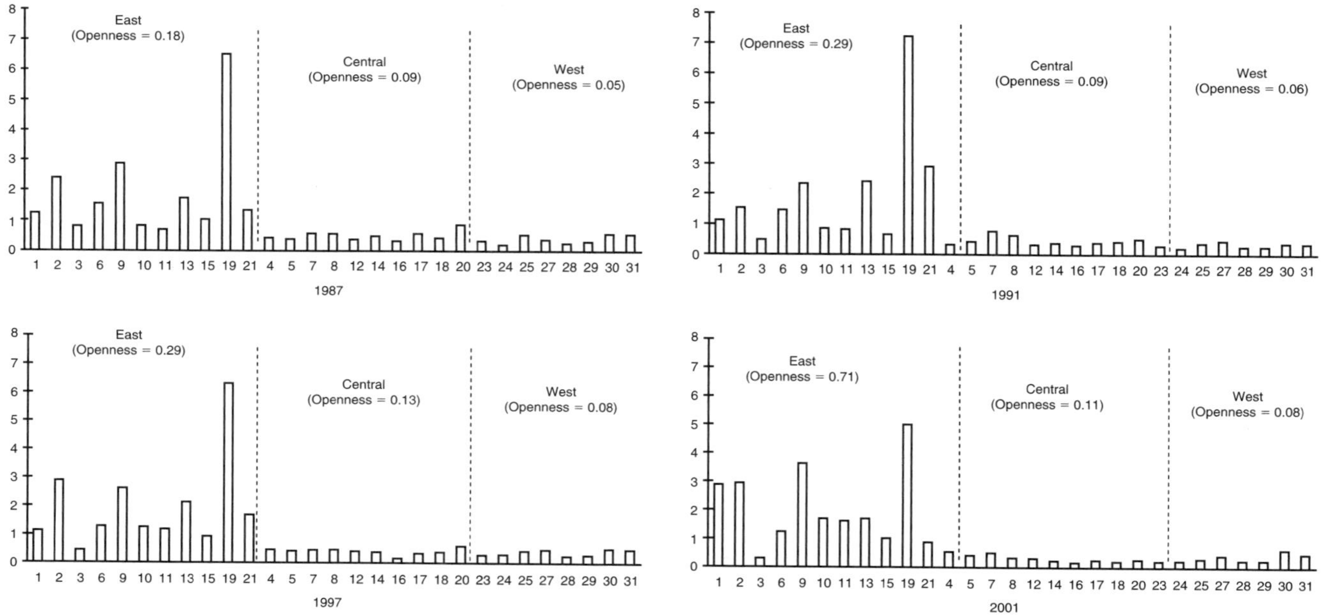

Figure 1.2 Ratio of regional openness to the national average (openness = trade/GDP)

Notes: Eastern: 1 = Beijing, 2 = Tianjin, 3 = Hebei, 6 = Liaoning, 9 = Shanghai, 10 = Jiangsu, 11 = Zhejiang, 13 = Fujian, 15 = Shandong, 19 = Guangdong, 21 = Hainan; Central: 4 = Shanxi, 5 = Inner Mongolia, 7 = Jilin, 8 = Heilongjiang, 12 = Anhui, 14 = Jiangxi, 16 = Henan, 17 = Hubei, 18 = Hunan; 20 = Guangxi; Western: 23 = Sichuan, 24 = Guizhou, 25 = Yunnan, 27 = Shaanxi, 28 = Gansu, 29 = Qinghai, 30 = Ningxia, 31 = Xinjiang.

despite the uniform national policy of opening up and the appeals of central government for local governments to embrace globalization actively.

Needless to say, globalization comes with both benefits and costs, which are not evenly distributed among regions or individuals. It is thus imperative to analyze the impact of globalization on income inequality before policy measures can be designed and implemented to curb the fast rising regional income inequality in China.

Accounting for China's inter-regional income inequality

As the first step of the regression-based decomposition, an income generating function must be obtained. Specification of such a function usually relies on the human capital theory. However, for modelling regional average income in China, consideration must be given to both human capital theory and production theory. This is because variables other than human capital are important in determining income levels across regions in China. These variables include capital input as argued by Yang (1994), government support as argued by Ma and Yu (2003), and deregulation or reform as argued by Démurger *et al.* (2002). Capital will be represented by per capita capital stock, government support by fiscal expenditure excluding administrative fees, and reform or deregulation by a privatization index defined as the proportion of non-state-owned enterprises employees in the total labour force. Meanwhile, it is accepted that geography is important in affecting regional economic development in China. Thus, dummy variables for east, central and west China will be used to control for geography and infrastructure (Démurger 2001). Further, urbanization differs from region to region, and such differences affect regional per capita income and, thus, inequality. This can be controlled by an urbanization index, defined as the proportion of the non-agricultural population. Finally, the conventional variables of labour and education must be considered. Given labour surplus in China and the linear relationship between the variables of labour and dependency ratio, we chose to include the latter. The converging trend in the dependency ratio implies a declining contribution of this variable to inequality.

The observations on capital stock are taken from Zhang, Wu and Zhang (2004, ZWZ hereafter). ZWZ do not include inventory as capital stock while Zhang and Zhang (2003, ZZ hereafter) do, although both studies use the same data estimation technique. Also, ZWZ construct the time series of capital stock as from 1952 rather than 1978, as in ZZ. Since the inventory represents only potential rather than effective production input, and biases in the estimate decrease as the time interval expands between the initial year and the current year, data from ZWZ will be used in this chapter. Other data are compiled from *Comprehensive Statistical Data and Materials for 50 Years of New China*, as well as various issues of the *China Statistical Yearbook*, both published by the National Bureau of Statistics (NBS). See the Appendix for details on data construction.

Largely due to the incompleteness of FDI statistics, the modelling exercise is confined to the period 1987–2001. With Taiwan, Hong Kong and Macau excluded, there are 31 provinces or regions in China, including four autonomous municipal cities. Chongqinq – the youngest region in China – was created in 1997 and is merged with Sichuan. Tibet is excluded because of a lack of complete data. Therefore, a total of 29 regions will be covered in this study.

In summary, the following variables are included in the underlying income generating function: per capita income (*Y*), per capita capital input (*K*), the dependency ratio as an alternative to labour (*Dep*),[5] average years of schooling (*Edu*), per capita FDI (*FDI*), trade/GDP ratio (*Trade*), reform or privatization defined as proportion of the labour force working in the non-state-owned enterprises (*Reform*), urbanization defined as the proportion of non-agricultural population (*Urb*) – which also serves as a proxy for industrialization, location dummies (*Central* and *West*),[6] and dummies for the period 1992 onwards (*D92*) and 1996 onwards (*D96*). *D92* is used to capture the effects of Deng Xiaoping's South-China tour and *D96* to capture a number of significant reforms initiated in 1996, especially the labour market reform characterized by the large-scale laying-off of redundant workers (*Xiagang*). Finally, government support is represented by per capita government expenditure excluding administrative fees (*Gov*). This is a proxy of government involvement in economic activities in general, and in public investment in particular. All observations in value terms are deflated by regional CPIs.

Regarding functional form, most empirical studies in human capital theory adopt the semi-log form or the Mincer model. If one relies on the production theory, Cobb–Douglas (double log), CES (constant elasticity of substitution) or translog specifications are the possible candidates (see Wan 1996; Wan and Cheng 2001). In the inequality decomposition literature, Fields and Yoo (2000:145) did not explicitly provide theoretical arguments supporting their semi-log specification, except for the casual remark 'based on human capital theory or some other underlying theoretical model'. Tsui (2007) did exactly the same, with a different remark: 'to render the estimation manageable'. On the other hand, Morduch and Sicular (2002:101) simply used a strictly linear function without much justification. In this paper, we decide to adopt the combined Box-Cox and Box-Tidwell model in order to minimize misspecification error:

$$Y^{(\lambda)} = a_0 + a_1 X_1^{(\theta)} + a_2 X_2^{(\theta)} + \cdots + a_K X_K^{(\theta)} + \textit{dummy terms} + u \qquad (1.1)$$

where λ and θ are transformation parameters; other notations are self-explanatory. In this specification, $Y^{(\lambda)} = Y^{\lambda} - 1/\lambda$ and $X_k^{(\theta)} = X_k^{\theta} - 1/\theta$. As λ approaches 0, the limit of $Y^{\lambda} - 1/\lambda$ is *Ln Y* by L'Hôpital's rule. Hence, $Y^{(\lambda)} = Ln\ Y$ when $\lambda = 0$ (Judge *et al.* 1988). The same arguments apply to $X_k^{(\theta)}$. Model (1.1) encompasses many functional forms, including the semilog income generating function of Fields and Yoo (2000) and Tsui (2007) if $\lambda = 0$ and $\theta = 1$, and the standard linear function of Morduch and Sicular (2002) if $\lambda = \theta = 1$. In the case that $\lambda = \theta = 0$, a double-log equation, as used by Zhang and Zhang (2003) is obtained. When $\lambda = -1$ or $\theta = -1$, the relevant variable becomes its reciprocal. Clearly, one can restrict each of the two transformation parameters to be 0, 1, −1 or unrestricted. The 4 by 4 combinations produce 16 different functional forms. Moreover, one can impose $\lambda = \theta$ although they are not restricted to a particular numerical value. Clearly, our specification (1.1) is more general and flexible than what has been used in the inequality decomposition literature as it encompasses at least 17 different models.

These 17 models are fitted to the Chinese data using Shazam, which employs an iterative maximum likelihood (ML) estimation procedure.[7] Model selection can be easily undertaken using the conventional χ^2 test where the test statistic is twice the difference in the loglikelihood values of model (1) and its restricted versions. As reported in Table 1.A1 of the Appendix, the test results indicate rejections of all models with two exceptions. The first case involves imposing $\lambda = 0$ while θ remains a free parameter. This amounts to a log-nonlinear model (the *X*s are subject to a nonlinear transformation). The second case involves restricting $\lambda = \theta$. Statistically speaking, these two models are equivalent to (1) and either of them can be used for inequality decomposition. We choose to use the log-nonlinear model, largely because it is consistent with the human capital theory where almost all empirical studies apply logarithm transformation to the dependent variable in modelling the wage or income generating process.

Could the log-nonlinear model be spurious? After all, the panel data we use contain fifteen years of time series observations, thus the variables may be non-stationary. Employing the popular unit-root test of Im, Pesaran and Shin (2003) or the IPS test for heterogeneous panel data, we found that FDI and education are stationary, but all other variables are non-stationary. Consequently, it is necessary to test for co-integration (McCoskey and Kao 1999). The literature on co-integration tests in panels is large and growing rapidly. Baltagi and Kao (2000) provide a comprehensive survey. For a more recent review, see Breitung and Pesaran (2005). Consequently, many testing procedures are available and each has its own merits and disadvantages. We chose to employ the residual-based test of Im, Pesaran and Shin (2003) or IPS due to its popularity.[8] Relying on IPS, the residual is found to be stationary when the order of lag is set to two. The test statistic is found to be −1.71 while the critical value is −1.66, indicating rejection of the null hypothesis of unit roots. According to this test result, the log-nonlinear model we obtained earlier can be said to represent a valid long-run regression relationship.[9]

One may argue that one or more of the independent variables could be endogenous, such as trade and FDI. Consequently, we re-estimate the log-nonlinear model using the generalized method of moment or GMM technique of Blundell and Bond (1998) and then apply the Hausman test (Hausman 1978). The resultant χ^2 statistic is 0.86, indicating absence of endogeneity in our log-nonlinear model. It is noted that all GMM estimates, except that for government support (*Gov*), possess the same signs as the ML estimates, confirming the robustness of the latter. However, most GMM estimates, including that for *Gov*, are insignificant. This is not surprising as GMM estimation can only guarantee consistency, but not efficiency. Consequently, we disregard the GMM estimation results hereafter as ML estimation of our model is both efficient and consistent.

Table 1.1 reports ML estimation results for the log-nonlinear model. No *t*-ratio is reported for the θ coefficient as it is obtained by grid search. Earlier rejection of the double-log model implies that θ is significantly different from zero. It is clear that the model fits the data quite well, as indicated by the high R^2. All parameters are different from 0 at the 1 per cent or 5 per cent level of significance. Further, the signs of all parameter estimates are consistent with expectations. In particular, the coefficient estimates for the location dummies match the fact that western regions are poorer than central regions, which, in turn, are poorer than eastern regions. In terms of elasticity estimates, income growth is quite responsive to reform, education, government support, urbanization and domestic capital. The low elasticity of FDI is acceptable given its small sample mean value (517 *yuan*) relative to domestic capital (4403 *yuan*). Since per capita domestic capital is 8.5 times that of per capita FDI, the

Table 1.1 Estimated income generating function (sample size = 435)

Variable	Coefficient estimate	*t*-ratio	*p*-value	Elasticity at means	Loglikelihood value	Adj-R^2
Capital	0.034	4.612	0.000	0.105		
Dependency	−0.064	−4.299	0.000	−0.118		
Education	0.151	2.545	0.011	0.195		
Government	0.054	4.976	0.000	0.110		
FDI	0.008	2.405	0.017	0.018		
Trade	0.038	4.350	0.000	0.058		
Reform	0.123	9.024	0.000	0.188	−2533.22	0.935
Urbanization	0.082	4.940	0.000	0.128		
Central	−0.072	−3.297	0.001	−0.025		
West	−0.168	−6.996	0.000	−0.046		
Year 1992	0.083	4.818	0.000	0.056		
Year 1996	0.170	9.527	0.000	0.068		
Constant	4.796	32.950	0.000	4.796		
θ	0.133					

marginal impact of FDI on income is 45 per cent larger than that of domestic capital, which corroborates well with conventional wisdoms.

To analyze inequality of income rather than inequality of logarithm of income, it is necessary to solve the estimated log-nonlinear income generating function for the income variable Y:

$$Y = \exp(\hat{a}_0) \cdot \exp(\hat{a}_1 X_1^{(\theta)} + \hat{a}_2 X_2^{(\theta)} + \cdots + \hat{a}_K X_K^{(\theta)}) \cdot \exp\,(\textit{dummy terms}) \cdot \exp(\hat{u}) \tag{1.2}$$

The term $\exp(\hat{a}_0)$ is a scalar in (1.2) and can be removed from the equation without any consequence when relative measures of inequality are used, as in this chapter. By the same token, year dummy terms can be removed since inequality will be measured and decomposed on a year-by-year basis.

To decompose total inequality in Y using (1.2), the first step is to identify the contribution of the residual term $\hat{u}$. This can be achieved by adopting the before–after principle of Cancian and Reed (1998). In other words, the contribution can be calculated as the difference between inequality of the original income Y and that of income given by (1.2) when assuming $\hat{u} = 0$. Denote this income by $\tilde{Y}$ and an inequality index by I, the residual contribution is simply equal to $I(Y) - I(\tilde{Y})$, where

$$\tilde{Y} = \exp(\hat{a}_0) \cdot \exp(\hat{a}_1 X_1^{(\theta)} + \hat{a}_2 X_2^{(\theta)} + \cdots + \hat{a}_K X_K^{(\theta)}) \cdot \exp\,(\textit{dummy terms}) \tag{1.3}$$

Table 1.2 Total inequality and explained proportion

Year	Total Gini	Contribution by		Proportion explained* = 100 × (1−|Residual|/Total)
		Independent variables	Residual	
1987	0.172	0.159	0.013	92.4
1988	0.176	0.163	0.012	93.2
1989	0.183	0.167	0.016	91.3
1990	0.174	0.173	0.001	99.4
1991	0.182	0.172	0.011	94.0
1992	0.187	0.172	0.014	92.5
1993	0.201	0.178	0.022	89.1
1994	0.206	0.187	0.019	90.8
1995	0.210	0.198	0.012	94.3
1996	0.206	0.202	0.004	98.1
1997	0.203	0.206	−0.003	98.5
1998	0.199	0.204	−0.004	98.0
1999	0.206	0.209	−0.003	98.5
2000	0.208	0.211	−0.003	98.6
2001	0.214	0.210	0.003	98.6

Note: * A negative (positive) residual contribution implies that variables not considered are (dis-)equalizing forces. As discussed in the chapter, the ratio of the absolute value of residual contribution to the total inequality indicates the proportion of inequality not explained and 1 minus this proportion can be defined as the explained proportion.

Again, the year dummy terms and $\exp(\hat{a}_0)$ can be removed from (1.3) without affecting the analytical results. In passing, it is noted that $\tilde{Y}$ differs from the usual predicted Y under a semilog econometric model by a factor of $\exp(0.5\,\hat{\sigma}^2)$, where $\hat{\sigma}^2$ is the estimated variance of the error term (see Wan 1996).

Using the Gini index as an example measure, total income inequality and the residual contribution for China are tabulated in Table 1.2 (for results using other measures, see Tables 1.A2–A5 in the Appendix). The total inequality displays a clear upward trend, increased over 24 per cent from 1987 to 2001. This increase is also evident when other inequality indices are used. The values of Gini may appear smaller than some would expect. This is because they represent the between component – inequality between regions only, excluding the within component. To calculate the latter requires data at the individual or household level. Also, deflation by regional CPIs produces smaller regional inequality estimates (Wan 2001).

To a large extent, the residual contribution can be interpreted as that part of inequality not accounted for by the included variables. That is, it represents the effect on inequality of excluded variables. In a hypothetical though unrealistic situation where all variables are included and there exists no model misspecification, the residual would disappear so that exactly 100 per cent of total inequality is explained.[10] Generally speaking, it is a rule, rather than exception, that the residual contribution is non-zero. Both negative and positive residual contributions indicate some lack of explanatory power of the estimated model. A positive (negative) contribution implies that the effects of excluded variables are more beneficial to the rich (poor).[11] It is thus reasonable to use the ratio of the absolute value of the residual contribution over total inequality to indicate the proportion of inequality not explained. Consequently, one minus this proportion can be defined as the explained proportion, which reflects the quality of the modelling work. When the model fits the data poorly, the explained proportion would be low and the corresponding research findings would be of little value, as policy initiatives based on these findings would be ineffective.[12] From this perspective, our modelling exercise is quite successful as we can explain up to 99.4 per cent of total inequality (last column of Table 1.2). Even in the worst case of 1993, almost 90 per cent of total inequality is explained.

The difference between the total inequality and the residual contribution equals the contributions of those independent variables included in the income generating function. To obtain contributions of individual variables, the Shapley value procedure of Shorrocks (1999) is adopted here.[13] The full decomposition results are presented in Table 1.4 and in the Appendix as Tables 1.A2–A5, with inequality measured respectively by the Gini coefficient, the generalized entropy measures (GE_0 and GE_1), the Atkinson index, and the squared coefficient of variation (CV). As expected, the decomposition results differ depending on the indicator of inequality used. This is not surprising because different indicators are associated with different social welfare functions and presume different aversions to inequality. They also place different weights to different segments of the underlying Lorenz curve. It is noted, however, that the squared CV violates the principle of transfer and the Atkinson index is ordinally equivalent to the GE measures as its entire family can be expressed as a monotonic transformation of the latter (Shorrocks and Slottje 2002). Consequently, we only use results under the Gini, the Theil Index (GE_1) and the mean logarithmic deviation (GE_0) in the following discussions.

Although pointing to a similar increasing trend in total inequality, different indicators of inequality rank individual variables differently (Table 1.3). Nevertheless, they are largely consistent in ranking the less

Table 1.3 Ranks of inequality contribution by alternative inequality measures

Year	K	Dep	Edu	Gov	FDI	Trade	Reform	Urb	Location
1987	3	9	7,7,6	4	8	5	6,6,7	1	2
1988	3	9	7,7,6	4	8	5	6,6,7	2,1,1	1,2,2
1989	3,3,2	9	7,7,6	4	8	5	6,6,7	2,1,1	1,2,3
1990	3,3,2	9	7,7,6	5,5,4	8	4,4,5	6,6,7	2,1,1	1,2,3
1991	3,3,2	9	7	5,5,4	8	4,4,5	6	2,1,1	1,2,3
1992	3,1,1	9	7,8,8	5,4,4	8,7,7	4,5,5	6	2,3,2	1,2,3
1993	2,1,1	9	7	6,4,4	8	5	4,6,6	3,3,2	1,2,3
1994	2,1,1	9	8	5,4,4	7	6,6,5	4,5,6	3	1,2,2
1995	1	9	8	4,3,2	7	6	3,5,5	5,4,4	2,2,3
1996	1	9	8	4,3,2	7	6	3,5,5	5,4,4	2,2,3
1997	1	9	8	3,2,2	7	6	4,4,5	5,5,4	2,3,3
1998	1	9	8	3,2,2	7	6,5,5	4,6,6	5,4,4	2,3,3
1999	1	9	8	5,2,2	7	4,3,3	3,5,5	6	2,4,4
2000	1	9	8	4,2,2	7	5,3,3	2,4,4	6	3,5,5
2001	1	9	8	5,3,2	7	4,2,3	3,4,4	6	2,5,5

Note: One number indicates consistent ranking; three numbers indicate ranks by Gini, GE_0 and GE_1, respectively.

important contributors. For example, all three indices show that the dependency ratio is the least important variable and they are broadly consistent in ranking FDI and education as the second and third least important factors. Further, some agreement is seen with respect to capital and urbanization as the most important contributors. In the early years, consistent ranking is evident for reform and trade, even government support. In later years, differences in the ranking emerge regarding contributions of variables such as location and government support for economic development.

Faced with the inconsistency, one can either choose a particular measure or take the average across different indicators (only applicable to the percentage contributions, not absolute contributions) and then proceed to interpretation and discussions. We chose to report the decomposition results under the Gini coefficient in Table 1.4. The contributions are calculated using the total explained portion as the denominator, thus they sum to 100 per cent. According to Table 1.4, the least important variable is still the dependency ratio. This is attributable to the converging trend in this variable, partly driven by the nationwide policy of birth control. This result also reflects the fact of surplus labour in China. Thus, differences in dependency ratio across regions are of little significance in driving regional inequality. It must be noted that this is only true at the

Table 1.4 Inequality decomposition results, Gini index

Year	Relative contribution (%)								
	K	Dep	Edu	Gov	FDI	Trade	Reform	Urb	Location
1987	13.49	3.85	6.56	13.35	4.45	11.66	11.03	17.92	17.69
1988	14.16	3.73	6.47	13.06	5.08	12.11	10.38	17.36	17.63
1989	14.67	3.34	6.38	12.59	5.49	12.42	10.43	17.05	17.62
1990	14.92	3.16	7.40	11.97	5.60	12.70	10.45	16.46	17.34
1991	15.39	3.10	6.24	11.91	6.04	12.67	10.64	16.40	17.61
1992	15.90	3.29	6.25	11.44	6.32	12.19	10.91	15.97	17.74
1993	16.04	3.23	6.96	11.29	6.30	11.81	11.87	15.26	17.23
1994	16.19	3.37	5.74	12.57	6.66	11.51	13.07	13.92	16.98
1995	16.72	3.05	5.80	13.51	6.75	10.96	13.85	13.12	16.23
1996	17.18	2.93	5.39	13.59	6.71	11.33	13.98	12.75	16.13
1997	17.30	2.69	5.32	14.20	6.81	11.66	13.94	12.20	15.88
1998	17.95	2.55	5.26	14.43	7.07	11.89	12.54	12.28	16.04
1999	18.08	0.81	5.10	13.72	6.94	13.77	14.28	11.92	15.38
2000	17.82	0.49	4.38	14.37	6.85	14.17	15.27	11.44	15.20
2001	18.37	0.90	4.77	13.32	6.98	14.34	14.77	11.44	15.12

highly aggregate level. Labour input and dependency ratio are still important for income generation and income disparity at the household level.

The stock of physical capital has always been important. Its importance has increased over time and it now constitutes almost 20 per cent of total inequality, making it the largest contributor since 1995. On the other hand, urbanization was rated as the number one or two factor until 1992, but its role quickly declined. It dropped to the third or fifth position and finally settled at the sixth position. This reflects well the converging trend in urbanization across China. Despite this, urbanization still contributes about 12 per cent to total inequality. Sharing a similar trend with urbanization, location has become less important, its ranking having dropped from first place until 1994 (second, in 1987) to second place since 1995. The declining contribution does not necessarily mean narrowing gaps in factors associated with location (natural resources, weather, proximity to markets and ports). It means that other factors have become more unequally distributed across China.

It is clear that FDI ranks as the second least important determinant of regional inequality in China up until the early 1990s. However, it has gained importance in recent years. The impact of trade on total inequality has been moderate. If one combines trade and FDI as an overall indicator of globalization, the contribution is quite substantial, particularly

Table 1.4 continued

				Absolute contribution				
K	**Dep**	**Edu**	**Gov**	**FDI**	**Trade**	**Reform**	**Urb**	**Location**
0.021	0.006	0.010	0.021	0.007	0.019	0.018	0.029	0.028
0.023	0.006	0.011	0.021	0.008	0.020	0.017	0.028	0.029
0.024	0.006	0.011	0.021	0.009	0.021	0.017	0.028	0.029
0.026	0.005	0.013	0.021	0.010	0.022	0.018	0.028	0.030
0.026	0.005	0.011	0.020	0.010	0.022	0.018	0.028	0.030
0.027	0.006	0.011	0.020	0.011	0.021	0.019	0.027	0.031
0.029	0.006	0.012	0.020	0.011	0.021	0.021	0.027	0.031
0.030	0.006	0.011	0.024	0.012	0.022	0.024	0.026	0.032
0.033	0.006	0.011	0.027	0.013	0.022	0.027	0.026	0.032
0.035	0.006	0.011	0.027	0.014	0.023	0.028	0.026	0.033
0.036	0.006	0.011	0.029	0.014	0.024	0.029	0.025	0.033
0.037	0.005	0.011	0.029	0.014	0.024	0.026	0.025	0.033
0.038	0.002	0.011	0.029	0.015	0.029	0.030	0.025	0.032
0.038	0.001	0.009	0.030	0.014	0.030	0.032	0.024	0.032
0.039	0.002	0.010	0.028	0.015	0.030	0.031	0.024	0.032

in the later years. The combined contribution was around 16 per cent earlier but now runs at around 22 per cent, surpassing the capital variable. It is important to note that this finding is robust to inequality measures. Therefore, globalization does deserve serious consideration owing to its large and increasing effects on regional inequality, which has implications for poverty and poverty reduction in China. The increasing contribution of globalization is a result of increased trade and FDI inflow.

Over time, a number of factors gained prominence. Reform or privatization was placed sixth in importance but moved up to third position, highlighting the unequal pace in privatizing state-owned entities and the importance of privatization on income growth. It is interesting to observe that government support for economic development is diverging. The positive contribution implies less (more) developed areas provide less (more) support. The diverging trend may have to do with the taxation reform initiated in 1994, which significantly enhances the budgeting and spending power of local governments. The reform allows rich regions to collect more taxes and fees to finance economic activities.

The small and stable contribution of education is most probably attributable to the many years of public provision of basic education in China, particularly in the urban areas. A surprising result is that the contribution of education only ranks the second or third from the last, a finding not inconsistent with ZZ. Conversely, the impacts of reform and urbanization on inequality are expected to decline in the long run because slow reformers or latecomers are bound to catch up. After all, these two variables have a maximum value of 100. It should be noted that the role of location will diminish as development of technology in the transportation and communications sectors are helping to downplay the importance of physical isolation or distance. This diminishing role is reinforced by the historical campaign of western development characterized by considerable investment in disadvantaged regions. As known, the effects of investment in infrastructure on development are typically lagged.

It is worth noting that a declining percentage contribution does not necessarily mean a decreasing absolute contribution. A careful examination of Table 1.4 and Tables 1.A2–A5 reveals that, apart from the dependency ratio and urbanization, all other variables contribute progressively more to total inequality. The dependency ratio is the only variable with declining contribution in both relative and absolute terms. Urbanization more or less maintained its absolute contribution but displayed a declining relative contribution because of the increasing trend in total inequality.

It may seem sensible to discuss our findings in relation to ZZ. However, this is not appropriate for a number of reasons. First, we focus on income inequality while ZZ focus on partial labour productivity. Second, ZZ employ a double log model which is rejected in this chapter. Third, ZZ relies on the logarithmic variance as the only measure of inequality. Our results are robust to inequality measures and based on a flexible modelling strategy. An indication of inadequacy of ZZ lies in that domestic capital is more productive than FDI, which is difficult to justify.

Conclusion

This chapter provides an accounting for China's regional income inequality, with a special emphasis on the impact of globalization. Relying on a carefully constructed panel data set, the flexible Box–Cox specification is adopted to minimize modelling errors. The income generating function is estimated successfully and the decomposition results are based on a recently developed methodology of Shorrocks (1999). It is found that (a) globalization constitutes a positive and substantial share of China's regional inequality and the share rises over time;[14] (b) capital is one of the largest and increasingly important contributors to regional inequality; (c) economic reform characterized by privatization exerts a significant impact on regional inequality; and (d) the relative contributions of education, location, urbanization and the dependency ratio to regional inequality have been declining.

A number of major policy implications are readily derivable from our empirical results. Further globalization will lead to higher regional inequality in China unless concerted efforts are devoted to promote trade in and FDI flows to west and central China. Thus, it is suggested that policy biases that promoted trade and FDI but which are gradually being phased out in coastal China should be implemented in other parts of China. Market potential and location considerations place the poor regions in a disadvantageous position with regard to attracting FDI and promoting trade. However, a converging trend in FDI and trade is encouraging. More important is the domestic capital, equalization of which across regions will cut regional inequality by 20 per cent. To narrow gaps in capital distribution, it is necessary – though difficult – to break the vicious circle existing in the creation of capital. This calls for the development of a financial market in China, especially in poor rural areas. Again, policy support for investment in the poor regions is needed in terms of tax concessions and bank lending. In particular, continued financial reforms are necessary in order to eliminate discrimination against small farmers and rural activities. Finally, changes are needed in the collection and allocation of fiscal resources that so far have favoured the developed regions. An equalization in fiscal support would lead to an almost 15 per cent drop in regional inequality and a progressive fiscal scheme would result in a considerably greater impact. Combined, globalization, domestic capital stock and government fiscal support contribute over half of the total regional inequality in China.

Notes

This study was prepared for the UNU-WIDER project on Inequality and Poverty in China, directed by Guanghua Wan. We are grateful to Tony Shorrocks, Stephan Klasen, Eric Thorbecke and Machiko Nissanke for helpful comments on earlier drafts of the paper. Financial support from the Chinese Natural Sciences Foundation (No. 70403004), and the China Center for Economic Studies of Fudan University are acknowledged.

1 The concept of globalization has many dimensions, ranging from interdependence of economic activities in different countries to flows of ideas across national borders. In this chapter, we focus on economic globalization through exchanges of goods and services, and flows of foreign capital. Flows of labour, information, ideology, culture and living styles are not considered, as relevant data are unavailable or incomplete. To be more precise, we use openness (trade/GDP ratio) and per capita FDI to represent globalization in this chapter.

2 Unless indicated otherwise, data quoted in this section are all from the National Bureau of Statistics (NBS) (various years).

3 Another SEZ was opened in Xiamen, Fujian province in 1980. See table 3 in Démurger *et al.* (2002) for the timeline of policy initiatives.

4 The stock market represents another avenue for attracting foreign capital.

5 We tried to add per capita labour input or household size, but neither of them is significant.

6 Consistent with most studies, central provinces refer to Shanxi, Guangxi, Inner Mongolia, Jilin, Heilongjiang, Anhui, Jiangxi, Henan, Hubei and Hunan, and western provinces include Sichuan, Guizhou, Yunnan, Shaanxi, Gansu, Qinghai, Ningxia and Xinjiang.

7 Ideally, one should estimate these models for each region or for every year. Due to the limited sample size, and also given the flexibility of our functional form, we choose to pool the data for model estimation. As shown later, a re-estimation by GMM under the specification of a dynamic panel data model supports our choice.

8 IPS is the only unit roots test for panel models that is coded in TSP and Stata.

9 Caution must be exercised here as the IPS test, as with many other co-integration tests, cannot guarantee co-integration in all units/groups in the panel when the null hypothesis of unit roots is rejected.

10 An identity, expressing total income as a sum of source incomes, can be thought of as a special income generating function (not an econometric function) with no residual term. In this case, our decomposition can explain 100 per cent of the total inequality.

11 It is possible, at least hypothetically, that the residuals are all positive for the poor and negative for the rich. In this case, the contribution of the residual term must be negative as it is an equalizing factor.

12 It can be shown that when $R^2 = 1$ or 0, the explained proportion is 100 or 0 per cent. In the case that CV^2 is used as the measure of inequality, the explained proportion is always identical to the R^2.

13 For this purpose, a Java programme has been developed by the World Institute for Development Economics Research of the United Nations University (UNU-WIDER). This programme allows decomposition of inequality of a dependent variable into components associated with any number of independent variables and under any functional form. Readers interested in the Shapley procedure should consult Shorrocks (1999) for technical details and Wan and Zhou (2005) for an intuitive explanation.

14 One of the referees suggested confirming this conclusion by running a regression of inequality on a set of regressors. This useful suggestion was not taken up because we can only have a total of fifteen observations on regional inequality (one for each year) for this kind of regression. Even with five or six explanatory variables, the degrees of freedom would drop below ten. Such a model is rather unreliable. More importantly, our decomposition results are sufficient for gauging the impact of globalization on regional inequality in China.

References

Atkinson, A.B. (2001) 'A Critique of the Transatlantic Consensus on Rising Income Inequality', *World Economy*, 24: 433–552.

Atkinson, A.B. and Brandolini, A. (2001) 'Promise and Pitfalls in the Use of "Secondary" Data-sets: Income Inequality in OECD Countries as a Case Study', *Journal of Economic Literature*, 39, 3: 771–99.

Baltagi, B.H. and Kao, C. (2000) 'Nonstationary Panels, Cointegration in Panels and Dynamic Panels: A Survey', Centre for Policy Research Working Paper 16, Syracuse University.

Ben-David, D. (1993) 'Equalizing Exchange: Trade Liberalization and Income Convergence', *Quarterly Journal of Economics*, 108, 3: 653–79.

Birdsall, N. (1999) 'Globalization and the Developing Countries: The Inequality Risk', Remarks at Overseas Development Council Conference, International Trade Center, Washington, DC.

Blundell, R. and Bond, S. (1998) 'Initial Conditions and Moment Restrictions in Dynamic Panel Data Models', *Journal of Econometrics*, 87: 115–43.

Bourguignon, F. and Morrisson, C. (2002) 'Inequality Among World Citizens: 1820–1992', *American Economic Review*, 92, 4: 727–44.

Breitung, J. and Pesaran, M.H. (2005) 'Unit Roots and Cointegration in Panels', Discussion Paper Series 1: Economic Studies 42/2005, Deutsche Bundesbank.

Cancian, M. and Reed, D. (1998) 'Assessing the Effects of Wives Earning on Family Income Inequality', *Review of Economics and Statistics*, 80: 73–9.

Démurger, S. (2001) 'Infrastructure Development and Economic Growth: An Explanation for Regional Disparities in China?', *Journal of Comparative Economics*, 29: 95–117.

Démurger, S., Sachs, J.D., Woo, W.T., Bao, S., Chang, G. and Mellinger, A. (2002) 'Geography, Economic Policy, and Regional Development in China', *Asian Economic Papers*, 1: 146–205.

Fields, G.S. and Yoo, G. (2000) 'Falling Labor Income Inequality in Korea's Economic Growth: Patterns and Underlying Causes', *Review of Income and Wealth*, 46: 139–59.

Fischer, S. (2003) 'Globalization and Its Challenges', *American Economic Review*, 93, 2: 1–30.

Hall, R.E. and Jones, C.I. (1999) 'Why do some Countries Produce So Much More Output Per Worker than Others?', *Quarterly Journal of Economics* 114, 1: 83–116.

Hausman, J. (1978) 'Specification Tests in Econometrics', *Econometrica* 46: 1251–71.

Hurrell, A. and Woods, N. (2000) 'Globalization and Inequality', in R. Higgott (ed.), *The New Political Economy of Globalization* (Cheltenham: Edward Elgar).

Im, K.S., Pesaran, M.H. and Shin, S. (2003) 'Testing for Unit Roots in Heterogeneous Panels', *Journal of Econometrics*, 115: 53–74.

Judge, G., Hill, R., Griffiths, W., Lütkepohl, H. and Lee, T. (1988) *Introduction to the Theory and Practice of Econometrics*, 2nd edn (New Jersey: Wiley).

Kanbur, R. and Zhang, X. (2005) 'Fifty Years of Regional Inequality in China: A Journey Through Central Planning, Reform and Openness', *Review of Development Economics* 9, 1: 87–106.

Kolenikov, S. and Shorrocks, A. (2005) 'A Decomposition Analysis of Regional Poverty in Russia', *Review of Development Economics*, 9, 1: 25–46.

Krugman, P. and Venables, A. (1995) 'Globalization and the Inequality of Nations', *Quarterly Journal of Economics*, 110, 4: 857–80.

Lin, Y. and Liu, P. (2003) 'China's Economic Development Strategy and Regional Income Disparity', (in Chinese), *Economic Research Journal (Jingji Yanjiu)*, 3: 19–25.

Lindert, P.H. and Williamson, J.G. (2001) 'Does Globalization Make the World More Unequal', NBER Working Paper 8228 (Cambridge, MA: NBER).

Ma, Shuanyou and Yu, H. (2003) 'Fiscal Transfer and Convergence of Regional Economy', (in Chinese), *Economic Research Journal (Jingji Yanjiu)*, 3: 26–33.
Mazur, J. (2000) 'Labor's New Internationalism', *Foreign Affairs*, 81, 1: 79–93.
McCoskey, S. and Kao, C. (1999) 'Testing the Stability of a Production Function with Urbanization as a Shift Factor', *Oxford Bulletin of Economics and Statistics*, 61: 671–90.
Morduch, J. and Sicular, T. (2002) 'Rethinking Inequality Decomposition, with Evidence from Rural China', *Economic Journal*, 112: 93–106.
NBS (National Bureau of Statistics) (various years) *China Statistical Yearbook* (Beijing: China Statistical Publishing House).
NBS (National Bureau of Statistics) (1999) *Comprehensive Statistical Data and Materials for 50 Years of New China* (Beijing: China Statistical Publishing House).
Sala-i-Martin, X. (2002a) 'The Disturbing "Rise" of Global Income Inequality', NBER Working Paper 8904 (Cambridge, MA: NBER).
Sala-i-Martin, X. (2002b) 'The World Distribution of Income', NBER Working Paper 8933 (Cambridge, MA: NBER).
Shorrocks, A.F. (1999) 'Decomposition Procedures for Distributional Analysis: A Unified Framework Based on the Shapley Value', Unpublished manuscript, Department of Economics, University of Essex.
Shorrocks, A.F. and Slottje, D. (2002) 'Approximating Unanimity Orderings: An Application to Lorenz Dominance', *Journal of Economics*, Supplement 9: 91–117.
Srinivasan, T.N. and Bhagwati, J. (1999) 'Outward-Orientation and Development: Are Revisionists Right?', Economic Growth Center Discussion Paper 806, Yale University.
Stiglitz, J.E. (1998) 'More Instruments and Broader Goals: Moving Toward the Post-Washington Consensus', WIDER Annual Lecture 2 (Helsinki: UNU-WIDER).
Tsui, K.Y. (2007) 'Forces Shaping China's Interprovincial Inequality', *Review of Income and Wealth*, 53, 1: 60–92.
Wade, R.H. (2001) 'The Rising Inequality of World Income Distribution', *Finance and Development*, 38, 4.
Wan, G.H. (1996) 'Measuring Input Substitution and Output Expansion Effects: A Nonparametric Approach with Application', *Empirical Economics*, 21, 3: 361–80.
Wan, G.H. (2001) 'Changes in Regional Inequality in Rural China: Decomposing the Gini Index by Income Sources', *Australian Journal of Agricultural and Resource Economics*, 45, 3: 361–82.
Wan, G.H. (2004) 'Accounting for Income Inequality in Rural China: A Regression Based Approach', *Journal of Comparative Economics*, 32, 2: 348–63.
Wan, G.H. and Cheng, E.J. (2001) 'Effects of Land Fragmentation and Returns to Scale in the Chinese Farming Sector', *Applied Economics*, 33, 2: 183–94.
Wan, G.H. and Zhou, Z.Y. (2005) 'Income Inequality in Rural China: Regression-based Decomposition Using Household Data', *Review of Development Economics*, 9, 1: 107–20.
Wei, S. and Wu, Y. (2003) 'Globalization and Inequality: Evidence from Within China', NBER Working Paper 8611 (Cambridge, MA: NBER).
Xing, Y. and Zhang, K.H. (2004) 'FDI and Regional Income Disparity in Host Countries: Evidence from China', *Economia Internazionale/International Economics*, 57, 4: 363–79.
Yang, K. (1994) 'On the Change in Regional Economic Disparity' (in Chinese), *Economic Research Journal (Jingji Yanjiu)*, 12: 19–33.

Yin, X. (1998) *The Procedure and Effects of China's Reform of International Trade* (in Chinese) (Shanxi: Shanxi Economic Publishing House).
Young, A. (2000) 'Gold into Base Metals: Productivity Growth in The People's Republic of China during the Reform Period', NBER Working Paper 7856 (Cambridge, MA: NBER).
Zhang, J., Wu, G. and Zhang, J.P. (2004) 'Estimation of Provincial Capital Stock in China: 1952–2000' (in Chinese), *Economic Research Journal (Jingji Yanjiu)*, 3: 35–44.
Zhang, X. and Zhang, K.H. (2003) 'How Does Globalization Affect Regional Inequality Within a Developing Country? Evidence from China', *Journal of Development Studies*, 39, 4: 47–67.

Appendix

(1) Unless indicated otherwise, data for the period 1987–98 are all from *Comprehensive Statistical Data and Materials for 50 Years of New China* (NBS, 1999). Data for years 1999–2001, unless indicated otherwise, are from *China Statistical Yearbook, 2000, 2001* and *2002* (NBS, various years).

(2) *Income*: Regional income is the weighted average of urban and rural per capita incomes, with non-agricultural and agricultural population shares as weights. Both urban and rural incomes are deflated by regional urban and rural CPIs. For Shanghai, Beijing and Tianjin, urban and rural CPIs are the same.

(3) *Capital*: Using the perpetual stock method, Zhang *et al.* (2004) constructed capital stock data at the 1952 price. They provide estimates for 1952–2000, and the authors extend the data to 2001. Capital stock in 1952 is given by

$$K_0 = \frac{I_0}{\delta + r}$$

where K_0 is the capital stock in 1952, I_0 investment in the same year, δ the depreciation rate, and r the average growth rate of real investment before 1952. This method is used in Hall and Jones (1999), Young (2000) and also ZZ.

(4) *Dependency*: The dependency ratio is computed as

$$Dependency = \frac{total\ population - employment}{employment} \times 100\%$$

(5) *Education (edu)*: *China Population Yearbooks* report regional population by educational attainment as from 1987. Unfortunately, such

data were not published for 1989, 1991 and 1992, and data for 1987 and 1988 are incomplete as the illiterate population are not reported. Also, unlike data for other years, the 1994 data did not consider members of the population below the age of 15. To estimate data for these years, we compute average years of schooling using data for the other years and then fit the model:

$$\ln(edu) = f(\cdot) \times \mu$$

where *edu* is per capita years of schooling, $f(\cdot)$ is simply a linear function of time trend and regional dummies, μ the error term. This model is estimated by the GLS technique, allowing for heteroscedasticity in the panel data. The R^2 of the estimated equation is 0.966. To denote the predicted value by ^, we have:

$$\hat{edu} = \exp[\ln(\hat{edu})]\exp(0.5\hat{\sigma}^2)$$

where $\ln(\hat{edu})$ denotes the predicted values of $\ln(edu)$ and $\hat{\sigma}^2$ is the estimated variance of μ. Data for 1987–89, 1991, 1992 and 1994 are estimated by the above model.

(6) *FDI*: *FDI* is defined as per capita FDI. The 1987–89 data for Sichuan are from the *China Statistical Yearbook*. The Qinghai data for 1988 and 2000 are the average of the neighbouring two years. FDI data are converted into RMB, using the medium exchange rate available in the *China Statistical Yearbooks*.

(7) *Trade*: *Trade* is computed as the trade/GDP ratio. Trade data are converted into RMB.

(8) *Reform*: *Reform* is computed as the proportion of workers and staff in non-state-owned entities.

(9) *Urbanization*: Urbanization is defined as the proportion of the non-agricultural population in the total. Except for Hebei, Heilongjiang and Gansu, the 1999–2001 data of the agricultural and non-agricultural population are from provincial statistical yearbooks. Total population of Hebei, Heilongjiang and Gansu in 2000 are from the *China Statistical Yearbook, 2001*. For these three regions, the 1999 population data are the averages of the neighbouring two years, and the 2001 data are forecast based on data in 2000 and the growth rate during 1999–2000.

(10) *Gov*: This is per capita government expenditure excluding administration fees, deflated by regional CPI.

Table 1.A1 Results of χ^2 test with H_0: model 1 = each of models 2–17

Model	Restrictions		Loglikelihood value	χ^2-value	Test result*
	Λ	θ			
1	Unrestricted	Unrestricted	−2531.93		
2	1	1	−2597.98	132.10	Reject H_0
3	0	1	−2549.73	35.60	Reject H_0
4	−1	1	−2626.91	189.96	Reject H_0
5	Unrestricted	1	−2548.54	33.22	Reject H_0
6	1	0	−2736.61	409.36	Reject H_0
7	0	0	−2538.43	13.00	Reject H_0
8	−1	0	−2639.73	215.60	Reject H_0
9	Unrestricted	0	−2537.98	12.10	Reject H_0
10	1	−1	−2881.56	699.26	Reject H_0
11	0	−1	−2623.64	183.42	Reject H_0
12	−1	−1	−2616.71	169.56	Reject H_0
13	Unrestricted	−1	−2585.36	106.86	Reject H_0
14	1	Unrestricted	−2590.62	117.38	Reject H_0
15	0	Unrestricted	−2533.22	2.58	**Not Reject H_0**
16	−1	Unrestricted	−2626.87	189.88	Reject H_0
17		$\lambda = \theta$	−2532.72	1.58	**Not Reject H_0**

Note: * level of significance = 1 per cent.

Table 1.A2 Inequality decomposition results, GE_0

Year	Relative contribution (%)								
	K	Dep	Edu	Gov	FDI	Trade	Reform	Urb	Location
1987	14.94	4.38	7.05	14.27	4.80	11.73	7.35	18.82	16.65
1988	15.53	4.14	6.91	13.85	5.47	12.20	7.06	18.15	16.69
1989	16.06	3.67	6.79	13.36	5.88	12.40	7.39	17.79	16.66
1990	16.24	3.42	7.79	12.60	6.01	12.62	7.82	17.12	16.37
1991	16.59	3.35	6.58	12.50	6.41	12.57	8.31	16.98	16.70
1992	16.99	3.55	6.53	12.09	6.66	12.07	8.86	16.46	16.79
1993	16.99	3.51	7.10	11.73	6.56	11.71	10.42	15.68	16.29
1994	17.06	3.71	5.85	13.45	6.87	11.52	11.60	14.21	15.73
1995	17.58	3.43	5.88	14.56	6.90	10.94	12.45	13.41	14.85
1996	18.13	3.17	5.49	14.69	6.90	11.30	12.56	13.01	14.75
1997	18.24	2.90	5.32	15.42	7.02	11.63	12.50	12.44	14.52
1998	18.94	2.62	5.27	15.61	7.29	11.83	11.19	12.57	14.68
1999	19.04	0.33	5.26	14.80	7.16	14.11	13.15	12.20	13.96
2000	18.81	−0.24	4.52	15.27	7.11	14.57	14.32	11.71	13.94
2001	19.34	0.25	4.84	14.17	7.24	14.65	14.16	11.55	13.80

Table 1.A3 Inequality decomposition results, GE_1

Year	Relative contribution (%)								
	K	Dep	Edu	Gov	FDI	Trade	Reform	Urb	Location
1987	15.42	4.91	7.04	14.74	4.99	11.62	6.28	19.01	16.00
1988	16.01	4.57	6.90	14.33	5.64	12.11	6.05	18.34	16.06
1989	16.52	4.10	6.80	13.85	6.05	12.26	6.45	17.96	16.01
1990	16.73	3.87	7.78	13.06	6.13	12.42	6.95	17.33	15.73
1991	17.06	3.76	6.62	12.91	6.52	12.34	7.51	17.19	16.09
1992	17.42	3.96	6.56	12.51	6.75	11.84	8.13	16.66	16.17
1993	17.36	4.00	7.05	12.10	6.62	11.50	9.86	15.88	15.62
1994	17.39	4.16	5.85	13.93	6.90	11.38	10.97	14.44	14.98
1995	17.89	3.92	5.89	15.06	6.91	10.81	11.82	13.64	14.06
1996	18.47	3.61	5.54	15.22	6.89	11.16	11.92	13.26	13.92
1997	18.61	3.32	5.31	16.01	7.00	11.49	11.87	12.71	13.67
1998	19.33	3.02	5.20	16.20	7.26	11.67	10.68	12.84	13.80
1999	19.35	0.48	5.33	15.34	7.13	14.06	12.71	12.45	13.16
2000	19.16	−0.09	4.56	15.74	7.09	14.50	13.95	11.95	13.14
2001	19.63	0.41	4.83	14.71	7.21	14.56	13.85	11.74	13.05

Table 1.A2 continued

Absolute contribution								
K	Dep	Edu	Gov	FDI	Trade	Reform	Urb	Location
0.006	0.002	0.003	0.006	0.002	0.005	0.003	0.008	0.007
0.007	0.002	0.003	0.006	0.002	0.005	0.003	0.008	0.007
0.007	0.002	0.003	0.006	0.003	0.005	0.003	0.008	0.007
0.008	0.002	0.004	0.006	0.003	0.006	0.004	0.008	0.008
0.008	0.002	0.003	0.006	0.003	0.006	0.004	0.008	0.008
0.008	0.002	0.003	0.006	0.003	0.006	0.004	0.008	0.008
0.009	0.002	0.004	0.006	0.003	0.006	0.005	0.008	0.008
0.010	0.002	0.003	0.008	0.004	0.006	0.006	0.008	0.009
0.011	0.002	0.004	0.009	0.004	0.007	0.008	0.008	0.009
0.012	0.002	0.004	0.009	0.004	0.007	0.008	0.008	0.010
0.012	0.002	0.004	0.010	0.005	0.008	0.008	0.008	0.010
0.012	0.002	0.003	0.010	0.005	0.008	0.007	0.008	0.010
0.013	0.000	0.004	0.010	0.005	0.010	0.009	0.008	0.010
0.013	0.000	0.003	0.011	0.005	0.010	0.010	0.008	0.010
0.014	0.000	0.003	0.010	0.005	0.010	0.010	0.008	0.010

Table 1.A3 continued

Absolute contribution								
K	Dep	Edu	Gov	FDI	Trade	Reform	Urb	Location
0.007	0.002	0.003	0.007	0.002	0.005	0.003	0.008	0.007
0.007	0.002	0.003	0.007	0.003	0.006	0.003	0.008	0.007
0.008	0.002	0.003	0.007	0.003	0.006	0.003	0.009	0.008
0.008	0.002	0.004	0.007	0.003	0.006	0.004	0.009	0.008
0.008	0.002	0.003	0.006	0.003	0.006	0.004	0.009	0.008
0.009	0.002	0.003	0.006	0.003	0.006	0.004	0.008	0.008
0.009	0.002	0.004	0.007	0.004	0.006	0.005	0.009	0.008
0.010	0.003	0.004	0.008	0.004	0.007	0.007	0.009	0.009
0.012	0.003	0.004	0.010	0.005	0.007	0.008	0.009	0.010
0.013	0.003	0.004	0.011	0.005	0.008	0.008	0.009	0.010
0.014	0.002	0.004	0.012	0.005	0.008	0.009	0.009	0.010
0.014	0.002	0.004	0.012	0.005	0.008	0.008	0.009	0.010
0.015	0.000	0.004	0.012	0.005	0.011	0.010	0.009	0.010
0.015	0.000	0.004	0.012	0.005	0.011	0.011	0.009	0.010
0.015	0.000	0.004	0.011	0.006	0.011	0.011	0.009	0.010

Table 1.A4 Inequality decomposition results, Atkinson index (e = 0)

Year	Relative contribution (%)								
	K	Dep	Edu	Gov	FDI	Trade	Reform	Urb	Location
1987	14.93	4.38	7.04	14.27	4.79	11.73	7.37	18.83	16.66
1988	15.53	4.13	6.89	13.84	5.46	12.20	7.08	18.16	16.70
1989	16.06	3.66	6.78	13.36	5.87	12.39	7.41	17.79	16.67
1990	16.24	3.42	7.78	12.60	5.99	12.62	7.84	17.13	16.39
1991	16.60	3.34	6.57	12.50	6.40	12.57	8.32	16.99	16.71
1992	17.00	3.54	6.51	12.08	6.65	12.06	8.87	16.46	16.81
1993	17.01	3.51	7.09	11.72	6.54	11.71	10.43	15.69	16.31
1994	17.08	3.70	5.84	13.45	6.85	11.51	11.62	14.21	15.74
1995	17.60	3.42	5.86	14.56	6.88	10.93	12.46	13.41	14.86
1996	18.16	3.16	5.47	14.69	6.89	11.29	12.58	13.01	14.76
1997	18.27	2.89	5.31	15.43	7.01	11.62	12.51	12.44	14.53
1998	18.96	2.62	5.25	15.62	7.27	11.82	11.20	12.56	14.70
1999	19.07	0.34	5.24	14.79	7.14	14.11	13.16	12.19	13.97
2000	18.83	−0.23	4.50	15.27	7.09	14.56	14.33	11.70	13.95
2001	19.37	0.25	4.82	14.17	7.22	14.65	14.17	11.54	13.81

Table 1.A5 Inequality decomposition results, squared CV

Year	Relative contribution (%)								
	K	Dep	Edu	Gov	FDI	Trade	Reform	Urb	Location
1987	15.90	5.47	7.06	15.20	5.18	11.52	5.12	19.19	15.36
1988	16.49	5.02	6.94	14.83	5.82	12.02	4.93	18.53	15.42
1989	16.99	4.55	6.85	14.35	6.23	12.11	5.41	18.15	15.36
1990	17.22	4.33	7.81	13.54	6.28	12.19	6.00	17.55	15.08
1991	17.54	4.19	6.70	13.33	6.63	12.08	6.63	17.42	15.47
1992	17.85	4.38	6.63	12.95	6.85	11.59	7.31	16.89	15.54
1993	17.73	4.52	7.06	12.49	6.69	11.26	9.23	16.10	14.91
1994	17.70	4.65	5.89	14.44	6.94	11.21	10.26	14.71	14.19
1995	18.18	4.43	5.95	15.57	6.92	10.65	11.12	13.92	13.25
1996	18.78	4.10	5.65	15.78	6.89	10.99	11.20	13.56	13.05
1997	18.95	3.79	5.34	16.63	7.00	11.29	11.18	13.04	12.78
1998	19.67	3.46	5.18	16.81	7.24	11.46	10.13	13.17	12.88
1999	19.65	0.60	5.46	15.91	7.12	13.94	12.18	12.78	12.36
2000	19.48	0.04	4.66	16.25	7.09	14.38	13.48	12.29	12.33
2001	19.90	0.54	4.88	15.28	7.21	14.42	13.45	12.04	12.28

Table 1.A4 *continued*

Absolute contribution								
K	Dep	Edu	Gov	FDI	Trade	Reform	Urb	Location
0.006	0.002	0.003	0.006	0.002	0.005	0.003	0.008	0.007
0.007	0.002	0.003	0.006	0.002	0.005	0.003	0.008	0.007
0.007	0.002	0.003	0.006	0.003	0.005	0.003	0.008	0.007
0.007	0.002	0.004	0.006	0.003	0.006	0.004	0.008	0.008
0.008	0.002	0.003	0.006	0.003	0.006	0.004	0.008	0.008
0.008	0.002	0.003	0.006	0.003	0.006	0.004	0.008	0.008
0.008	0.002	0.003	0.006	0.003	0.006	0.005	0.008	0.008
0.009	0.002	0.003	0.007	0.004	0.006	0.006	0.008	0.009
0.011	0.002	0.004	0.009	0.004	0.007	0.008	0.008	0.009
0.011	0.002	0.003	0.009	0.004	0.007	0.008	0.008	0.009
0.012	0.002	0.003	0.010	0.005	0.008	0.008	0.008	0.009
0.012	0.002	0.003	0.010	0.005	0.008	0.007	0.008	0.009
0.013	0.000	0.004	0.010	0.005	0.009	0.009	0.008	0.009
0.013	0.000	0.003	0.010	0.005	0.010	0.010	0.008	0.009
0.013	0.000	0.003	0.010	0.005	0.010	0.010	0.008	0.009

Table 1.A5 *continued*

Absolute contribution								
K	Dep	Edu	Gov	FDI	Trade	Reform	Urb	Location
0.016	0.005	0.007	0.015	0.005	0.011	0.005	0.019	0.015
0.017	0.005	0.007	0.015	0.006	0.012	0.005	0.019	0.016
0.018	0.005	0.007	0.015	0.007	0.013	0.006	0.019	0.016
0.019	0.005	0.009	0.015	0.007	0.014	0.007	0.020	0.017
0.019	0.005	0.007	0.015	0.007	0.013	0.007	0.019	0.017
0.020	0.005	0.007	0.014	0.008	0.013	0.008	0.019	0.017
0.021	0.005	0.008	0.015	0.008	0.014	0.011	0.019	0.018
0.024	0.006	0.008	0.020	0.009	0.015	0.014	0.020	0.019
0.028	0.007	0.009	0.024	0.011	0.016	0.017	0.021	0.020
0.030	0.007	0.009	0.025	0.011	0.018	0.018	0.022	0.021
0.032	0.006	0.009	0.028	0.012	0.019	0.019	0.022	0.022
0.032	0.006	0.009	0.028	0.012	0.019	0.017	0.022	0.021
0.035	0.001	0.010	0.028	0.013	0.024	0.021	0.022	0.022
0.035	0.000	0.008	0.029	0.013	0.026	0.024	0.022	0.022
0.035	0.001	0.009	0.027	0.013	0.025	0.024	0.021	0.022

2
The Urban–Rural Income Gap and Income Inequality in China

Terry Sicular, Yue Ximing, Björn Gustafsson and Shi Li

Introduction

Studies of China's inequality almost universally report that the gap between urban and rural household incomes in China is large, has increased over time, and contributes substantially to overall inequality. According to most estimates, mean per capita income in urban China is more than triple that in rural areas, giving China one of the highest urban–rural income ratios in the world. The size of this gap has been discussed in the Chinese official media, is noted in government and Communist Party reports, and is the motivation for major policy initiatives such as the 'Build a Socialist New Countryside' campaign of 2006, which aims to reduce the gap by boosting public spending in rural areas.

China's urban–rural income gap is often attributed to policies that have inhibited labour mobility, most importantly the household registration or *hukou* system. The household registration system was established during the Maoist period to control population movement. It has continued to the present and is reinforced by a range of complementary policies such as taxation of urban employers that hire migrants, prohibition of urban employment of migrants in some trades, and the denial of urban public services such as education to unregistered households.[1] In recent years, the government has carried out reforms of the *hukou* system so as to allow greater mobility, but substantial barriers remain (Wang 2004). These barriers are thought to protect the welfare of registered urban residents, a politically sensitive group, but at the same time they create political concerns of a different sort.

Whether or not concerns about the urban–rural income gap are justified depends, among other things, on the true magnitude of the gap as well as on the factors that underlie the gap. To date, a range of studies have examined China's urban–rural income gap (for example, Knight and Song 1999; Yang and Zhou 1999; Zhao and Tong 2000; Shi 2004; Sicular, Zhao and Shi 2004; Benjamin *et al.* 2005). For several reasons, most linked to data constraints, past estimates of the income gap are probably biased. First, most income data for China do not include certain components. One missing component is housing related income; specifically, the imputed rental value of owner-occupied housing and imputed subsidies on publicly-owned rental housing. Housing related income is likely to differ systematically between urban and rural areas, and it is of recent interest because in the late 1990s China privatized urban housing (Khan and Riskin 2007). Also missing from income is the value of household consumption of public services in areas such as education, health care and local infrastructure. Consumption of public services is, again, likely to be higher in urban than rural areas, and so its exclusion would cause understatement of China's urban–rural gap.

Second, most studies do not control for spatial differences in the cost of living. This is understandable, as systematic information on spatial price differences has been scarce. Still, if the cost of living in urban areas is substantially higher than that in rural areas, then the real gap in incomes may be smaller than that reported in the literature.

Third, most estimates of China's urban–rural income gap are based on data that exclude unregistered migrants resident in urban areas. Since rural-to-urban migration is generally considered an important mechanism for narrowing the urban–rural income gap, excluding rural-to-urban migrants is problematic. Excluding this group, which in China has a mean income below that of registered urban and above that of rural residents, causes overstatement of the urban–rural income gap. Including migrants is increasingly relevant in studies of China, because restrictions on migration have been loosened and migration has grown accordingly. Moreover, incorporating migrants into the estimation of inequality measures is relevant for international comparisons as, in most countries, measurement of inequality includes migrants.

With these considerations in mind, here, we recalculate the size of China's urban–rural income gap, estimate the contribution of the revised gap to overall inequality and analyze the factors underlying the gap. For our analysis, we use household and individual data from Chinese Household Income Project (CHIP) household income surveys for 1995 and 2002. These surveys were conducted under the auspices of the Chinese Academy of Social Sciences (CASS). They are large, nationally representative, and contain detailed information on household income and other relevant household and individual characteristics. The CHIP data have certain advantages. They are relatively recent, and so provide more up-to-date information than is generally available. Other data with wide regional coverage, most notably from the National Bureau of Statistics (NBS) household survey, are typically only available to researchers in tabulated or aggregated form. Alternative datasets that provide household level survey data such as the China Health and Nutrition Survey (CHNS) have narrower regional coverage than the CHIP survey. Finally, the CHIP dataset is unusual in that it contains information on housing-related income components and on rural-to-urban migrants.

The first step of our analysis is to recalculate the size of the urban–rural gap and its contribution to national inequality. We do so for China as a whole and for its three major regions – the east, the central region and the west. In this recalculation, we make three modifications that bring our measurement of the gap closer to international best practice and allow more comparability with studies for other countries. First, we use a fuller measure of income which includes housing related components of income. Unfortunately, we cannot measure the implicit subsidies associated with household consumption of public services. From a theoretical standpoint this should be included to capture fully the urban–rural differences, but the necessary information is unavailable. More generally, data on household consumption of public services is unavailable for most countries and rarely included in international calculations of household income.[2]

Second, we adjust for spatial differences in the cost of living. Costs of living can differ systematically among regions and between urban and rural areas so, ideally, studies of inequality should use incomes that have been adjusted using spatial price deflators. Due to lack of data on regional price levels, spatial price deflation is rare in studies on China. An exception is Ravallion and Chen (2004), which uses estimates of the urban and rural poverty lines to adjust for cost of living differences, and then recalculates national inequality. More recently, Benjamin *et al.* (2005) use new spatial price indices from a study by Brandt and Holz (2004) to recalculate the level of national inequality. Neither of these studies, however, uses spatial price deflation for a detailed analysis of the urban–rural income gap. Here, we use the Brandt and Holz (2004) spatial price indices to deflate incomes and then recalculate the urban–rural income gap and its contribution to inequality. Where relevant, we compare our findings with those of Ravallion and Chen (2004) and Benjamin *et al.* (2005).[3]

Third, we include rural-to-urban migrants. Past analyses exclude unregistered rural migrants living in cities. The 2002 CHIP survey data contain information for a sample of rural migrants resident but not registered in urban areas. Using this sample, we are able to provide some indicative findings that include migrants. We discuss the coverage of our migrant sample in more detail below, as well as some broader methodological concerns regarding the measurement of China's urban and migrant populations.

The second step of our analysis is an investigation of the factors underlying the urban–rural gap. Here, we use the Oaxaca–Blinder decomposition. The Oaxaca–Blinder method cannot identify how particular policies (such as the household registration system) contribute to the gap, but it gives information on the extent to which the gap reflects differences between urban and rural areas in household characteristics as opposed to simple location of residence. The proportion of the urban–rural gap due to differences between urban and rural areas in household characteristics is usually called 'explained' differences, while the proportion due to simple locale of residence is called the 'unexplained' differences. One interpretation of the 'unexplained' proportion is that it reflects discrimination, as this proportion comes solely from group categorization (location, here), rather than from differences in household characteristics, which are considered fair reasons for an income differential.

This decomposition method also gives a measure, albeit from a partial equilibrium perspective, of how large the gap would be if rural and urban groups had similar characteristics. Such information is useful from a policy perspective. For example, if differences in educational characteristics between rural and urban areas contribute substantially to the gap – as we find they do – then policy makers may wish to focus their attention on the determinants, and consequences, of education levels in the two sectors. As in our calculations of the urban–rural income gap, the Oaxaca–Blinder decomposition is similarly carried out with and without the migrant sample included. The decomposition results with and without migrants provide different information. The results without migrants are especially useful if one is interested in extent to which urban residents are favoured over rural residents due to long urban biased governmental policies. The results with migrants are useful if one focuses on the urban–rural divide, as this work does, because migrants comprise an increasing share of the urban population and, in the broader development process, migration serves as a mechanism that erodes the urban–rural income gap.

Several key findings emerge from our analysis. We find that, after recalculation, the urban–rural income gap is substantially reduced. While including housing related income components increases the income gap somewhat, adjusting for spatial price differences dramatically reduces it. Including migrants narrows the gap further. With these revisions, China still has a relatively large urban–rural income ratio, but that ratio is within the range of most other countries.

It follows that these adjustments also reduce the contribution of China's urban–rural gap to overall inequality. After recalculating income and including migrants, we find that in 2002 the urban–rural gap contributes about one quarter of overall inequality, as compared to estimates of 50 per cent or more in most studies.

The Oaxaca–Blinder decomposition reveals that household and individual characteristics such as education, age, and household demographics, indeed contribute to the urban–rural income gap. Differences in the endowments of such characteristics, holding the returns to these characteristics constant, contributed about half of the income gap. Location of residence, including differences between urban and rural areas in the returns to household and individual characteristics, contributed the other half. Interestingly, the contribution of location declined between 1995 and 2002, although only modestly. This is consistent with the increase in spatial mobility during this time.

The decomposition reveals further that education is the most important non-location characteristic underlying the urban–rural income gap. In 2002, differences in education levels between urban and rural areas contributed one quarter of the income gap. Differences in the endowments of and returns to other household characteristics (such as family size and composition, landholdings and Party membership) are, on balance, less important. That said, in the long term, education levels are endogenous and current investments in human capital are probably affected by other household characteristics, such as family size and composition.

Definitions and data

The data used for the analysis in this chapter come from two rounds of the CHIP survey conducted in 1996 and 2003 for the reference periods of 1995 and 2002. These surveys were carried out under the direction of a team of researchers consisting of scholars at the Institute of Economics, Chinese Academy of Social Sciences, and researchers from other countries. The data were collected by the NBS using survey instruments designed by the project research team. A detailed description of the data can be found in Li *et al.* (2007). Here, we point out some of the main features of the data set and discuss aspects most relevant to our analysis.

Regional coverage changed somewhat between the two years of the survey. To ensure comparability between the results for the two years, we use a sub-sample having the property that each location (province*rural, province*urban) was present in the survey for both years under investigation. The rural sample covers Anhui, Beijing, Gansu, Guangdong, Guizhou, Hebei, Henan, Hubei, Hunan, Liaoning, Jiangsu, Jiangxi, Jilin, Shaanxi, Shandong, Shanxi, Sichuan, Yunnan and Zhejiang. The urban sample covers Anhui, Beijing, Gansu, Guangdong, Henan, Hubei, Jiangsu, Liaoning, Shanxi, Sichuan and Yunnan.[4]

Since urban residents were over-sampled in 1995 and under-sampled in 2002, we weight the urban and rural sub-samples so that their population shares are equal those in the total population according to official NBS census based population data. With this adjustment, the sample distribution between rural and urban areas is consistent with the official population distribution between urban and rural areas for all of China. All analyses using the combined urban and rural samples use this population weight adjustment.

A limitation of most household survey data for China is that rural-to-urban migrants who do not have an urban residence permit are excluded. For 2002, the CHIP survey includes a special sample of migrants, making it possible to produce more complete estimates for that year. Below, we describe the migrant sample and explore how including migrants influences the size of the rural–urban gap and its contribution to inequality. We also offer a more general discussion of China's urban population statistics.

The target variable for this study is household per capita disposable income.[5] This includes cash income, retained in-kind income (important in rural China, particularly at the beginning of the period studied), and other income in kind (relevant in urban China in the past, although declining in importance in recent years). Net taxes and fees are subtracted.

Most economists believe that income should include housing related components. The NBS does not include these components in disposable income, nor do most other household income data for China. Our estimates of average household income in China use the NBS definition but add in housing subsidies and imputed rent. Income levels here are therefore higher than those obtained using the NBS definition. Depending on the distributional profile of housing subsidies and imputed rent, our definition of income could show larger or smaller inequality than the NBS definition. In fact, we find that including housing increases inequality, which is not surprising, as higher-income and urban households tend to enjoy larger housing subsidies and imputed rents.

During the period under investigation, China carried out housing reform in urban China. In the past, most urban households had lived in public housing and paid low rent, implying that they received subsidies for rental housing. These subsidies largely benefited better-off households (Khan *et al.* 1993). In the late 1990s, the government privatized urban public housing. By 2002, most urban residents owned their homes and no longer received rental housing subsidies. Rather, they now received the imputed rents from owned housing. For urban China and China as a whole, inclusion of housing components and changes in these components due to the housing reform could influence the measured urban–rural gap and inequality.[6]

Our analysis treats the household as the income-receiving unit and divides the disposable income of each household by the number of household members. Following what is now common practice in the analysis of income distributions, we assign this household average to each member of the household. Individuals are thus the unit of analysis, and we abstract from intra-household allocation issues.[7]

Since price levels have changed over time, and differentially among provinces and between rural and urban areas, we use official provincial consumer price indices to express 2002 incomes in 1995 prices. Note that separate indices are available for rural versus urban areas in each province. We use these separate indices so that deflation factors can differ between urban and rural areas within provinces as well as among provinces.

Prices differ not only across time, but also spatially at any point in time. This is especially true in a geographically large country such as China. Analyses of income inequality for China typically do not adjust for spatial price differences because price data by region have been unavailable. A recent study for China by Brandt and Holz (2004) gives estimates of regional differences in the costs of living among provinces and between urban and rural areas. Their study uses raw regional price data for 1990 to calculate baseline spatial cost of living indices for that year. The 1990 spatial price indices are then extrapolated to later years using provincial urban and rural consumer price indices.

The Brandt–Holz spatial price deflators have some limitations. One is that their estimates of housing costs are based on the costs of housing construction materials, and the difference in the costs of construction materials between urban and rural areas is typically smaller than the difference in costs of housing services. For this reason, the Brandt–Holz estimates may understate the price differential between urban and rural areas. Also, they only have raw price data for 1990, and they use a basket of consumption quantities for 1990. The accuracy of extrapolations from 1990 will obviously decline the longer the intervening time period because the structure of consumption and also the quality of goods and services consumed changes over time. Here, we are extrapolating a fairly long way, to 2002.

Despite these limitations, the Brandt–Holz estimates provide an opportunity to correct, albeit imperfectly, for spatial price differences, and to see how such corrections affect the level and composition of inequality. Below, we present findings calculated both with and without spatial price adjustments. In most cases, the differences are substantial.

The urban–rural income gap: magnitude and trends

Table 2.1 gives average household per capita income for all of China, and separately for urban and rural households. The statistics in this table

Table 2.1 Mean household disposable per capita incomes: national, urban, rural and the urban–rural gap (units: *yuan*, ratios)

	1995			2002			
	NBS, unadjusted	**Unadjusted**	**PPP**	**NBS, unadjusted**	**Unadjusted**	**PPP**	**PPP, 1995 prices**
National	2,396	2,921	2,584	4,770	5,826	5,139	4,554
Urban	4,429	5,635	4,259	8,038	10,004	7,798	6,910
Rural	1,564	1,810	1,899	2,673	3,145	3,434	3,043
Ratio urban to rural	2.83	3.11	2.24	3.01	3.18	2.27	2.27
Urban minus rural	2,865	3,825	2,360	5,366	6,858	4,364	3,867

Notes:

1 As urban households were over-sampled in 1995 and rural households over-sampled in 2002, national mean incomes are calculated using weights that reflect the proportions of urban and rural individuals in the Chinese population as given by NBS census-based data (Table 2.5).

2 Except for columns labelled NBS, income includes housing components of income (rental subsidies and imputed rents on owner-occupied housing). Migrants are not included in these calculations.

3 PPP numbers are adjusted for spatial price differences using the Brandt–Holz (B–H) spatial cost of living estimates. The numeraire is the nationwide average cost of living for a joint basket of consumer goods, which we calculate as a weighted average of the B–H mean urban and rural costs of living where the weights are current population shares. Choice of population weights in calculating this numeraire affects income levels somewhat, but not the ratios or inequality levels.

4 In the last column, 2002 incomes are deflated to 1995 prices using NBS consumer price indices for each provincial urban and rural location, and then adjusted for spatial price differences using the 1995 spatial cost of living estimates from B–H. This is equivalent to first converting 2002 incomes into PPP terms using the B–H spatial price indices and then deflating them using the CPI for the nationwide average cost of living between 1995 and 2002.

exclude the migrant sub-sample, which is incorporated starting in the section on urbanization and migrants (p. 42).

Table 2.1 provides two measures of the urban–rural income gap; the ratio of urban to rural mean incomes (relative gap) and the difference between urban and rural mean incomes (absolute gap). For both 1995 and 2002, the first columns give income calculated according to the NBS definition, which excludes housing components of income. The second columns give NBS income plus housing components of income. These numbers are in current prices with no spatial price adjustments.[8] Not surprisingly, adding in housing related income increases mean incomes for both the rural and urban samples. Urban incomes increase more than rural incomes because the imputed value of urban owner-occupied housing and housing subsidies exceeds those in rural areas. Consequently, including this component enlarges the urban–rural income ratio, by 10 per cent in 1995 and by 6 per cent in 2002. In ensuing sections, we only present findings calculated using the more complete measure of income that includes housing components of income.

Whether including housing components or not, at current, unadjusted prices the urban–rural income ratio is substantial, close to or exceeding 3 in both years. This is high by international standards. Eastwood and Lipton (2004) give ratios for other Asian countries in the 1990s that fall between 1.3 and 1.8, with the Philippines a high outlier at 2.17. Similarly, Knight and Song (1999: 338) give urban–rural ratios for income and consumption in twelve countries, mostly in Asia but also in the Middle East and Africa. China's ratio exceeds those in all the other countries listed except Zimbabwe and South Africa. Note that most of the ratios for other countries reported in these sources include housing components of income but are not adjusted for spatial price differences.

The next columns give income adjusted to control for spatial differences in the cost of living. *Yuan* units in these columns reflect purchasing price parity (PPP) with national average consumer prices over both urban and rural areas. We refer to incomes after adjustment for spatial price differences as purchasing price parity incomes. To allow comparison with 1995, for 2002 Table 2.1 also gives PPP incomes in constant 1995 prices.

Adjustments for spatial price differences reduce the relative gap substantially because costs of living are higher in urban areas. According to Brandt and Holz's cost of living estimates, prices in urban areas were, on average, 36 per cent higher than in rural areas in 1995 and 39 per cent higher in 2002. With spatial price deflation the relative gap declines markedly from 3.1 to 2.2 in 1995 and from 3.2 to 2.3 in 2002. Even so, China's ratios remain relatively high by international standards.

Comparison of the PPP figures in constant prices (shown in the last columns for both 1995 and 2002) reveals that China's urban–rural income gap has increased little over time. Between 1995 and 2002, the adjusted relative gap rose by a mere 1 per cent. However, the absolute gap increased by 64 per cent from 2360 to 3867 *yuan* in 1995 constant prices.

China's urban–rural gap is not uniform regionally. As shown in Table 2.2, the relative gap is highest in the west where, in both 1995 and 2002, the unadjusted ratios exceeded 4, as compared to 3 or less for the central region and the east. As above, adjusting for spatial price differences greatly reduces the relative gaps. Urban/rural differentials in the cost of living are highest in the west, so PPP adjustments narrow the gap more in the west than elsewhere. Nevertheless, even in PPP terms the west's urban–rural income ratios remain well above 3, as compared to around 2 in the central region and the east.

Table 2.2 Regional differences in income per capita and the urban–rural gap (units: *yuan*, ratios)

	1995		**2002**		
	Unadjusted	**PPP**	**Unadjusted**	**PPP**	**PPP, 1995 prices**
Western region	2,105	1,987	4,138	3,864	3,424
Urban	4,963	4,198	8,662	7,498	6,644
Rural	1,167	1,261	2,005	2,150	1,905
Ratio of urban to rural	4.25	3.33	4.32	3.49	3.49
Urban minus rural	3,796	2,937	6,658	5,348	4,739
Central region	2,229	2,170	4,550	4,382	3,883
Urban	4,175	3,400	7,995	6,790	6,017
Rural	1,558	1,747	2,644	3,050	2,702
Ratio of urban to rural	2.68	1.95	3.02	2.23	2.23
Urban minus rural	2,617	1,653	5,350	3,740	3,314
Eastern region	4,246	3,411	8,480	6,762	5,992
Urban	7,555	5,148	13,029	9,038	8,009
Rural	2,527	2,509	4,520	4,781	4,236
Ratio of urban to rural	2.99	2.05	2.88	1.89	1.89
Urban minus rural	5,028	2,640	8,509	4,258	3,773

Notes:

1 Notes to Table 2.1 apply.

2 For each region, mean income is calculated using weights that reflect the proportion of urban to rural individuals within that region as given by the NBS census-based data.

3 Western provinces are Sichuan (including Chongqing), Guizhou, Yunnan, Shaanxi and Gansu; central provinces are Shanxi, Jilin, Anhui, Jiangxi, Henan, Hubei and Hunan; eastern provinces include Beijing, Hebei, Liaoning, Jiangsu, Shandong, Zhejiang and Guangdong.

Between 1995 and 2002, the relative gap rose in the west and the central region, but declined in the east. These trends in the west and the central region indicate that those parts of China where poverty is most concentrated are falling further behind, at least in relative terms. Yet trends in the east, China's most developed region, hint that perhaps in the long term, as China becomes more developed, the urban–rural gap could stabilize or even narrow.

The contribution of the urban–rural gap to inequality

The standard method of measuring the contribution of spatial income differences to inequality is decomposition of inequality by subgroup. Discussion of this approach and its application to the analysis of spatial inequality are available elsewhere (see Shorrocks 1984; Shorrocks and Wan 2005), so here we summarize only the main elements. Subgroup inequality decomposition is typically carried out using inequality indices from the entropy family. We employ two commonly used entropy measures, the Theil L (Mean Logarithmic Deviation) and the Theil T. The Theil L is defined as

$$I_{TL} = \frac{1}{n}\sum_{i=1}^{n} \ln\left(\frac{\mu}{y_i}\right) \tag{2.1}$$

and the Theil T as

$$I_{TT} = \frac{1}{n\mu}\sum_{i=1}^{n} \left[\ln\left(\frac{y_i}{\mu}\right)\right] y_i \tag{2.2}$$

where μ is mean income, y_i income of the ith individual, and n the total number of individuals.

These inequality indices can be decomposed among subgroups using the general formula:

$$I = \sum_{g=1}^{k} w_g I_g + I(\mu_1, \mu_2, \ldots, \mu_k) \tag{2.3}$$

where w_g is a weight attached to the gth group, I_g inequality within the gth group, and μ_g mean income of the gth group. Equation (2.3) states that overall inequality is equal to the weighted sum of inequality within

Table 2.3 Inequality decomposition by urban and rural subgroups

	1995				2002			
	Theil L		Theil T		Theil L		Theil T	
	Unadjusted	PPP	Unadjusted	PPP	Unadjusted	PPP	Unadjusted	PPP
Total	0.363	0.264	0.398	0.287	0.368	0.275	0.355	0.263
Between	0.149	0.074	0.158	0.078	0.164	0.083	0.160	0.083
Within	0.214	0.190	0.240	0.209	0.204	0.193	0.195	0.180
Contribution of between and within effects (%)								
Total	100.0	100.0	100.0	100.0	100.0	100.0	100.0	100.0
Between	41.0	27.9	39.7	27.3	44.6	30.0	45.1	31.6
Within	59.0	72.1	60.3	72.7	55.4	70.0	54.9	68.4

Notes:
1 The notes to Table 2.1 apply.
2 PPP figures are comparable across years because deflation involves multiplication by a constant, and the inequality indices and decompositions are scale invariant.

each subgroup plus inequality measured across mean incomes of the subgroups. The weighted sum of inequality within each subgroup is referred to as 'within-group' inequality. Inequality measured across mean incomes of the subgroups is referred to as 'between-group' inequality.

Since we are interested in the contribution to inequality of the urban–rural income gap, we divide the sample into urban and rural subgroups. The contribution of the urban–rural income gap to inequality is the between-group component of the decomposition and equals inequality measured across mean incomes of the urban and rural groups.

Table 2.3 gives values of the two Theil indices and the results of inequality decompositions for 1995 and 2002. These are calculated using both unadjusted and PPP incomes. The overall level of inequality shows no clear trend between 1995 and 2002. The Theil L increases slightly, while the Theil T decreases. This is true regardless of whether or not incomes are adjusted for spatial price differences. The contrasting trends in the Theil L and Theil T indices arise because the underlying Lorenz curves for these two years cross.

Adjustments for spatial price differences substantially reduce the level of overall inequality. The extent of the reduction is similar for the two indices. In 1995, the price adjustment reduces inequality by about 27 per cent and, in 2002, by about 25 per cent. Therefore, roughly one quarter of inequality in unadjusted incomes is attributable to spatial price differences. This finding is consistent with that of Ravallion and Chen (2004), who also find that correcting for spatial price differences reduces overall inequality.[9] The fact that correcting for spatial price differences reduces inequality reflects that spatial price differences are positively correlated with levels of income.[10]

The lower half of Table 2.3 shows the percentages of inequality contributed by between-versus within-group inequality. The results for the Theil L and Theil T are very similar. For unadjusted incomes, between-group inequality contributes about 40 per cent of total inequality in 1995, increasing to 45 per cent in 2002. These numbers would suggest that the urban–rural gap is an increasingly important source of inequality, approaching half of the total.[11]

Adjusting for spatial price differences, however, reduces the contribution of between-group inequality noticeably, to less than 30 per cent in 1995 and about 30–32 per cent in 2002.[12] In real terms, then, perhaps one third of all inequality is due to the urban–rural gap; furthermore, the contribution of the real income gap has increased somewhat over time.

Disaggregating by region provides further information on the structure underlying the urban–rural income gap's contribution to inequality. Table 2.4 gives inequality decompositions for each of the three regions. For simplicity, the table contains only results calculated using PPP incomes. The regional differences are marked. In the west, between-group inequality contributes roughly half of total inequality, as compared to less than a quarter in the east (bottom of Table 2.4). The central region lies in between.

Indeed, the absolute levels of between-group inequality in the east and the central region are relatively low (top of Table 2.4). In these areas, then, if policy makers wish to reduce inequality, they should focus their efforts on income differentials within urban or within rural areas. The situation is different in western China. Overall inequality is markedly higher in the west, and the numbers in Table 2.4 suggest that the reason for this, and the distinguishing feature of inequality in the west, is the high level of between-group inequality. The level of between-group inequality in western China is two to three times that in the other regions, while within-group inequality is roughly similar to that in the other regions. Concerns about the urban–rural gap, then, should focus on western China.

Urbanization, migrants and the rural–urban gap

During the reform period, the level of urbanization in China has increased substantially. As shown in Table 2.5, according to official statistics the urban population share rose from about 26 per cent in 1990 to 29 per cent in 1995, and further to 39 per cent in 2002. This increase

Table 2.4 Inequality decomposition of PPP incomes by urban and rural subgroups by region

	1995		2002	
	Theil L	**Theil T**	**Theil L**	**Theil T**
Western region				
Total	0.308	0.409	0.352	0.342
Between	0.157	0.173	0.186	0.191
Within	0.151	0.235	0.166	0.151
Central region				
Total	0.165	0.164	0.215	0.215
Between	0.046	0.050	0.077	0.079
Within	0.118	0.114	0.138	0.135
Eastern region				
Total	0.267	0.264	0.229	0.220
Between	0.062	0.064	0.050	0.049
Within	0.205	0.200	0.179	0.171
Contribution of between and within effects (%)				
Western region				
Total	100	100	100	100
Between	51	42	53	56
Within	49	58	47	44
Central region				
Total	100	100	100	100
Between	28	31	36	37
Within	72	69	64	63
Eastern region				
Total	100	100	100	100
Between	23	24	22	22
Within	77	76	78	78

Notes:
1 The notes to Table 2.1 apply.
2 PPP results are comparable across years because deflation involves multiplication by a constant and the inequality indices and decompositions are scale invariant.

Table 2.5 Urbanization in China

	Urban population as % of total	**Urban natural rate of increase**
1990	26.41	1.043
1995	29.04	0.923
2000	36.22	0.510
2001	37.66	na
2002	39.09	na

Sources: Urban population shares are from NBS (2003). Note that these numbers include unregistered rural migrants residing in urban areas. The urban natural rates of increase are from NBS (1996) and Chan and Hu (2003).

holds implications for estimates of the urban–rural gap and inequality. Mean incomes for urban and rural areas depend on who is classified as urban and who as rural. Also, in the calculation of inequality using sample survey data, urban and rural samples are typically assigned weights based on their shares in the national population.

Growth in China's urban population is the result of two trends; natural increase in the urban population and reclassification of the rural population. Reclassification occurs when rural residents migrate to urban places and when rural places (and their resident populations) are reclassified as urban places.[13] All of these mechanisms have contributed to China's urban population growth, but migration appears to be the most important. Chan and Hu (2003) note that the urban natural rate of increase has been low (Table 2.5). They estimate that, in the 1990s, the natural rate of increase of the urban population contributed only about one third of total growth in the urban population. They estimate further that, of total growth in the urban population in the 1990s, 22 per cent was due to reclassification of rural places. The remaining 55 per cent was due to migration. In other words, during the 1990s migration probably contributed more than half of China's urban growth.

How should the reclassification of rural into urban places be treated in analyses of inequality? Most would argue that classifications of places should remain unchanged; that is, that an area classified as rural in one or more years should be counted as rural for the duration of the period under study, or that an area classified as urban in one or more years should be counted as urban for the duration. So, for example, residents of a rural area where farmland is converted to industrial and other non-agricultural uses would be counted as either rural or urban for the entire period. Chan and Hu (2003), however, point out that one reason for allowing classifications to change is that, in some cases, the reclassification is driven by migration from villages to towns prior to their re-designation as urban.

The NBS population statistics incorporate changes in the classification of rural places and almost all studies of China follow suit, primarily because the data required to keep classifications constant are unavailable. An exception is Benjamin *et al.* (2005), which provides an alternative estimate of the urban–rural income gap that keeps place classifications constant. That study concludes that reclassification tends to slow the convergence of mean incomes between urban and rural places, because reclassified rural areas tend to be those that have experienced the fastest income growth. Residents of the now richer, previously rural places are counted as urban, and residents of those places that grow more slowly and remain relatively poor continue to be counted as rural.

While, in principle, it would be desirable to redo our analysis holding place classifications constant, our data do not permit it. Benjamin *et al.* (2005) conduct the analysis using panel data, which makes it possible to keep the urban and rural classifications unchanged over time. The CHIP survey data are not panel. In our analysis, then, we are constrained to rely on the standard NBS approach, under which rural places are reclassified as urban when they evolve to meet the criteria used to delineate urban places. As mentioned above, however, it is thought that less than one quarter of the growth in China's urban population is caused by the reclassification of places.

More important is the treatment of migrants. Rural-to-urban migration is the major factor causing China's rising levels of urbanization. Researchers universally agree that rural migrants who have moved to urban places should be counted in the urban population. Unfortunately, migrant populations are difficult to count, and estimates of inequality for China do not adequately incorporate this group. Most household surveys for China, including the NBS household survey, do not count the great majority of migrants because the sample frames are based on place of registration rather than place of residence, and most migrants are not registered in the cities in which they live. Consequently, unregistered migrants living in cities are absent in urban survey samples.

Unregistered rural-to-urban migrants are also largely absent from the rural samples. When an entire rural household migrates, it is not included in the rural survey because no family member is present to be surveyed. Individuals who migrate without their families are often also not included in the rural sample. Rural surveys only count such individuals if they reside at home for a substantial portion of the year (more than six months in the NBS survey), or are the primary source of income for their rural households. These criteria apply to the CHIP urban and rural sub-samples, which follow the NBS sampling frame and use the same criteria for household membership.

In order to improve coverage of migrants, for 2002 the CHIP researchers added a special survey of rural migrants in urban areas. Lack of information on migrants makes sample design for this group difficult, especially for large, nationwide surveys. The CHIP migrant sub-sample is not strictly representative of the migrant population nationwide; however, it is large and has broad geographical coverage, containing 2,005 households and 5,327 individuals.[14] The CHIP migrant survey covers all the provinces, although not all the cities, in the regular CHIP urban survey. As rural–urban migrants are concentrated in large cities, the two provincial level municipalities (Beijing, Chongqing) and all the provincial capital cities (plus one or two middle-sized cities in each of the provinces) were included in the migrant survey. The sample contains 100 migrant households in each of Beijing and Chongqing, 200 migrant households from each of the coastal and interior provinces, and 150 households in each of the western provinces. Within each province, 100 migrant households were in the capital city and the rest were in the other cities. Within cities, the migrant households were selected from within the same urban resident committees (*jumin weiyuan hui*) used for sampling in the regular urban household survey. Selection into the migrant survey sample is not affected by place of origin or length of residence in the city, but the household head must be registered as rural, not urban.

As the sampling frame is based on urban residential neighbourhood committees, the CHIP migrant sample does not contain migrants who were not living in residential neighbourhoods; for example, those living in construction sites, factories and on the street. Included are migrants who live in urban residential neighbourhoods; that is, migrant individuals and families that live in apartments or other urban housing or who rent rooms in such buildings. This group includes both short- and long-term migrants, but probably contains a disproportionately high share of long-term migrants and also of migrant families. With these limitations in mind, the migrant sub-sample provides information that can be used to explore the effects of including migrants in analysis of the urban–rural gap.

In order to analyze the urban–rural gap, we must assign a weight to the migrant sample that reflects its share in the larger population. Information on the number of migrants in China's cities is weak, but a few studies provide estimates. Using data from China's 2000 census, in which efforts were made to count migrants in their place of residence, Liang and Ma (2004) estimate that in 2000 the migrant population resident in cities was equal to 13 per cent of the urban population.[15] This estimate includes urban-to-urban migrant households and so may be high; however, the number of migrants probably increased between 2000 and 2002, so Liang and Ma's number would understate the migrant population in the year of study here.

Mo (2004) gives estimates for 2002 based on a special, nationwide survey of rural households that included detailed questions about employment and labour movement. This study reports a number for rural-to-urban migrant workers equal to 16 per cent of the urban population.[16] This number does not include dependents. The CHIP migrant survey data gives 24 per cent of the members in migrant households as dependants, which we use to adjust the Mo (2004) figure. On this basis, we obtain an estimate of the rural-to-urban migrant population equivalent to 21 per cent

Table 2.6 Mean household per capita incomes including migrants, 2002 (units: *yuan*, ratios)

	Unadjusted	**PPP**
National	5,566	4,942
Urban	9,337	7,293
Urban registered	10,004	7,798
Urban migrant	6,083	4,831
Rural	3,145	3,434
Ratio of migrant to registered urban	0.61	0.62
Ratio of migrant to rural	1.94	1.41
Ratio of urban to rural	2.97	2.12

Notes:

1 Population weights are rural 60.91 per cent, urban non-migrant 32.445 per cent, and urban migrant 6.645 per cent. These shares maintain the official urban/rural population shares for 2002, with migrants constituting 17 per cent of the urban population (see discussion in the text).

2 Price adjustments are explained in the notes to Table 2.1.

3 See the text for discussion of the migrant sample.

of the urban population. This estimate is probably high, as the dependency ratio in the CHIP migrant sub-sample probably includes a disproportionate number of dependants.

Based on this information, we conclude that in 2002 the migrant share in China's urban population probably fell between 13 and 21 per cent. In most of our calculations, we use the mid-point in this range, 17 per cent, as the migrant share of the urban population. We also conduct sensitivity analyses to explore how the choice of the migrant population share affects the findings.

Table 2.6 gives mean household per capita incomes including migrant households, with migrants assumed to constitute 17 per cent of the urban population. After adjusting for spatial price differences, mean income per capita of migrant households is about 60 per cent below that of the urban registered and about 40 per cent above that of the rural sample.[17] Not surprisingly then, including migrants reduces the size of the urban–rural gap. With migrants the relative gap is 2.12 (PPP incomes), as opposed to 2.27 without migrants (see Table 2.1). For both unadjusted and PPP incomes, including migrants reduces the relative gap by about 10 per cent.

Table 2.7 gives inequality levels and decompositions with and without the migrants, and also with and without PPP adjustments. The impact of including migrants is fairly modest. Including migrants does not

Table 2.7 Inequality levels and decomposition, with and without migrants and spatial price adjustments, 2002

	Theil L				Theil T			
	Unadjusted	**With migrants**	**PPP**	**All adjustments**	**Unadjusted**	**With migrants**	**PPP**	**All adjustments**
Total	0.368	0.354	0.275	0.268	0.355	0.356	0.263	0.268
Between	0.164	0.145	0.083	0.070	0.160	0.143	0.083	0.070
Within	0.204	0.209	0.193	0.198	0.195	0.213	0.180	0.198
Contributions (%)								
Between	44.6	41.1	30.0	26.1	45.1	40.1	31.6	26.3
Within	55.4	58.9	70.0	73.9	54.9	59.9	68.4	73.7

Notes:
1 The notes to Table 2.1 apply.
2 Except for the last columns (All adjustments), this table shows the effects of carrying out each adjustment separately; that is, the columns labelled 'With migrants' are not adjusted for spatial price differences, and the columns labelled 'PPP' do not include migrants.
3 In columns including migrants, migrants are assumed to constitute 17 per cent of the urban population.

substantially change the level of overall inequality for China. The Theil L registers a decrease and the Theil T a small increase, indicating that the Lorenz curves cross. For both indices, the level of between-group inequality declines and that of within-group inequality increases. Including migrants causes the between-group contribution to total inequality in PPP incomes to decline by about four percentage points. This change is smaller than that resulting from spatial price deflation.

The data in Table 2.7 show the impact of including both migrants and spatial price deflation on the inequality decomposition. With both these adjustments, overall inequality declines by about 25 per cent, which is due primarily to spatial price deflation. With both adjustments, the level of between-group inequality falls by more than 50 per cent. Its contribution to total inequality declines from 45 per cent to only 26 per cent. Most of this decline is again due to spatial price deflation.

Table 2.8 gives sensitivity analyses using different migrant shares in the urban population. All numbers here are based on the PPP incomes. For purposes of illustration, we use the following shares: 0 per cent, the share implicitly assumed by analyses that do not include migrants; a low estimate of 13 per cent; our mid-range choice of 17 per cent; and a high estimate of 21 per cent. We also show results for a yet higher share of 25 per cent so as to show the possible impact of an even larger migrant population.

As expected, increasing the migrant share reduces the urban–rural income ratio. With zero migrants, the ratio is 2.27. With a migrant share

Table 2.8 Migrant population share sensitivity analysis, 2002

Urban population, migrants (%)	**Theil L**					**Theil T**				
	0	**13**	**17**	**21**	**25**	**0**	**13**	**17**	**21**	**25**
Urban–rural income ratio	2.27	2.16	2.12	2.09	2.06	2.27	2.16	2.12	2.09	2.06
Total inequality	0.275	0.270	0.268	0.266	0.264	0.263	0.267	0.268	0.269	0.270
Between	0.083	0.073	0.070	0.067	0.064	0.083	0.073	0.070	0.067	0.064
Within	0.193	0.197	0.198	0.199	0.200	0.180	0.194	0.198	0.202	0.205
Contributions (%)										
Between	30.0	27.0	26.1	25.1	24.2	31.6	27.5	26.3	25.1	23.9
Within	70.0	73.0	74.0	74.9	75.8	68.4	72.5	73.7	75.0	76.1

Notes:
1 This table shows results for inequality of PPP incomes.
2 The notes to Table 2.7 apply.
3 See the text for discussion of migrant population shares.

of 25 per cent, the ratio falls to 2.06. This ratio remains fairly high by international standards.

Overall inequality shows no clear upward or downward trend as the migrant population share increases. The Theil L decreases and the Theil T increases. Between-group inequality declines steadily as the migrant share rises. Yet, the impact of changes in the migrant share is not overly large. A near doubling in the migrant share from 13 per cent to 25 per cent causes the contribution of between inequality to fall by fewer than 4 percentage points, from about 27 per cent to 24 per cent.

These results demonstrate that including migrants can have an impact on measured patterns of inequality. The impact, however, is fairly modest, even when using relatively high estimates of the size of the migrant population. This might reflect that migrants tend to have characteristics more similar to urban residents (younger, better educated, smaller households), so that movement of this subset of the rural population does not reduce the urban–rural gap as much as would movement of 'average' rural residents. Note, moreover, that these calculations hold constant the incomes of other groups. That is, the calculations do not take into account the fact that migration can affect the incomes of those remaining behind in rural areas as well as of the registered urban population.

Factors underlying the urban–rural income gap

Even after the adjustments outlined above, the urban–rural income gap in China remains relatively large and contributes substantially to overall inequality. The gap reflects a variety of factors, including differences in household characteristics and also in economic environments and policies. The Oaxaca–Blinder decomposition provides an empirical methodology for investigating some of the factors that underlie the gap. This method allows us to calculate the extent to which income differences between the urban and rural groups reflect differences in individual characteristics as opposed to other factors. We carry out the decomposition first without migrants and then with migrants included in the urban sample. As we discussed earlier, the decomposition results with and without migrants provide different pictures. Without migrants, the 'unexplained' proportion of the urban–rural income gap gives a measure of the extent to which urban residents are favoured over rural residents under long-standing urban biased government policy in China. Inclusion of migrants provides information on how migration is affecting the income gap and captures the increasing importance of migrants in the urban population.

Table 2.9 Composition of mean incomes and of the urban–rural income gap (*yuan*; unadjusted, current prices)

	1995				2002			
	Urban	**Rural**	**Urban–rural**	**Difference (%)**	**Urban**	**Rural**	**Urban–rural**	**Difference (%)**
Mean income per capita	5,635	1,810	3,825	100.0	10,004	3,145	6,859	100.0
Labour earnings per capita	3,487	1,466	2,021	52.8	6,421	2,524	3,897	56.8
Non-labour income per capita	2,148	344	1,804	47.2	3,583	621	2,962	43.2
of which:								
Asset income	71	8	63	1.6	49	18	31	0.4
Pension income	660	7	653	17.1	1,265	13	1,252	18.3
Government transfers minus taxes	613	−53	667	17.4	237	−81	318	4.6
Housing income	643	201	442	11.5	1,765	426	1,339	19.5
Private transfers, remittances	160	181	−20	−0.5	267	245	23	0.3

Notes:

1 Labour earnings per capita include wages and net income from self-employment, including both agricultural and non-agricultural self-employment. Note that net income from self-employment probably overstates labour earnings from this source, as it includes some returns to entrepreneurship and to capital used in such activities.

2 Non-labour earnings include all other forms of income, of which the components are shown here. Percentages are of the difference in total income.

3 Rent subsidies on public housing are counted as part of housing income, not as part of government transfers. Similarly, all pension income regardless of its source is counted as part of pensions and is not included in government transfers.

The Oaxaca–Blinder method is often used to analyze differences in earnings or the returns to labour. Here, we use it to analyze differences in per capita income, including both labour earnings and other income. We analyze income rather than labour earnings because a large proportion of income in China, especially in urban areas, is non-labour income. In addition, non-labour income accounts for well over 40 per cent of the absolute gap between urban and rural incomes (Table 2.9). Analysis of labour earnings alone would therefore miss much of the story. Table 2.9 shows the composition of urban and rural incomes. Labour earnings include wages and net income from self-employment, and non-labour income includes asset income, pensions, net government transfers, housing components of income, and private transfers and remittances. Of non-labour income, pensions, net government transfers, and housing income have been the most important. Net government transfers declined substantially between 1995 and 2002.

The Oaxaca–Blinder decomposition requires two steps. The first step is to estimate income equations separately for the two groups. These equations typically take the form:

$$\ln(y^g) = \alpha_g + \beta_g X^g + \varepsilon^g \text{ for } g = u, r \qquad (2.4)$$

where g indicates the group (urban or rural here), y is a vector of per capita incomes of individuals, and X a matrix of individual characteristics.

The second step is to use the regression results to decompose the difference in mean incomes between the groups. The difference in mean log incomes between the higher income urban and lower income rural group can be written as

$$\begin{aligned}\overline{\ln y}^u - \overline{\ln y}^r &= (\hat{\alpha}_u - \hat{\alpha}_r) + (\hat{\beta}_u \bar{X}^u - \hat{\beta}_r \bar{X}^r) \\ &= (\hat{\alpha}_u - \hat{\alpha}_r) + \hat{\beta}_u(\bar{X}^u - \bar{X}^r) + (\hat{\beta}_u - \hat{\beta}_r)\bar{X}^r \qquad (2.5)\end{aligned}$$

The first term in the right-hand side of equation 2.5 gives the proportion of the urban–rural income gap due to differences in the constants. The second term gives the proportion due to differences between the two groups in their endowments of characteristics. The third term is the proportion due to differences in the estimated regression coefficients or 'returns' to characteristics. The first and third terms are typically considered the 'unexplained' proportion of the gap, and the second term the 'explained' proportion of the gap.

Equation 2.5 uses the coefficients of the richer (urban) group as weights for the differences in characteristics and uses the mean poorer (rural) characteristics as the weights for the differences in coefficients. This is the standard approach. The reverse decomposition would be

$$\overline{\ln y}^u - \overline{\ln y}^r = (\hat{\alpha}_u - \hat{\alpha}_r) + \hat{\beta}_r(\bar{X}^u - \bar{X}^r) + (\hat{\beta}_u - \hat{\beta}_r)\bar{X}^u \tag{2.6}$$

This reverse decomposition uses the rural coefficients to weight the differences in characteristics and uses mean urban characteristics to weight the differences in coefficients. We present results for both the standard and reverse decompositions.

Estimation of the income equations for the urban and rural subgroups

A variety of characteristics can influence per capita household incomes (Miles 1997; Gustafsson and Li 1998 and 2001; Knight and Song 1999: ch. 3; Morduch and Sicular 2000). These include demographic characteristics such as household size, the proportion of dependants versus working-age household members, the ethnic composition of household members, and the age of household members. The education of household members may also be important, as it influences the returns to labour and also to some assets.

Household assets generate income. Holdings of many assets, however, are dependent on the level of household income and, so, endogenous. In China, an important asset that is not dependent on the level of household income is farmland allocated to households by villages under the household responsibility or contracting system: such land is allocated administratively by the village or township on the basis of household size, and reallocations are infrequent.

Another set of factors considered potentially important in explaining household incomes in China is political status and connections (Bian and Logan 1996; Morduch and Sicular 2000; Lam 2003). Political status and connections are difficult to measure directly, but might be associated with the presence of a Communist Party member or cadre within the household. Here, we focus on Party membership, as cadre status is often attached to employment: disentangling the extent to which political connections as opposed to the wages from cadre employment explain income is difficult. Note that Party membership's relationship with income could reflect not only political connections, but also unobserved ability or ambition that may be associated with Party membership (Gerber 2000; Lam 2003).

Finally, location of residence is commonly thought to affect income levels, especially in China, where mobility is limited. Here, we include provincial dummy variables to capture the effects of location.

Tables 2.10a and 2.10b present descriptive statistics on per capita income and household characteristics for the urban and rural sub-samples. For 2002, we give two columns of urban statistics, one excluding and one including the migrant sub-sample (assumed to constitute 17 per cent of the urban population). Household characteristics differ noticeably between the urban and rural groups, suggesting that these variables explain at least part of the urban–rural income gap. Mean education for the urban sample is about 50 per cent higher than that for the rural sample. Urban households tend to be older and smaller, and they contain proportionately more working-age members. They also have a higher incidence of Party membership and a lower proportion of members with poor health or minority ethnicity. Only rural households have farmland.

The regression results for urban and rural income equations appear in Table 2.11. Estimation is carried out using OLS. We include squared terms for education, age, household size, and land to allow for potential nonlinearities. Spatial price adjustments do not affect the estimated coefficients for the variables shown in this table, but they alter the estimated constant term and coefficients for the provincial dummy variables (not shown). They also influence the overall explanatory power of

Table 2.10a Household characteristics of individuals in the regression samples, 1995

Variable	Urban		Rural		Ratio of urban to rural
	Mean	Standard deviation	Mean	Standard deviation	
Income per capita	5633	6444	1810	1462	3.11
Income per capita (PPP)	4256	4938	1898	1373	2.24
Average education of working-age adults	10.27	2.54	6.20	2.07	1.66
Average age of working-age adults	39.48	7.88	35.50	5.74	1.11
Household size	3.37	0.88	4.73	1.37	0.71
Household members of working age (16–65) (%)	77.48	18.54	70.15	21.24	1.10
Working-age members in the Party (%)	22.32	28.79	5.28	13.31	4.23
Family members that are ethnic minority (%)	3.35	14.94	5.12	18.20	0.66
Contracted farm land per capita (mu)	0.0	0.0	1.17	1.13	–
Observations	21378		34682		

Table 2.10b Household characteristics of individuals in the regression samples, 2002

Variable	Urban without migrants		Urban with migrants		Rural		Ratio of urban (no migrants) to rural	Ratio of urban (with migrants) to rural
	Mean	Standard deviation	Mean	Standard deviation	Mean	Standard deviation		
Income per capita	9937	6473	9346	6533	3145	2597	3.16	2.97
Income per capita (PPP)	7712	4503	7268	4650	3426	2725	2.25	2.12
Average education of working-age adults	10.85	2.56	10.35	2.77	7.11	1.97	1.53	1.46
Average age of working-age adults	40.49	7.37	39.44	7.64	37.07	6.56	1.09	1.06
Household size	3.25	0.84	3.21	0.86	4.41	1.24	0.74	0.73
Household members of working age (16–65) (%)	80.35	19.17	79.75	19.33	75.47	19.92	1.06	1.06
Working-age members in the Party (%)	23.92	29.66	20.43	28.64	7.20	15.67	3.32	2.84
Working-age members in poor health (%)	0.26	3.71	0.61	5.05	0.65	4.90	0.40	0.93
Family members that are ethnic minority (%)	3.48	14.83	4.06	16.24	6.08	20.23	0.57	0.67
Contracted farm land per capita (mu)	0.0	0.0	0.0	0.0	1.36	1.73	–	–
Observations	20,173		25,272		33,803			

Notes:

1 The statistics in these tables are calculated over individuals rather than households. One can interpret them as weighted household averages, with the weights being the number of household members. The number of observations is the number of individuals in households surveyed.

2 Urban means including migrants are calculated using a migrant share in the urban population of 17 per cent.

3 Income values shown here are in current *yuan*.

4 Information on health was not collected in 1995. Health status is self-reported.

Table 2.11 Per capita income OLS regression estimates (dependent variable: ln household per capita income, unadjusted and PPP)

Variable	1995		2002		
	Urban	Rural	Urban w/out migrants	Urban w/ migrants	Rural
Average education of working-age adults	0.0454***	0.0483***	0.0289***	0.0474***	0.0463***
Education squared	0.0001	−0.0017***	0.0023***	0.0018***	0.0008*
Average age of working-age adults	0.0415***	0.0451***	0.0187***	0.0265***	0.0318***
Age squared	−0.0004***	−0.0005***	−0.0001*	−0.0002***	−0.0004***
Household size	−0.3054***	−0.2041***	−0.3392***	−0.2696***	−0.2335***
Household size squared	0.0231***	0.0100***	0.0286***	0.0221***	0.0130***
Household members of working age (16–65) (%)	0.0047***	0.0037***	0.0031***	0.0037***	0.0032***
Working-age members in the Party (%)	0.0014***	0.0024***	0.0023***	0.0025***	0.0032***
Working-age members in poor health (%)			−0.0029***	−0.0024***	−0.0028***
Family members that are ethnic minority (%)	−0.0015***	−0.0014***	0.0014***	0.0007***	0.0009***
Contracted farm land per capita (mu)		0.0346***			0.0351***
Land squared		−0.0042***			−0.0003*
Observations	21378	34682	20173	25272	33803
F-statistic (unadjusted)	914.50***	789.48***	765.78***	954.53***	741.18***
Adjusted R^2 (unadjusted)	0.45	0.40	0.43	0.43	0.40
F-statistic (PPP)	611.51***	666.39***	554.52***	731.95***	770.46***
Adjusted R^2 (PPP)	0.35	0.36	0.35	0.37	0.41

Notes:
1 *** indicates significance at the 1 per cent confidence level; ** at 5 per cent; and * at 10 per cent.
2 Spatial price adjustments do not affect the estimated coefficients of the variables shown here, only those of the provincial dummy variables and constant term. Spatial price adjustments also affect the regressions' explanatory power, so we provide F-statistics and adjusted R^2s for both cases.
3 The constant term and estimated coefficients for provincial dummies are not shown due to space limitations. These coefficients were, for the most part, significant.
4 Observations represent individuals rather than households. In the regression for the urban sample that includes migrants, weights are used to reflect that the migrant share of the urban population is 17 per cent.
5 The percentage of working-age adults that is male was included as an explanatory variable in initial regressions, but was not significant and so was dropped.
6 Information on health was not collected in 1995. Health status is self-reported.

the equations. We report F-statistics and adjusted R^2 statistics for both cases.

The estimated coefficients are almost all highly significant and for the most part of the expected signs. The coefficients clearly differ between the urban and rural samples. Including migrants moves most of the urban coefficients values closer to those of the rural sample, although differences remain. For example, in 2002 the relationship between education and income in rural areas is close to linear, while for the urban sample (with and without migrants) the marginal returns to education increase with the level of education. Also, the returns to Party membership are higher in rural areas than in urban areas. Differences in returns to characteristics, then, may also contribute to the urban–rural income gap.

Decomposition of the urban–rural wage gap

Tables 2.12a–c contain summary results from Oaxaca–Blinder decompositions of the urban–rural income gap for 1995 and 2002. Both the standard and reverse decompositions are shown, and the decomposition is carried out both for unadjusted and PPP incomes. For 2002, we present decomposition results with migrants included in the urban sample. As explained in the table notes, the Oaxaca–Blinder method cannot identify the separate contributions of the constant term and indicator variables. Therefore, the tables give only the sum contribution of the constant and provincial dummy variables.

We begin with discussion of the results without migrants. Here, we are mainly interested in the results for PPP incomes. As most studies do not adjust for spatial price differences, however, some comments about how spatial price adjustments affect the results may be of interest. As noted above, spatial price deflation reduces the urban–rural gap. In 2002, for example, the gap in unadjusted ln incomes is 1.205 and in adjusted log incomes 0.887 (Table 2.12b). In the decompositions, this reduction in the gap is fully matched by the reduction in the sum contribution of the constant term and provincial dummy variables. That is, correcting for spatial price differences only affects the contributions of the constant term and provincial dummy variables, and does not affect the contributions of other explanatory variables. This reflects the fact that adjusting for spatial prices only alters mean differences among locations, which differences are captured by the constant term and provincial dummy variables.

While correcting for spatial price differences does not change the absolute size of the contributions of non-geographic explanatory variables, it increases their proportional contributions to the gap. In 2002, for example, spatial deflation increases the percentage contribution of

Table 2.12a Decomposition of the difference between mean urban (excluding migrants) and rural incomes, 1995

	Standard decomposition		Reverse decomposition	
	Unadjusted	PPP	Unadjusted	PPP
Difference in ln incomes	1.169	0.848	1.169	0.48
Contributions to difference (values):				
Constant term and provincial dummies	0.708	0.387	0.708	0.387
Other explanatory variables	0.461	0.461	0.461	0.461
Of which:				
Coefficients	0.020	0.020	0.174	0.174
Endowments	0.441	0.441	0.286	0.286
Contributions to difference (%):				
Constant term and provincial dummies	60.6	45.6	60.6	45.6
Other explanatory variables	39.4	54.4	39.4	54.4
Of which:				
Coefficients	1.7	2.4	14.9	20.5
Endowments	37.7	52.0	24.5	33.7

Table 2.12b Decomposition of the difference between mean urban (excluding migrants) and rural incomes, 2002

	Standard decomposition		Reverse decomposition	
	Unadjusted	PPP	Unadjusted	PPP
Difference in ln incomes	1.205	0.887	1.205	0.887
Contributions to difference (values):				
Constant term and provincial dummies	1.039	0.722	1.039	0.722
Other explanatory variables	0.165	0.165	0.165	0.165
Of which:				
Coefficients	−0.313	−0.313	−0.238	−0.238
Endowments	0.479	0.479	0.405	0.405
Contributions to difference (%):				
Constant term and provincial dummies	86.2	81.4	86.2	81.4
Other explanatory variables	13.7	18.6	13.7	18.6
Of which:				
Coefficients	−26.0	−35.3	−19.8	−26.8
Endowments	39.8	54.0	33.6	45.7

Table 2.12c Decomposition of the difference between mean urban (including migrants) and rural incomes, 2002

	Standard decomposition		**Reverse decomposition**	
	Unadjusted	**PPP**	**Unadjusted**	**PPP**
Difference in ln incomes	1.111	0.793	1.111	0.793
Contributions to difference (values):				
Constant term and provincial dummies	0.484	0.168	0.484	0.168
Other explanatory variables	0.625	0.625	0.625	0.625
Of which:				
Coefficients	0.192	0.192	0.272	0.272
Endowments	0.435	0.435	0.354	0.354
Contributions to difference (%):				
Constant term and provincial dummies	43.6	21.2	43.6	21.2
Other explanatory variables	56.3	78.8	56.3	78.8
Of which:				
Coefficients	17.3	24.2	24.5	34.3
Endowments	39.2	54.9	31.9	44.6

Notes:
1 Numbers in these tables may not add up exactly due to rounding.
2 The standard decomposition weights endowment differences between the two groups by the urban group's estimated coefficients and weights differences in coefficients by rural mean endowments. The reverse decomposition weights endowment differences by the rural group's coefficients and weights differences in coefficients by urban mean endowments.
3 Some explanatory variables are uniformly equal to zero for the urban subgroup. These variables include a few provincial dummy variables and, importantly, farm land. Urban households have no contracted land. In principle, the contributions of these variables should be attributed entirely to differences in endowments, as is done by the reverse decomposition. The standard decomposition attributes the contributions of these variables entirely to differences in coefficients, which does not make much sense. We therefore prefer the reverse decomposition results.
4 As discussed by Jones (1983) and Oaxaca and Ransom (1999), when dummy variables are included in the regression equations, the constant terms and the coefficients of the dummy variables will depend on the choice of reference group or groups for the dummy variables. For this reason, identification of the separate contributions of the constant terms and dummy variables is impossible in the decomposition, and we do not present them separately.

non-geographic explanatory variables from 14 per cent to 19 per cent in 2002. More generally, if incomes are not adjusted for spatial price variation, the proportional contribution of location and the constant term will be overstated; that of other explanatory variables such as age, education and so on will be understated.

For PPP incomes, in 1995 about 46 per cent of the urban–rural gap in ln incomes was due to location dummy variables and the constant term, and 54 per cent due to differences in the returns to and endowments of non-geographic explanatory variables. This contribution of non-geographic explanatory variables dropped markedly between 1995 and 2002, from 54 per cent to only 19 per cent. This decline is due to the fact that, in 2002, the differences in coefficients between the two groups had the effect of substantially decreasing inequality. In 1995, differences in the coefficients widened the gap, while in 2002 they reduced the gap by more than 25 per cent. As shown in Table 2.13b, this negative contribution of the 2002 coefficients is largely attributable to the returns on household size, which are more negative in urban than rural areas. The returns to most other variables are higher in urban than in rural areas.

Endowments of non-geographic household characteristics contribute between one third and one half of the urban–rural income gap. Table 2.13a–c gives the separate contribution of each such characteristic to the income gap. Education endowments make a sizable contribution, especially in 2002 when they account for more than one quarter of the income gap. All else held constant, if average education levels in rural areas were increased to be on a par with those in urban areas, then in 2002 the urban–rural income gap would decline by 26 to 30 per cent.

The only other characteristic for which endowments make a sizable contribution to the income gap is household size. In 1995, differences in household size accounted for 16–19 per cent of the gap, and in 2002 for 13–16 per cent of the gap. This endowment effect, however, is offset by the negative contribution of differences in the coefficient on household size.

The contributions of the endowments of most other variables are small. The endowments of farmland to rural households reduce the income gap by 5 per cent or less in both years. The higher incidence of Party membership in urban China increases the gap by 6 per cent or less in both years.

Including migrants in the urban sample has a noticeable impact on the decomposition results (Tables 2.12c and 2.13c). Including migrants reduces the per cent contribution of the constant term and provincial dummy variables markedly. The contribution of the coefficients, however, increases and becomes positive. The contribution of endowments remains relatively unchanged.

The sharp reduction in the per cent contribution of the constant term and provincial dummy variables when migrants are included deserves some comment. This reduction can be seen as a reflection of the equalizing effect of rural-to-urban migration on the urban–rural income gap.

Table 2.13a Contributions of individual explanatory variables to the PPP urban–rural gap, 1995 (%)

	Total	Standard decomposition		Reverse decomposition	
		Endowment	Coefficient	Endowment	Coefficient
Average education of working-age adults	30.8	22.9	7.1	9.4	20.6
Average age of working-age adults	15.1	5.7	9.4	1.1	14.0
Household size	−2.8	16.0	−18.9	18.5	−21.5
Household members of working age (%)	12.9	4.1	8.7	3.2	9.7
Working-age members in the Party (%)	2.4	2.9	−0.6	4.7	−2.4
Working-age members in poor health (%)					
Family members that are ethnic minority (%)	0.3	0.3	−0.0	0.2	0.0
Contracted farm land per capita (mu)	−3.3	0.0	−3.4	−3.4	0.0

Table 2.13b Contributions of individual explanatory variables to the PPP urban–rural gap, 2002 (%)

	Total	Standard decomposition		Reverse decomposition	
		Endowment	Coefficient	Endowment	Coefficient
Average education of working-age adults	25.4	30.3	−5.0	26.2	−0.8
Average age of working-age adults	−3.3	4.8	−8.0	0.7	−3.9
Household size	−2.7	13.1	−15.8	16.3	−18.9
Household members of working age (%)	0.8	1.7	−0.9	1.8	−1.0
Working-age members in the Party (%)	3.7	4.4	−0.7	6.1	−2.4
Working-age members in poor health (%)	0.1	0.1	0.0	0.1	0.0
Family members that are ethnic minority (%)	−0.1	−0.4	−0.3	−0.2	0.2
Contracted farm land per capita (mu)	−5.3	0.0	−5.3	−5.3	0.0

Table 2.13c Contributions of individual explanatory variables to the PPP urban–rural gap including migrants, 2002 (%)

	Total	**Standard decomposition**		**Reverse decomposition**	
		Endowment	**Coefficient**	**Endowment**	**Coefficient**
Average education of working-age adults	39.2	31.8	7.4	24.5	14.7
Average age of working-age adults	18.0	3.8	14.2	0.2	14.1
Household size	17.3	13.4	3.9	15.4	−2.0
Household members of working age (%)	7.2	2.0	5.3	1.6	5.5
Working-age members in the Party (%)	3.4	4.0	−0.6	5.0	−1.6
Working-age members in poor health (%)	0.0	0.0	0.0	0.0	0.0
Family members that are ethnic minority (%)	−0.3	−0.1	−0.1	−0.3	−0.1
Contracted farm land per capita (mu)	−5.9	0.0	−5.9	−5.9	0.0

Notes:

1 The notes to Table 2.12 apply.

2 For education, age, household size and land, the contributions shown are the sum contributions of the linear and squared terms.

3 Due to rounding, numbers do not always add up exactly.

We also note that the inclusion of migrants as urban residents in the Oaxaca–Blinder decomposition would lead to understatement of discrimination of current urban biased income generating policies in favour of registered urban residents. Consequently, the decomposition results without migrants are most relevant if one is interested in how urban residents are favoured under urban biased government policies. A closely related issue is discrimination against rural migrants in urban areas. This discrimination takes many forms; such as job opportunities based on *hukou*, inaccessibility to migrants of many social programmes and so on. Further discussion of discrimination against rural migrants in urban areas is beyond the scope of this work, but has been the focus of many studies; Démurger *et al.* (2007), for instance.

Conclusion

In this chapter, we have explored China's urban–rural income gap. Several key findings emerge. First, China's urban–rural income gap is considerable by international standards, even after various adjustments; such as fuller measurement of income, spatial price deflation and including migrants in the urban sample. Still, these adjustments – especially spatial price deflation – reduce the size of the gap substantially. With respect to trends over time, we find the adjusted relative gap widened little between 1995 and 2002. This conclusion differs from that reported elsewhere.[18,19]

Second, the contribution of the urban–rural income gap to overall inequality has been relatively large and has increased somewhat – although, again, its level is reduced by the adjustments. If we use 2002 unadjusted incomes and include migrants, between-group inequality contributes more than 40 per cent of overall inequality. If we further correct for spatial price differences, the contribution decreases to 26 per cent.

With or without adjustments, this contribution is sizable relative to that in other countries. Shorrocks and Wan (2005) review international evidence on this question. Citing available studies based on household-level data and using similar methodology to that used here, they report that the contribution of the urban–rural gap ranges from less than 20 per cent in Greece to 26–30 per cent in the Philippines. Eastwood and Lipton (2004) give estimates for earlier years for developing countries. Excepting China, in all cases the contribution of the urban–rural gap is less than 25 per cent of total inequality.[20] All of these estimates are calculated using nominal prices, unadjusted for spatial price differences. Our unadjusted estimates for China exceed the highest numbers for other countries by 10 percentage points.

Third, regional differences in China's urban–rural gap are considerable. The urban–rural income gap is much greater in western China than in the eastern or central regions, as is its contribution to inequality. Indeed, the urban–rural gap's contribution to overall inequality in the east and central is fairly small.

These regional differences suggest that efforts to bridge the urban–rural divide should target the west. Further research is required to identify what sorts of targeted interventions would be most effective, but some recent studies provide complementary evidence. Fan, Zhang and Zhang (2004) and Zhang and Fan (2004) examine the impact of public investments on regional poverty and inequality in GDP per capita. Their findings suggest that public investment targeted to western China would have the most impact, especially investments in rural education, agricultural research, and development. Investments in irrigation and poverty loans, however, would be less effective.

Our analysis highlights several measurement issues: one issue being spatial differences in prices and the cost of living, which has a substantial impact on the measured size of the gap and its contribution to inequality. Our findings here parallel those in Brandt and Holz (2004). As the study of income inequality is ultimately interested in real differences in incomes, spatially adjusted estimates of the urban–rural gap and its contribution are most meaningful.

A second measurement issue is the delineation of urban versus rural populations. Here, various problems arise, but probably most important for China is the treatment of migrants. Including migrants in the urban sample reduces the size of the urban–rural income gap and that gap's contribution to inequality, but only modestly. Including migrants has little impact on the overall level of inequality, because lower between-group inequality is offset by higher within-group inequality. Migration increases inequality within urban areas, which brings with it a new set of challenges.

Further research and better data are needed to explore fully the impact on inequality measurement of including migrants, but these results provide some indication of the magnitude and direction. The impact is, however, noticeably smaller than that of correcting for spatial price differences. Efforts to improve information on geographic price differences, then, are equally important.

What explains the urban–rural gap? Differences in endowments of household characteristics contribute roughly half the gap in PPP ln income. Most important here is education. Differences in education levels contribute 25–30 per cent of the gap. These estimates imply that, all else equal, if rural education levels were increased to be on a par with urban levels, the urban–rural income gap would decline by 25–30 per cent.

Location of residence contributes the other half of the PPP income gap. Here, location's contribution is defined as the sum contribution to the gap of differences between urban and rural areas in the constant terms, coefficients on provincial dummy variables, and coefficients on household and individual characteristics. Spatial price deflation makes a difference here, reducing location's contribution by more than 10 percentage points. Over time, the contribution of location declines somewhat, which is consistent with increased mobility and market integration.

Our analysis points to the need for further research in several areas: one is education. Studies on education in China generally report large differences in the levels of education not only between urban and rural areas, but also among provinces (Hannum, Behrman and Wang 2005). Such spatial differences in education probably reflect multiple factors, including differences in incomes, in public expenditures on education, and in patterns of migration. Evidence provided here and elsewhere suggests that the private returns to education are also lower in rural areas

(Cai, Park and Zhao 2005; Yue *et al.* 2007). Further information is needed to understand why private returns to education differ geographically. To what extent, for example, do such geographic differences reflect differences in the industrial structure of employment and specificity of human capital? To what extent might they reflect correlation with unobserved community or individual characteristics?

A second topic for further research is spatial location. Why, after controlling for observed characteristics, does location of residence remain so important in explaining income differences? The *hukou* (or household registration system) and related policies that continue to hinder rural-to-urban movement are obvious culprits. Yet, the persistence of urban–rural gaps in other countries suggests that, even without such artificial restrictions, migration is unlikely to eliminate the urban–rural income gap or to equalize the returns to education and other individual characteristics.

China's urban–rural income gap has shown little sign of declining, despite substantial easing of the restrictions on migration and the growing number of migrants. A variety of factors could contribute to the persistence of spatial differences. One factor is non-labour income, which accounts for nearly half the income gap. Migration is not likely to reduce gaps in some forms of non-labour income, such as housing-related income and pensions. Also, migration may not be able to eliminate the gap because variables other than income may affect decisions to move. Other relevant factors include access to community networks and support systems, farm labour requirements, job discrimination, incomplete information about living conditions and employment opportunities, higher costs of living (especially housing) in cities, and access to schooling and other public services.

Notes

We are grateful to Anthony Shorrocks and other participants of the UNU-WIDER project meeting 'Inequality and Poverty in China', 26–27 August 2005, Helsinki, Finland, for their comments, and to two anonymous referees for their detailed suggestions. We thank the Swedish International Development Cooperation Agency (Sida), Ford Foundation, Centre for International Governance Innovation (CIGI) and University of Western Ontario for the funding that facilitated this work.

1 See Chan and Zhong (1999) and Solinger (1999) for details on the *hukou* system and related policies.
2 In their review of household income survey data for twenty-five countries, Smeeding and Weinberg (2001) report that only one country collects information on consumption of public education services (Australia), and only

three on government subsidized health care services (Australia, Germany and the USA). Note that some studies (for example, Eastwood and Lipton 2000; Sahn and Stifel 2003) look directly at urban–rural gaps in levels of education, health and other welfare-related variables. Some information on urban–rural gaps in such variables for China can be found in China Development Research Foundation and UNDP (2005) and Zhang and Kanbur (2005).

3 Note that these two studies use different data than those used here. Ravallion and Chen (2004) use tabulated data provided by the NBS, which has broader geographical coverage than the CHIP dataset but is not at the household level. Benjamin *et al.* (2005) use household level data from the China Health and Nutrition Survey, which has narrower regional coverage than the CHIP survey.

4 The sample also includes Chongqing, which was part of Sichuan province in 1995 but became a separate province in 1997. For consistency, in the analysis Chongqing observations are treated as part of the Sichuan sample in both 1995 and 2002.

5 The advantages and disadvantages of using income as the target variable in studies of inequality have been discussed extensively in the literature (see, for example, Deaton 1997; Atkinson and Bourguignon 2000; Gradín *et al.* 2004; World Institute for Development Economics Research 2005). One disadvantage of using income is that income fluctuates over the lifecycle and can vary from year to year. If households can save and borrow, however, then, in the face of such income fluctuations, they can smooth consumption. Therefore, consumption expenditures may better reflect expected permanent income. The use of consumption, however, also has its drawbacks. Consumption, as with income, can fluctuate over time as needs might vary over the lifecycle. Consumption also depends heavily on the habits and preferences of individuals, so that some measured inequality will be spurious. From a practical standpoint, using consumption raises difficulties in the treatment of infrequently purchased consumer durables.

We would argue that certain features of China provide reasons to use income rather than consumption. In China, financial markets are still undeveloped and households have limited opportunities to borrow and save. The theoretical advantages of using consumption, then, are not fully applicable. Availability of consumption data is also an issue, and, where available, Chinese consumption data count the entire cost of consumer durable purchases as current year expenses. Perhaps for these reasons, inequality measured over consumption per capita is often higher than that measured over income per capita, and few inequality studies for China use consumption data (we know of only two, Jalan and Ravallion, 1998, and Wu and Perloff, 2005). In view of these considerations, and so that our findings are comparable to most other studies of inequality in China, we use income as the target variable.

6 In addition, and probably at least as important as its impact on income distribution, housing reform has led to a redistribution of wealth. Changes in the distribution of wealth are not the topic of this chapter, but interested readers will find discussion of this topic in Zhao and Ding (2007).

7 Some analyses of inequality use equivalence scales to adjust for differences in household composition and size. Unfortunately, no recent estimates of equivalence scales for urban and rural China are available, and we do not have the information needed to estimate them.

8 The numbers in Table 2.1, including those that follow the NBS definition of income, are calculated using the CHIP survey data. Due to differences in sample size and geographical distribution, our numbers using the NBS income definition differ somewhat from the numbers published by the NBS, which are calculated using data from the NBS household surveys. The NBS reports an urban–rural income ratio of 2.7 for 1995 and 3.3 for 2002 (NBS 2003).

9 Ravallion and Chen (2004) find that using the urban and rural poverty lines to correct for urban–rural differences in the cost of living reduces the Gini coefficient by about 12 per cent in both 1995 and 2001. This reduction is less than ours, but we use spatial price deflators that are more finely disaggregated, capturing price differences between urban and rural areas in each province and also among provinces. Their spatial price deflation only differentiates between urban and rural areas for the nation as a whole. Also, they use a different inequality index. Note that Benjamin *et al.* (2005) provide estimates of the Gini coefficient with spatial deflation, but they do not provide the undeflated numbers for comparison.

10 The correlation between incomes and costs of living for 1995 is 0.92 and for 2002 is 0.85.

11 Kanbur and Zhang (1999) also calculate the contribution of the urban–rural income gap to overall inequality for 1995 and report a between contribution of 71 per cent, much higher than our estimate. They calculate inequality using provincial level data. Such an approach understates the importance of intra-urban and intra-rural inequality, as inequality among provincial means will always be lower than inequality among households or individuals.

12 Adjusting for spatial price differences increases the contribution of between-group inequality, because less of between-group than within-group inequality is due to spatial price differences (as shown by the indices for between- and within-group inequality in the top half of Table 2.3).

13 Reclassification can also occur if the definition of urban places changes, which, in fact, it has. The NBS adopted a new definition of urban places for the 2000 census that replaces the definition adopted for the 1990 census and used during the 1990s. This change in definition is fairly complex, and we refer interested readers to the literature for details (see, for example, Zhou and Ma 2003). Starting with the 2002 statistical yearbook, the NBS has been publishing data for the 1990s that is adjusted to conform to the new definition of urban places. Some recent studies, however, criticize the NBS adjustments and provide alternative population estimates (Chan and Hu 2003; Zhou and Ma 2003). In their thorough analysis, Chan and Hu (2003) conclude that the NBS number for the urban population in 1995 (29.04 per cent) is too low. They propose an alternative estimate of 31.72 per cent, almost 3 percentage points higher than the NBS number. Using Chan and Hu's alternative estimate for 1995, we have recalculated inequality levels and the contributions of between- and within-group inequality. Using these alternative estimates has little impact on the results, so, in this chapter, we use the NBS population statistics for our calculations.

14 For more details about the migrant subsample, see Li *et al.* (2007).

15 This estimate includes all inter-county migrants in cities and towns who have resided in their destination for six or more months and who do not have local household registration status.

16 In Mo (2004) migrants are defined as workers employed outside their township of residence for more than six months; movements for marriage, study, and to join the army are excluded. The 16 per cent figure includes only rural migrants employed in urban areas.

17 The gap in income between registered urban residents and rural-to-urban migrants does not fully capture the gap in their economic welfare, as migrants have little access to urban social services and, on average, work longer hours than do registered urban residents.

18 Note that the Brandt and Holz spatial price indices probably understate the difference in housing prices between urban and rural areas, and perhaps increasingly so over time if urban areas have experienced speculative housing bubbles.

19 As mentioned earlier, our income variable does not include the value of household consumption of subsidized public services because no data are available on such consumption. Inclusion of this component would probably increase the size of the urban–rural income gap. It would probably also affect the measured trends in the gap, although the direction of the effect is not clear. Statistics for welfare indicators such as infant mortality rates, life expectancies, and education levels give a mixed picture. Overall, however, they do not indicate deterioration in the relative status of the rural population between 1995 and 2002. See China Development Research Foundation and UNDP (2005), National Bureau of Statistics (2003), World Bank (2003), and Zhang and Kanbur (2005).

20 For China they refer to a study by Zhang (1997), which gives a contribution of 38 per cent in 1988. This contribution is comparable to the unadjusted contribution in this study. Zhang's estimate for 1988 is calculated using household data from an earlier round of the CHIP survey.

References

Atkinson, A.B. and Bourguignon, F. (2000) 'Introduction: Income Distribution and Economics', in A.B. Atkinson and F. Bourguignon (eds), *Handbook of Income Distribution*, Volume 1, Elsevier North Holland, Amsterdam.

Benjamin, D., Brandt, L., Giles, J. and Wang, S. (2005) 'Income Inequality in the Transition Period', in Loren Brandt and Thomas G. Rawski (eds), 'China's Great Transition: Origins, Mechanisms and Consequences of the Post-Reform Economic Boom', Manuscript, Department of Economics, University of Pittsburgh, Pittsburgh.

Bian, Y. and Logan, J.R. (1996) 'Market Transition and the Persistence of Power: The Changing Stratification System in Urban China', *American Sociological Review*, 61, 5: 739–58.

Brandt, L. and Holz, C.A. (2004) 'Spatial Price Differences in China: Estimates and Implications', Mimeo, University of Toronto, Toronto.

Cai, F., Park, A. and Zhao, Y. (2005) 'The Chinese Labor Market', in Loren Brandt and Thomas G. Rawski (eds), 'China's Great Transition: Origins, Mechanisms and Consequences of the Post-Reform Economic Boom', Manuscript, Department of Economics, University of Pittsburgh, Pittsburgh.

Chan, K.W. and Hu, Y. (2003) 'Urbanization in China in the 1990s: New Definition, Different Series, and Revised Trends', *China Review* 3, 2, Fall: 49–71.
Chan, K.W. and Zhong, L. (1999) 'The Hukou System and Rural–Urban Migration in China', *China Quarterly*, 160, December: 818–65.
China Development Research Foundation and UNDP (2005) *China Human Development Report 2005: Towards Human Development with Equity*, http://www.hdr.undp.org/docs/reports/national/CPR_China/China_2005_en.pdf
Deaton, A. (1997) *The Analysis of Household Surveys: A Microeconometric Approach to Development Policy* (Baltimore: Johns Hopkins University Press).
Démurger, S., Gurgand, M., Li, S. and Yue, X. (2007) 'Migrants as Second-class Workers in Urban China? A Decomposition Analysis', Mimeo (Groupe d'Analyse et de Théorie Economique: Ecully).
Eastwood, R. and Lipton, M. (2000) 'Rural–Urban Dimensions of Inequality Change', Working Paper 200, UNU-WIDER, Helsinki, September.
Eastwood, R. and Lipton, M. (2004) 'Rural and Urban Income Inequality and Poverty: Does Convergence between Sectors Offset Divergence within Them?', in G.A. Cornia, *Inequality, Growth and Poverty in an Era of Liberalization and Globalization*, (Oxford: Oxford University Press for UNU-WIDER): 112–41.
Fan, S., Zhang, L. and Zhang, X. (2004) 'Reforms, Investment and Poverty in Rural China', *Economic Development and Cultural Change*, 52, 2, January: 395–421.
Gerber, T.P. (2000) 'Membership Benefits or Selection Effects? Why Former Communist Party Members Do Better in Post-Soviet Russia', *Social Science Research*, 29, 1: 25–50.
Gradín, C., Cantó, O. and del Río, C. (2004) 'Inequality, Poverty and Mobility: Choosing Income or Consumption as Welfare Indicators', Working Paper, P.T. 18/04, Instituto de Estudios Fiscales, Universidade de Vigo, Vigo, Spain.
Gustafsson, B. and Li, S. (1998) 'Inequality in China at the End of the '80s – Locational Aspects and Household Characteristics', *Asian Economic Journal*, 12, 1: 35–63.
Gustafsson, B. and Li, S. (2001) 'A More Unequal China? Aspects of Inequality in the Distribution of Equivalent Income', in C. Riskin, R. Zhao and S. Li, *China's Retreat from Equality: Income Distribution and Economic Transition*, 44–83 (Armonk, NY: M.E. Sharpe): 44–83.
Hannum, E., Behrman, J. and Wang, M. (2005) 'Human Capital in China', in Loren Brandt and Thomas G. Rawski (eds), 'China's Great Transition: Origins, Mechanisms and Consequences of the Post-Reform Economic Boom', Manuscript, Department of Economics, University of Pittsburgh, Pittsburgh.
Jalan, J. and Ravallion, M. (1998) 'Transient Poverty in Post-reform Rural China', *Journal of Comparative Economics*, 26, 2, June: 338–57.
Jones, F.L. (1983) 'On Decomposing the Wage Gap: A Critical Comment on Blinder's Method', *Journal of Human Resources*, 18, 1: 126–30.
Kanbur, R. and Zhang, X. (1999) 'Which Regional Inequality? The Evolution of Rural–Urban and Inland–Coastal Inequality from 1983 to 1995', *Journal of Comparative Economics*, 27, 4, December: 686–701.
Khan, A.R., Griffin, K., Riskin, C. and Zhao, R. (193) 'Household Income and Its Distribution in China', in Keith Griffin and Renwei Zhao (eds), *The Distribution of Income in China* (Basingstoke: Macmillan).
Khan, A.R. and Riskin, C. (2007) 'Growth and Distribution of Household Income in China Between 1995 and 2002', in Björn Gustafsson, Shi Li and Terry Sicular

(eds), *Inequality and Public Policy in China* (New York: Cambridge University Press).

Knight, J. and Song, L. (1999) *The Urban–Rural Divide: Economic Disparities and Interactions in China* (New York: Oxford University Press).

Lam, K.C. (2003) 'Earnings Advantage of Party Members in Urban China', Working Paper, Business Research Centre, Hong Kong Baptist University, Hong Kong.

Li, S., Luo, C., Wei, Z. and Yue, X. (2007) 'Appendix: The 1995 and 2002 Household Surveys: Sampling Methods and Data Description', in Björn Gustafsson, Shi Li and Terry Sicular (eds), *Inequality and Public Policy in China* (New York: Cambridge University Press).

Liang, Z. and Ma, Z. (2004) 'China's Floating Population: New Evidence from the 2000 Census', *Population and Development Review*, 20, 3: 467–88.

Miles, D. (1997) 'A Household Level Study of the Determinants of Incomes and Consumption', *Economic Journal*, 107, 440: 1–25.

Mo, R. (2004) *2003–2004 Nian: Zhongguo Jiuye Baogao* (Beijing: Ministry of Labour and Public Security Press).

Morduch, J. and Sicular, T. (2000) 'Politics, Growth and Inequality in Rural China: Does it Pay to Join the Party?', *Journal of Public Economics*, 77, 3: 331–56.

NBS (National Bureau of Statistics) (China) (1996) *China Statistical Yearbook 1996* (Beijing: China Statistical Press).

National Bureau of Statistics (China) (2003) *China Statistical Yearbook 2003* (Beijing: China Statistical Press).

Oaxaca, R.L. and Ransom, M.R. (1999) 'Identification in Detailed Wage Decompositions', *Review of Economics and Statistics*, 8, 1: 154–7.

Ravallion, M. and Chen, S. (2004) 'China's (Uneven) Progress Against Poverty', World Bank Policy Research Working Paper 3408, September.

Sahn, D. and Stifel, D. (2003) 'Urban–Rural Inequality in Living Standards in Africa', *Journal of African Economies*, 12, 4: 564–97.

Shi, X. (2004) 'Urban–Rural Income Differentials Decomposition in China 1990s', M.A. Thesis, China Center for Economic Research, Peking University, Beijing.

Shorrocks, A. (1984) 'Inequality Decomposition by Population Subgroups', *Econometrica*, 52, 6, November: 1369–85.

Shorrocks, A. and Wan, G. (2005) 'Spatial Decomposition of Inequality', *Journal of Economic Geography*, 5, 1: 59–81.

Sicular, T., Zhao, Y. and Shi, X. (2004) 'Urban–Rural Income Inequality in China in the 1990s', Mimeo, China Center for Economic Research, Peking University, Beijing.

Smeeding, T.M. and Weinberg, D.H. (2001) 'Toward a Uniform Definition of Household Income', *Review of Income and Wealth*, 47, 1, March: 1–24.

Solinger, D. (1999) *Contesting Citizenship in Urban China: Peasant Migrants, the State, and the Logic of the Market* (Berkeley, CA: University of California Press).

Wang, F.-l. (2004) 'Reformed Migration Control and New Targeted People: China's Hukou System in the 2000s', *China Quarterly*, 177, March: 115–32.

World Bank (2003) 'China: Promoting Growth with Equity', Country Economic Memorandum, Report 24169-CHA, September.

World Institute for Development Economics Research (WIDER) (2005) 'World Income and Inequality Database, v 2.0a: User Guide and Data Sources', June, http://www.wider.unu.edu/wiid/wiid.htm

Wu, X. and Perloff, J.M. (2005) 'China's Income Distribution, 1985–2001', *Review of Economics and Statistics*, 87, 4: 763–75.

Yang, D.T. and Zhou, H. (1999) 'Rural–Urban Disparity and Sectoral Labor Allocation in China', *Journal of Development Studies*, 35, 3: 105–33.

Yue, X., Sicular, T., Li, S. and Gustafsson, B. (2007) 'Explaining Incomes and Inequality in China', in Björn Gustafsson, Shi Li and Terry Sicular (eds), *Inequality and Public Policy in China* (New York: Cambridge University Press).

Zhang, P. (1997) 'Income Distribution during the Transition in China', Working Paper 138, UNU-WIDER, Helsinki.

Zhang, X. and Fan, S. (2004) 'Public Investment and Regional Inequality in Rural China', *Agricultural Economics*, 30, 2: 89–100.

Zhang, X. and Kanbur, R. (2005) 'Spatial Inequality in Education and Health Care in China', *China Economic Review*, 16, 2: 189–204.

Zhao, R. and Ding, S. (2007) 'The Distribution of Wealth in China', in Björn Gustafsson, Shi Li and Terry Sicular (eds), *Inequality and Public Policy in China* (New York: Cambridge University Press).

Zhao, X.B. and Tong, S.P. (2000) 'Unequal Economic Development in China: Spatial Disparities and Regional Policy Reconsideration, 1985–1995', *Regional Studies*, 34, 6: 549–61.

Zhou, Y. and Ma, L.J.C. (2003) 'China's Urbanization Levels: Reconstructing a Baseline from the Fifth Population Census', *China Quarterly*, 173: 176–96.

3
Financial Development and Income Inequality in Rural China 1991–2000

Zhicheng Liang

Introduction

The Chinese economy has experienced impressive growth over the last two decades. However, this rapid growth has been accompanied by remarkable increases in inequality. According to the World Bank (1997), China's Gini coefficient rose from 0.288 in 1981 to 0.388 in 1995. Similarly, the Chinese official statistics indicate that the Gini coefficient rose from 0.330 in 1980 to 0.458 in 2000 (Chang 2002). More recently, Ravallion and Chen (2007) find that, after adjusting for difference in the cost-of-living between urban and rural China, the Gini coefficient for China as a whole climbed up from 0.280 in 1981 to 0.394 in 2001.

Rising inequality in China has received considerable attention. Earlier attempts mainly focused on the measurement of inequality (Rozelle 1994). Later, efforts were made to decompose overall inequality into within- and between-group components in terms of income, consumption or other social indicators (Tsui 1998; Kanbur and Zhang 1999; Gustafsson and Li 2002). More recently, Wan (2004) and Wan, Lu and Chen (Chapter 1, this volume) explored the contributions of various factors to China's rising inequality. While these studies provide important insights into the evolving pattern of inequality in China, little research has been conducted to address the role of financial development in the dynamic changes in Chinese income distribution. This chapter attempts to fill this gap by employing the recently released provincial data to explore the relationship between finance and inequality in China.

A growing body of literature on finance and income distribution has shown that financial development can exert important influence on inequality. However, there exist alternative theories that make different predictions concerning the finance–inequality linkage. For instance, in the dynamic model of Greenwood and Jovanovic (1990), an inverted U-shaped relationship is depicted; that is, financial development could widen income inequality during the early period, then tend to lessen it as average income rises and more households gain access to financial intermediaries and services. By contrast, other theoretical models suggest a negative and linear relationship (for example, Galor and Zeira 1993; Banerjee and Newman 1993), showing that development of financial market and financial intermediation helps reduce income inequality.

Based on a panel data set covering Chinese provinces over the period of 1991–2000, we examine the impact of financial development on income inequality in rural China. The rest of this chapter is organized as follows. The next section provides a brief review on the relationship between finance and income distribution. We then highlight the recent trend of income inequality and financial development in rural China. Empirical analyses are presented and the chapter concludes with a discussion of our findings.

Financial development and income distribution: a brief literature review

How does financial development affect income distribution? Two different schools of thought offer quite contrasting answers to this question. The first suggests an inverted U-shaped relationship between finance and inequality. Based on the pioneering work of Greenwood and Jovanovic (1990), two production technologies are assumed: a safe technology with constant but relatively low returns to investment, and a risky technology with expected high returns; further assuming that entry into the financial market is costly at a fixed price. Due to this entry fee, access to the financial sector may be restricted to agents with an amount of wealth above a certain threshold level. Their model shows that the development of financial intermediaries helps overcome the information friction on risky investment through collecting and analyzing information on investment projects. It also contributes to smoothing away idiosyncratic shock through risk diversification, trading and pooling.

Therefore, Greenwood and Jovanovic (1990) predict that, along with the financial intermediary development, the evolution of income inequality follows an inverted U-shaped path: in the early stage of development when financial intermediaries are less developed, the economy grows slowly with low inequality; in the intermediate stage of development, widening income inequality coincides with more rapid economic growth and further deepening financial development; by maturity, when an extensive financial structure is fully developed with more agents gaining access to the financial intermediary sector, the degree of income inequality will decline and ultimately become stable in the final stage of development.

The second school of thought suggests a negative and linear relationship between financial development and income inequality (e.g., Galor and Zeira 1993; Banerjee and Newman 1993). Galor and Zeira (1993) model the dynamic evolution of income distribution in an economy with indivisibility in human capital investment, where agents live for two periods, and generations are linked through bequests. Agents can either work as unskilled labour for both periods, or make an indivisible investment in human capital when they are young in the first period and then work as skilled labour in the second period. Due to financial market imperfections, only agents with a sufficiently large inheritance will invest in human capital and become skilled labour, while other agents will remain unskilled. Therefore, initial wealth distribution matters for the long-run level of income, and inequality will be perpetuated through bequests between generations. In the long run, there will be a polarization of wealth between high-income skilled labourers and low-income unskilled ones: rich, educated families will converge to the high-income steady state; poor, uneducated families will converge to the low-income steady state.

Similar predictions can also be found in the Banerjee and Newman model (1993), which concerns the dynamics of wealth distribution with financial market imperfections and indivisible investment. Banerjee and Newman (1993) show that opportunity for investment in high-return projects may be restricted to rich individuals with wealth over a threshold level. More specifically, under imperfect financial markets, only agents with wealth in excess of this threshold level may undertake high-return investment while those with inadequate wealth will not. The initially rich will become richer through their investment in high-return investment projects; the initially poor, with no access to credit markets, will remain poor. Based on these theoretical analyses, a negative and linear relationship between finance and inequality is predicted; a relationship in which the development of financial markets and financial intermediaries can help reduce income inequality by reducing capital market imperfections and providing more opportunities for the poor to borrow and invest in high-return projects.

However, few empirical studies have been conducted to test these alternative theories. The work of Li, Squire and Zou (1998) and that of Clarke, Xu and Zou (2003) are two notable exceptions. Using a dataset of Gini coefficients for 40 developed and developing countries from 1947 to 1994, Li, Squire and Zou (1998) examine the relationship between financial depth and income inequality. They find that better-functioning financial markets are strongly associated with lower income inequality. Similarly, by employing panel data from both developing and developed countries between 1960 and 1995, Clarke, Xu and Zou (2003) find that inequality is lower in countries with better-developed financial sectors, and that inequality decreases as economies develop their financial intermediaries. It is apparent that these empirical results support the linear hypothesis suggested by Galor and Zeira (1993) and Banerjee and Newman (1993), rather than an inverted U-shaped pattern, as predicted by Greenwood and Jovanovic (1990).

In this chapter, using Chinese provincial data, we attempt to test the alternative predictions made by different schools of thought concerning the finance–inequality linkage. To the best of our knowledge, this is the first study looking at the relationship between finance and inequality for rural China.

Financial reforms and income inequality in rural China

Two decades of rural reforms in China have successfully stimulated rural economic growth, and greatly improved the living standards of rural households. Rapid development of the rural economy altered the pattern of income distribution in rural China (Wan 2004). Meanwhile, in order to establish a more efficient mechanism to support investment, in order to meet the financial demands of rural households and better serve the rural sector, a series of policy measures has been introduced to reform and strengthen China's rural financial system.

Reforms in the rural financial system

Before economic reforms, a mono-banking system was established under the centrally planned economy, and the People's Bank of China (PBC) was the only formal financial institution in China. However, the traditional financial system failed to provide sufficient financial support to meet the needs arising from expanded production in such economic sectors as agriculture, industry, construction, transport and commerce. The abandoning of the mono-banking system in the late 1970s marked the beginning of China's financial reforms. Four specialized banks, authorized with specialized functions concerning different scopes of economic activities, were separated from the traditional system, and the PBC was then reorganized as the Central Bank of China.[1]

Among the four state-owned specialized banks, the Agricultural Bank of China (ABC) plays the most important role in serving the rural sector, and acts as the key institution in China's rural financial system. Another important financial institution has been the rural credit cooperatives (RCCs), located at the township and county level, and subject to the monitoring of the branches of the ABC. In the 1980s, the focus of reforms to the RCCs was to revive their role in collective organization, democratic management and administration, and to expand their autonomy in business operations. Since the beginning of the 1990s, the government has begun to accelerate the process of commercializing the state-owned banks. To facilitate the transformation of the ABC into competitive, autonomous, and self-accountable commercial banks, the Agricultural Development Bank of China (ADBC), a policy-lending bank responsible for financial loans on the purchase and sale of agricultural products, was established in 1994. The promulgation of the Commercial Bank Law in 1995 ensured independent operations for the commercial banks, which considerably strengthened the commercializing reforms of the state-owned specialized banks. The process of commercialization was further advanced by the separation of the RCCs from the branches of the ABC in 1996, and the RCCs were subject to the direct supervision and monitoring of the PBC. Meanwhile, rural cooperative foundations (RCFs) – which were created at the beginning of the 1980s and organized by local governments as informal financial institutions to fill the credit vacuum of formal finance in the rural sector – have also experienced rapid development during this period. Therefore, a multi-institutional financial system was formed in rural China, including the formal financial institutions and various types of informal financial organizations.

Recently, significant changes have occurred in the market orientation and operational strategy of the ABC. In order to improve efficiency and profitability, the ABC began to reduce its rural financial business. The focus of the ABC has been shifted from rural to urban areas. Meanwhile, along with the expansion of the ABC's credit business into non-agricultural sectors, the role of the ABC in promoting rural development has been weakened sharply. As for the other state-owned commercial banks, they also gradually withdrew from rural areas. Moreover, the Chinese government and the PBC have recently implemented a series of policy measures to control the development of informal finance in rural China. As a result, the RCFs were either abolished or merged into the RCCs in 1999.

Consequently, the RCCs have become the dominant financial institution serving China's rural sector. The ratio of the RCCs' agriculture loans in total agricultural credits has increased rapidly from 26 per cent in

1979 to 54 per cent in 1997, and then to 77 per cent in 2001. As for the loans to the township and village enterprises (TVEs), the proportion of the RCCs has also expanded from 32.1 per cent in 1979 to 69.5 per cent in 1997, and to 77.3 per cent in 2001.[2] These results indicate that the monopoly of the RCCs in rural finance has been gradually strengthened over the last several years.

Due to the important role of the RCCs in the rural financial system, the Chinese government and the PBC have launched a series of reforms to transform the RCCs into viable financial institutions that operate independently, bear risks on their own, and take responsibility for their own profits and losses. In addition, policy measures have also been advanced to make the RCCs true cooperatives that better serve their members and the rural sector. A pilot programme for further reforming the RCCs has been implemented in several areas. Eight counties were selected for a pilot reform project on interest rate liberalization within the RCCs, with the deposit rates being allowed to float up to 30 per cent of the official deposit rate, and their lending rate up to 70 per cent of the reference level. In some areas, the RCCs at the township and county level were merged into the county financial union, which in turn would be transformed into rural commercial banks according to the shareholding system principle. So far, three rural commercial banks have been established in Jiangsu province. In addition, efforts were made to organize rural cooperative banks in certain advanced areas. In 2003, the first rural cooperative bank was set up in Zhejiang province. In the long run, however, to strengthen rural financial systems and to promote economic growth in rural areas, fundamental financial reforms in the structure of ownership and corporate governance are required.

Income inequality in rural China

Two decades of market-oriented transition have altered the patterns of income distribution in rural China significantly. Figure 3.1 presents the official Gini coefficient for rural China. During the early stage of rural reforms (1978–84), the Household Responsibility System (HRS) successfully released farmers' potential and significantly raised production efficiency. Along with improvement in agricultural productivity, increased agricultural prices also contributed to rural income growth over this period. Due to egalitarian land distribution, the gains of rural reforms were widely shared among rural households; thus, the rural Gini coefficient increased only slightly from 0.212 in 1978 to 0.244 in 1984.

However, rural China has witnessed significant changes in household income structure since 1985, due mainly to stagnant agricultural

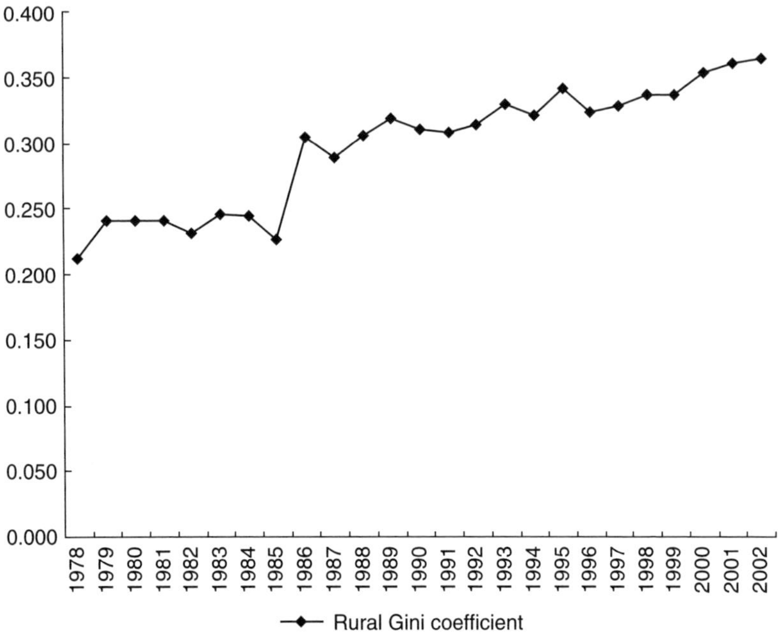

Figure 3.1 Rural income inequality in China, 1978–2002 (Gini coefficient)
Source: Compiled by the author based on NBS data.

production, unbalanced growth of Township and Village Enterprises (TVEs), and the rapid development of off-farm opportunities. In the second half of the 1980s, China's rural Gini coefficient rose from 0.227 in 1985 to 0.319 in 1989. This mainly resulted from the changed nature of income gains and the growing differential in rural non-farm opportunities among regions (Rozelle 1994; Wan 2001; Fan, Zhang and Zhang 2004).

During the early 1990s, China's rural Gini coefficient increased from 0.310 in 1990 to 0.341 in 1995, and then fell to 0.323 in 1996. An important reason for this may be the rapid increases in farm procurement prices between 1994 and 1995, which disproportionately benefited low-income rural households for whom farming was an important source of income, and helped to offset the impact on inequality of the rapid growth of non-agricultural incomes (Benjamin *et al.* 2005).

Since 1997, however, China has recorded once again significant increases in rural inequality, with the rural Gini coefficient rising from 0.329 in 1997 to 0.365 in 2002. Unequal access to off-farm employment, as well as falling agricultural income due to a sharp decline in agricultural product prices in the late 1990s were important factors that contributed to the deterioration in rural income distribution.

Worsening income distribution has become a serious challenge to the Chinese government as it may undermine long-run economic growth and social stability (Wan, Lu and Chen 2006). Clearly, in order to reduce rural inequality, it is necessary to identify its determinants.

A number of studies emphasized the role of rural industrialization and the emerging non-agricultural sector (especially the development of the TVEs) in influencing rural income distribution (Rozelle 1994; Hare 1994; Kung and Lee 2001). More recently, other potential driving factors were examined. These include migration, fiscal decentralization, irrigation, roads, telecommunications, education, and rural research and development (Khan and Riskin 1998; Huang *et al.* 2003; Fan, Zhang and Zhang 2004). In addition, efforts have been made to assess the contribution of spatial income differences to recent rises in rural inequality (Cheng 1996; Gustafsson and Li 2002; Wan 2004).

However, few empirical studies have considered the important role of the financial market in determining China's rural inequality. The recent work of Wan (2004) and Wan and Zhou (2005) are two notable exceptions. Utilizing the regression-based approach to inequality decomposition, Wan (2004) concluded that the absence of formal capital markets in the less developed areas of rural China has been detrimental to capital formation in these regions, which significantly contributes to widening regional inequalities in rural China. This finding is further confirmed in Wan and Zhou (2005). Both Wan (2004) and Wan and Zhou (2005) find that disparities in capital stock is the most important contributor to rural inequality in China, and they recommend the strengthening of the rural financial market as being the strategy to curb rising inequality.

The central government has implemented a series of policy measures to lower income inequality in rural China. Such policies include price support for agricultural products; policy aid to stimulate the development of rural industry, especially in the least developed provinces; and the increase in public investment in roads, irrigation, electrification, education, agricultural R&D and other public services in rural areas. To implement these policies requires further development of the rural financial system.

It is imperative to note, however, that unless finance itself is unrelated to or negatively associated with inequality, the development of credit markets may not help improve income distribution. It is in this context that an examination of the finance–inequality nexus takes on significance and it is to this that we now turn in the next section.

Econometric modelling

Data and variables

To explore empirically the impact of financial development on income inequality in rural China, the logarithm of provincial rural Gini coefficients (*GINI*) will be employed as the dependent variable.[3] In order to measure the level of financial development in rural China, we construct an indicator (*FINANCE*), defined as the ratio of total rural loans to rural GDP. Unfortunately, official data on rural loans and rural GDP are not available. To obtain these variables, we first divide the rural sector into two subsectors: the agricultural sector and the non-agricultural sector. Rural loans are computed as the sum of credit allocated to the agricultural sector and the TVEs. For the rural GDP, we follow the procedure of Fan, Zhang and Zhang (2004), in which the GDP of the agricultural sector is equivalent to the GDP of the primary sector used by China's National Bureau of Statistics (NBS). The value-added for rural industry (including construction) and services is used as a proxy of non-agricultural GDP from rural China. Finally, rural GDP is computed as the sum of GDP for these two subsectors.[4]

Another explanatory variable is the per capita rural net income at 1985 constant prices (expressed in logarithmic terms in the model and to be denoted by *RY*). In order to test the inverted Kuznets' U-shaped hypothesis on the relationship between economic development and income inequality (Kuznets, 1955), we include both the linear term of *RY* as well its squared term.

Given the role of public investments in rural development, we include the variable of government investment in the agricultural sector (*AGEXP*), defined as the ratio of government expenditures in the agricultural sector to rural GDP.[5] In addition, we introduce the variable *TVED*, defined as the ratio of TVE output to total rural output.

To capture the impacts of investment on rural inequality, the variable *INV*, measured by the ratio of fixed assets investment to GDP, is included. Finally, demographic changes may also exert influences on rural income distribution. Therefore, we introduce the variable of *RLAB*, defined as the ratio of the number of rural labourers to total rural population.

The data to be used cover 21 Chinese provinces over the period 1991–2000. This is because computable and complete summary statistics of rural household surveys for the calculation of the rural Gini coefficient are only available for these provinces over these years. The 21 provinces included in our sample are: Tianjin, Hebei, Shanxi, Inner Mongolia, Liaoning, Heilongjiang, Shanghai, Jiangsu, Zhejiang, Anhui, Fujian, Jiangxi,

Henan, Hubei, Hunan, Guangdong, Guangxi, Yunnan, Shaanxi, Qinghai and Xinjiang. The primary sources of our data are from the *China Statistical Yearbook* (NBS, various years), *Almanac of China's Finance and Banking* (PBC, various years), *China Rural Statistical Yearbook* (NBS, various years), and *Comprehensive Statistical Data and Materials on 50 Years of China* (NBS, 1999), plus individual provincial statistical yearbooks.

Regression model

To test the linear hypothesis suggested by Galor and Zeira (1993) and Banerjee and Newman (1993), we adopt the following regression model:

$$\begin{aligned} GINI_{i,t} &= \alpha_0 + \alpha_1 GINI_{i,t-1} + \alpha_2 FINANCE_{i,t} + \alpha_3 RY_{i,t} + \alpha_4 RY_{i,t}^2 \\ &\quad + \alpha_5 TVED_{i,t} + \alpha_6 AGEXP_{i,t} + \alpha_7 INV_{i,t} + \alpha_8 RLAB_{i,t} + \mu_i + \varepsilon_{i,t} \end{aligned} \tag{3.1}$$

Similarly, to test the Greenwood–Jovanovic hypothesis of an inverted U-shaped relationship between finance and inequality, we introduce a squared term of the financial variable ($FINANCE_{i,t}^2$) into our model, and thus the regression model can be rewritten as follows:

$$\begin{aligned} GINI_{i,t} &= \beta_0 + \beta_1 GINI_{i,t-1} + \beta_2 FINANCE_{i,t} + \beta_3 FINANCE_{i,t}^2 + \beta_4 RY_{i,t} + \beta_5 RY_{i,t}^2 \\ &\quad + \beta_6 TVED_{i,t} + \beta_7 AGEXP_{i,t} + \beta_8 INV_{i,t} + \beta_9 RLAB_{i,t} + \mu_i + \varepsilon_{i,t} \end{aligned} \tag{3.2}$$

In both of these models, $GINI_{i,t}$ is the logarithm of the Gini coefficient for province i at year t, and $FINANCE_{i,t}$ is the financial indicator. Table 3.1 lists the variables, while Table 3.2 reports their descriptive statistics. Meanwhile, correlations between the explanatory variables can be found in Table 3.3. As expected, high correlation is found between *RY* and RY^2 and between *FINANCE* and $FINANCE^2$. It seems that necessary measures should be taken to address these problems.

The generalized method of moments (GMM) methodology, proposed by Arellano and Bond (1991) and further developed by Blundell and Bond (1998), is employed here to control for endogeneity in our regression model. The GMM estimator has been widely employed, particularly in the studies of macroeconomics and finance. This method has a number of advantages. For instance, Beck, Levine and Loayza (2000) argue that the GMM panel estimator is good in exploiting the time-series variation in the data, accounting for unobserved individual specific effects,

Table 3.1 Definitions of variables

Variable	Definition
GINI	The logarithm of Gini coefficient
FINANCE	Rural financial development level, measured by the ratio of total rural loans to rural GDP
RY	The logarithm of real per capita rural net income
AGEXP	Government investment in the agricultural sector (AGEXP), measured by the ratio of government expenditures in the agricultural sector to rural GDP
TVED	Development level of the township and village enterprises (TVEs), measured by the ratio of TVEs' output to the total rural output
INV	Investment rate, measured by the ratio of fixed assets investment to GDP
RLAB	The ratio of the number of rural labourers to total rural population

Table 3.2 Descriptive statistics of variables

	Mean	Std dev.	Minimum	Maximum	Observations
GINI	−1.3006	0.1411	−1.6809	−0.9140	210
FINANCE	0.2850	0.1767	0.0936	1.3006	206
RY	6.3424	0.3994	5.5430	7.1842	210
AGEXP	0.0251	0.0211	0.0041	0.1133	206
TVED	0.6833	0.1891	0.1565	0.9304	210
INV	0.3253	0.0827	0.1729	0.6726	210
RLAB	0.4758	0.0683	0.2954	0.6977	210

and therefore providing better control for endogeneity of all the explanatory variables.

Empirical results

The empirical results are reported in Table 3.4. For each regression, we test model specification in terms of over-identifying restrictions for instrument validity, and second order serial correlation. For the validity of over-identifying restrictions, the Hansen test or the Sargan test can be applied, where the null hypothesis is that the instruments are uncorrelated with the residuals. In the present study, we report the Hansen test statistics (rather than the Sargan test statistics) because the Hansen test is more consistent and robust in the presence of heteroscedasticity and autocorrelation (for example, Hansen 1982; Newey and West 1987;

Table 3.3 Correlations between the explanatory variables

	$FINANCE_{i,t}$	$FINANCE^2_{i,t}$	$RY_{i,t}$	$RY^2_{i,t}$	$AGEXP_{i,t}$	$INV_{i,t}$	$RLAB_{i,t}$	$TVED_{i,t}$
$FINANCE_{i,t}$	1.0000							
$FINANCE^2_{i,t}$	0.9427*	1.0000						
	(0.0000)							
$RY_{i,t}$	0.4019*	0.3383*	1.0000					
	(0.0000)	(0.0000)						
$RY^2_{i,t}$	0.4074*	0.3419*	0.9995*	1.0000				
	(0.0000)	(0.0000)	(0.0000)					
$AGEXP_{i,t}$	0.0181	0.0195	−0.4768*	−0.4674*	1.0000			
	(0.7961)	(0.7811)	(0.0000)	(0.0000)				
$INV_{i,t}$	0.3933*	0.2694*	0.3093*	0.3177*	0.1301*	1.0000		
	(0.0000)	(0.0001)	(0.0000)	(0.0000)	(0.0624)			
$RLAB_{i,t}$	0.2485*	0.2138*	0.2757*	0.2880*	−0.0622	0.1276	1.0000	
	(0.0003)	(0.0020)	(0.0001)	(0.0000)	(0.3742)	(0.0649)		
$TVED_{i,t}$	0.2684*	0.2454*	0.6718*	0.6699*	−0.6904*	0.0995	0.3699*	1.0000
	(0.0001)	(0.0004)	(0.0000)	(0.0000)	(0.0000)	(0.1506)	(0.0000)	

Note: * significant at the 1 per cent level; * significant at the 5 per cent level; * significant at the 10 per cent level; *p*-values are presented in parentheses.

Arellano 2002). Note that a significant χ^2 value for this test indicates that the over-identifying restrictions are not valid. Results in Table 3.4 show that all the regressions pass the Hansen tests, which suggests that our instruments are valid. In addition, there exists no evidence of second serial correlation in our estimations.

Under Regression I of Table 3.4, we report the estimated model (1). The coefficients of *FINANCE* are negative and statistically significant, suggesting that financial development helps reduce rural income inequality in China. On the contrary, the impact of TVEs development (*TVED*) on the rural Gini coefficient is positive, confirming rural industrialization as a disequalizing factor. Interestingly, regions with higher value of *RLAB* (the ratio of rural labourers to rural population) tend to have lower rural inequality. However, both the coefficients of *RY* and RY^2 are statistically insignificant. Thus, there exists little support to the inverted Kuznets' U-shaped relation between economic development and income inequality.

Since the variables of *RY* and RY^2 are highly correlated, we decide to delete RY^2 from the model, and the new estimation results are reported under Regression II of Table 3.4. Now, the variable of *RY* is positively and significantly correlated with rural inequality, indicating that rural income distribution tends to be less egalitarian in regions with higher per capita income. As for the variable *FINANCE*, it remains statistically significant and negatively correlated with rural inequality, which highlights the important contribution of rural financial development in the reduction of income inequality. In other words, the linear and negative relationship between finance and inequality is confirmed.

Regression III of Table 3.4 presents the results for model (1). Since both *RY* and RY^2 are statistically insignificant in Regression III, we also report under Regression IV the estimated results after deleting RY^2. As for the financial variables, we find that the coefficients of squared term $FINANCE^2$ are always statistically insignificant. Therefore, the inverted U-shaped hypothesis is rejected in the case of rural China.

Conclusion

Rising income inequality in rural China have been at the centre of public concerns and subject to passionate debate. Recent studies show that unequal capital inputs emerges as the most significant determinant of income inequality in rural China, and the contribution of the capital inputs to regional inequality is likely to continue to increase, unless

Table 3.4 Financial development and income inequality in rural China (dependent variable = $GINI_{i,t}$: the logarithm of rural Gini coefficient)

	Regression I	Regression II	Regression III	Regression IV
$GINI_{i,t-1}$	0.8173* (9.61)	0.7079* (7.51)	0.8154* (10.76)	0.6033* (6.27)
Financial development:				
$FINANCE_{i,t}$	−0.1930* (−1.93)	−0.1590* (−1.89)	−0.2155 (−1.48)	−0.4928* (−1.90)
$FINANCE^2_{i,t}$			0.0226 (0.20)	0.3572 (1.34)
Per capita income:				
$RY_{i,t}$	−0.6324 (−0.47)	0.0823* (2.08)	−0.4610 (−0.37)	0.1573* (2.27)
$RY^2_{i,t}$	0.0507 (0.49)		0.0376 (0.40)	
Other control variables:				
$AGEXP_{i,t}$	2.3676* (2.89)	3.0924* (3.48)	2.3965* (3.33)	3.9453* (4.80)
$TVED_{i,t}$	0.2344* (2.18)	0.1625 (1.53)	0.2287* (2.05)	0.0942 (0.69)
$INV_{i,t}$	0.1441 (1.33)	0.1082 (0.88)	0.1600 (1.50)	0.1552 (0.89)
$RLAB_{i,t}$	−0.4177* (−2.36)	−0.3901* (−2.83)	−0.4021* (−2.30)	−0.3756* (−2.57)
Constant	1.7206 (0.39)	−0.8889* (−2.68)	1.1542 (0.29)	−1.4434* (−3.00)
Hansen test	Chi2 = 16.21 Prob. > Chi2 = 0.368	Chi2 = 14.81 Prob. > Chi2 = 0.320	Chi2 = 17.45 Prob. > Chi2 = 0.424	Chi2 = 12.37 Prob. > Chi2 = 0.651
AR(2)	Z = 1.50 Prob. > Z = 0.133	Z = 1.44 Prob. > Z = 0.149	Z = 1.41 Prob. > Z = 0.158	Z = 1.34 Prob. > Z = 0.180
Observations	186	186	186	186
Provinces	21	21	21	21

Notes: * significant at the 1 per cent level; * significant at the 5 per cent level; * significant at the 10 per cent level.
For all regressions, T-statistics values are presented in parentheses.

governments establish rural credit markets to assist poor regions and poor farmers to obtain capital (Wan 2004; Wan and Zhou 2005). Therefore, the development of China's rural financial systems, through effective capital mobilization and resource allocation to meet the investment required for rural development, will promote rural economic growth, as well as improve rural income distribution.

In this study, using panel data over the period 1991–2000, we apply the generalized method of moment (GMM) technique to investigate empirically the impacts of rural financial development on the distribution of income in rural China. It is found that rural financial development significantly contributes to the reduction of rural inequality. Our findings strongly support the linear relationship – rather than the Greenwood–Jovanovic inverted U-shaped relationship – between finance and inequality. Thus, to lower China's rural inequality, the Chinese government should make greater efforts to strengthen rural financial systems, paying particular attention to development of viable credit markets in poor areas of rural China.

Nevertheless, our results should be interpreted with caution. More studies that cover a longer time period will be useful to deepen our understanding of the finance–inequality linkage in post-reform China. Further research based on data at the micro-level is also highly recommended. A better understanding of the relationship between financial development and income inequality can shed light on future development not only for China, but also for other developing countries.

Notes

1 The four state-owned specialized banks are the Agricultural Bank of China (ABC), the Construction Bank of China (CCB), the Bank of China (BOC) and the Industrial and Commercial Bank of China (ICBC).
2 See *Almanac of China's Finance and Banking*, 1986–2002.
3 China's National Bureau of Statistics (NBS) has annually conducted well-established national household surveys covering both rural and urban areas for all regions of the country in the post-reform period. These data are ideal for the analysis of China's evolving pattern of income distribution. However, we do not have comprehensive access to these survey data. Fortunately, summary statistics for various income intervals of rural households are still available at the provincial level, and we use them to calculate China's provincial rural Gini coefficients.
4 Please see Fan, Zhang and Zhang (2004) for more details on this procedure.
5 Government expenditures in the agricultural sector include the expenditures for supporting agricultural production, investments for comprehensive development of agriculture, and operating expenses in relation to agriculture, forestry, water conservancy and meteorology.

References

Arellano M. (2002) 'Sargan's Instrumental Variables Estimation and the Generalized Method of Moments', *Journal of Business & Economic Statistics*, 20, 4: 450–9.

Arellano, M. and Bond S. (1991) 'Some Tests of Specification for Panel Data: Monte Carlo Evidence and an Application to Employment Equations', *Review of Economic Studies*, 58, 2: 277–97.

Banerjee, A.V. and Newman, A.F. (1993) 'Occupational Choice and the Process of Development', *Journal of Political Economy*, 101, 2: 274–98.

Beck T., Levine, R. and Loayza, N. (2000) 'Finance and the Sources of Growth', *Journal of Financial Economics*, 58, 1–2: 261–310.

Benjamin, D., Brandt, L., Giles, J. and Wang, S. (2005) 'Income Inequality During China's Economic Transition', University of Toronto (Department of Economics) Working Paper tecipa-238, University of Toronto, Canada.

Blundell, R. and Bond, S. (1998) 'Initial Conditions and Moment Restrictions in Dynamic Panel Data Models', *Journal of Econometrics*, 87, 1: 115–43.

Chang, G.H. (2002) 'The Cause and Cure of China's Widening Income Disparity', *China Economic Review*, 13: 335–40.

Cheng, Y.-S. (1996) 'A Decomposition Analysis of Income Inequality of Chinese Rural Households', *China Economic Review*, 7, 2: 155–67.

Clarke, G., Xu, L.C. and Zou, H. (2003) 'Finance and Income Inequality: Test of Alternative Theories', Policy Research Working Paper 2984 (Washington, DC: World Bank).

Fan, S., Zhang, L. and Zhang, X. (2004) 'Reform, Investment and Poverty in Rural China', *Economic Development and Cultural Change*, 52, 2: 395–422.

Galor, O. and Zeira, J. (1993) 'Income Distribution and Macroeconomics', *Review of Economic Studies*, 60, 1: 35–52.

Greenwood, J. and Jovanovic, B. (1990) 'Financial Development, Growth, and the Distribution of Income', *Journal of Political Economy*, 98, 5: 1076–107.

Gustafsson, B. and Li, S. (2002) 'Income Inequality within and across Counties in Rural China 1988 and 1995', *Journal of Development Economics*, 69, 1: 179–204.

Hansen, L. (1982) 'Large Sample Properties of Generalized Method of Moments Estimators', *Econometrica*, 50: 1029–54.

Hare, D. (1994) 'Rural Nonagricultural Activities and Their Impact on the Distribution of Income: Evidence from Farm Households in Southern China', *China Economic Review*, 5, 1: 59–82.

Huang, Q., Dawe, D., Huang, J., Rozelle, S. and Wang, J. (2003) 'Irrigation, Poverty and Inequality in Rural China', CCAP Working Paper 03-E14 (Beijing: CCAP).

Kanbur, R. and Zhang, X. (1999) 'Which Regional Inequality? The Evolution of Rural–Urban and Inland/Coastal Inequality in China', *Journal of Comparative Economics*, 27: 686–701.

Khan, A.R. and Riskin, C. (1998) 'Income and Inequality in China: Composition, Distribution and Growth of Household Income, 1988 to 1995', *China Quarterly*, 154: 221–53.

Kung, J. and Lee, Y. (2001) 'So What If There Is Income Inequality? The Distributive Consequence of Nonfarm Employment in Rural China', *Economic Development and Cultural Change*, 50, 1: 19–46.

Kuznets, S. (1955) 'Economic Growth and Income Inequality', *American Economic Review*, 45, 1: 1–28.
Li, H., Squire, L. and Zou, H. (1998) 'Explaining International and Intertemporal Variations in Income Inequality', *Economic Journal*, 108, 446: 26–43.
NBS (National Bureau of Statistics) (various years) *China Rural Statistical Yearbook* (Beijing: China Statistics Press).
NBS (National Bureau of Statistics) (various years) *China Statistical Yearbook* (Beijing: China Statistics Press).
NBS (National Bureau of Statistics) (1999) *Comprehensive Statistical Data and Materials on 50 Years of China* (Beijing: China Statistics Press).
Newey, W. and West, K. (1987) 'Hypothesis Testing with Efficient Method of Moments Estimation', *International Economic Review*, 28: 777–87.
PBC (People's Bank of China) (various years) *Almanac of China's Finance and Banking* (Beijing: China Financial Publishing House (*Zhongguo Jinrong Chubanshe*)).
Ravallion, M. and Chen, S. (2007) 'China's (Uneven) Progress against Poverty', *Journal of Development Economics*, 82: 1– 42.
Rozelle, S. (1994) 'Rural Industrialization and Increasing Inequality: Emerging Patterns in China's Reforming Economy', *Journal of Comparative Economics*, 19, 3: 362–91.
Tsui, K.Y. (1998) 'Trends and Inequality of Rural Welfare in China: Evidence from Rural Households in Guangdong and Sichuan', *Journal of Comparative Economics*, 26: 783–804.
Wan, G.H. (2001) 'Changes in Regional Inequality in Rural China: Decomposing the Gini Index by Income Sources', *Australian Journal of Agricultural and Resource Economics*, 45, 3: 361–82.
Wan, G.H. (2004) 'Accounting for Income Inequality in Rural China', *Journal of Comparative Economics*, 32, 2: 348–63.
Wan, G.H., Lu, M. and Chen, Z. (2006) 'The Inequality-Growth Nexus in the Short Run and Long Run, Empirical Evidence from China', *Journal of Comparative Economics*, 34: 654–67.
Wan, G.H., Lu, M. and Chen, Z. (2008) 'Globalization and Regional Inequality in China', Chapter 1, this volume.
Wan, G.H. and Zhou, Z.Y. (2005) 'Income Inequality in Rural China: Regression-based Decomposition Using Household Data', *Review of Development Economics*, 9, 1: 107–20.
World Bank (1997) *Sharing Rising Incomes: Disparities in China* (Washington, DC: World Bank Publications).

4

Regional Income Inequality in Rural China, 1985–2002: Trends, Causes and Policy Implications

Guanghua Wan

Introduction

It is widely recognized that regional inequality in China has been on the rise since economic reforms were initiated in the late 1970s (Kanbur and Zhang 2005; Wan 2005). In addition to its repercussions on social and political stability, such a rise has hampered poverty alleviation (Ravallion and Chen 2004; Zhang and Wan 2006) and is found to be detrimental to long-run economic growth (Wan, Lu and Chen 2006). Many Chinese scholars also consider high inequality as a major contributor to the sluggish domestic demand in China. It is thus not surprising to witness a broad and growing interest in China's regional inequality. Earlier studies largely focused on the measurement of regional inequality. Subsequent efforts were devoted to break down total inequality into various components, either by population subgroups (Tsui 1991) or by factor components (Wan 2001). Recently, the technique of regression-based decomposition has gained popularity (Fields and Yoo 2000; Morduch and Sicular 2002; Wan 2002) and has been applied to China (Morduch and Sicular 2002; Wan 2004; Wan and Zhou 2005).

Despite a large volume of literature on regional inequality in China, few existing studies constructed time profiles of inequality among rural regions in China.[1] This is surprising, given that a dominant proportion of China's population live in the countryside and, as discussed later, rural inequality is a large component of overall regional inequality. More importantly, rural inequality is fundamentally different from its urban counterpart in terms of causes, trends and policy implications. For example, geography is much more important in driving rural inequality than urban inequality. When encompassing weather, infrastructure and other natural resources, the geography variable would account for a very significant share of total rural inequality. This is not necessarily the case for the urban sector, despite the probable relevance of location as a determinant of wages. Needless to say, in China the distribution of arable land is relevant to rural inequality but not to its urban counterpart. Clearly, while studies on the whole of China or urban China are important, there exist obvious justifications for separate focus on rural China.

This chapter will fill such a gap in the literature by providing a time profile of regional income inequality in rural China for the period 1985–2002, this profile having been appealed for by Rozelle (1994). Another purpose of the chapter is to identify the components of rural regional inequality. This is accomplished by undertaking conventional as well as regression-based inequality decompositions. These decompositions offer different insights into the determinants of the total inequality. Also, policy implications will be explored.

The chapter is organized as follows. The next section describes the data and the time profile of rural regional inequality. Therein, conventional and newly proposed methods will be employed to decompose total inequality into two broad components: between regional belts (that is, eastern-central-western China) and within these belts. The subsequent section applies the regression-based decomposition to rural China, which helps reveal the root sources of regional inequality. Finally, we discuss policy implications in our conclusion.

Data and preliminary analysis

As a precursory note, it is useful to mention that a substantial proportion of China's regional inequality – in the order of 25 per cent or so – is attributable to the urban–rural gap.[2] The remainder is due to inequalities within urban and rural regions. In accounting for the total regional inequality for China as a whole, these so-called within-components are given by their respective Theil L index estimates, weighted by their population shares. Since unweighted rural regional inequality is found to be greater than its urban counterpart (Wan 2005), and a major percentage of the population lives in the rural areas, the contribution of rural regional inequality to total inequality must be substantial.

To accomplish the research objectives of this chapter, most of our data are compiled from the *China Rural Household Survey Yearbook* (NBS various years) for the period 1985–2002. Earlier data are incomplete. Ideally, the rural population should be used, as our income observations are for rural residents. However, we failed to find consistent rural population series for all regions. Instead, agricultural population statistics are used.[3] It is expected that they will be highly correlated with the rural population and are available from the *China Rural Statistical Yearbook* (NBS various years). Excluding Hong Kong, Taiwan and Macao, there are 31 regions (provinces, autonomous regions or metropolitan cities) in China. However, our sample contains data for 28 regions with Hainan merged with Guangdong, Chongqing merged with Sichuan, and Xizang (Tibet) excluded. Data for Tibet are not complete. As argued by Wan (2001), such exclusion is not expected to distort the analytical results. All data in value terms are deflated by regional rural consumer price indices (CPIs) as well as the regional price indices compiled by Brandt and Carsten (2004).

The deflated regional income data are plotted against years in Figure 4.1; for each year the plot contains per capita real incomes for all 28 regions. This figure shows that while real income has been increasing over time, its dispersion is also on the rise, as indicated by the expanding height of the plots over time. According to Figure 4.1, regional incomes increased over 1985–89. After a setback for most regions in 1989–90, the increasing trend resumed: this setback was probably caused by the austerity programme initiated by the Chinese government in 1989 (Wan 2001).

Reasonably assuming no changes in the composition of regions in the rich and poor groups, the poor (lower segments of the plots) consistently

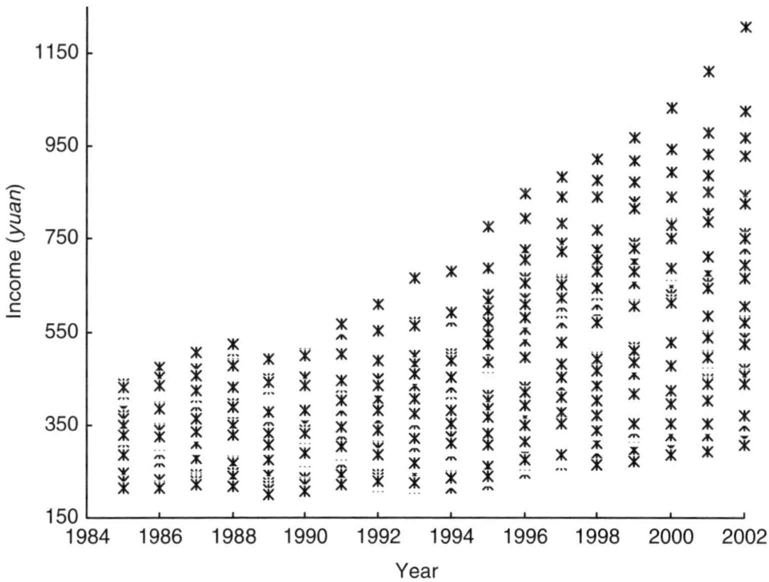

Figure 4.1 Regional per capita real income, by year

experienced slower income growth than the rich (upper segments of the plots). In fact, for the poor regions as a group, real income declined or was stagnant before 1996. Even after a small rise in 1996, this group's income rose little over 1996–2002. In contrast, income increased over the period 1985–88 for the rich regions. For this group, there was a small drop in income in 1989, but the increasing trend resumed immediately after and continued strongly until 2002. Judging from these observations, one may conclude that regional income inequality in rural China has been increasing in both absolute as well as relative terms, respectively indicated by the expanding height of the plots over time, and by the differing growth rates for the poor and rich regions.

A careful examination of Figure 4.1 reveals that the gaps between the income groups (top, middle and bottom segments of the plots) seem to have expanded more than those within these groups or segments. This clustering of regional income in recent years implies some form of polarization in China. In other words, income has probably been diverging more between income groups than within income groups. Nevertheless, Figure 4.1 may be misleading as far as the gathering inequality trend is concerned because the expansion in income dispersion had been accompanied by changes in income levels. It is known that an identical income growth for all regions can also result in increased dispersions, as in Figure 4.1, but such growth leaves inequality unchanged as long as relative rather than absolute inequality measures are used.

A formal way to analyze inequality is to construct Lorenz curves and conduct stochastic dominance analysis. For this purpose, Lorenz curves are obtained for each of the 18 years. Although there is a tendency for the Lorenz curve to move downwards over time, any first-degree stochastic dominance is not clearly visible when they are all displayed in one diagram. On the one hand, this may be caused by 'too much information' – many curves are squeezed onto one diagram. On the other, this is understandable as inequality changes are usually small from one year to the next. To reduce distractions caused by 'too much information', we average Lorenz curves over a 3-year interval and present these curves in Figure 4.2. Unfortunately, even Figure 4.2 does not exhibit any particularly clear first-degree stochastic dominance. As a consequence, pair-wise comparisons of these curves have to be made (these are not shown, in order to economize space) and they indicate that nine out of the fifteen pairs of the Lorenz curves cross, mostly at the top or bottom ends of the distributions.

When Lorenz curves cross, they cannot be used to rank income distributions. In this case, a second or higher degree of stochastic dominance

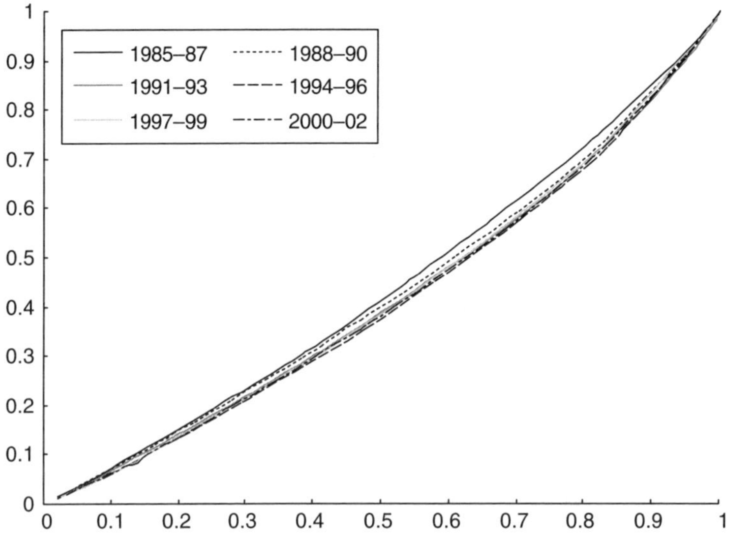

Figure 4.2 Lorenz curves

can be introduced. Alternatively, summary inequality measures could be used instead (Fields 2001). To minimize possible sensitivities to inequality measures,[4] we compute most relative inequality indices that are commonly in use; namely the Gini, Theil L, Theil T and half CV^2.[5]

Let Z denote the target variable, μ denote the mean of Z, j index observations ($j = 1, 2, \ldots, N$); the following formulae can be used: Atkinson $= 1 - \Pi_j(Z_j/\mu)^{1/N}$, Theil $L = (1/N)\sum_j Ln(\mu/Z_j)$, and Theil T $= (1/N)\sum_j(Z_j/\mu)Ln(Z_j/\mu)$. The Atkinson index is not considered here because it can be expressed as a monotonic transformation of Theil L (Shorrocks and Slottje 2002).

The computed values are tabulated in Table 4.1 (left panel). Since CV^2 violates the principle of transfer, values in the last column are reported only for comparison purpose as there are many studies in China using the measure CV^2. Results in Table 4.1 show that all measures are consistent in demonstrating a rising trend in regional inequality in rural China. In particular, the inequality increased rather dramatically until 1995–96. After that, the increasing trend became moderate. This finding is consistent with Figure 4.1, which shows that income in poor regions experienced little growth before 1995–96 but some improvement afterwards, while the rich regions exhibited growth throughout the period. The slowing down in inequality increases after 1995–96, which may be caused by

Table 4.1 Regional inequality in rural China

	Deflated data				Undeflated data			
	Gini	Theil L	Theil T	CV^2	Gini	Theil L	Theil T	CV^2
1985	0.109	0.020	0.019	0.037	0.152	0.038	0.042	0.095
1986	0.123	0.025	0.024	0.047	0.171	0.047	0.050	0.114
1987	0.129	0.027	0.026	0.052	0.180	0.052	0.056	0.127
1988	0.134	0.029	0.028	0.057	0.187	0.056	0.061	0.138
1989	0.137	0.030	0.029	0.059	0.194	0.060	0.065	0.148
1990	0.141	0.032	0.031	0.062	0.198	0.063	0.069	0.162
1991	0.142	0.032	0.032	0.065	0.208	0.070	0.078	0.185
1992	0.151	0.036	0.036	0.072	0.215	0.074	0.082	0.194
1993	0.164	0.043	0.042	0.086	0.231	0.084	0.094	0.226
1994	0.170	0.046	0.045	0.090	0.228	0.082	0.089	0.210
1995	0.186	0.056	0.054	0.107	0.234	0.085	0.092	0.211
1996	0.188	0.058	0.055	0.109	0.221	0.076	0.080	0.180
1997	0.186	0.057	0.054	0.106	0.214	0.072	0.076	0.169
1998	0.186	0.056	0.053	0.105	0.208	0.067	0.071	0.158
1999	0.188	0.058	0.055	0.109	0.212	0.070	0.074	0.164
2000	0.188	0.057	0.055	0.110	0.219	0.075	0.080	0.181
2001	0.195	0.061	0.059	0.118	0.225	0.079	0.084	0.190
2002	0.195	0.062	0.059	0.119	0.226	0.080	0.085	0.194

the implementation of the grain price support policy, which benefited poor regions more (Zhang 2005). Since the trend was only moderated, not really reversed, other forces must be stronger than the policy change in pushing up the long-run inequality trend. Identifying these other forces is crucial for policy makers if rural regional inequality is to be brought down.

As a by-product, we calculated inequality values using undeflated data (see the right panel in Table 4.1). As is expected, not taking into consideration inflation and regional price levels leads to upward biases in inequality measurement. The biases are quite substantial. What is interesting, and perhaps surprising, is that the biases are larger in the early years, a finding consistent with Brandt and Carsten (2004). Also, the biases are less severe when using Gini relative to other measures, possibly due to the differing sensitivities of these measures to different sections of the underlying Lorenz curves.

Spatial decomposition

To assess whether the rising inequality is due to enlarged gaps between regional belts or within regional belts, we undertake subgroup decomposition following Shorrocks (1984). As in most studies, we divide China into three belts. The central belt includes Shanxi, Guangxi, Inner Mongolia, Jilin, Heilongjiang, Anhui, Jiangxi, Henan, Hubei and Hunan. The western belt includes Sichuan, Guizhou, Yunnan, Shaanxi, Gansu, Qinghai, Ningxia, and Xinjiang. The eastern belt consists of the remaining regions, all along the coast. The inequality index we use is the Theil L coefficient. Other inequality measures are not appropriate for the conventional subgroup decomposition; see Shorrocks and Wan (2005).

The decomposition results are shown in Figure 4.3 (numerical values are tabulated in Table 4.A1 in the Appendix). It is found that:

(a) all individual components (within each belt and between belts) exhibit increasing trends, clearly demonstrating income divergence within belts as well as divergence between belts;
(b) the divergence between belts expanded faster than divergence across regions within belts, resulting in a growing share of the between-component;
(c) there is an oscillatory cycle around the total inequality trend and it is largely driven by the between component. This implies that there are forces driving inter-belt income divergence, and that they fluctuate from year to year. These forces may include cyclical weather conditions, the 'cobweb phenomena' often present in the agricultural sector, and biological cycles of perennial crops or plants. For example, differences in production structure across the belts may contribute to the cyclical pattern. The western and central regions produce more grain and fruits. Fruits typically have a bumper year followed by a lean year and this contributes to the income correlation between regions within these belts. In a bumper year, the income gaps between the coast and inland regions will narrow; in other conditions, they will expand. Weather and market conditions also vary from year to year. In bad years, regions producing similar products will suffer income drops together, leading to larger income gaps between belts. In good years, these gaps may narrow down;
(d) the year 1995 deserves special attention. In this year, total inequality jumped more than usual and all components seem to have reached their peak values. After 1995, the between-component stayed more or less constant but all within-components continued to rise, particularly that within the western belt. It would be interesting to explore whether this is related to the major taxation reform implemented in 1994. Also, grain price support policy was introduced in 1995. Such a nationwide policy shift certainly helped raise income levels of the poor regions more, leading to smaller gaps between regional belts.

One can add up all the within-components and compute their overall percentage contribution to total inequality (see Figure 4.4). Figure 4.4 confirms the early observation that the total within-belts contribution has declined in relative terms, although the total absolute contribution has not. It is also clear that the declining trend was contained from 1995

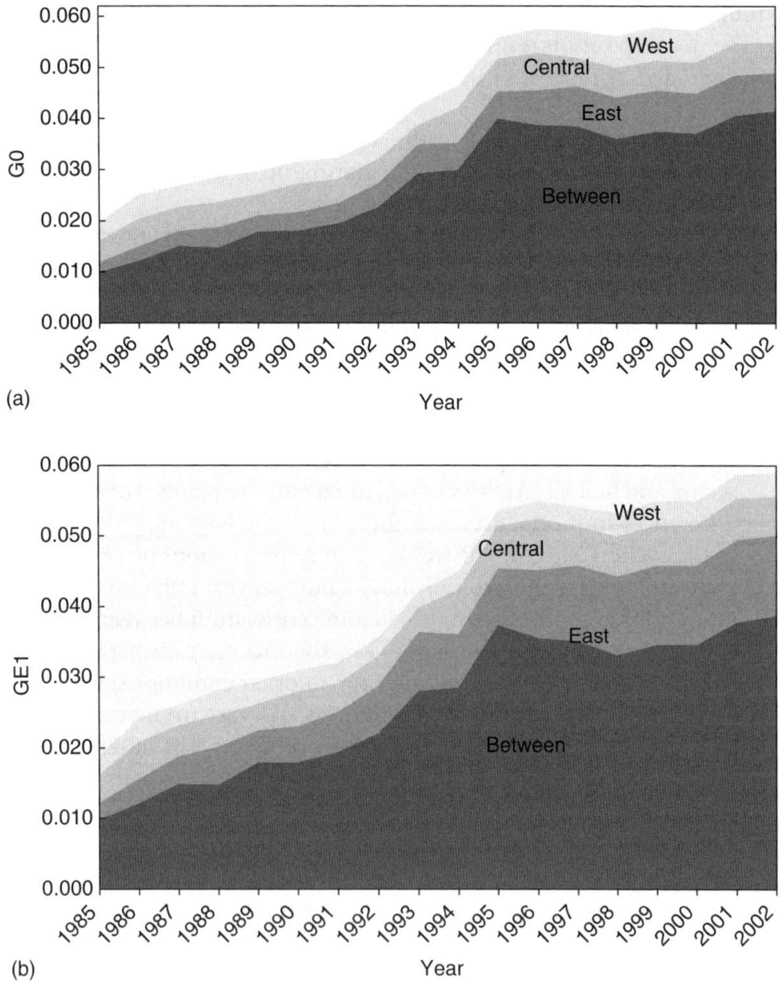

Figure 4.3 Theil L, Theil T, Gini and CV^2 decompositions for the eastern, central and western areas of China. (a) Traditional eastern–central–west decomposition. (b) Eastern–central–western decomposition: Theil T (c) Eastern–central–west decomposition: Gini (d) Eastern–central–western decomposition: CV^2

to 1998 and resumed after 1999. Given the finding that the between-component is a positive function of the number of groups involved in subgroup decompositions (Shorrocks and Wan 2005), such a large and increasing between-component is rather surprising.[6] Here, there are only three groups and yet the between-component is considerable, which must imply very substantial inter-belt income gaps. Note that current literature points to a small between-component with only a few exceptions (Shorrocks and Wan 2005).

Looking into the individual within-components (see Appendix Table 4.A1), dispersions within the western belt were rather small and those

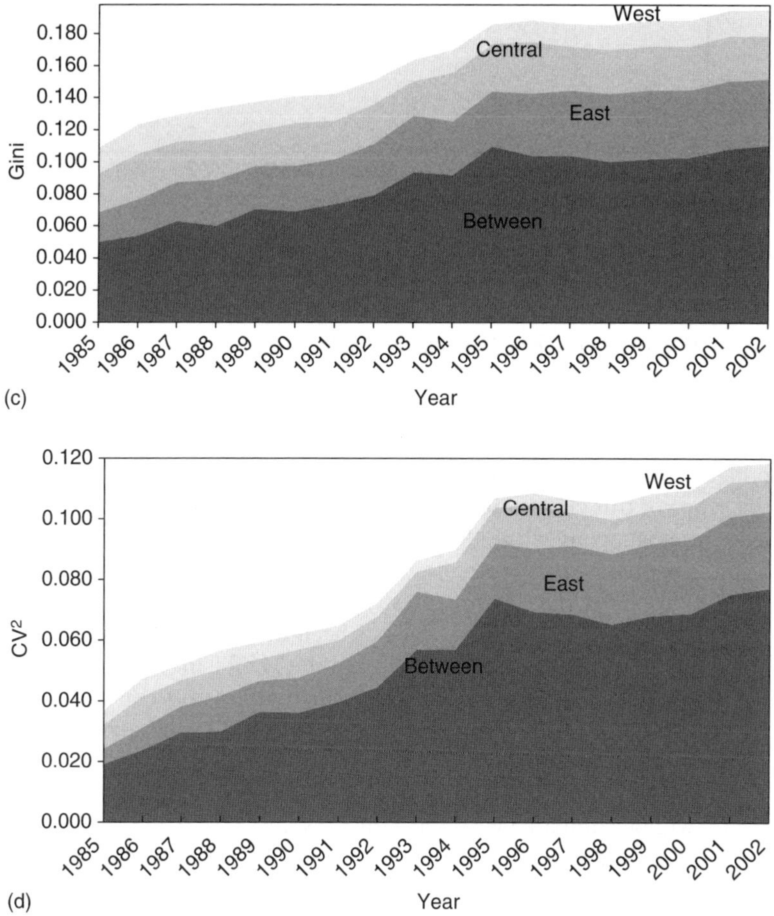

Figure 4.3 continued

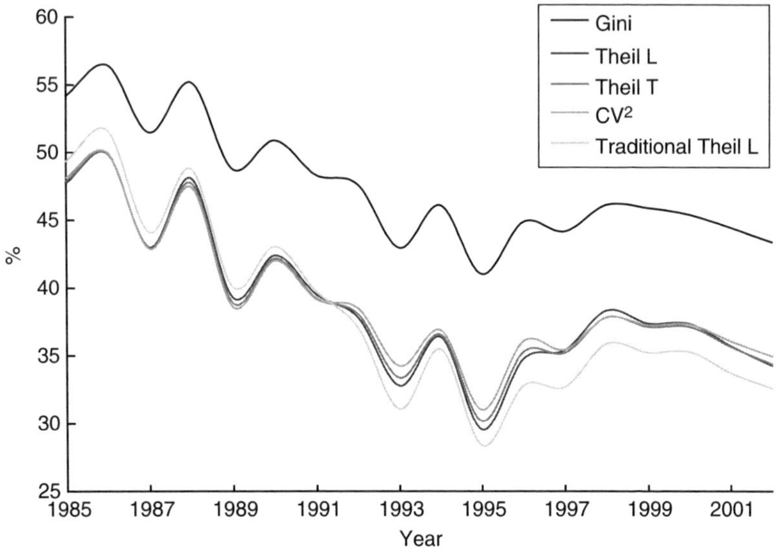

Figure 4.4 Overall within-belt contribution to regional inequality (%)

within the central belt were sizable until the late 1990s and early 2000s. The within-component of the eastern belt was moderate in the 1980s. It increased to a level more or less compatible to that of the central belt around the mid-1990s. Since then, the contribution of the eastern belt dominated the total within-component. Thus, as far as the within components are concerned, the eastern region is more important. It is beyond the scope of this chapter to explore why the eastern regions became the least homogeneous while the western regions were consistently more homogeneous.

Let us consider the sensitivity of the above decomposition results to inequality measures. Previously, it has been uncommon or inappropriate to use inequality measures other than the Theil L index for subgroup decomposition. Therefore, examining sensitivity in this context has so far been rare, or not possible. In what follows, we propose a subgroup decomposition procedure that can be used with any inequality measures. We then apply this approach to the Chinese data. Empirical outcomes will be compared with the earlier results.

Our approach is inspired by the Shapley procedure of Shorrocks (1999). Briefly put, applying this procedure requires a function between the target variable, such as income and its determinants. Expressing the function as Y = f(X), one can then apply any operator to both sides of the equation and attribute the total value, as defined by the operator, to the contributions made by individual elements in X. For example, given an income generating function, one can apply an inequality operator to both sides of the function, and attribute total income inequality to various components associated with income determinants. Since an identity is a special function, we will rely on a defined identity to decompose regional inequality into the between-belt and within-belt components.

The identity we define must express regional income as a function – being linear or nonlinear – of income gaps between regional belts and income gaps across regions within belts. This can be achieved by defining u_i as the average income of, and d_i as the dummy variable for, belt i. Also, let δ_1 denote deviations of per capita income of eastern regions from the average income of the eastern belt. Similarly, we can define δ_2 and δ_3. Now, regional income Y can be written as:

$$Y = u_i + d_1\delta_1 + d_2\delta_2 + d_3\delta_3 \tag{4.1}$$

It is noted that u_i take identical values for those regions belonging to the same belt. Therefore, it can be used to represent income gaps between belts. The other three terms in (4.1) capture income gaps across regions within individual belts.

We can proceed by constructing various counterfactuals. Assume absence of income gaps between belts (that is, all three belts have the same mean income, say national average, as denoted by u) as well as absence of income gaps within belts. This is equivalent to replacing u_i by u and $d_1\delta_1$, $d_2\delta_2$, $d_3\delta_3$ by 0. Substituting these into (4.1) will produce an identical income for every region. In this case, regional inequality is zero. Now, permit the presence of income gaps between belts only (that is, u_i take their defined values) while ensuring income gaps within individual belts remain absent (that is, $d_1\delta_1 = d_2\delta_2 = d_3\delta_3 = 0$). We can substitute these values into (4.1) and calculate the corresponding inequality. This inequality is only caused by income gaps between belts, not within belts. By the same token, we can replace u_i by u and any two of $d_1\delta_1$, $d_2\delta_2$, $d_3\delta_3$ by 0 (only one of them taking its defined values); the corresponding inequality must be due to income gaps within the relevant belt. This kind of counterfactual can be constructed under all possible combinations of replacements. Alternative estimates of the same inequality component can be obtained; they are averaged to reach the final estimate. This is essentially what Shapley decomposition does (see Shorrocks 1999; Wan and Zhou 2005).

Applying the above decomposition to Chinese data produces results that are quite consistent with the earlier decomposition results (see Appendix

Table 4.A2). For comparison purposes, we plot the between-component in Figure 4.4 as well. The plot resembles the traditional decomposition results quite well, indicating the robustness of earlier decomposition results. For example, they show a clear declining trend in the percentage contribution of the overall within-components. As the number of regions in each belt is kept constant for the decomposition, the more rapid increases in the between-component are indicative of more enlarging income gaps between belts than within belts, confirming the early finding of polarization. Interestingly, the results are slightly different when the Gini index is used. The other three give almost indistinguishable percentage contributions. According to the Gini decomposition, the within- component was almost 50 per cent in 1985, and became smaller over time, reaching 45 per cent in 2002. The other indicators show similar declining trends, but starting with 45 per cent in 1985 declining to 35 per cent in 2002.

Sources of rural regional inequality

Given the consistent rises in regional inequality in rural China, one naturally wonders what factors drive this trend. It is not difficult to speculate about possible determinants of regional inequality in China. What is more interesting and challenging is to quantify the contributions of these determinants. Kanbur (2002) appealed for the linking of inequality with fundamental variables because simply breaking down total inequality into the usual within- and between-components (as done in the preceding section) is insufficient. To quantify contributions of various determinants to total inequality, we follow the regression-based decomposition approach of Wan (2004), which has a number of advantages. In particular, it does not depend on inequality measures; it is applicable irrespective of functional form for the regression equation, and it permits interactive terms of independent variables. Interested readers are referred to Wan (2002).

Intuitively, if every region possesses the same amount of every input as well as same returns to factors, there would be no inequality. Same returns may not be realistic, but have been presumed in most, if not all, previous studies. Assuming same returns, it is the spatial distributions of factor inputs that matter. Postulating, without loss of generality, that the marginal impact of a factor is positive on income generation, its dispersion would contribute positively to inequality if the input variable were positively correlated with total income. On the contrary, if rich regions possess less of this factor than poor regions, it would help reduce regional inequality. In the unlikely case of a linear income function

$Y = \Sigma\ \beta_i X_i + \beta_0$, it is possible to express the Gini index of income as a weighted sum of concentration indices of factor inputs:

$$\text{Gini (Y)} = \Sigma\ \beta_i E(X_i)/E(Y)\ C(X_i) \tag{4.2}$$

where β_i denotes marginal income of X_i, E is the expectation operator, and $C(X_i)$ denotes the concentration index of X_i. Resembling the Gini coefficient, $C(X_i)$ is a measure of dispersion of X_i. It takes values between 1 and -1. Broadly speaking, if X_i and Y are positively correlated, $C(X_i) > 0$. Otherwise, $C(X_i) < 0$. Although equation (4.2) may not be derivable under other inequality indices or when the income function is not strictly linear, it does help demonstrate our point that total inequality can be accounted for by dispersions of factor inputs.

Turning to empirical factor–income relationships in China, we plot income against each of the input variables – see Figure 4.5. The trend lines in this figure indicate that capital, schooling and industrialization are positively correlated with income, while land is perhaps unrelated to income. Section (d) of Figure 4.5 depicts a nonlinear curve between income and schooling or education. To a lesser extent nonlinearity also appears in section (b) of Figure 4.5, where the correlation does not seem to exist. Of course, such bivariate correlations may not reveal the true relationship, as other factors are not controlled for. Also, the impact of factor dispersions on total inequality cannot be directly discerned from Figure 4.5. To account for rural regional inequality in China, we now turn to the regression-based decomposition technique.

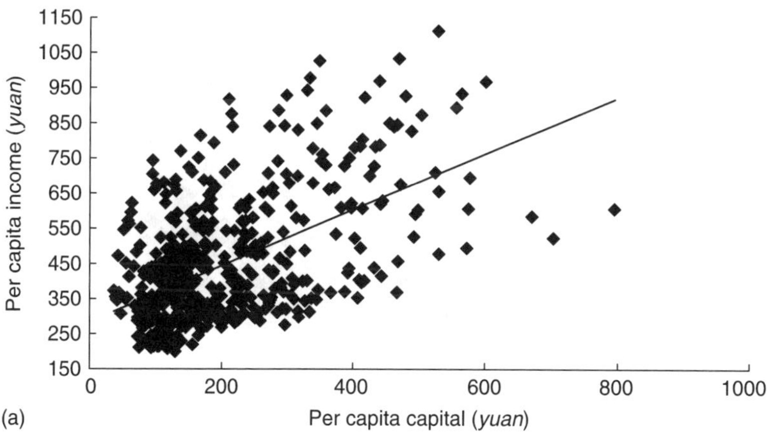

(a)

Figure 4.5 Distribution of income in relation to capital, land, industrialization and education. (a) Income and capital (b) Income and land (c) Industrialization and income (d) Education and income

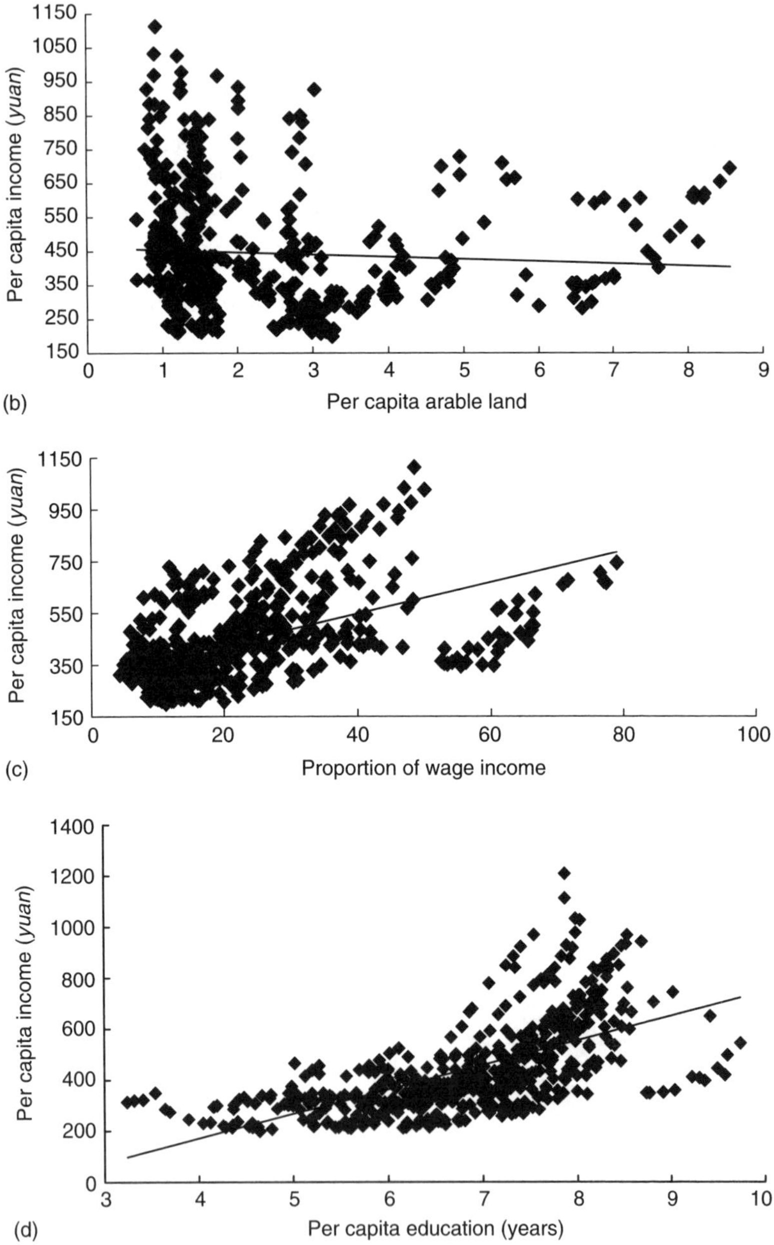

Figure 4.5 *continued*

Essentially, the regression-based decomposition combines a regression model with the Shapley value framework of Shorrocks (1999). The basic idea is to attribute inequality in the dependent variable to contributions of the residual and independent variables in the regression equation. Following the before–after principle of Cancian and Reed (1998), Wan (2004) proposed to define the contribution of the residual by $I(Y) - I(\hat{Y})$, where $\hat{Y}$ is the predicted value based on the estimated regression model and I denotes any inequality measure. To obtain the contributions of independent variables to $I(\hat{Y})$, the Shapley procedure developed by Shorrocks (1999) can be applied. The procedure is founded on cooperative game theory (see Shapley 1953) and is applicable irrespective of the functional form or inequality measure (for technical details, see Shorrocks 1999).

To estimate the empirical income generation function, we start with human capital theory, which dictates that income is a function of education and experience. At the aggregate regional level, it is not possible to define experience or its proxy. Further, rural income also depends on production inputs such as land, capital and so on. Consequently, we consider the following variables:

Y	=	per capita net income (*yuan*/head)
K	=	capital stock (1000 *yuan*/head)
Land	=	arable land (mu/head, 1 mu = 1/15 Ha)
DEP	=	dependency ratio
HH	=	household size
IND	=	degree of industrialization = wage income/net income
EDU	=	average years of schooling of working age members (years/head)

Note that DEP and HH are included to control for labour input since these three variables are linearly related, thus inclusion of any two of the three is sufficient. In addition, regional dummy variables (to account for geographic location and location related factors) and dummy variables for the years 1992 (marking Deng Xiaoping's tour of southern China) and 1995 (marking the start of the grain price support policy) are included. Also, a time trend variable is incorporated to control for possible changes in macro-economic environment and technology or other shifts over time.

Regarding functional form, the conventional practice is to specify a log-linear form, the so-called Mincer function. We experimented with log-linear, linear-linear, double-log and linear-log (that is, the dependent variable is untransformed but independent variables are in logarithms).

Table 4.2 Estimation results of income functions

	log-log			linear-log		
	Estimate	***t*-ratio**	***p*-value**	**Estimate**	***t*-ratio**	***p*-value**
K	0.2033	9.74	0.00	75.7670	6.51	0.00
K^2	0.0000	3.16	0.00	0.0003	4.17	0.00
Land	−0.0596	−4.16	0.00	−22.4760	−2.57	0.01
EDU	−1.1840	−3.19	0.00	−939.3500	−3.70	0.00
EDU^2	0.4569	4.32	0.00	305.1200	4.41	0.00
HH	0.0592	1.13	0.26	21.6230	0.83	0.41
DEP	−0.0226	−2.14	0.03	−8.5414	−1.78	0.08
IND	0.0067	7.34	0.00	2.5553	4.93	0.00
Constant	5.6803	13.94	0.00	792.1800	3.03	0.00
Buse R2		0.9994			0.9465	
Log-likelihood value		613.84			−2503.42	
RSS		2.47			572260.00	

Given our panel data model, the disturbance term is proposed to be heteroscedastic across regions and autoregressive over time for individual regions. Denote the disturbance term by ε_{it}, the error process satisfies:

$$\begin{aligned}
&\varepsilon_{it} = \rho_i \varepsilon_{it-1} + u_{it} \quad \text{for all } i \text{ and } t,\\
&E(u_{it}) = 0 \quad \text{for all } i \text{ and } t,\\
&E(u_{it}^2) = \sigma_i^2(1-\rho_j^2) \quad \text{for all } i,\\
&E(u_{it}u_{js}) = 0 \quad \text{for } i \neq j \text{ or } t \neq s
\end{aligned}$$

Consequently, the variance–covariance matrix becomes (see Kmenta 1986):

$$\begin{bmatrix} R_1\sigma_1^2 & 0 & \dots & 0 \\ 0 & R_2\sigma_2^2 & \cdot & 0 \\ \cdot & \cdot & \cdot & \cdot \\ 0 & 0 & \dots & R_N\sigma_N^2 \end{bmatrix}, \quad \text{where } R_i = \begin{bmatrix} 1 & \rho_i & \rho_i^2 & \cdot & \rho_i^{T-1} \\ \rho_i & 1 & \rho_i & \cdot & \rho_i^{T-2} \\ \cdot & \cdot & \cdot & \cdot & \cdot \\ \cdot & \cdot & \cdot & \cdot & \cdot \\ \rho_i^{T-1} & \rho_i^{T-2} & \cdot & \rho_i & 1 \end{bmatrix}$$

ρ_i denotes the correlation coefficient between successive errors for region *i*. The estimation can be easily implemented using the econometric software Shazam.

Estimation results for the income generation functions are presented in Table 4.2 (dummy variable and time trend terms are not reported but

Table 4.2 continued

log-linear			linear-linear		
Estimate	*t*-ratio	*p*-value	Estimate	*t*-ratio	*p*-value
0.19	10.60	0.00	80.96	8.08	0.00
−0.013	−5.16	0.00	−4.5988	−3.43	0.00
−0.0174	−3.04	0.00	−7.6558	−2.43	0.02
0.0036	0.09	0.93	−41.3810	−1.68	0.09
0.0052	1.70	0.09	5.1783	2.88	0.00
0.0093	0.87	0.39	6.2726	1.19	0.24
−0.0226	−2.17	0.03	−8.6538	−1.83	0.07
0.0065	6.87	0.00	2.5312	4.89	0.00
5.6361	32.95	0.00	424.5800	4.30	0.00
	0.9994			0.9469	
	617.83			−2496.62	
	2.43			555290.00	

are available from the author upon request). The usual χ^2 test can be employed to choose between the log-linear and double-log models, and between the linear-linear and linear-log models. The test statistic is given by twice the absolute difference in the loglikelihood values of relevant models, with degrees of freedom equal to the difference in the number of parameters in these models. Since all the models have the same number of parameters, one can simply compare the relevant loglikelihood values and make a choice. As a consequence, the linear-linear and log-linear models are preferred.

Selection between the two preferred models can be implemented by the χ^2 test derived by Box and Cox (1964), where the null hypothesis is the equivalence of the log-linear and linear-linear models, and the test statistic is given by

$$l = \frac{N}{2}\left|\ln\left[\frac{RSS_1/C^2}{RSS_2}\right]\right|$$

which is distributed as $\chi^2(1)$, where $C = \exp[(\sum \log Y_i)/N]$, N is the sample size and RSS_1 (RSS_2) denotes the residual sum of squares from the linear-linear (log-linear) models. Substituting the relevant values into the above expression, we obtained $l = 73.3$. When the null hypothesis is rejected, as in this chapter, the log-linear model is selected if $RSS_1/C^2 > RSS_2$. Otherwise, the linear-linear model is selected. Since the ratio of RSS_1/C^2 to RSS_2 is 1.34, the log-linear model is the finally chosen income generating function for rural China.

The log-linear model possesses expected signs for most of the estimated coefficients. After controlling for the dependency ratio, any increase in household size (HH) implies more labour input. From this perspective, the positive sign associated with HH is justified and is consistent with Wan (2004). The negative estimate for the land variable is not unexpected, as cropping is known to make a loss or merely a small profit (Wan and Cheng 2001). Nonlinearity is present for capital input, and possibly the schooling variable. The model fits the data quite well, as indicated by the reasonably high R^2 and *t*-ratios. We decided not to drop the non-significant variables, in order to minimize data mining.

Before proceeding to inequality decomposition, it is necessary to solve the estimated equation for income Y, so inequality is measured over income rather than logarithm of income. Solving the log-linear model, we have:

$$\begin{aligned} Y = \exp(5.64) \cdot \exp(&0.19\,\mathrm{K} - 0.013\,\mathrm{K}^2 - 0.017\,\mathrm{Land} + 0.0036\,\mathrm{EDU} \\ &+ 0.0052\,\mathrm{EDU}^2 + 0.0093\,\mathrm{HH} - 0.0226\,\mathrm{DEP} + 0.0065\,\mathrm{IND} \\ &+ Loc) \cdot \exp(other\ terms) \end{aligned}$$

where *Loc* is the sum of all regional dummy variable terms and *other terms* is the sum of all year dummy variable terms, time trend and the residual terms. *Loc* represents geographical conditions, weather, water and other non-removable natural resources as well as infrastructure. When relative inequality indicators are used, as in this chapter, terms associated with the constant and time trend terms (including year dummy variables) can be removed from the equation without affecting the decomposition results. This is because inequality is measured for each year and these terms are all scalars of the income variable Y (recall the homogeneity theorem of relative inequality measures). Also, the contribution of residual is given by $I(Y) - I(\hat{Y})$, where $\hat{Y}$ is the predicted value based on the estimated regression model. Thus, the final equation for Shapley decomposition is

$$\begin{aligned} \hat{Y} = \exp(&0.19\,\mathrm{K} - 0.013\,\mathrm{K}^2 - 0.017\,\mathrm{Land} + 0.0036\,\mathrm{EDU} \\ &+ 0.0052\,\mathrm{EDU}^2 + 0.0093\,\mathrm{HH} - 0.0226\,\mathrm{DEP} \\ &+ 0.0065\,\mathrm{IND} + Loc) \end{aligned}$$

The decomposition is implemented using a Java programme developed by the World Institute for Development Economics Research (UNU-WIDER). Decomposition results are presented in Table 4.3.[7] Judging from the proportions of inequality explained by the estimated model, our analytical results are quite satisfactory. We can explain 80 per cent or

Table 4.3 Sources of regional inequality in rural China explained by the regression model (%)

	K	Land	EDU	HH	IND	DEP	Loc	Sum	K	Land	EDU	HH	IND	DEP	Loc	Sum
	Gini								*Theil L*							
1985	14.98	2.16	18.68	−0.70	15.04	0.95	78.71	129.82	11.06	0.30	23.44	−2.03	17.91	0.86	110.91	162.46
1986	7.93	1.90	16.96	−0.63	13.90	1.47	69.73	111.26	0.12	0.56	18.35	−1.55	15.01	1.59	86.70	120.77
1987	7.03	2.17	15.94	−0.47	14.05	0.50	66.47	105.69	−1.08	0.78	17.05	−1.30	14.92	0.48	81.32	112.10
1988	8.07	2.30	14.38	−0.60	14.04	0.61	64.71	103.51	0.66	0.98	14.53	−1.43	13.98	0.63	76.12	105.44
1989	8.44	2.21	14.26	−0.63	14.63	0.63	64.02	103.56	1.82	0.88	14.58	−1.48	15.69	0.67	76.40	108.55
1990	9.87	2.02	15.90	−0.61	13.25	0.60	63.60	104.62	4.36	0.70	16.60	−1.49	13.25	0.60	74.57	108.63
1991	12.31	1.96	14.73	−0.54	13.73	0.61	61.48	104.28	6.96	0.46	15.24	−1.39	14.47	0.65	73.50	109.89
1992	11.90	2.31	15.88	−0.65	15.02	0.54	59.52	104.51	7.94	0.94	16.78	−1.56	15.83	0.56	70.31	110.83
1993	13.88	2.59	12.51	−0.59	14.59	0.54	54.91	98.43	10.73	1.29	11.86	−1.32	14.04	0.56	60.64	97.84
1994	15.00	2.67	12.69	−0.58	15.27	0.56	52.89	98.51	12.31	1.36	11.81	−1.27	14.55	0.58	57.40	96.74
1995	16.31	1.87	13.10	−0.47	11.60	0.49	47.37	90.27	12.50	0.43	11.80	−0.88	10.11	0.47	47.92	82.36
1996	17.95	2.06	12.16	−0.39	12.10	0.47	45.92	90.26	13.71	0.59	10.88	−0.76	10.67	0.45	46.30	81.84
1997	18.37	2.48	13.02	−0.42	13.17	0.46	46.60	93.69	14.31	1.01	12.31	−0.82	11.33	0.45	47.52	86.11
1998	20.20	2.41	11.76	−0.38	12.54	0.39	46.20	93.12	15.91	0.94	10.54	−0.75	10.75	0.37	46.87	84.62
1999	20.86	2.19	11.67	−0.28	11.32	0.42	45.03	91.21	16.86	0.67	10.44	−0.60	9.38	0.41	45.61	82.79
2000	23.14	2.24	11.26	−0.22	12.28	0.41	44.98	94.09	19.91	0.80	10.55	−0.58	10.67	0.42	46.70	88.47
2001	24.20	2.20	9.43	−0.27	11.06	0.41	44.01	91.05	20.41	0.65	8.01	−0.60	8.89	0.41	44.09	81.88
2002	25.06	2.06	10.93	−0.29	9.45	0.38	43.49	91.08	21.55	0.33	9.80	−0.63	7.01	0.39	43.81	82.25
	Theil T								CV^2							
1985	11.83	0.11	23.56	−2.11	18.33	0.79	111.99	164.55	13.00	−0.24	24.15	−2.22	18.90	0.73	113.84	168.18
1986	−0.83	0.70	18.09	−1.61	15.61	1.61	87.48	121.07	−1.83	0.84	18.05	−1.73	16.35	1.66	88.31	121.70
1987	−2.11	0.92	16.54	−1.34	15.39	0.50	80.97	110.87	−3.24	1.08	16.25	−1.37	15.96	0.54	80.67	109.86

(*Continued*)

Table 4.3 continued

	K	Land	EDU	HH	IND	DEP	Loc	Sum	K	Land	EDU	HH	IND	DEP	Loc	Sum
	Theil T								CV^2							
1988	0.00	1.06	14.32	−1.52	14.46	0.64	75.47	104.50	−0.65	1.16	14.21	−1.59	15.04	0.67	74.73	103.58
1989	1.26	0.95	14.17	−1.53	15.95	0.68	75.26	106.75	0.69	1.06	13.92	−1.60	16.30	0.73	74.15	105.25
1990	3.71	0.81	16.26	−1.48	13.71	0.65	74.15	107.81	3.09	0.90	16.03	−1.51	14.24	0.66	73.63	107.06
1991	5.97	0.53	14.57	−1.34	14.57	0.63	71.96	106.88	5.00	0.60	13.99	−1.31	14.70	0.65	70.25	103.88
1992	7.24	1.15	15.95	−1.52	16.23	0.56	69.17	108.82	6.68	1.38	15.22	−1.53	16.75	0.59	68.02	107.13
1993	10.21	1.50	11.23	−1.28	14.34	0.57	59.66	96.23	9.87	1.68	10.58	−1.25	14.66	0.60	58.30	94.43
1994	12.35	1.62	11.37	−1.27	15.24	0.60	57.75	97.64	12.65	1.89	10.91	−1.28	16.07	0.64	58.00	98.89
1995	12.68	0.58	11.40	−0.91	10.56	0.50	48.31	83.12	13.00	0.75	10.92	−0.93	11.13	0.52	48.41	83.80
1996	13.77	0.82	10.49	−0.80	11.33	0.47	46.75	82.84	13.96	1.04	10.10	−0.83	12.09	0.51	46.95	83.83
1997	14.49	1.29	11.83	−0.85	12.13	0.48	48.21	87.60	14.78	1.59	11.37	−0.87	13.05	0.50	48.64	89.05
1998	16.48	1.24	10.23	−0.81	11.71	0.39	47.85	87.12	17.14	1.54	9.88	−0.86	12.79	0.41	48.52	89.44
1999	17.35	0.95	10.01	−0.64	10.16	0.42	46.32	84.56	17.90	1.24	9.56	−0.68	11.08	0.42	46.78	86.32
2000	20.39	1.09	10.16	−0.60	11.54	0.44	47.15	90.15	20.89	1.40	9.80	−0.64	12.56	0.46	47.35	91.81
2001	21.11	0.94	7.61	−0.63	9.64	0.43	44.82	83.91	21.79	1.23	7.18	−0.65	10.47	0.45	45.18	85.66
2002	22.19	0.63	9.25	−0.68	7.54	0.39	44.12	83.45	22.72	0.91	8.69	−0.71	8.16	0.40	43.98	84.14

Source: See text.

more of total inequality. It is not unexpected that decomposition outcomes vary with inequality measures. However, they are broadly consistent in ranking contributors and in portraying the time trends of individual contributions. Consequently, discussion hereafter will be based on those under Gini only.

For large countries such as China, the variable *Loc* (representing geography, non-removable resources, weather conditions and so on) is expected to make a very substantial contribution to total regional inequality. This is particularly true for rural China, and more so for the early years. In a subsistence society with a closed economy, no market exists and proximity to markets and ports is irrelevant to income. In such cases, a dominant proportion of regional inequality can be explained by the *Loc* variable. In the early days of rural China, markets were fragmented and rural income was almost entirely derived from farming, which heavily depends on soil, water and weather conditions. Therefore, it is not surprising to see overwhelming contributions of the *Loc* variable in the 1980s. As non-farming income increased and as markets developed and infrastructure was improved in poor areas, the percentage contribution of *Loc* started to decline, a finding consistent with a priori expectations.[8]

Despite the reduction in its percentage contribution, the importance of *Loc* cannot be overlooked. This is so for several reasons. First, its absolute contribution has been maintained over time. Even in terms of relative contributions, it has ranked as of foremost importance throughout the period under consideration. Second, *Loc* in this chapter not only means local natural resources, but also access to market, information and technology – or even investment. The latter directly affects productivity and resource endowment, and indirectly affects efficiency of resource use. Finally, natural resources in terms of the quality and quantity of land, the weather and water are not subject to market development or the improvement of infrastructure. It is true that as infrastructure improves for poor regions, locational disadvantages for the inland regions might be alleviated. Nevertheless, these disadvantages could never be eliminated, since transportation and communication costs would always be non-decreasing functions of distance to ports and major markets.

Uneven distribution of capital ranked third in the 1980s, but its contribution gradually increased to over 25 per cent, making it the second largest contributor to regional inequality in rural China after 1996. This result is in line with Wan and Zhou (2005) who used household data instead of aggregate regional data. On the other hand, education was the second largest contributor and its position has more or less matched that of industrialization since 1996. The contribution of industrialization is considerable but is smaller than that suggested by the earlier studies of Rozelle (1994) and Wan (2001). Such an inconsistency is most probably due to contamination in early analytical frameworks, where other factors were not controlled for. Wan (2004) obtained a smaller contribution than Rozelle (1994) and Wan (2001) after controlling for certain variables. However, Wan (2004) did not incorporate regional dummy variables in his income function. When location dummies are included, as in this study, the contribution of industrialization is bound to become even smaller.

The only negative contributor is household size. As it represents labour input and labour is more abundant in poor regions, such a finding is justified. In reality, the household size may imply extra income from sideline activities (Wan 2004). Unfortunately, this sole equalizing factor makes negligible impact on total inequality. Furthermore, as household size converges in China, this minimal equalizing contribution will disappear in the long run. Related to the household size variable, the dependency ratio makes a negligible but positive contribution. Land is found to be a contributor to increased inequality. This is caused by the negative returns to land in China for many of the years under study. It is known that poor regions possess more land and poor households are those that mainly engage in farming. If government support is sufficiently effective in reversing the marginal production from land, land would be an equalizing factor in rural China.

Conclusion

In this chapter, we constructed a time profile of rural regional inequality in China over the period 1985–2002. We further decomposed total regional inequality into between (eastern-central-western) belts contribution and contributions due to regional income gaps within these belts. Both the conventional decomposition and the proposed Shapley value decomposition yielded similar results. Finally, we applied the inequality accounting framework of Wan (2004) to identify the root sources of total inequality. Several findings deserve special mention.

First, regional income is found to diverge, more so between regional belts than within these belts. In other words, inequality between regional belts as well as that within these belts has been on the rise. The fast increase in regional inequality is accompanied by worsening polarization. Second, while the eastern-central-western divide constituted some 50 per cent of the total regional inequality in the mid-1980s, its contribution increased to around 60 per cent as from 1996. Third, location and location related factors comprise the greatest contributor to total regional inequality, although its percentage contribution has decreased over time. Fourth, capital and rural industrialization are the second and third grreatest contributors to total inequality. Finally, schooling or human capital has been gaining importance as a determinant of regional inequality. Based on these findings, we can derive the following policy implications:

National policy must target regional belts, not only individual regions. As farming structure becomes more homogenous in neighbouring regions, policy induced and other shocks are likely to enhance polarization unless supplementary measures are taken at the stage of policy design.

While investment in the infrastructure of inland regions is necessary, more attention should be given to capital accumulation at the household level in the poor regions. It is possible that capital accumulation may become the greatest contributor to regional inequality in the not too distant future. Thus, development of the rural capital market, particularly credit access for the poor, should be placed on the top of the agenda of central and local governments.

Further concerted efforts must be devoted to human capital accumulation in poor areas. Schooling might not have mattered so much in largely subsistence China in the 1970s or early 1980s, but this is no longer the case. The growing contribution of schooling to regional inequality appeals for serious government educational input in the interior regions.

Continued support for generating non-farming incomes in the poor regions can lead to substantial reduction in regional inequality. Fiscal and budgetary policies should make allowance for the initiation and growth of rural industries in the inland regions as far as inequality reduction is concerned.

Finally, much more is needed than the abolition of agricultural tax in providing assistance to grain farmers. This not only has bearing on the food security of the nation, but, potentially, is also effective for combating the high level of regional inequality in China.

Notes

1 A search in Econlit using keywords 'China', 'region', 'rural' and 'inequality' produced 59 journal article entries and only a few of them touched on, but did not focus on, rural regional inequality.

2 If differences in price levels and inflation between urban and rural areas were not considered, this proportion would be over-estimated as in Kanbur and Zhang (1999).

3 Rural population refers to those whose *hukou* (household registration) is in rural rather than urban China, while agricultural population refers to those who derive their livelihood from rural economic activities, including town and village enterprises.

4 Different measures imply different social welfare functions and different aversions to inequality; see Dagnum (1990).
5 There exist alternative ways to calculate the Gini coefficient. We follow Silber (1989) by defining Gini = $P'QI$, where P is the vector containing population shares and I is the vector containing income shares, both sorted in ascending order by the per capita income variable. Q is a square matrix with 0 on the diagonal, 1 above the diagonal and -1 below the diagonal.
6 As the between-component and within-components always add up to 100 per cent, we only plotted the within-components in Figure 4.4.
7 The results are different from Wan (2004), who did not use the regional price deflators of Brandt and Carsten (2004). Also, different modelling strategy was followed in Wan (2004), where location was not fully accounted for.
8 The decomposition results for 1985 and 1986 seem to produce unusually large contributions of the residual term. However, our results look more acceptable than those of Morduch and Sicular (2002) and they are consistent over years in terms of trends of the individual contributions.

References

Box, G.E.O. and Cox, D.R. (1964) ‘An Analysis of Transformation’, *Journal of the Royal Statistical Society*, A26: 211–52.

Brandt, L. and Carsten, A.H. (2004) ‘Spatial Price Differences in China: Estimates and Implications’, Mimeo, Social Science Division, University of Science and Technology, Hong Kong.

Cancian, M. and Reed, D. (1998) ‘Assessing the Effects of Wives Earning on Family Income Inequality’, *Review of Economics and Statistics*, 80: 73–9.

Dagnum, C. (1990) ‘On the Relationship between Income and Inequality Measures and Social Welfare Functions’, *Journal of Econometrics*, 43: 91–102.

Fields, G.S. (2001) *Distribution and Development: A New Look at the Developing World* (Cambridge, MA: MIT Press).

Fields, G.S. and Yoo, G. (2000) ‘Falling Labour Income Inequality in Korea’s Economic Growth: Patterns and Underlying Causes’, *Review of Income and Wealth*, 46: 139–59.

Kanbur, R. (2002) ‘Notes on the Policy Significance of Inequality Decompositions’, Mimeo, Cornell University, Ithaca, NY.

Kanbur, R. and Zhang, X. (1999) ‘Which Regional Inequality: Rural–Urban or Coast–Inland? An Application to China’, *Journal of Comparative Economics*, 27: 686–701.

Kanbur, R. and Zhang, X. (2005) ‘Fifty Years of Regional Inequality in China: A Journey Through Central Planning, Reform and Openness’, *Review of Development Economics*, 9, 1: 87–106.

Kmenta, J. (1986) *Elements of Econometrics* (New York: Prentice-Hall).

Morduch, J. and Sicular, T. (2002) ‘Rethinking Inequality Decomposition, with Evidence from Rural China’, *Economic Journal*, 112: 93–106.

NBS (National Bureau of Statistics) (various) *China Rural Statistical Yearbook* (Beijing: China Statistical Publishing House).

NBS (National Bureau of Statistics) (various) *China Rural Household Survey Yearbook* (Beijing: China Statistical Publishing House).

Ravallion, M. and Chen, S. (2004) 'China's (Uneven) Progress Against Poverty', Policy Research Working Paper 3408 (Washington DC: World Bank).
Rozelle, S. (1994) 'Rural Industrialization and Increasing Inequality: Emerging Patterns in China's Reforming Economy', *Journal of Comparative Economics*, 19: 362–91.
Shapley, L.S. (1953) 'A Value for N-person Games', in H.W. Kuhn and A.W. Tucker (eds), *Annals of Mathematics Studies*, 28: 307–17, Princeton University Press, *Contributions to the Theory of Games*, Volume 2.
Shorrocks, A.F. (1984) 'Inequality Decomposition by Population Subgroups', *Econometrica*, 52, 6: 1369–85.
Shorrocks, A.F. (1999) 'Decomposition Procedures for Distributional Analysis: A Unified Framework Based on the Shapely Value', Unpublished manuscript, Department of Economics, University of Essex, Colchester.
Shorrocks, A.F. and Slottje, D. (2002) 'Approximating Unanimity Orderings: An Application to Lorenz Dominance', *Journal of Economics*, (Supplement 9): 91–118.
Shorrocks, A.F. and Wan, G.H. (2005) 'Spatial Decomposition of Inequality', *Journal of Economic Geography*, 5, 1: 59–82.
Silber, J. (1989) 'Factor Components, Population Subgroups and the Computation of the Gini Index of Inequality', *Review of Economics and Statistics*, 71, 1: 107–15.
Tsui, K.Y. (1991) 'China's Regional Inequality, 1952–85', *Journal of Comparative Economics*, 15: 1–21.
Wan, G.H. (2001) 'Changes in Regional Inequality in Rural China: Decomposing the Gini Index by Income Sources', *Australian Journal of Agricultural and Resource Economics*, 43: 361–81.
Wan, G.H. (2002) 'Regression-based Inequality Decomposition: Pitfalls and a Solution Procedure', WIDER Discussion Paper 2002/101, UNU-WIDER, Helsinki.
Wan, G.H. (2004) 'Accounting for Income Inequality in Rural China', *Journal of Comparative Economics*, 32, 2: 348–63.
Wan G.H. (2005) 'Rising Inequality in Post Reform China', WIDER *Angle* 2/2005, UNU-WIDER, Helsinki.
Wan, G.H. and Cheng, E.J. (2001) 'Effects of Land Fragmentation and Returns to Scale in the Chinese Farming Sector', *Applied Economics*, 33, 2: 183–94.
Wan, G.H., Lu, M. and Chen, Z. (2006) 'The Inequality–Growth Nexus in the Short- and Long-run: Empirical Evidence from China', *Journal of Comparative Economics*, 34, 4: 654–7.
Wan, G.H. and Zhou, Z. (2005) 'Income Inequality in Rural China: Regression-based Decomposition Using Household Data', *Review of Development Economics*, 9: 107–20.
Zhang, X. (2005) 'Sang Nong Problems and Rural Development', Online paper, http://www.ccrs.org.cn/article_view.asp?id=108.
Zhang, Y. and Wan, G.H. (2006) 'The Impact of Growth and Inequality on Rural Poverty in China', *Journal of Comparative Economics*, 34, 4: 694–712.

Appendix

Table 4.A1 Composition of regional inequality in rural China

Year	Between belts	Within belt of			Total Theil L
		Eastern	Central	Western	
1985	0.010	0.002	0.004	0.004	0.020
1986	0.012	0.003	0.006	0.005	0.025
1987	0.015	0.003	0.005	0.004	0.027
1988	0.015	0.004	0.005	0.005	0.029
1989	0.018	0.003	0.004	0.004	0.030
1990	0.018	0.004	0.006	0.004	0.032
1991	0.019	0.004	0.005	0.004	0.032
1992	0.023	0.005	0.005	0.004	0.036
1993	0.029	0.006	0.004	0.004	0.043
1994	0.030	0.005	0.007	0.004	0.046
1995	0.040	0.005	0.007	0.004	0.056
1996	0.039	0.007	0.007	0.005	0.058
1997	0.038	0.008	0.006	0.005	0.057
1998	0.036	0.008	0.006	0.006	0.056
1999	0.037	0.008	0.006	0.006	0.058
2000	0.037	0.008	0.006	0.006	0.057
2001	0.041	0.008	0.006	0.006	0.061
2002	0.041	0.008	0.006	0.007	0.062

Table 4.A2 Shapley decomposition of regional inequality into between- and within-components

Year	Between belts	Within belt of			Total	Between belts	Within belt of			Total
		East	Central	West			East	Central	West	
	Gini					*Theil L*				
1985	0.050	0.019	0.024	0.016	0.109	0.010	0.002	0.004	0.003	0.020
1986	0.054	0.023	0.029	0.018	0.123	0.013	0.003	0.005	0.004	0.025
1987	0.063	0.025	0.025	0.017	0.129	0.015	0.004	0.005	0.003	0.027
1988	0.060	0.029	0.025	0.019	0.134	0.015	0.005	0.005	0.004	0.029
1989	0.070	0.027	0.022	0.018	0.137	0.018	0.004	0.004	0.004	0.030
1990	0.069	0.028	0.027	0.017	0.141	0.018	0.005	0.005	0.003	0.032
1991	0.074	0.028	0.024	0.017	0.142	0.020	0.005	0.004	0.003	0.032
1992	0.079	0.032	0.025	0.015	0.151	0.022	0.006	0.004	0.003	0.036
1993	0.094	0.035	0.022	0.013	0.164	0.029	0.008	0.004	0.003	0.043
1994	0.092	0.034	0.030	0.014	0.170	0.030	0.007	0.007	0.003	0.046
1995	0.110	0.034	0.030	0.012	0.186	0.039	0.007	0.006	0.003	0.056
1996	0.104	0.039	0.032	0.013	0.188	0.038	0.009	0.007	0.003	0.058
1997	0.104	0.041	0.027	0.014	0.186	0.037	0.011	0.006	0.004	0.057
1998	0.100	0.042	0.028	0.016	0.186	0.035	0.011	0.006	0.004	0.056
1999	0.102	0.043	0.028	0.016	0.188	0.036	0.011	0.006	0.005	0.058
2000	0.103	0.042	0.027	0.016	0.188	0.036	0.011	0.006	0.004	0.057
2001	0.108	0.042	0.028	0.016	0.195	0.039	0.011	0.006	0.005	0.061
2002	0.110	0.042	0.027	0.016	0.195	0.040	0.011	0.006	0.005	0.062
	Theil T					CV^2				
1985	0.010	0.002	0.004	0.003	0.019	0.019	0.005	0.008	0.005	0.037
1986	0.012	0.003	0.005	0.003	0.024	0.024	0.008	0.010	0.006	0.047

(Continued)

Table 4.A2 continued

Year	Between belts	Within belt of			Total	Between belts	Within belt of			Total
		East	Central	West			East	Central	West	
	Theil T					CV^2				
1987	0.015	0.004	0.004	0.003	0.026	0.030	0.009	0.009	0.005	0.052
1988	0.015	0.005	0.005	0.004	0.028	0.030	0.012	0.009	0.006	0.057
1989	0.018	0.005	0.004	0.003	0.029	0.036	0.010	0.007	0.005	0.059
1990	0.018	0.005	0.005	0.003	0.031	0.036	0.012	0.009	0.005	0.062
1991	0.019	0.006	0.004	0.003	0.032	0.040	0.013	0.007	0.005	0.065
1992	0.022	0.007	0.004	0.003	0.036	0.045	0.015	0.008	0.004	0.072
1993	0.028	0.008	0.003	0.002	0.042	0.057	0.019	0.007	0.004	0.086
1994	0.029	0.008	0.006	0.003	0.045	0.057	0.017	0.012	0.004	0.090
1995	0.037	0.008	0.006	0.002	0.054	0.074	0.018	0.012	0.003	0.107
1996	0.036	0.010	0.007	0.003	0.055	0.069	0.021	0.014	0.004	0.109
1997	0.035	0.011	0.006	0.003	0.054	0.069	0.023	0.011	0.004	0.106
1998	0.033	0.011	0.006	0.003	0.053	0.065	0.023	0.011	0.005	0.105
1999	0.035	0.011	0.006	0.003	0.055	0.068	0.024	0.011	0.006	0.109
2000	0.035	0.011	0.006	0.003	0.055	0.069	0.024	0.011	0.005	0.110
2001	0.038	0.012	0.006	0.003	0.059	0.075	0.026	0.012	0.005	0.118
2002	0.039	0.011	0.006	0.003	0.059	0.077	0.025	0.011	0.005	0.119

5

Human Capital and Wage Determination in Different Ownerships, 1989–97

Chunbing Xing

Introduction

In the 1990s, China experienced far-reaching transition from a central planning system to a market oriented economy, and the coexistence of different types of ownership was one prominent feature of this process. In particular, the role of private economy as an important complementary part of the whole economy was officially recognized at the 14th CCP congress (1992), and the private sector subsequently made enthusiastic progress. In contrast to state-owned enterprises (SOEs), private enterprises are market oriented, and employers have autonomy to set wages according to employees' productivity. Conversely, SOEs suffer from soft-budget constraints and overstaffing as a by-product (Kornai 1980). In transition economies, SOEs are often the means by which government provides public goods and services (Lin and Tan 1999). While China attempted to improve the financial performance of SOEs through various reforms in the 1990s, the government has been hesitant to relieve SOEs of their traditional role as providers of job security and welfare for their employees. As a result, the SOEs did not have the autonomy to dismiss surplus workers and, consequently, they were unable to set wages according to employee's productivity (Dong and Putterman 2003). Clearly, the wage-setting mechanism differs between different types of ownership and such differences may translate into different rates of returns to human capital, which in turn imply segmentation of the labour market in China.

There is a sizable literature on the returns to education in China, among which two are closely related to the present study. Zhao (2002) finds that in 1996 returns to education in foreign invested enterprises were higher than those in SOEs, urban collective enterprises and domestic private enterprises. Using survey data from Dalian and Xiamen, Dong and Bowles

(2002) examine wage-setting in China's light consumer goods industry in 1998 for (i) state-owned enterprises; (ii) township and village enterprises; (iii) joint ventures; and (iv) foreign-invested firms. They find no significant difference in the returns to education among the four types of firms. Some other studies, such as Zhao (2001) and Chen, Démurger and Fournier (2005), also investigate the systems of wage determination or the wage structure of different types of ownership.

This chapter contributes to the existing literature by estimating returns to education in different ownerships. Using the *China Health* and *Nutrition Survey* (CHNS), we find that the returns are around 0–2 per cent in the early 1990s in all sectors, for both rural and urban regions. In 1997, the returns rose to above 4 per cent in the private sector but remained low in other sectors. The main departures of the study include a more representative sample of data and an adoption of a two-step switching model, which can be used to estimate wage equations for more than two categories simultaneously.

In the next section of this chapter we describe the data used in the empirical analysis and discuss patterns of human capital and wage distribution in different types of ownership. The basic results of regression analysis are then presented, and we subsequently address selection bias and the rural–urban divide. We then go on to use the multinomial logit regression in order to analyze the role of human capital in sector choice and close the chapter with the conclusions.

Data and model specification

Data description

The CHNS survey covers about 16,000 individuals from more than 3,000 households in nine provinces: Liaoning, Heilongjiang, Jiangsu, Shandong, Henan, Hubei, Hunan, Guangxi and Guizhou. These provinces vary greatly in terms of geography and economic development. This chapter uses four waves of this dataset: 1989, 1991, 1993 and 1997. Heilongjiang was not included in the survey in the first three waves and, in 1997, Liaoning was replaced by Heilongjiang.

Because we focus on wage determination, only wage earners are considered. The observations are divided into four subsets: state-owned enterprises (SOEs), small collective enterprises (SCEs), large collective enterprises (LCEs), and private enterprises (PRIs). Whether a collective enterprise is small or large mainly depends on the level of government control applied to it. Most SCEs function at town and village government level, and can also be referred to as TVEs; LCEs function at or above county level government. The PRIs category comprises 'individual or private' businesses, incorporating 'joint ventures' in 1991, and 'family contract' and 'joint venture' enterprises in 1993. For the 1997 survey, PRIs includes three subcategories: 'family contract', 'private or individual' and 'joint venture'. Although all three waves contain the joint venture category – which may have different wage determination mechanisms than other components – we still classify them as belonging to the private sector. Table 5.1 reports the labour shares of different types of ownership from 1989 to 1997. In the rural regions, the private sector accounts for a considerable proportion of the labour force, which increased slightly from 23 per cent in 1989 to 26 per cent in 1997. In urban areas, the public sector dominated through 1989 to 1997, with the state-owned sector taking 60–70 per cent of the labour force. The share of the private sector rose, however, from 5 per cent in 1989 to 12 per cent in 1997. If Liaoning had not been replaced by Heilongjiang, the labour share in the private sector would have been higher in 1997, because SOEs were more dominant in Heilongjiang than in Liaoning.[1]

Table 5.2 presents summary statistics. As for years of schooling (also depicted in Figure 5.1), several points need to be mentioned. First, the education level is the highest in SOEs from 1989 to 1997. Taking 1991 as

Table 5.1 Labour shares of different ownerships

Ownership	**1989**		**1991**		**1993**		**1997**	
	Persons	**%**	**Persons**	**%**	**Persons**	**%**	**Persons**	**%**
Rural								
State-owned (SOEs)	478	35.83	504	35.07	450	33.28	586	40.89
Small collective (SCEs)	404	30.28	396	27.56	377	27.88	311	21.7
Large collective (LCEs)	145	10.87	184	12.8	211	15.61	164	11.44
Private (PRIs)	307	23.01	353	24.57	314	23.22	372	25.96
Total	1,334	100.00	1,437	100.00	1,352	100.00	1,433	100.00
Urban								
State-owned (SOEs)	1,294	64.22	1,185	66.05	919	65.83	809	60.87
Small collective (SCEs)	246	12.21	212	11.82	143	10.24	169	12.72
Large collective (LCEs)	373	18.51	320	17.84	255	18.27	195	14.67
Private (PRIs)	102	5.06	77	4.29	79	5.66	156	11.74
Total	2,015	100.00	1,794	100.00	1,396	100.00	1,329	100.00

Source: Compiled by the author, based on data from CHNS.

Table 5.2 Summary statistics

		SOEs		SCEs		LCEs		PRIs	
		Mean	s.e.	Mean	s.e.	Mean	s.e.	Mean	s.e.
Rural									
1989	Hourly wage (*yuan*)	1.1	2.3	0.7	1.4	0.6	1.1	1.1	1.6
	Working hours per day	7.9	0.8	8.0	1.5	8.1	0.9	7.6	2.6
	Schooling (years)	8.7	3.8	7.3	3.5	7.5	3.1	6.5	3.1
	Height (cm)	165.1	7.8	163.2	7.4	163.8	7.6	163.3	6.8
	Age	35.8	11.9	31.9	11.0	32.3	10.6	34.1	12.0
1991	Hourly wage (*yuan*)	0.5	0.3	0.6	0.4	0.5	0.2	1.1	2.0
	Working hours per day	8.0	0.8	8.2	1.1	8.1	0.8	8.0	2.5
	Schooling (years)	9.0	3.5	7.3	3.3	7.5	2.9	7.1	3.1
	Height (cm)	163.6	10.8	162.3	7.2	162.8	10.5	161.7	11.3
	Age	34.1	11.0	33.3	11.2	32.9	10.7	32.1	11.6
1993	Hourly wage (*yuan*)	0.7	0.4	0.8	0.4	0.8	0.5	1.4	1.8
	Working hours per day	7.9	0.9	8.1	2.9	8.6	5.2	8.2	3.9
	Schooling (years)	9.1	3.6	7.6	3.1	7.7	2.6	7.0	2.8
	Height (cm)	164.5	8.1	162.8	7.6	161.6	7.4	162.3	7.3
	Age	35.6	11.2	34.3	11.2	32.1	11.4	33.3	11.4
1997	Hourly wage (*yuan*)	1.0	0.6	1.1	1.1	1.2	1.2	1.4	1.4
	Working hours per day	7.7	1.0	7.9	1.5	8.0	1.7	8.5	1.8
	Schooling (years)	10.3	2.5	8.2	2.7	9.1	2.8	8.0	3.0
	Age	36.2	10.4	39.3	10.5	35.8	10.5	35.9	13.0
Urban									
1989	Hourly wage (*yuan*)	0.6	1.3	0.6	1.3	0.7	1.8	0.7	0.7
	Working hours per day	7.9	1.0	8.0	1.5	8.0	1.2	8.3	2.2
	Schooling (years)	9.5	3.6	6.9	3.5	8.0	3.2	6.7	3.4
	Height (cm)	162.9	8.0	162.2	8.4	162.0	7.6	160.4	7.4
	Age	36.1	12.1	35.5	12.5	35.2	12.4	35.5	15.1
1991	Hourly wage (*yuan*)	0.5	0.2	0.5	0.3	0.4	0.3	0.8	0.5
	Working hours per day	7.9	0.7	8.2	1.2	7.9	0.9	8.2	1.9
	Schooling (years)	9.9	3.2	7.1	3.2	8.3	3.0	7.5	3.4
	Height (cm)	163.5	8.7	162.1	7.5	161.6	12.0	161.0	7.5
	Age	35.8	11.2	36.5	11.7	33.4	11.3	37.1	12.8
1993	Hourly wage (*yuan*)	0.7	0.8	0.7	0.5	0.7	2.1	2.7	10.8
	Working hours per day	7.9	2.0	8.4	2.2	7.7	1.1	8.1	2.1
	Schooling (years)	9.9	3.3	7.2	3.1	8.5	2.8	7.9	3.3
	Height (cm)	163.4	9.6	162.2	14.6	163.0	8.1	162.0	7.7
	Age	37.5	10.9	37.5	10.4	34.4	10.6	35.6	12.1
1997	Hourly wage (*yuan*)	1.1	0.6	1.3	1.6	1.0	0.4	1.5	1.5
	Working hours per day	7.8	0.9	7.7	1.8	8.0	0.8	8.7	2.0
	Schooling (years)	10.9	3.0	8.2	3.3	9.7	2.8	9.0	3.1
	Age	37.5	10.3	38.8	11.4	36.4	9.7	34.2	11.0

Source: Compiled by the author, based on data from CHNS.

an example, the sequence in descending order is SOEs, LCEs, SCEs and PRIs in the rural regions, with average education levels being 9.0, 7.5, 7.3 and 7.1 years, respectively. The case of the urban areas is different, with the SCEs and PRIs reversing their position after 1991. Second, except for

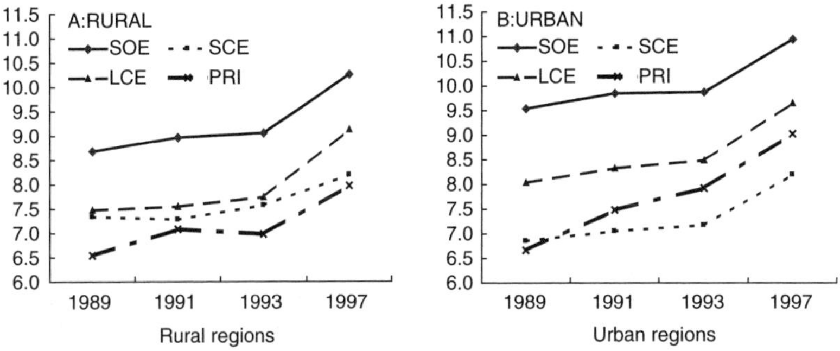

Figure 5.1 Years of schooling of labourers in different ownerships, 1989–97
Source: Computed by the author, based on data from CHNS.

the SCEs, education levels in all sectors are higher in urban than rural areas. Third, education levels increased in all sectors during this period. Another component of human capital is health, for which height is an indicator (for example, Fogel 1994; Duncan and Strauss 1997; Strauss and Duncan 1998). Height is invariably greater in the SOEs than in other sectors (depicted in Figure 5.2). Table 5.2 also reports the hours worked per day. Daily working hours in SOEs tend to be less than those in other ownership firms.

Although the public sector, especially SOEs, has an advantage in terms of human capital, their wage levels are low compared to the private sector. For example, in 1991 in rural China, hourly wages are 0.5, 0.6, 0.5, and 1.1 *yuan* in SOEs, SCEs, LCEs, and PRIs, respectively. With the exception of 1989, the standard errors of hourly wages are greater for the private sector than for other types of ownership. Table 5.3 also tabulates various wage percentiles for different types of ownership. It is obvious that wages in the private sector show greater dispersion than is found in other sectors. In 1991 in rural China, the 10 per cent percentile wage level is around 0.3 *yuan*/hour in all sectors. At the 90 per cent percentile, however, the wage level in the private sector is about 1.9 *yuan*/hour, 2.5, 1.9, and 2.5 times that of SOEs, SCEs, and LCEs, respectively. The patterns in the urban areas and for other survey years are similar.

These patterns of wage distribution may not be compatible with those of personal income that have been reported in other studies, as wage does not include bonuses and subsidies. However, wage constitutes an important part of personal income, and wage setting is of interest in its own right. Thus, most of our discussions in this chapter are confined purely to wage. However, as discussed later, our results are robust to the inclusion or exclusion of bonuses and subsidies.

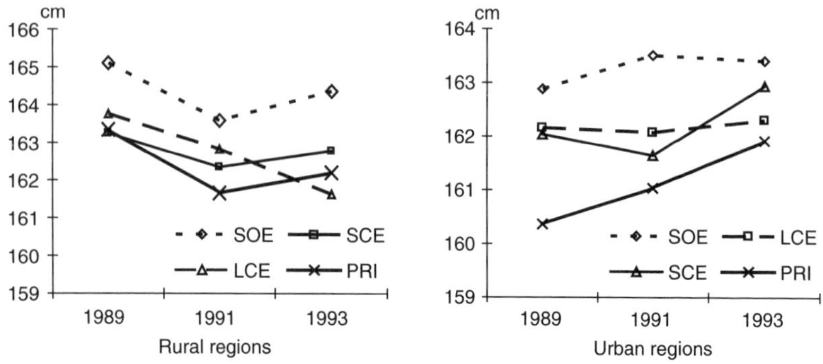

Figure 5.2 Height of labourers in different ownerships (unit: cm)
Source: Computed by the author, based on data from CHNS.

Table 5.3 Wage distributions (unit: *yuan*)

Percentiles of wage distributions (%)	Rural				Urban			
	SOEs	SCEs	LCEs	PRIs	SOEs	SCEs	LCEs	PRIs
1989								
10	0.281	0.222	0.264	0.274	0.238	0.173	0.208	0.233
25	0.352	0.308	0.305	0.412	0.295	0.257	0.259	0.280
50	0.472	0.453	0.382	0.611	0.381	0.367	0.343	0.467
75	0.625	0.622	0.486	0.977	0.513	0.490	0.431	0.707
90	0.918	1.070	0.686	1.946	0.674	0.881	0.582	1.167
1991								
10	0.310	0.253	0.299	0.307	0.285	0.211	0.259	0.344
25	0.377	0.350	0.368	0.446	0.354	0.305	0.315	0.431
50	0.481	0.499	0.453	0.708	0.450	0.416	0.395	0.629
75	0.610	0.724	0.577	1.152	0.566	0.567	0.503	0.922
90	0.774	0.993	0.760	1.900	0.701	0.834	0.629	1.391
1993								
10	0.352	0.342	0.345	0.406	0.318	0.231	0.282	0.446
25	0.444	0.503	0.478	0.635	0.391	0.446	0.346	0.528
50	0.576	0.703	0.712	1.005	0.514	0.641	0.492	0.957
75	0.822	0.919	0.936	1.645	0.717	0.867	0.664	1.760
90	1.070	1.319	1.260	2.865	0.967	1.190	0.970	2.733
1997								
10	0.424	0.402	0.438	0.552	0.505	0.536	0.498	0.528
25	0.618	0.591	0.613	0.721	0.707	0.693	0.661	0.711
50	0.873	0.804	0.901	1.047	1.010	0.932	0.892	1.113
75	1.192	1.308	1.348	1.495	1.398	1.334	1.186	1.620
90	1.555	1.864	1.957	2.157	1.848	2.097	1.448	2.386

Source: Compiled by the author, based on data from CHNS.

Model specification

The model to be estimated is an extended Mincer (1974) equation:

$$\ln(wage_{si}) = \beta_{s0} + H_{si}\beta_{s1} + X_{si}\beta_{s2} + u_{si} \quad (5.1)$$

where s refers to different sectors or SOEs, SCEs, LCEs, and PRIs; H is the human capital vector, which includes education, health, experience and experience squared. We use the years of formal schooling and height as proxies of education and health. Experience is defined as: experience = age − (years of schooling) − 6; $\ln(wage)_{si}$ can be observed only when individual i is in sector s (selection bias is discussed later). In addition, X controls for factors such as gender, location (province dummies) and occupation. We estimate wage equations separately for each year and for each type of ownership.

OLS results

Pooling results

Assuming that wage determination is identical in all sectors, all observations can then be pooled to estimate one regression model, with ownership dummies included. The results are presented in Table 5.4. When the ownership dummies are not added, the adjusted r-squares are around 0.13, 0.25, 0.17 and 0.15 in 1989, 1991, 1993, and 1997, respectively. They increase by 2.2, 1.7, 6.1 and 1.4 percentage points when the ownership dummies are included. The results also indicate that differences in the wage levels exist mainly between the private and public sectors. Holding other factors constant, the average wages of the private sector (for different years) were 51.9 per cent, 35.9 per cent, 65.7 per cent, and 20.7 per cent higher than those of the SOEs. The effect of human capital on wages seems to evolve over time. The returns to education are 1.4 per cent, 1.6 per cent, 2.3 per cent and 1.3 per cent, respectively in 1989, 1991, 1993, and 1997. These estimates are low compared to those of Appleton, Song and Xia (2005) and Zhang *et al.* (2005). Note that our estimates refer to returns to wage while others represent returns to total personal income. Health (for which height is a proxy) is also positively related to wages. Labourers who are taller tend to earn more wages, but the effects are statistically significant only in 1993.

Other factors are also important in wage determination. Females earn significantly less than their male counterparts. Wage levels also vary significantly between regions, thus the labour market is geographically segmented.

Table 5.4 Wage equation (pooling results) (dependent variable = log (hourly wage))

	1989		1991		1993		1997	
	1	2	3	4	5	6	7	8
Schooling	0.011	0.014**	0.015***	0.016***	0.016***	0.023***	0.013**	0.013**
	(0.007)	(0.007)	(0.003)	(0.003)	(0.005)	(0.005)	(0.005)	(0.005)
Experience	0.022***	0.023***	0.026***	0.026***	0.028***	0.028***	0.027***	0.030***
	(0.008)	(0.008)	(0.002)	(0.002)	(0.003)	(0.003)	(0.004)	(0.004)
Experience squared/100	−0.015	−0.015	−0.030***	−0.031***	−0.037***	−0.035***	−0.048***	−0.052***
	(0.021)	(0.020)	(0.004)	(0.004)	(0.006)	(0.006)	(0.007)	(0.007)
Ln(height)	0.135	0.261	0.244	0.277	0.666**	0.622**		
	(0.214)	(0.212)	(0.205)	(0.203)	(0.284)	(0.273)		
Female	−0.095***	−0.085**	−0.120***	−0.121***	−0.092***	−0.081***	−0.155***	−0.155***
	(0.036)	(0.035)	(0.022)	(0.022)	(0.031)	(0.030)	(0.023)	(0.023)
Liaoning ('89, '91, '93) or Heilongjiang ('97) omitted								
Jiangsu	−0.103*	−0.141***	−0.059*	−0.077**	0.120***	0.047	0.310***	0.320***
	(0.054)	(0.055)	(0.030)	(0.031)	(0.043)	(0.043)	(0.049)	(0.049)
Shandong	0.157**	0.127*	0.000	−0.011	0.126***	0.115**	0.141**	0.167***
	(0.064)	(0.067)	(0.032)	(0.032)	(0.048)	(0.047)	(0.055)	(0.056)

Henan	0.139**	0.082	0.065*	0.055	−0.026	−0.067	0.186***	0.194***
	(0.064)	(0.064)	(0.039)	(0.039)	(0.054)	(0.052)	(0.056)	(0.056)
Hubei	0.053	0.021	0.126***	0.116***	0.087*	0.077*	0.196***	0.213***
	(0.058)	(0.058)	(0.033)	(0.033)	(0.046)	(0.045)	(0.052)	(0.052)
Hunan	0.273***	0.219***	0.123***	0.097***	0.282***	0.241***	0.458***	0.442***
	(0.059)	(0.059)	(0.033)	(0.032)	(0.047)	(0.045)	(0.054)	(0.054)
Guangxi	−0.013	−0.051	−0.056	−0.080**	0.137***	0.071	0.108**	0.093*
	(0.072)	(0.071)	(0.036)	(0.036)	(0.049)	(0.047)	(0.053)	(0.052)
Guizhou	0.094	0.055	−0.071*	−0.073*	0.094*	0.045	0.098*	0.101*
	(0.066)	(0.066)	(0.038)	(0.038)	(0.052)	(0.051)	(0.057)	(0.057)
State-owned sector omitted								
Small collective		0.075		0.050**		0.122***		−0.031
		(0.047)		(0.025)		(0.035)		(0.041)
Large collective		−0.003		0.003		0.073**		−0.025
		(0.046)		(0.025)		(0.034)		(0.036)
Private sector		0.519***		0.359***		0.657***		0.207***
		(0.082)		(0.046)		(0.049)		(0.044)
Adj-R^2	0.134	0.156	0.245	0.262	0.165	0.226	0.154	0.168
N	1506	1506	2688	2688	2302	2302	2233	2233

Note: Occupation and urban dummy are controlled; * significant at the 10 per cent level, ** significant at the 5 per cent level, *** significant at the 1 per cent level; standard errors in parenthesis, constants not reported.
Source: Compiled by the author, based on data from CHNS.

Wage determination in different types of ownership

Assuming identical returns to education in all sectors is, of course, restrictive. In what follows, we estimate wage equations by type of ownership and by year. The top panel of Table 5.5 reports OLS results, while the bottom panel reports results of switching regressions. It is noted that the results for 1989 are dropped because, for that year, the sample size of the private sector is rather small.

The results of early 1990s

In 1991, the returns were about 2 per cent in SOEs and only 1 per cent in other types of ownership. Experience seems to be an important wage determinant in all sectors. However, the wage–experience profiles are different between the SOEs and the private sector. The marginal impacts of experience on wages for those with zero years of experience were 2.6 per cent and 3.5 per cent in SOEs and the private sector, respectively. The coefficients of experience squared are negative, implying a concave wage–experience relationship. Based on the estimates of Table 5.5, it would take 30 years or so for workers in the private sector to reach the peak wage level. In SOEs, however, it would take as long as 60 years. Thus, wages in SOEs were almost constantly increasing during the entire working life of employees. This finding is consistent with the fact that seniority is an important factor in setting wages in SOEs. The results in Table 5.5 also indicate the role of health in wage determination. The wage elasticity with respect to height is about 2.0 in PRIs, much higher than that in other sectors.

The results for 1993 are very similar to those of 1991. It is useful to note, however, that from 1991 to 1993 returns to education increased and experience remained an important wage determinant in all ownership types except LCEs. The premium associated with experience for those with a low level of experience also increased.

These results seem to indicate a peculiar labour market in the early 1990s, as education was not significant in determining wage in any ownership type except SOEs. The returns in SOEs, although significant, are extremely low. Clearly, wage determination was not wholly based on productivity. According to Lardy (1997), the early 1990s coincide with the end of the second stage reforms, which were initiated in the mid-1980s and focused on establishing responsibilities between managers and the government. Although some research (Groves *et al.* 1995) shows that the managerial labour market improved during this period, our results tell a different story.

Table 5.5 Wage equations of different sectors (dependent variable = log (hourly wage))

	1991				1993				1997			
	SOEs	SCEs	LCEs	PRIs	SOEs	SCEs	LCEs	PRIs	SOEs	SCEs	LCEs	PRIs
OLS												
Schooling	0.020***	0.006	0.012	0.011	0.023***	0.014	0.005	0.024	0.006	0.008	0.004	0.041***
	(0.003)	(0.010)	(0.008)	(0.017)	(0.005)	(0.012)	(0.013)	(0.021)	(0.006)	(0.015)	(0.015)	(0.013)
Experience	0.026***	0.018***	0.017***	0.035***	0.029***	0.028***	0.012	0.046***	0.035***	0.026**	0.022**	0.028***
	(0.002)	(0.006)	(0.005)	(0.012)	(0.004)	(0.007)	(0.008)	(0.015)	(0.004)	(0.011)	(0.010)	(0.007)
Experience squared/100	−0.020***	−0.031***	−0.011	−0.063***	−0.031***	−0.050***	−0.011	−0.072***	−0.064***	−0.048**	−0.034	−0.045***
	(0.004)	(0.011)	(0.009)	(0.022)	(0.007)	(0.013)	(0.014)	(0.027)	(0.009)	(0.020)	(0.023)	(0.012)
Ln(height)	−0.039	0.663	−0.164	1.964*	0.633**	1.210**	−0.319	2.447				
	(0.201)	(0.534)	(0.384)	(1.032)	(0.310)	(0.539)	(0.606)	(1.633)				
Adj-R^2	0.392	0.147	0.162	0.071	0.184	0.217	0.114	0.186	0.199	0.148	0.074	0.292
N	1437	522	433	296	1180	431	393	298	1201	383	299	350
Switching												
Schooling	0.015***	0.001	−0.003	−0.009	0.017***	0.002	−0.021	0.000	0.010	0.006	−0.001	0.033**
	(0.004)	(0.011)	(0.011)	(0.020)	(0.007)	(0.014)	(0.014)	(0.026)	(0.007)	(0.015)	(0.016)	(0.015)
Experience	0.025***	0.020***	0.014**	0.031**	0.027***	0.026***	0.000	0.042**	0.036***	0.032***	0.021**	0.024***
	(0.003)	(0.007)	(0.006)	(0.013)	(0.005)	(0.009)	(0.009)	(0.017)	(0.004)	(0.011)	(0.010)	(0.008)
Experience squared/100	−0.020***	−0.037***	−0.011	−0.059**	−0.032***	−0.049***	0.001	−0.073**	−0.065***	−0.060***	−0.036	−0.039***
	(0.005)	(0.013)	(0.010)	(0.023)	(0.009)	(0.016)	(0.016)	(0.031)	(0.009)	(0.021)	(0.023)	(0.013)
Ln(height)	0.085	1.001*	−0.277	2.523**	0.655**	0.992	−0.892	2.674				
	(0.238)	(0.602)	(0.447)	(1.075)	(0.321)	(0.737)	(0.593)	(1.773)				
Mills	−0.053	0.060	0.131	0.251	0.001	0.250	0.340**	0.514***	0.070	0.014	0.199	0.111
	(0.040)	(0.099)	(0.102)	(0.154)	(0.066)	(0.180)	(0.144)	(0.193)	(0.061)	(0.083)	(0.139)	(0.089)
Adj-R^2	0.388	0.157	0.137	0.109	0.148	0.180	0.180	0.200	0.206	0.165	0.064	0.292
N	1080	463	345	265	953	333	307	249	1165	359	290	345

Note: Occupation and province dummies are controlled; * significant at the 10 per cent level, ** significant at the 5 per cent level, *** significant at the 1 per cent level; standard errors in parenthesis, constants not reported.
Source: Compiled by the author, based on data from CHNS.

Wage determination in 1997

From 1993 onward, China's reform entered a critical stage. In 1992, 'building a socialist market economy' was established as the main objective of economic reforms at the 14th CCP Congress. The private was recognized as an important complementary part of the whole economy and, subsequently, it developed significantly. How does this affect wage determination in different ownerships?

The most striking result is that returns to education in the private sector increased to 4.1 per cent (significant at the 1 per cent level), while those of other sectors remained low and insignificant. As for experience, however, it is interesting to point out that, unlike in 1991 or 1993, it would only take 27 years for an SOE employee to reach the peak wage level as of 1997.

Our results are consistent with other studies, in that returns to education in China were lower than in other countries in the early 1990s, and have subsequently been increasing (Psacharopoulos 1994; and Zhang *et al.* 2005, for example). Nevertheless, our estimates are lower than earlier estimates (see de Brauw *et al.* (2002) for rural areas, and Appleton, Song and Xia (2005) and Zhang *et al.* (2005) for urban areas). There are two possible reasons for this difference. First, the sample data are different. Take Zhang *et al.* (2005) as an example: their data were for Beijing, Liaoning, Zhejiang, Sichuan, Guangdong and Sha'anxi, and these provinces (except Sha'anxi) are more developed relative to those provinces covered by CHNS. Second, as mentioned before, we exclude bonuses and subsidies; most others include both.

Could the difference in the returns to education be driven by occupation not ownership? The answer is 'no', because we have controlled occupation in our models. Nevertheless, our data show that the occupational compositions in the public sector are different from the private sector. Based on Xing (2007), 24 per cent of employees in SOEs are professional/technical workers, while in private sectors this figure is only 3 per cent.

What really matters is the problem of self-selection. That is, individuals are not randomly assigned to different types of ownership. It is possible that a worker chooses a particular type of ownership because s/he perceives more favourable returns than are perceived by those who choose otherwise. In this case, estimating wage equations separately may be problematic. We look into this problem in the following section.

Self-selection and the rural–urban divide

Switching regression

An individual chooses his/her job partly based on their personal characteristics, both observable and unobservable, which cannot be fully controlled for in the wage equation. When unobservable (uncontrollable) characteristics are correlated with education, the estimates may be biased. In China, those who are more capable or possess who greater entrepreneurial spirit tend to work in the private sector because of the wage gap (Li 1997). To correct this bias, we resort to the switching model (Maddala 1983).

The starting point is a latent variable model:

$$I^{*}_{si} = z_{si}\gamma + \eta_{si} \tag{5.2}$$

where z_{si} are exogenous variables and I^{*}_{si} is unobservable. Let I be a polychotomous variable and $I = s$ ($s = 1, 2, 3, 4$), when the sth category is chosen, then:

$$I = s \text{ if and only if } I^{*}_{s} > Max\ I^{*}_{j}\ (j = 1, 2, 3, 4, \text{ and } j \neq s)$$

Further assuming $\varepsilon_s = Max\ I^{*}_{j} - \eta_s$ ($j = 1, 2, 3, 4$, and $j \neq s$) so $I = s$ if and only if $\varepsilon_s < z_s\gamma$. If η_j is identically and independently distributed with a cumulative distribution function $F(\eta_i < c) = \exp[-\exp(-c)]$ we have

$$F_s(\varepsilon) = \Pr(\varepsilon_s < \varepsilon) = \frac{\exp(\varepsilon)}{\exp(\varepsilon) + \sum_{j \neq s} \exp(z_j\gamma)}$$

For the wage equation of sector s, $\ln(wage_{si})$ can be observed if and only if $\varepsilon_s < z_s\gamma$. Now, assume:

$$\varepsilon^{*}_{s} = J_s(\varepsilon_s) = \Phi^{-1}[F_s(\varepsilon)]$$

Then, OLS can be used to estimate the following equation to obtain returns to education for all sectors:

$$\begin{aligned} E[\ln(wage_s)|H_s, X_s, \varepsilon_s < z_s\gamma] = {} & \beta_{s0} + H_s\beta_{s1} + X_s\beta_{s2} \\ & - \sigma_s\rho_s\phi[J_s(z_s\gamma)]/F_s(z_s\gamma) + \nu_s \end{aligned} \tag{5.3}$$

where $\sigma^2_s = \text{var}(u_s)$, ρ_s is the correlation coefficient between u_s and ε^{*}_{s}, $\hat{\gamma}$ and $m = \phi[J_s(z_s\hat{\gamma})]/F_s(z_s\hat{\gamma})$ can be obtained by first estimating a multinomial logit model.[2]

The selection bias is essentially caused by the correlation between u_s and ε^{*}_{s}. If $\rho_s = 0$, model (5.3) reduces to (5.1). When $\rho_s \neq 0$, the unobservable component in the sector choice stage is correlated with the unobservable component at the wage determination stage. For example, the more capable may choose to work in the private sector, and they are also better educated and earn higher wages. In this case, the return differentials are merely a result of sorting, rather than labour market segmentation. The switching regression or Heckman's two-stage model utilizes the predicted probability of sector choice to serve as a proxy for the unobserved component in the wage equation. Thus, the coefficient of *m* reflects the existence of sample selection.

To identify the sector choice behaviour, vector *z* contains information such as family size, household income per capita, community population density and infrastructure, proportions of the labour force in agriculture and in other employment. For 1997, we only have information on family size, gender ratio, marital status, urban dummy and family assets. Most of these factors influence sector choice behaviour, but have little direct impact on wage. It is noted that including household income per capita for selectivity correction may be problematic, because wage forms part of household income. As will be discussed, the final modelling results are robust to its inclusion or exclusion.

The results of the switching regression can be found at the bottom panel of Table 5.5. Although the returns to education in the switching models are slightly lower than their OLS counterparts, the coefficient differentials between different sectors remain the same as before. And, as in the OLS regressions, the wage–experience profiles have different shapes in different years and in different types of ownership. In the early 1990s, it would take 40 years (results for 1993) or 60 years (results for 1991) to reach the peak wage level in an SOE, but only 25–30 years in the private sector.

Our results indicate that the returns to education and to experience vary in different types of ownership, even after considering the selection bias. In fact, these results confirm the existence of segmentation in the Chinese labour market, where labour mobility is insufficient. Free movement between sectors was not common, so there should not be much change once we have corrected for the selection bias.

Urban–rural divide

As is known, China is a typical dual economy. In particular, the majority of the rural labour force does not comprise wage earners. Also, the reform processes were not homogeneous in urban and rural areas. Thus, we need to examine wage determinations in urban and rural areas separately. Because the results of the switching model are similar to those of OLS, only OLS results are reported in Table 5.6. Results for 1991 are not reported because they are similar to those of 1993.

In 1993 in rural China, returns to education are all insignificant. The 1997 results show that education had become a critical factor in the wage determination of the private sector, and the differentials in the returns constitute one of the main differences in wage-setting between different types of ownership. Returns to education in the private sector stands at 4.2 per cent (significant at the 5 per cent level), while the returns to education of other

	1993				1997			
	SOEs	SCEs	LCEs	PRIs	SOEs	SCEs	LCEs	PRIs
Rural								
Schooling	0.013	0.015	−0.005	0.018	0.012	−0.007	−0.005	0.042**
	(0.008)	(0.014)	(0.022)	(0.025)	(0.011)	(0.022)	(0.029)	(0.017)
Experience	0.015**	0.030***	0.015	0.051***	0.034***	0.028*	−0.006	0.027***
	(0.007)	(0.008)	(0.012)	(0.017)	(0.007)	(0.016)	(0.026)	(0.009)
Experience squared/100	−0.016	−0.054***	−0.028	−0.083***	−0.057***	−0.046	0.032	−0.036**
	(0.013)	(0.016)	(0.022)	(0.032)	(0.016)	(0.028)	(0.060)	(0.016)
Female	−0.062	−0.048	−0.211**	0.060	−0.079	−0.420***	−0.185	−0.185**
	(0.056)	(0.081)	(0.095)	(0.172)	(0.049)	(0.108)	(0.131)	(0.086)
Adj-R^2	0.15	0.152	0.079	0.158	0.198	0.141	0.043	0.257
N	367	308	168	232	469	224	117	225
Urban								
Schooling	0.026***	0.023	0.022	0.023	−0.000	0.014	0.017	0.040*
	(0.007)	(0.022)	(0.018)	(0.036)	(0.007)	(0.022)	(0.016)	(0.021)
Experience	0.036***	0.031**	0.011	0.023	0.037***	0.030*	0.027***	0.041***
	(0.005)	(0.015)	(0.010)	(0.032)	(0.005)	(0.016)	(0.010)	(0.011)
Experience squared/100	−0.040***	−0.054**	0.006	−0.031	−0.074***	−0.068**	−0.040*	−0.091***
	(0.009)	(0.027)	(0.019)	(0.055)	(0.011)	(0.032)	(0.022)	(0.020)
Female	−0.015	−0.205*	−0.151*	−0.563*	−0.113***	−0.147	−0.132*	−0.237**
	(0.045)	(0.111)	(0.089)	(0.297)	(0.035)	(0.105)	(0.068)	(0.103)
Adj-R^2	0.207	0.368	0.066	0.383	0.222	0.126	0.15	0.436
N	813	123	225	66	732	159	182	125

Note: Occupation and province dummies are controlled; log form of height is also controlled in 1993;
* significant at the 10 per cent level; ** significant at the 5 per cent level; *** significant at the 1 per cent level; standard errors in parenthesis, constants not reported.
Source: Compiled by the author, based on data from CHNS.

sectors remain low and insignificant. The estimated wage–experience profiles all display an inverted-U shape, except LCEs in 1997.

The urban picture is quite different, with the majority of the labour force working in the public sector, especially SOEs. The share of the private sector is low. Based on Table 5.6, in 1993 the returns to education are all above 2 per cent, with that of the SOEs being the highest and only significant figure. In 1997, the case is reversed to some extent, with the returns to education in the private sector becoming the highest, 4.0 per cent (significant at the 10 per cent level), while those of SOEs, SCEs and LCEs' are −0.0 per cent, 1.4 per cent and 1.7 per cent, respectively. As in the rural areas, the estimated wage–experience profiles are all inverted-U shaped in 1993 (except for LCEs). As of 1993, it took less time to reach peak wage levels in the private and collective-owned sectors than in SOEs. By 1997, however, the same number of years are required to achieve the top wage for SOEs and private sector employees.

One point is worth noting: despite the urban–rural divide, the returns to education of different sectors in different years are very similar in urban and rural China. This can be attributed to the fact that wage earners are working in the relatively more modern sectors irrespective of locations.

Sector choice and human capital allocation

In this section, we consider the multinomial logit regression (first step of the switching model), which examines the effect of education on sector choice and, hence, the allocation of human capital. In particular, we are interested in whether human capital is allocated to sectors where the returns are higher. Let SOEs be the base choice, thus the probability of SOEs, SCEs, LCEs or PRIs being chosen is

$$\Pr(I = 1|z) = \frac{1}{1+\sum_{j\neq s}\exp(z\gamma_j)}$$

and

$$\Pr(I = s|z) = \frac{\exp(z\gamma_s)}{1+\sum_{j\neq s}\exp(z\gamma_j)}$$

where $s = 2$, 3 and 4 stands for SCEs, LCEs and PRIs, respectively; z is a vector of independent variables defined previously (pp. 128–30); and γ is the coefficient vector. The ratio of the probability of choosing s over the probability of choosing SOEs becomes

$$\Pr(I = s|z)/\Pr(I = 1|z) = \exp(z\gamma_s)$$

The relative risk ratio or RRR can be defined as

$$RRR \equiv \frac{\Pr(I = s|z')/\Pr(I = 1|z')}{\Pr(I = s|z)/\Pr(I = 1|z)} = \exp((z' - z)\gamma_s)$$

When schooling increases by one year (holding other variables constant), $RRR \equiv \exp((z' - z)\gamma_s) = \exp(\gamma_{schooling})$. The *ratio* of the probability of choosing sector *s* to that of choosing SOEs will increase if $RRR > 1$, and the reverse will be true when $RRR < 1$.

Without losing generality, we tabulate the 1997 results only (see the top panel of Table 5.7). Education is a significant factor in sector choice (which can alternatively be stated as: education is a significant factor when employers recruit employees). All estimates of RRR are less than unity (0.81, 0.85 and 0.79 for SCEs, LCEs and PRIs). Literally interpreted, the probabilities of choosing other sectors decrease as education increases. This finding runs contrary to the suggestion that returns to education are generally lower in SOEs, a puzzle worth further investigation.

Since different age groups may face different job opportunities, it is useful to examine whether earlier findings are robust in this regard. To this end, the whole sample is divided into five age groups: less than or equal to 25 years, 26–30 years, 31–35 years, 36–40 years and above 40 years. The results are reported at the bottom panel of Table 5.7. The results are similar to those in the top panel. The better educated tend to choose SOEs. For the youngest group, the RRRs of SCEs, LCEs and PRIs relative to SOEs are 0.57 (significant at the 1 per cent level), 0.82 (not significant) and 0.61 (significant at the 1 per cent level). The differences in the magnitude and significance of RRRs indicate that SOEs and LCEs are more or less the same as far as sector choice is concerned. The same can be said in relation to SCEs and PRIs. The only exception is the 36–40 years group, for whom education is not a significant factor in sector choice. Also, those with more education tend to choose the non-state sectors (RRR > 1).

It seems that individuals with more human capital tend to be allocated to the SOEs, even though both the average wage level and the return to education is lower there. To some extent, these contradictory results are likely to be caused by the exclusion of bonuses and subsidies in our study, which constituted a much more important part of personal income in SOEs than in other ownership types. In the 1997 survey of CHNS, about 60 per cent of employees in SOEs received bonuses, while in PRIs this figure was only 10 per cent. Besides bonuses, there are various subsidies in SOEs. It is reasonable for individuals with more human capital to choose SOEs if these benefits are sufficiently large to fill the wage gap. Our results (not reported here as they are similar to those reported in the preceding section,

Table 5.7 Ownership choice model (1997, multinomial logit) (dependent variable = ownership: SOEs = 1/SCEs = 2/LCEs = 3/PRIs = 4)

	SCEs/SOEs		LCEs/SOEs		PRIs/SOEs			
	Beta	**RRR**	**Beta**	**RRR**	**Beta**	**RRR**	**Pseudo-R^2**	**Obs**
A: Full sample	−0.2053***	0.8144	−0.1610***	0.8513	−0.2356***	0.7901	0.2318	2176
B: <=25	−0.5580***	0.5724	−0.1973	0.821	−0.4948***	0.6097	0.3167	345
26–30	−0.3168	0.7285	−0.1651	0.8478	−0.5429**	0.581	0.2943	318
31–35	−0.3644**	0.6946	0.0763	1.0793	−0.1589	0.8531	0.3172	373
36–40	0.0262	1.0265	0.1673	1.1821	0.0502	1.0515	0.4591	308
>40	−0.2138***	0.8075	−0.2267***	0.7971	−0.2940***	0.7453	0.2618	829

Note: Experience, experience squared, family size, gender ratio, marital status, urban dummy, family asset, etc. are controlled. Constants and standard errors are not reported neither. * Significant at the 10% level, ** significant at the 5% level, *** significant at the 1% level.
Source: Compiled by the author, based on data from CHNS.

pp. 128–32) indicate that even when bonuses and subsidies are added to wages, both the income level and returns to education are still higher in PRIs, holding other factors constant. These contradictory results may also be related to the fact that SOEs often offer better job security, health insurance and pension coverage than other ownerships. We leave this for further research.

Conclusion

Using CHNS data, this chapter aims to investigate the wage-setting mechanisms in state-owned, collective-owned and private enterprises. It is revealed that returns to education are different across different types of ownership, and that in 1997 the returns were highest in the private sector. Our results are robust to selection bias, the rural–urban divide, and the inclusion of bonuses and subsidies. In a competitive and integrated economy, resources are allocated so that returns in different sectors are identical. We can therefore conclude that, in terms of wage determination, China's labour market is segmented according to types of ownership.

One factor underlying this segmentation is the lack of worker mobility between different ownership types. We find that better educated workers are reluctant to move to non-state sectors, even though both wage level and returns to education are higher there. This may be closely related to the institutional arrangement of the social security system. Workers in SOEs choose not to move to the private sector because the former provide more social security than the latter (Zhao 2002). In order to develop a more competitive labour market, an integrated social security system must first be established.

Notes

1 In 1996, the labour shares of SOEs were 39 per cent and 33 per cent in Heilongjiang and Liaoning respectively (NBS 1997: tables 4.3 and 4.10).

2 To be precise, what we should estimate is the conditional logit model (see Maddala 1983). Because we have information only at the individual level, we use the multinomial logit, which is a special version of the conditional logit model (Wooldridge 2002: 501).

References

Appleton, S., Song, L. and Xia, Q. (2005) 'Has China Crossed the River? The Evolution of Wage Structure in Urban China during Reform and Retrenchment', *Journal of Comparative Economics*, 33, 4: 644–63.

Chen, Y., Démurger, S. and Fournier, M. (2005) 'Earnings Differentials and Ownership Structure in Chinese Enterprises', *Economic Development and Cultural Change*, 53, 4: 933–58.
deBrauw, A., Huang, J., Rozelle, S., Zhang, L. and Zhang, Y. (2002) 'The Evolution of China's Rural Labour Markets during the Reforms: Rapid, Accelerating, Transforming', *Journal of Comparative Economics*, 30, 2: 329–53.
Dong, X., and Bowles, P. (2002) 'Segmentation and Discrimination in China's Emerging Industrial Labour Market', *China Economic Review*, 13, 2–3: 170–96.
Dong, X., and Putterman, L. (2003) 'Soft Budget Constraints, Social Burdens, and Labor Redundancy in China's State Industry', *Journal of Comparative Economics*, 31, 1: 110–33.
Duncan, T., and Strauss, J. (1997) 'Health and Wages: Evidence on Men and Women in Urban Brazil', *Journal of Econometrics*, 77: 159–85.
Fogel, R.W. (1994) 'Economic Growth, Population Theory, and Physiology: The Bearing of Long-Term Processes on the Making of Economic Policy', *American Economic Review*, 84, 3: 369–95.
Groves, T., Hong, Y., McMillan, J. and Naughton, B. (1995) 'China's Evolving Managerial Labour Market', *Journal of Political Economy*, 103, 4: 873–92.
Kornai, J. (1980) *Economics of Shortage* (Amsterdam: North-Holland).
Lardy, N. (1997) *China's Unfinished Economic Reform* (Washington, DC: Brookings Institution Press).
Li, S. (1997) 'A Model of Labour Mobility in Transition China', *Economic Research Journal* (*Jingji Yanjiu*), January (in Chinese).
Lin, J., and Tan, G. (1999) 'Policy Burdens, Accountability, and the Soft Budget Constraints', *American Economic Review*, 89, 2: 426–31.
Maddala, G.S. (1983) *Limited-dependent and Qualitative Variables in Econometrics*, (Cambridge: Cambridge University Press).
Mincer, J. (1974) *Schooling, Experience and Earnings* (New York: Columbia University Press).
NBS (National Bureau of Statistics) (1997) *China Statistical Yearbook* (Beijing: China Statistic Publishing House), available at: www.stats.gov.cn/ndsj/information/nj97/dml.htm
Psacharopoulos, G. (1994) 'Returns to Investment in Education: a Global Up-date', *World Development*, 22: 1325–43.
Strauss, J. and Duncan, T. (1998) 'Health, Nutrition and Economic Development', *Journal of Economic Literature*, 36, 2: 766–817.
Wooldridge, J.M. (2002) *Econometric Analysis of Cross Section and Panel Data* (Cambridge, MA: MIT Press).
Xing, C. (2007) 'Wage Determination and Returns to Education in Different Ownerships of China: Evidence from Quantile Regressions', *Frontiers of Economics in China*, 2, 1: 114.
Zhang, J., Zhao,Y., Park, A. and Song, X. (2005) 'Economic Returns to Schooling in Urban China, 1988 to 2001', *Journal of Comparative Economics*, 33, 4: 730–52.
Zhao, Y. (2001) 'Foreign Direct Investment and Relative Wages: The Case of China'. *China Economic Review*, 12, 1: 40–57.
Zhao, Y. (2002) 'Earnings Differentials between State and Non-State Enterprises in Urban China', *Pacific Economic Review*, 7, 1: 181–97.

6

Income, Income Inequality and Health: Evidence from China

Hongbin Li and Yi Zhu

Introduction

China has recorded impressive growth over the past 25 years since the introduction of the market economy, and there has been a substantial increase in average living standards. However, in recent years there has been growing concern about the large increase in income inequality over the same period. For example, Bramall (2001) shows that the Gini coefficient for rural China has increased by almost 50 per cent from 1980 to 1999. The rising inequality has had and will have important impacts on various aspects of social life, resulting, for example, in frequent social conflicts (Alesina and Perotti 1996), higher levels of violent crime (Hsieh and Pugh 1993), and ultimately in a slowing down of economic growth (Aghion, Caroli and Garcia-Penalosa 1999). While inequality may affect society and its economic development in many ways, we focus in this chapter on a particular aspect of the socioeconomic effects of inequality; that is, its impact on health.

The relationship between income, income inequality and health is an issue that has attracted the attention of a variety of social science disciplines; such as economics, sociology and public health. From an early stage in the debate, it was argued that income has a positive effect on health (Grossman 1972; Preston 1975). This is called the absolute income hypothesis. However, some researchers assert that relative income or income inequality plays an equally important role in determining health. According to the relative income hypothesis (or the weak income inequality hypothesis), people who feel more economically disadvantaged than their peers in a reference group are more likely to have poorer health (Marmot *et al.* 1991; Wilkinson 1997). Low relative income may cause stress and depression leading to illness (Cohen *et al.* 1997) or weaken one's power in the allocation of local health-related resources (Deaton 2003). Some (Wilkinson 1996) go even further and argue that income inequality may affect the health of both the poor and the well-off in a society (referred to as the strong income inequality hypothesis), possibly through disinvestment in public health and human capital, the erosion of social capital, or stressful social comparisons (Kawachi and Kennedy 1999).

The relative income or income inequality hypotheses have been empirically tested, but almost exclusively drawing on data from industrialized countries, and the results have been mixed.[1] The tests have been conducted at both the aggregate and individual levels. At the aggregate level, a number of studies have shown a robust association between income inequality and public health (for example, Waldmann 1992; Kaplan *et al.* 1996; Kawachi, Kennedy and Prothrow-Stith 1997; Lynch *et al.* 1998). However, the use of aggregate data may be unconvincing. As noted by Gravelle (1998), income inequality may be spuriously correlated with the aggregate measure of health if individual health is a concave function of income. It is therefore difficult to discriminate between the effects of income and income inequality using aggregate data. To differentiate between the absolute income and income inequality effects, recent studies employ individual data. Among these studies, some support the income inequality hypothesis (for example, Kennedy *et al.* 1998a; Soobader and LeClere 1999; Blakely, Kennedy and Kawachi 2001), while others find no significant effects of inequality (for example, Meara 1999; Blakely, Lochner and Kawachi 2002; Mellor and Milyo 2002).

The aim of this chapter is to test the above hypotheses and investigate the relationship between income, income inequality and health in China, using the individual data from the *China Health and Nutrition Survey* (CHNS). We find evidence supporting the absolute income hypothesis that income has a positive effect on self-reported health status. Consistent with findings by Daly *et al.* (1998), we also find evidence supporting the strong version of the income inequality hypothesis but not the weak version. However, unlike previous findings of a linear relationship, our results show an inverted-U association between self-reported health status and inequality; that is, the detrimental effect of income inequality on health only appears in communities with high inequality. We also test the effect of relative deprivation and income rank on health but find little effect of relative income on health. This is in contrast with the work of Eibner and Evans (2005), who find relative deprivation important in explaining individual health with the exception of rank. Finally, we also show that rising inequality can significantly increase one's probability of engaging in health-compromising behaviour such as smoking and alcohol abuse.

We contribute to the literature studying the relationship between income inequality and health in the following ways. First, this chapter is one of the first studies to use individual data from a developing country. Although poor health and high inequality are key features of many developing countries, the earlier literature has studied their association drawing mainly on data from the United States and other industrialized countries.[2] Moreover, as pointed out by Gerdtham and Johannesson (2004), industrial countries such as Sweden may not be the best places for studying the effects of income inequality, because these countries are typically more egalitarian and do not have sufficient variation in income inequality across regions. In contrast, China has both rising inequality and a large variation in inequality across localities (Gustafsson and Li 2002). Second, we extend the previous work by explicitly distinguishing between the relative income hypothesis and the income inequality hypothesis in the same study. Previous studies have tested either the relative income hypothesis (Deaton 2001; Eibner and Evans 2005) or the income inequality hypothesis (for example, Mellor and Milyo 2002).[3] Finally, we measure income inequality at the community level, so that our focus is more locally defined than in most previous studies, which focus on the state or county level. Using community-level inequality not only facilitates the empirical test by allowing us to work with a larger variation in inequality, but also permits us to examine the potential impacts of inequality within a society by taking a set of people who are more closely related.

Hypotheses and previous research

In our study, we attempt to examine whether health outcomes and behaviour are correlated with income and income inequality in China. We begin with a discussion of several hypotheses that link income and income distribution to health, followed by a selected review of previous empirical work. We then specify the empirical test for each hypothesis.

Hypothesis 1: Absolute income hypothesis

The absolute income hypothesis argues that people with higher incomes have better health outcomes, but income inequality or relative income has no direct effect on health. A related concept is the poverty hypothesis, which emphasizes that ill health is a consequence of low income or extreme poverty. The idea that health improves with income goes back a long way in the literature. One of the most influential works in this area is by Preston (1975), who finds that the impact of additional income on mortality is greater among the poor than the rich. In other words, there is a concave relationship between income and health.

A large number of empirical studies in a variety of disciplines (such as economics, sociology and epidemiology) demonstrate a robust association between income and health (no matter how income and health are measured) using individual data, and most of the evidence points to a nonlinear relationship.[4] We follow the literature and test whether per capita income has a positive effect on individual health.[5] However, since the protective effect of absolute income on health is relatively uncontested (compared with the effect of income inequality or relative income), we do not place too much emphasis on this test.

Hypothesis 2: Income inequality hypothesis

The income inequality hypothesis presumes that income inequality per se is a threat to the health of individuals within a society, even holding their incomes constant. It focuses on the direct tie between health and income inequality, regardless of a person's particular income level. There are several potential pathways through which income inequality might harm an individual's health directly. For example, high levels of inequality might produce instabilities in the social capital by increasing mistrust and stress, or declining social cohesion, which in turn adversely influence an individual's own health through psychosocial responses such as violent crime or self-destructive behaviour.[6]

This hypothesis has two versions (Mellor and Milyo 2002). The strong version states that inequality affects all members in a society equivalently, irrespective of their income levels. The weak version suggests that income inequality may harm the health of only the least well off in a society, or that the harmful effect of inequality on health decreases with one's income rank.

Early studies use aggregate data to test the correlation between income inequality and health. Various works by Wilkinson over the past decade (for example, Wilkinson 1992, 1996) present evidence of a relationship between income inequality and life expectancy across a number of industrialized countries, both at a point in time and over time. While Wilkinson reports correlation coefficients, a growing body of literature tests this hypothesis using regression frameworks. A link between income inequality and health measures (mortality, morbidity and so on) has been discerned repeatedly at the level of countries (Waldmann 1992; Wennemo 1993), and across states, counties and cities within nations (Ben-Shlomo, White and Marmot 1996; Kaplan *et al.* 1996; Kennedy, Kawachi and Prothrow-Stith 1996; Kawachi and Kennedy 1997; Kawachi,

Kennedy and Prothrow-Stith 1997; Lynch *et al.* 1998). In addition, some studies find an association between income distribution across states in the US and state-level measures of smoking (Kaplan *et al.* 1996), alcohol consumption (Marmot 1997), and firearm crimes (Kennedy *et al.* 1998b).

Although these studies are informative, they use aggregate data, making it hard to differentiate between the hypotheses for absolute income and income inequality. The aggregate association between income inequality and health may merely reflect the nonlinear relationship between income and health at the individual level. For example, if a transfer of one dollar from the rich to the poor improves the health of the poor more than it diminishes the health of the rich, this income-equalizing transfer will increase the average health of the whole society.[7] If all that matters to individual health is income, then for two communities with identical average income, the community with a more equal income distribution tends to have better average health than the one with greater inequality. Thus, in aggregate studies, it is hard to distinguish this statistical artefact (Gravelle 1998) from mechanisms in which income inequality has a direct effect on individual health. In order to identify the true effect of inequality, one should employ individual data.

A number of studies using US data find that income inequality does indeed have a negative effect on individual health. For instance, Kennedy *et al.* (1998a, 1998b); Soobader and LeClere (1999); Fiscella and Franks (2000); and Blakely, Kennedy and Kawachi (2001) all show a significant association between inequality (at state or county level) and self-rated health status. Daly *et al.* (1998) examine the effects of several measures of state-level income inequality on individual mortality, and find supporting evidence for the income inequality hypothesis in a particular time period. Using county and tract-level inequality data, LeClere and Soobader (2000) find supporting evidence as well, but only for some specific subgroups in counties experiencing high inequality.

In contrast, some studies indicate no association between income inequality and individual health. Measuring inequality by the proportion of income earned by the poorest 50 per cent of the population, Fiscella and Franks (1997) find no effects of county-level inequality on mortality. Meara (1999) examines the relationship between state-level inequality and birth outcomes (such as infant mortality and low birth weight), and finds no significant relation. Mellor and Milyo (2002) construct several inequality measures both at the level of states and metropolitan areas, and show that their effects on self-rated health status are eliminated once individual income and locality effects are controlled.

Using the same data as Mellor and Milyo (2002), Blakely, Lochner and Kawachi (2002) draw a similar conclusion, finding that, after controlling for income, there is little association between income inequality and individual health. A few studies using data outside the United States provide further evidence against the income inequality hypothesis (Osler *et al.* 2002; Shibuya *et al.* 2002; Gerdtham and Johannesson 2004).

Most of the existing literature focuses on the strong version of the income inequality hypothesis. Only a few studies (Daly *et al.* 1998; Meara 1999; Mellor and Milyo 2002; Gerdtham and Johannesson 2004) implicitly or explicitly test the weak version, but none of their findings support the hypothesis.

In this chapter, we test both the strong and weak versions of the inequality hypothesis. The strong version of the income inequality hypothesis is specified as follows:

$$H_{ij} = \beta_0 + \beta_1 Q_j + \beta_2 Q_j^2 + I_{ij}\Gamma + X_{ij}\Theta + \varepsilon_{ij} \tag{6.1}$$

where i and j are subscripts for individual and community, respectively. H_{ij} denotes a number of health outcomes and behaviour (self-reported health status, objective body conditions, smoking, alcohol use and so on); Q_j stands for community-level income inequality; I_{ij} is the vector of per capita income and income squared; and X_{ij} is the vector of other individual, household and community variables. We also include the squared term of inequality to capture the potential nonlinear effect. We hypothesize that health outcomes deteriorate with income inequality ($\beta_1 < 0$), but the relation might not be linear ($\beta_2 \neq 0$).

To test the weak version, we extend equation (6.1) by introducing the interaction between inequality and a person's rank (in the ascending order of income), denoted by R_{ij}, to allow the effects of income inequality to vary by the relative income level. The model is

$$H_{ij} = \beta_0 + \beta_1 Q_j + \beta_2 Q_j^2 + \delta R_{ij} + \eta Q_j \cdot R_{ij} + I_{ij}\Gamma + X_{ij}\Theta + \varepsilon_{ij} \tag{6.2}$$

We expect a positive coefficient of the interaction term ($\eta > 0$), or that the negative effect of inequality on health outcomes is smaller for people with higher income rankings.

Hypothesis 3: Relative income hypothesis

The relative income hypothesis states that health depends on an individual's income relative to others in his or her group, rather than an individual's absolute income. According to this hypothesis, health declines when one is financially deprived relative to one's peers, and improves when one is prosperous relative to others. A similar hypothesis is the relative position hypothesis, which stresses that one's relative rank in a group is related to health outcomes.[8]

Some psychosocial and material factors may play a role in the mechanisms connecting relative income to health. Perceptions of being relatively deprived compared to their peers may make people stressed and depressed, thus diminishing their health directly through diseases or indirectly via health-compromising behaviour.[9] Another possibility is that within a community, relative income (or rank) may be more important in determining an individual's access to material goods or services that are correlated with health.[10]

The relative income hypothesis is consistent with an effect of income inequality, but the two are not totally equivalent. If inequality increases, the poor are made even poorer in relative terms, and the rich become relatively more prosperous. Thus, the harmful effect of income inequality is greater among the least well off. In this sense, the relative income theory parallels the weak version of the income inequality hypothesis. However, the strong version of the income inequality hypothesis goes further than the relative income hypothesis. According to the strong version, even rich people, who are least deprived in terms of relative income, may still suffer the adverse impacts of high level income inequality. Thus, the strong version suggests that income inequality might directly influence health through channels independent of relative income.

Studies using different measures of relative income generate mixed results. Some recent research uses the mean (or median) income of a community as a proxy for relative income, but finds no evidence supporting the hypothesis (for example, Robert 1998; Gerdtham and Johannesson 2004). However, the Whitehall study in Britain (Marmot, Shipley and Rose 1984; Marmot *et al.* 1991), one of the most widely known studies on relative income (position), finds higher rates of morbidity and mortality among civil servants in the lower administrative ranks. The contributions by Deaton (2001) and Eibner and Evans (2005) are more interesting, since they measure the level of relative income more specifically by the differences between an individual's income and the incomes of the richer members of the group. Using these measures, which are called relative deprivation (RD),[11] they both find a significant relative income effect on individual mortality from US data. Moreover, Eibner and Evans (2005) show that relative deprivation also influences the probability that an individual will engage in health-compromising behaviour, such as smoking and not wearing a seatbelt while driving.

Following Eibner and Evans (2005), we test the relative income hypothesis using the following specification:

$$H_{ij} = \beta_0 + \beta_1 RD_{ij} + I_{ij}\Gamma + X_{ij}\Theta + \varepsilon_{ij} \qquad (6.3)$$

Equation (6.3) is similar to equation (6.1), except that we replace Q_j with RD_{ij}, which stands for relative deprivation indices that measure an individual's relative income (see the section on 'Income inequality and relative income measures' for details). The difference in subscripts between Q_j and RD_{ij} means that income inequality is an aggregate measure for the whole community, while the relative income measures that we use are individual specific. We hypothesize that higher relative deprivation of income (or lower relative rank) reduces the probability of being healthy, and increases the probability of participating in health-compromising behaviour.

Data

In this chapter, we use the China Health and Nutrition Survey (CHNS) data, which were collected by the Carolina Population Center (CPC) at the University of North Carolina at Chapel Hill, the Institute of Nutrition and Food Hygiene, and the Chinese Academy of Preventive Medicine.[12] The CHNS was a longitudinal survey with five waves in 1989, 1991, 1993, 1997 and 2000. The sample households were randomly drawn from eight provinces including Liaoning, Shandong, Jiangsu, Henan, Hubei, Hunan, Guangxi and Guizhou.[13] Two cities and four counties were sampled in each province. We then randomly selected: four neighbourhoods in each city, one county-town neighbourhood, and three villages in each county. We define a neighbourhood or village as a community unit.[14] Approximately 20 households were sampled per community.

The CHNS data contain detailed information on household and individual characteristics as well as health-related information such as self-reported health status, physical functions, activities of daily living and health behaviour. We use the wave of 1993 for our basic cross section analysis because the 1993 CHNS has the richest set of health variables. We restrict our sample to men and women who were at least 20 years old in 1993 and had a complete set of data on health and demographic variables (age, sex, marital status, education and so on). As we need to construct income inequality and relative deprivation indices, we also exclude those with non-positive household income. In total, we have 7286 observations in the 1993 sample.

We also conduct some panel analysis using four waves of 1991 to 2000, though the panel analysis is limited by the data. Although the CHNS data are longitudinal, some health measures are not consistently reported across all the rounds. For example, the 1989 survey did not report many health outcomes, such as the self-reported health status. The 1991 survey did not have questions on activities of daily living, while the 1997 and 2000 waves changed physical functions to rarer diseases. The only health variables consistently available through the later four waves are self-reported health status, blood pressure and health behaviour.

Table 6.1 summarizes the definitions of key variables in our sample. We now discuss a variety of measurement issues that need to be clarified before we present the estimation results.

Health indicators

The CHNS data offer several potential health measures, as shown in the top panel of Table 6.1. Self-reported health status (SRHS) is the main health measure we use. Although SRHS is a subjective measure of individual health,[15] previous studies show that SRHS is highly correlated with subsequent mortality, even when controlling for more objective health measures (Idler and Benyamini 1997; Deaton and Paxson 1998). We construct a binary variable, *SRHS*, which equals 1 if excellent or good health is reported and equals 0 if fair or poor health is reported.[16]

We also use several objective health measures such as physical functions (PF) and activities of daily living (ADL), which are recorded in the physical examination section of the survey. PF provides information on the status of various body functions associated with heart, hearing, eyesight, arms, legs and so on. We construct five indicators as PF measures: heart, lungs and stomach condition (henceforth *heart*); blood pressure (*blood*); upper extremities condition (*upper*); lower extremities condition (*lower*); and urine and bowel control (*urine*). As with *SRHS*, we define them as binary variables that equal 1 if the function is normal and 0 otherwise. ADL measures whether or not the individual is physically restricted or unable to perform daily activities, such as walking for a certain distance (*walk*), lifting a certain weight (*lift*), climbing a staircase (*climb*), taking a bath alone (*shower*), and eating and drinking alone (*eat*). Again, we create binary variables that are equal to 1 if respondents were able to perform the activities, and equal to 0 if respondents reported any difficulty in these activities. However, ADL measures are unavailable for individuals under 50; thus, we can only use this measure for a smaller sample of the elderly.

In addition to these direct measures, the CHNS data also contain information on certain health compromising behaviours, such as smoking and

Table 6.1 Definitions of key variables

Variables	Definition
Self-reported health status (SRHS)	1 if health is excellent or good, 0 if fair or poor
Physical functions (PF)	
Heart	1 if normal in condition of heart, lungs, and stomach, 0 if otherwise
Blood	1 if normal blood pressure, 0 if high blood pressure
Upper	1 if normal in upper extremities, 0 if otherwise
Lower	1 if normal in lower extremities, 0 if otherwise
Urine	1 if normal in urine and bowel control, 0 if otherwise
Activities of daily living (ADL) (for 50+ years old)	
Walk	1 if able to walk for a kilometre, 0 if with limitation
Lift	1 if able to lift a 5 kg bag, 0 if with limitation
Climb	1 if able to climb a staircase, 0 if with limitation
Shower	1 if able to take the shower alone, 0 if needs help
Eat	1 if able to eat alone, 0 if needs help
Health behaviours	
Current smoker	1 if smokes at the survey time, 0 if not
Cigarettes per day	Average number of cigarettes smoked per day
Current drinker	1 if drinks alcoholic beverage in the previous year of the survey, 0 if not
Drinking frequency	0 if does not drink, 1 if no more than once a month, 2 if once or twice a month, 3 if once or twice a week, 4 if 3–4 times a week, 5 if daily or almost everyday
Inequality and relative deprivation	
Gini	Gini coefficient of income within the community
Rank	Centile rank (in the ascending order of income) within the community
RDA	Yitzhaki's relative deprivation index: $RDA_i = \Sigma(y_j - y_i)/N$, for all $y_j > y_i$ where y_i is the income of person i and N is the size of the community
RDL	Substituting log(y) for y in RDA
RDI	RDA/y; that is, dividing RDA by one's own income
Other variables	
Income	Deflated per capita household income
Education	Years of formal schooling
Family size	Number of household members
Tap water	1 if pipe or tap water inside house or courtyard, 0 if otherwise
Distance	Average distance (km) from the community to frequently used facilities
Rural	1 if the community is a village unit, 0 if an urban unit

alcohol consumption. Regarding smoking behaviour, we have knowledge of whether or not an individual smoked at the time of the survey, and the number of cigarettes smoked per day. Regarding drinking behaviour, we know whether or not an individual had drunk any alcoholic beverage in the year prior to the survey, and the frequency of drinking. In total, we have four variables to measure health behaviour; that is, *current smoker*, *cigarettes per day*, *current drinker*, and *drinking frequency*, as illustrated in Table 6.1. As most of the smokers and drinkers were men in our sample, we limit the analysis of health behaviour to men who had non-missing behaviour variables.

Table 6.2 (column 1) provides descriptive statistics concerning these health measures. SRHS and PF measures are available for the whole sample, but ADL and health behaviour variables are only available for smaller samples. Among all individuals, 73 per cent reported being in good health. Examining the data in two gender groups, we find that men are more healthy than women, with 76 per cent of men but only 70 per cent of women reporting themselves in good health. The proportion declines with age, as only 56 per cent of those over 50 report themselves to be in good health. By contrast, higher normal rates are reported for the PF measures, all exceeding 90 per cent for the whole sample. The proportion of people with no limitations in ADL is closer to that for SRHS, although it should be remembered that the sample is much smaller. Finally, 69 per cent of men were smoking at the time of the survey, and 63 per cent reported that they drank during the year prior to the survey.

Income inequality and relative income measures

In this chapter, we use the Gini coefficient to measure the community-level income inequality.[17] For every community, we calculate the Gini based on household income weighted by the family size.[18] In total, there are about 180 communities in our sample. The Gini ranges from 0.1 to 0.6, with the average value around 0.32 (Table 6.2).

Following Eibner and Evans (2005), we construct several relative deprivation indices as the proxy for relative income; that is, relative deprivation of absolute income (*RDA*), relative deprivation of log income (*RDL*), relative deprivation over individual income (*RDI*), and individual rank. Based on the theory developed by Yitzhaki (1979), *RDA* is defined as:

$$\text{RDA}_i = \frac{1}{N}\sum_j (y_j - y_i) \quad \forall \quad y_j > y_i \tag{6.4}$$

It measures the relative deprivation of person i with income y_i in a reference group of N people by the normalized total incomes of other group

Table 6.2 Descriptive statistics of health, inequality and other variables in China

Variables	Mean and (standard deviation)			
		Healthy versus unhealthy		
	Full sample (1)	SRHS = 1 (2)	SRHS = 0 (3)	*t*-statistics (4)
SRHS all	0.730 (0.444)	–	–	–
SRHS men	0.757 (0.429)	–	–	–
SRHS women	0.703 (0.457)	–	–	–
SRHS 50+ years old	0.556 (0.497)	–	–	–
Heart	0.928 (0.259)	–	–	–
Blood	0.948 (0.221)	–	–	–
Upper	0.936 (0.245)	–	–	–
Lower	0.936 (0.245)	–	–	–
Urine	0.995 (0.070)	–	–	–
Walk[a]	0.758 (0.428)	–	–	–
Lift[a]	0.726 (0.446)	–	–	–
Climb[a]	0.661 (0.473)	–	–	–
Shower[a]	0.938 (0.242)	–	–	–
Eat[a]	0.989 (0.103)	–	–	–
Current smoker[b]	0.688 (0.463)	–	–	–
Cigarettes per day[b]	10.82 (10.07)	–	–	–
Current drinker[b]	0.629 (0.483)	–	–	–
Drinking frequency[b]	2.275 (2.008)	–	–	–
Gini	0.323 (0.099)	0.323 (0.098)	0.322 (0.100)	0.61
Rank	0.498 (0.303)	0.508 (0.304)	0.471 (0.300)	4.65***
RDA (/1000)	0.429 (0.408)	0.423 (0.414)	0.443 (0.392)	1.84*
RDL	0.377 (0.512)	0.367 (0.514)	0.405 (0.505)	2.86***
RDI	1.224 (5.066)	1.177 (4.666)	1.353 (6.015)	1.32
Income (1000 *yuan*)	1.373 (1.246)	1.411 (1.271)	1.273 (1.171)	4.20***
Age	43.47 (14.85)	40.89 (13.69)	50.44 (15.62)	25.43***
Male	0.498 (0.500)	0.516 (0.500)	0.448 (0.497)	5.20***
Married	0.834 (0.372)	0.845 (0.362)	0.803 (0.398)	4.30***
Education	6.052 (4.381)	6.536 (4.219)	4.742 (4.541)	15.78***
Family size	4.414 (1.590)	4.463 (1.541)	4.283 (1.706)	4.29***
Tap water	0.629 (0.483)	0.631 (0.482)	0.621 (0.485)	0.81
Distance (km)	1.495 (2.767)	1.438 (2.592)	1.650 (3.187)	2.90***
Rural	0.676 (0.468)	0.686 (0.464)	0.651 (0.477)	2.81***
Households per community	18.37 (2.04)	–	–	–
Individuals per community	75.78 (16.09)	–	–	–
Sample size	7286	5320	1966	–

Notes: Standard deviations are shown in parentheses; *, **, and *** represent significance levels of 10, 5, and 1 per cent; [a] reported only by individuals aged 50+; [b] women are excluded.
Source: 1993 CHNS, adults 20+ years old.

members who earn more than *i*. *RDL* is the same as *RDA* except that it uses log(y) rather than y in (6.4). *RDI* equals RDA_i/y_i; namely the ratio of *RDA* relative to person *i*'s own income. The final index we use is the individual's centile rank within the reference group (where income is sorted in the ascending order). In contrast to the first three measures, the rank ignores the magnitude of the income difference between individuals. While larger values in *RDA*, *RDL* and *RDI* indicate higher levels of relative deprivation, a higher centile rank indicates a lower level.

As the Gini coefficient depicts the overall income distribution of a society, relative deprivation reflects a person's position or rank relative to the incomes of others within a reference group. In order to be consistent with the Gini coefficient, we use households in the same community as the reference group to generate these *RD* measures.[19] The summary statistics of our relative deprivation measures are reported in Table 6.2. Unlike the Gini, which is bounded between 0 and 1, relative deprivation measures (*RDA*, *RDL*, and *RDI*) are not limited in value and therefore have larger variations in the sample.

Other explanatory variables

In the individual level analysis, we control for variables including per capita income and income squared, age and age squared, education, indicators for gender and marital status, family size, source of drinking water (tap water or not), the distance from the community to nearby medical facilities,[20] and rural and provincial indicators. We show the descriptive statistics for these variables in the bottom panel of Table 6.2. Individuals in our sample have an average income of 1373 *yuan*,[21] an average age of 43 and, on average, 6 years of schooling.

In Table 6.2, we also divide the sample into two sub-samples: good health and poor health (columns 2 and 3). The differences in personal characteristics between the two sub-samples are what we would intuitively expect. Specifically, we find that, on average, healthy people have higher levels of per capita income and education, and are much younger than unhealthy ones. Those in good health also live in larger families and closer to medical facilities. The role of income inequality is less explicit, as the average Gini coefficients for the two groups are very close. On the other hand, the poor health group on average is slightly more deprived, as indicated by its smaller mean of individual ranks and larger mean of the other three indices. The *t*-ratios in column 4 show that most of the means are significantly different between the two sub-samples, except for some inequality and relative deprivation variables.

Estimation results

In this section, we use the 1993 CHNS sample to test various hypotheses previously discussed in a systematic manner. The main purpose of our study is to examine the correlation between individual health and income inequality or relative income. We also perform panel data analysis using four rounds of the CHNS data from 1991 to 2000.

Income, income inequality and health

We first employ a probit model to test the income inequality hypothesis (Hypothesis 2), in both the strong and weak versions. We apply models (6.1) and (6.2) to various health measures (such as *SRHS*, *PF*, *ADL*) and health behaviour, using individual level data. Our specifications also allow for a test of the absolute income hypothesis (Hypothesis 1), even though it is not our focus.

Self-reported health status

Table 6.3 presents the results of probit regressions using *SRHS* as the dependent variable. The results exhibit an inverted-U; that is, a quadratic relationship between *SRHS* and income inequality. We report d*F*/d*x*, or the marginal change of probability of reporting excellent or good health, when the independent variable increases.[22] In the first column, we have the Gini as the only independent variable. The coefficient of the Gini is positive but not significant. When we add the squared term in the second column, the correlation is still insignificant. However, in column 3, the coefficients of the Gini and Gini squared both become significant at the 5 per cent level, after we include other control variables such as per capita income, and personal and household characteristics. The positive coefficient of the Gini and negative coefficient of Gini squared mean that *SRHS* increases with inequality when Gini is less than 0.42 (75 percentile in the sample) and decreases with inequality for larger Gini. The results suggest that the strong version of the income inequality hypothesis (Hypothesis 2) is only supported for communities with considerable inequality.[23]

We also find evidence supporting the absolute income hypothesis (Hypothesis 1). Column 3 shows that there is a concave relationship between individual health and per capita income. The positive coefficient of income and negative coefficient of income squared are both significant at the 1 per cent level. The critical point of the health–income quadratic curve is about 7667 *yuan*, but 99 per cent of the values for income in our sample are below this figure. This means that, for most of our sample, health increases with absolute income, but at a decreasing rate.

Table 6.3 Probit regressions measuring the effects of income inequality on self-reported health status

	Dependent variable: self-reported health status (1 = excellent or good, 0 = fail or poor)			
	(1)	(2)	(3)	(4)
Gini	0.032	0.313	1.029**	1.147**
	(0.46)	(0.80)	(2.33)	(2.51)
Gini squared		−0.416	−1.236**	−1.176*
		(−0.73)	(−1.96)	(−1.87)
Rank				0.140*
				(1.78)
Gini*rank				−0.352
				(−1.54)
Income			0.046***	0.038**
			(3.81)	(2.34)
Income squared			−0.003***	−0.003*
			(−2.59)	(−1.83)
Education			0.004**	0.004**
			(2.00)	(1.98)
Male			0.037***	0.037***
			(4.26)	(4.25)
Married			0.043**	0.043**
			(2.28)	(2.32)
Family size			0.011**	0.011**
			(2.12)	(2.20)
Tap water			0.030*	0.032*
			(1.72)	(1.80)
Distance			−0.002	−0.002
			(−0.71)	(−0.76)
Rural			0.013	0.012
			(0.70)	(0.64)
Provincial indicators	No	No	Yes	Yes
Number of observations	7286	7286	7286	7286
Pseudo *R*-squared	0.00	0.00	0.09	0.09

Note: *, **, and *** represent significance levels of 10, 5, and 1 per cent; robust *t*-statistics, which allow for correlation of errors within household, are shown in parentheses; regressions 3 and 4 include age and age squared.

Other control variables also have the expected signs in column 3. The probability of being in good health decreases with age at a rate of 1 percentage point per year (not shown). One more year of schooling increases the probability of being in good health by 0.4 percentage points. Men have a 3.7 percentage points higher probability of being in good health than women, and married people have a 4.3 percentage points higher probability than single people. A one standard deviation increase in family size (1.6) raises the probability by 1.8 percentage points. Having access to tap water increases the probability of reporting good health by 3 percentage points. Finally, the distance to medical facilities has a negative sign but is statistically insignificant.

Next, in column 4, we test the weak version of the income inequality hypothesis; that is, whether the effects of inequality differ by relative income. As in the previous regression, the Gini has a quadratic form of effect on health. Although the individual rank has a positive effect (significant at the 10 per cent level), the interaction between the Gini and the rank is negative and not statistically different from zero. The result implies that the effect of income inequality does not vary with relative income, and the negative sign on the interaction seems to contradict what is predicted by the weak version of the income inequality hypothesis, that income inequality harms the health of the poor more than the rich.

In short, the results in Table 6.3 show that community level income inequality influences individual health status in a nonlinear way. According to the estimated coefficients, income inequality tends to have a detrimental impact on health when a community has considerable inequality (the Gini above 0.40, in column 3). The higher individual rank is beneficial to one's health, but income inequality has the same effect for each community member, regardless of his or her rank.

Physical functions

Table 6.4 reports estimations using two PF variables as dependent variables: the condition of heart, lungs and stomach (*heart*), and the condition of blood pressure (*blood*).[24] We find a nonlinear relationship between the Gini and heart function (columns 1 to 3), but no correlation between the Gini and blood pressure (columns 4 to 6). The effects are not altered by one's relative income position, as the coefficients of the interaction term are both insignificant (columns 3 and 6). Compared to previous estimates for *SRHS*, fewer control variables remain significant. These results are probably due to the lack of variation for the PF measures. For example, the proportion of people reporting normal heart condition is 93 per cent, and the proportion reporting normal blood pressure is 95 per cent.

Activities of daily living

As another check, we estimate the influence of income inequality on ADL measures in a restricted sub-sample of elderly people in Table 6.5. The two dependent variables we use here are indicators of whether one

Table 6.4 Probit regressions measuring the effects of income inequality on physical functions

	Dependent variable: heart (1 = normal in heart, lung, and stomach, 0 = otherwise)			**Dependent variable: blood (1 = normal blood pressure, 0 = high blood pressure)**		
	(1)	(2)	(3)	(4)	(5)	(6)
Gini	0.051	0.423**	0.441**	0.005	−0.069	−0.050
	(1.42)	(2.51)	(2.53)	(0.33)	(−0.81)	(−0.57)
Gini squared		−0.543**	−0.548**		0.112	0.106
		(−2.20)	(−2.23)		(0.90)	(0.86)
Rank			0.003			−0.001
			(0.08)			(−0.09)
Gini*rank			−0.023			−0.020
			(−0.23)			(−0.43)
Income	0.004	0.005	0.006	−0.004*	−0.004*	−0.002
	(0.84)	(0.91)	(0.93)	(−1.83)	(−1.83)	(−0.61)
Income squared	−0.000	−0.000	−0.000	0.000	0.000	0.000
	(−0.52)	(−0.53)	(−0.65)	(0.64)	(0.59)	(0.00)
Education	0.000	0.000	0.000	−0.000	−0.001	−0.001
	(0.07)	(0.23)	(0.21)	(−1.21)	(−1.26)	(−1.34)
Male	0.013**	0.012**	0.012**	0.004	0.004	0.004
	(2.05)	(1.98)	(1.98)	(1.37)	(1.37)	(1.45)

(*Continued*)

Table 6.4 continued

	Dependent variable: heart (1 = normal in heart, lung, and stomach, 0 = otherwise)			Dependent variable: blood (1 = normal blood pressure, 0 = high blood pressure)		
	(1)	(2)	(3)	(4)	(5)	(6)
Married	0.006	0.005	0.005	−0.007*	−0.007*	−0.007*
	(0.66)	(0.59)	(0.59)	(−1.68)	(−1.66)	(−1.67)
Family size	0.000	0.000	0.000	0.000	0.000	0.000
	(0.17)	(0.10)	(0.08)	(0.11)	(0.16)	(0.12)
Tap water	0.016**	0.017**	0.016**	−0.007*	−0.007*	−0.007**
	(2.03)	(2.05)	(1.99)	(−1.86)	(−1.87)	(−2.02)
Distance	−0.002**	−0.002**	−0.002**	0.000	0.000	0.000
	(−2.24)	(−2.34)	(−2.31)	(0.13)	(0.20)	(0.25)
Rural	0.017**	0.014	0.014*	0.011***	0.011***	0.011***
	(2.00)	(1.64)	(1.66)	(3.00)	(3.08)	(3.15)
Number of observations	6349	6349	6349	6033	6033	6033
Pseudo R-squared	0.08	0.08	0.08	0.21	0.21	0.21

Note: *, **, and *** represent significance levels of 10, 5, and 1 per cent; robust *t*-statistics, which allow for correlation of errors within household, are shown in parentheses; all regressions include age and age squared, and provincial indicators.

Table 6.5 Probit regressions measuring the effects of income inequality on activities of daily living

	Dependent variable: walk (1 = able to walk for 1 km, 0 = having limitation)			**Dependent variable: lift (1 = able to lift a 5 kg bag, 0 = having limitation)**		
	(1)	(2)	(3)	(4)	(5)	(6)
Gini	−0.484***	0.145	0.208	−0.281**	1.267*	1.316*
	(−4.43)	(0.24)	(0.34)	(−2.28)	(1.88)	(1.87)
Gini squared		−0.897	−0.850		−2.218**	−2.191**
		(−1.08)	(−1.03)		(−2.38)	(−2.34)
Rank			0.122			0.083
			(1.13)			(0.66)
Gini*rank			−0.237			−0.166
			(−0.76)			(−0.46)
Income	0.005	0.006	−0.009	0.028	0.031	0.021
	(0.32)	(0.35)	(−0.37)	(1.45)	(1.59)	(0.79)
Income squared	0.001	0.001	0.002	−0.000	−0.000	0.000
	(0.45)	(0.45)	(0.92)	(−0.20)	(−0.19)	(0.17)
Education	0.003	0.003	0.003	−0.003	−0.002	−0.002
	(0.98)	(1.05)	(1.05)	(−0.87)	(−0.70)	(−0.70)
Male	0.127***	0.127***	0.127***	0.160***	0.159***	0.159***
	(6.17)	(6.14)	(6.13)	(7.49)	(7.42)	(7.45)

(*Continued*)

Table 6.5 continued

	Dependent variable: walk (1 = able to walk for 1 km, 0 = having limitation)			**Dependent variable: lift (1 = able to lift a 5 kg bag, 0 = having limitation)**		
	(1)	**(2)**	**(3)**	**(4)**	**(5)**	**(6)**
Married	−0.009	−0.010	−0.009	0.023	0.022	0.022
	(−0.35)	(−0.39)	(−0.37)	(0.83)	(0.79)	(0.80)
Family size	0.007	0.007	0.007	0.005	0.005	0.005
	(1.20)	(1.16)	(1.22)	(0.87)	(0.78)	(0.82)
Tap water	−0.055**	−0.055**	−0.051**	0.039	0.038	0.041
	(−2.15)	(−2.16)	(−1.96)	(1.31)	(1.28)	(1.37)
Distance	0.001	0.001	0.000	−0.002	−0.003	−0.003
	(0.24)	(0.14)	(0.13)	(−0.47)	(−0.63)	(−0.64)
Rural	−0.003	−0.007	−0.009	0.037	0.027	0.026
	(−0.11)	(−0.26)	(−0.33)	(1.32)	(0.95)	(0.91)
Number of observations	2007	2007	2007	1988	1988	1988
Pseudo *R*-squared	0.17	0.17	0.17	0.19	0.19	0.19

Note: *, **, and *** represent significance levels of 10, 5, and 1 per cent; robust *t*-statistics, which allow for correlation of errors within household, are shown in parentheses; all regressions include age and age squared, and provincial indicators.

is able to walk for 1 km and lift a 5 kg bag without difficulty. We follow the estimation specifications that were previously applied to PF indicators.

The regression results in Table 6.5 further confirm our finding that income inequality has an impact on individual health. The community Gini has a negative effect on both walking and lifting abilities (columns 1 and 4). Moreover, inequality has a nonlinear effect on lifting ability (columns 5 and 6). The estimates imply that the probability of being able to lift the bag decreases with income inequality when the Gini is greater than 0.29 (about 38 percentile in the sub-sample). The impacts of income inequality on ADL limitations are independent of the individual rank, since the interaction of Gini and rank is not significant in columns 3 and 6.

Health behaviour

Previous results show that income inequality is strongly correlated with health outcomes. We now explore one of the potential mechanisms of their correlation by examining whether an increase in income inequality raises the probability that an individual engages in behaviour that compromises health; that is, smoking and alcohol consumption. The estimation results using different dependent variables are reported in Table 6.7 (see also Table 6.8).[25]

Table 6.7 suggests a strong correlation between inequality and smoking habits (columns 1 and 2). In the first column, we have the current smoker indicator as the dependent variable. The coefficient of the Gini is positive and significant at the 5 per cent level. It predicts that a one standard deviation increase in community Gini (0.10) will increase the probability of smoking by 2.1 percentage points. We then use the Tobit model to estimate the effects on cigarettes consumed per day in the second column. As with the estimation on *current smoker*, the Gini has a strong positive effect.

However, columns 3 and 4 show that the association between inequality and drinking behaviour is not as strong. The effect of income inequality on the probability of being a *current drinker* is positive and significant at the 10 per cent level, but the effect on drinking frequency appears marginally insignificant, albeit the same sign. In particular, the coefficient of the Gini indicates that a rise in the Gini by one standard deviation (0.10) will increase the probability of drinking alcohol by 1.8 per cent.

Relative income and health

We now test the relative income theory (Hypothesis 3) by replacing the independent variables of inequality with relative deprivation measures: *RDA*, *RDL*, *RDI*, and *individual rank*. The model to be estimated is equation (6.3).

Table 6.6 Probit regressions measuring the effects of income inequality on

	Dependent variables: physical functions (1 = normal, 0 = otherwise)					
	Upper		Lower		Urine	
	(1)	(2)	(3)	(4)	(5)	(6)
Gini	−0.029	−0.207	0.021	0.020	−0.004	−0.049**
	(−1.02)	(−1.27)	(0.72)	(0.12)	(−0.97)	(−2.37)
Gini squared		0.259		0.002		0.068**
		(1.11)		(0.01)		(2.22)
Income	−0.003	−0.003	−0.001	−0.001	−0.000	−0.000
	(−0.75)	(−0.75)	(−0.13)	(−0.13)	(−0.42)	(−0.51)
Income squared	−0.000	−0.000	−0.000	−0.000	0.000	0.000
	(−0.15)	(−0.18)	(−0.45)	(−0.45)	(0.55)	(0.51)
Number of observations	6447	6447	6443	6443	6444	6444
Pseudo *R*-squared	0.13	0.13	0.14	0.14	0.15	0.16

Note: *, **, and *** represent significance levels of 10, 5, and 1 per cent; robust *t*-statistics, regressions include age and age squared, education, gender, marital status, family size, tap

Because these measures are highly correlated with each other, their effects are estimated separately.

The estimation results with *SRHS* as the dependent variable (Table 6.9) show that the relative income hypothesis is not supported for any relative deprivation measure examined.[26] Across all the columns, none of the coefficients of *RDA*, *RDL*, *RDI*, or *rank* is statistically different from zero at the 10 per cent level. We conduct the same estimations taking PF/ADL and health behaviour measures as dependent variables, and again do not find any significant correlations with the relative deprivation indices (hence, not reported). Our results differ from those of Eibner and Evans (2005), who find that the relative deprivation has a strong impact on health when it reflects income differences between individuals (measured in *RDA*, *RDL*, and *RDI*), although their results are imprecise in many cases when they measure relative deprivation using rank.

Lagged inequality measures

Although the above results show a significant correlation between community level inequality and individual health, it may not have shown a

other objective health measures

Dependent variables: activities of daily living (1 = no limitation, 0 = otherwise)					
Climb		Shower		Eat	
(1)	(2)	(3)	(4)	(5)	(6)
−0.040	0.109	0.010	0.194	0.023**	0.011
(−0.29)	(0.14)	(0.24)	(0.91)	(2.05)	(0.23)
	−0.214		−0.268		0.019
	(−0.20)		(−0.90)		(0.28)
0.032	0.032	−0.006	−0.006	0.001	0.001
(1.56)	(1.57)	(−0.87)	(−0.86)	(0.96)	(0.96)
−0.001	−0.001	0.000	0.000	−0.0002*	−0.0002*
(−0.50)	(−0.51)	(0.36)	(0.42)	(−1.77)	(−1.82)
2001	2001	1971	1971	1764	1764
0.13	0.13	0.23	0.23	0.22	0.22

which allow for correlation of errors within household, are shown in parentheses; all water, distance to the medical facility, rural dummy, and provincial indicators.

causal effect. It could be that individual health affects income and, thus, income inequality, in which case there is a reverse causality. There could also be some unobserved variables that have effects on both income inequality and individual health. Generally, it is very difficult to solve these problems given the limitations of data. Nonetheless, we attempt to address these concerns in part using the panel structure of the CHNS data. Specifically, we replace the income and income inequality measures with lagged values.

In Table 6.10, we report the same regressions as in Tables 6.3, 6.4, 6.5 and 6.7, except that we substitute the lagged value of income and income inequality (from the 1991 CHNS) for the current value. Using lagged variables can help us to identify the causal effect from inequality to health, because current health status should not affect past income levels or income inequality. Due to space limitation, we only report the coefficients of inequality and income variables, and suppress the coefficients of other control variables. As shown by Table 6.10, the lagged income inequality has a highly significant effect on *SRHS* (column 2).[27] Similar to the estimates in Table 6.3, the effect takes a quadratic form

Table 6.7 Estimations of the effects of income inequality on health behaviour

	Dependent variable: smoking		Dependent variable: drinking	
	Current smoker	**Cigarettes per day**	**Current drinker**	**Drinking frequency**
	Probit (1)	**Tobit (2)**	**Probit (3)**	**OLS (4)**
Gini	0.206**	8.212***	0.177*	0.645
	(2.11)	(2.84)	(1.73)	(1.61)
Income	0.011	0.423*	0.030***	0.135***
	(1.50)	(1.91)	(3.68)	(4.41)
Education	−0.010***	−0.315***	0.005**	0.003
	(−3.66)	(−4.00)	(2.01)	(0.25)
Married	0.123***	4.514***	0.060**	0.410***
	(4.20)	(5.06)	(1.96)	(3.55)
Family size	0.001	0.051	0.001	0.016
	(0.20)	(0.30)	(0.17)	(1.61)
Tap water	0.009	0.814	0.032	0.293***
	(0.44)	(1.28)	(1.46)	(3.32)
Distance	−0.010***	−0.452***	0.001	−0.013
	(−2.97)	(−4.45)	(0.42)	(−1.04)
Rural	0.039*	1.789***	0.011	0.153
	(1.76)	(2.69)	(0.45)	(1.61)
Number of observations	3004	2899	3092	3083
(Pseudo) *R*-squared	0.04	0.01	0.04	0.04

Note: *, **, and *** represent significance levels of 10, 5, and 1 per cent; robust *t*-statistics, which allow for correlation of errors within households, are shown in parentheses; all regressions include age and age squared, and provincial indicators.

with the critical value of the Gini at 0.35. Lagged inequality also has a significant effect on the blood pressure, but not on other dependent variables.[28]

Conclusion

In this chapter, we employ micro data from China to test several hypotheses linking income and income inequality to individual health status. We find some evidence supporting these hypotheses. First, our results show a concave relationship between self-reported health status and per capita income (the absolute income hypothesis). Additional

Table 6.8 Probit regressions measuring the effects of income inequality on SRHS with control of behaviour

	Dependent variable: self-reported health status (1 = excellent or good, 0 = fail or poor)					
	(1)	(2)	(3)	(4)	(5)	(6)
Gini	0.959*	1.068*	1.047*			
	(1.95)	(1.97)	(1.90)			
Gini squared	−1.186*	−1.290*	−1.271			
	(−1.67)	(−1.65)	(−1.61)			
Income	0.042***	0.037***	0.032**			
	(3.28)	(2.57)	(2.10)			
Income squared	−0.003**	−0.003*	−0.002			
	(−2.30)	(−1.76)	(−1.10)			
Smoker		0.018	0.017			
		(0.67)	(0.63)			
Cigarettes per day		0.002	0.001			
		(1.29)	(0.95)			
Drinker			−0.046			
			(−1.38)			
Drinking frequency			0.023***			
			(2.80)			
Lagged Gini				1.748***	1.600***	1.673***
				(4.30)	(3.62)	(3.70)
Lagged Gini squared				−2.537*	−2.371***	−2.459***
				(−4.11)	(−3.49)	(−3.53)
Lagged income				0.030	0.022	0.025
				(1.64)	(0.99)	(1.12)

(*Continued*)

Table 6.8 continued

	Dependent variable: self-reported health status (1 = excellent or good, 0 = fail or poor)					
	(1)	(2)	(3)	(4)	(5)	(6)
Lagged income squared				0.001	0.001	0.000
				(0.19)	(0.27)	(0.10)
Lagged smoker					0.026	0.010
					(1.06)	(0.41)
Lagged cigarettes per day					0.001	0.001
					(1.07)	(1.13)
Lagged drinker						0.044
						(1.45)
Lagged drinking frequency						0.000
						(0.06)
Number of observations	3626	2899	2875	3626	2987	2928
Pseudo *R*-squared	0.09	0.09	0.10	0.10	0.10	0.10

Note: *, **, and *** represent significance levels of 10, 5, and 1 per cent; robust *t*-statistics, which allow for correlation of errors within household, are shown in parentheses; lagged variables are obtained from 1991 CHNS; all regressions include age and age squared, education, gender, marital status, family size, tap water, distance to the medical facility, rural dummy, and provincial indicators.

Table 6.9 Probit regressions measuring the effects of relative deprivation on self-reported health status

	Dependent variable: self-reported health status (1 = excellent or good, 0 = fail or poor)			
	(1)	**(2)**	**(3)**	**(4)**
RDA (/1000)	0.006 (0.30)			
RDL		−0.001 (−0.05)		
RDI			0.000 (0.78)	
Rank				0.048 (1.49)
Income	0.040*** (3.23)	0.038*** (2.77)	0.038*** (3.32)	0.023 (1.50)
Income squared	−0.003** (−2.10)	−0.003* (−1.87)	−0.003** (−2.08)	−0.002 (−1.08)
Education	0.003 (1.58)	0.003 (1.60)	0.003 (1.59)	0.003* (1.71)
Male	0.039*** (4.50)	0.039*** (4.49)	0.039*** (4.50)	0.038*** (4.42)
Married	0.044** (2.34)	0.044** (2.35)	0.044** (2.34)	0.044** (2.37)
Family size	0.011** (2.17)	0.011** (2.18)	0.011** (2.18)	0.012** (2.23)
Tap water	0.025 (1.41)	0.026 (1.50)	0.025 (1.50)	0.031* (1.75)
Distance	−0.002 (−0.71)	−0.002 (−0.74)	−0.002 (−0.74)	−0.002 (−0.84)
Rural	0.025 (1.40)	0.024 (1.38)	0.024 (1.38)	0.021 (1.20)
Number of observations	7286	7286	7286	7286
Pseudo *R*-squared	0.09	0.09	0.09	0.09

Note: *, **, and *** represent significance levels of 10, 5, and 1 per cent; robust *t*-statistics, which allow for correlation of errors within households, are shown in parentheses; all regressions include age and age squared, and provincial indicators.

income brings about greater improvement in the health of the poor than of the rich. Second, we find a significant association between self-reported health status and community-level income inequality (the income inequality hypothesis). In fact, the relationship we find appears as an inverted-U shape. That is to say, rising inequality tends to improve

Table 6.10 Probit regressions measuring the effects of lagged income inequality

	Dependent variables					
	SRHS		Heart		Blood	
	(1)	(2)	(3)	(4)	(5)	(6)
Lagged Gini	0.108	2.130***	−0.022	−0.003	0.036*	0.080
	(1.12)	(5.61)	(−0.54)	(−0.02)	(1.84)	(1.09)
Lagged Gini squared		−3.082***		−0.029		−0.071
		(−5.31)		(−0.13)		(−0.62)
Lagged income	0.020	0.022	0.011*	0.011*	−0.004	−0.004
	(1.15)	(1.24)	(1.76)	(1.76)	(−1.45)	(−1.42)
Lagged income squared	0.002	0.002	−0.001*	−0.001*	0.000	0.000
	(0.60)	(0.67)	(−1.93)	(−1.92)	(0.87)	(0.86)
Number of observations	7286	7286	6349	6349	6033	6033
Pseudo R-squared	0.09	0.09	0.08	0.08	0.21	0.21

Note: *, **, and *** represent significance levels of 10, 5, and 1 per cent; robust *t*-statistics, income and income inequality are obtained from 1991 CHNS; all regressions include to the medical facility, rural dummy, and provincial indicators.

health when inequality is low, and to harm health when inequality is above a certain level. We also find evidence that income inequality increases the likelihood and frequency of health-compromising behaviour such as smoking and alcohol consumption. However, our findings do not support the relative income hypothesis, or that the effect of inequality varies with income rank.

While this study has its own limitations, it is among the first to provide evidence from a developing country on the negative association between inequality and health, both of which are important issues for the field of development. Although the sample size is relatively small compared to the data in many US studies, the set of CHNS data we have used is so far one of the best data sets used in studying inequality and health in the context of developing economies, and is probably the best Chinese data set. Another limitation is that we only focus on one dimension of inequality: that is, community level inequality. We do not claim that community level inequality is necessarily more important than inequality at county or provincial level; rather, our purpose is to examine the socioeconomic impacts of inequality in a local setting, where we can see the people interacting with each other more closely. Focusing on the community level can also facilitate the empirical tests by allowing a larger variation of inequality

on health

Dependent variables					
Walk		Lift		Smoker	Drinker
(1)	(2)	(3)	(4)	(5)	(6)
−0.165	−0.499	0.036	−0.112	0.086	0.076
(−1.24)	(−0.86)	(0.25)	(−0.19)	(0.76)	(0.66)
	0.510		0.231		
	(0.58)		(0.27)		
0.024	0.024	0.038	0.038	−0.001	0.000
(1.14)	(1.12)	(1.55)	(1.54)	(−0.12)	(0.03)
−0.000	−0.000	−0.000	−0.000		
(−0.08)	(−0.08)	(−0.00)	(−0.00)		
2007	2007	1988	1988	3004	3092
0.16	0.16	0.19	0.19	0.04	0.03

which allow for correlation of errors within households, are shown in parentheses; lagged age and age squared, education, gender, marital status, family size, tap water, distance

in the sample. Finally, strictly speaking, our empirical tests are tests of correlations between community level inequality and individual health. The causal link may not be established until more evidence becomes available regarding the intermediate mechanisms through which inequality affects health.

China began its economic reform by abandoning the principle of absolute equality, 'eating from the same kitchen system', in agriculture (Lin 1992), in industry (Li 1997) and even in government (Qian and Weingast 1997). The reforms have improved incentives in most workplaces, which in turn has led to historic levels of growth in the past 25 years. However, the ever-increasing inequality that accompanies growth will ultimately slow it down. A recent study by Benjamin, Brandt and Giles (2006) finds that village level inequality is negatively associated with village economic growth in the long run. While there are many channels through which inequality could affect growth, our chapter shows one particular instance – poor health, which is itself a direct indicator of underdevelopment.

The Chinese government has apparently taken note of the serious issue of inequality. Wen Jiabao, the new premier, has repeatedly told the public that the goal of this government is to achieve equitable growth. The

Table 6.11 Fixed effects estimations of the effects of income inequality on health

	Dependent variables					
	SRHS		Blood		Smoker	Drinker
	(1)	(2)	(3)	(4)	(5)	(6)
Gini	0.087	0.428	0.014	−0.017	−0.012	0.044
	(1.51)	(1.60)	(0.72)	(−0.17)	(−0.22)	(0.68)
Gini squared		−0.506		0.047		
		(−1.28)		(0.31)		
Income	0.024***	0.024***	0.001	0.001	−0.007	0.008
	(2.79)	(2.80)	(0.29)	(0.29)	(−0.89)	(0.84)
Income squared	−0.001	−0.001	−0.000	−0.000	0.001	−0.001
	(−1.28)	(−1.26)	(−0.27)	(−0.28)	(1.24)	(−0.58)
Number of observations	23,597	23,597	21,067	21,067	10,429	10,620
R-squared	0.03	0.03	0.01	0.01	0.02	0.01
Lagged Gini	0.011	0.599**	0.027	−0.058	−0.002	−0.045
	(0.20)	(2.40)	(1.59)	(−0.67)	(−0.04)	(−0.70)
Lagged Gini squared		−0.811**		0.118		
		(−2.38)		(1.02)		
Lagged income	−0.001	−0.002	−0.005*	−0.005*	−0.014	−0.006
	(−0.15)	(−0.17)	(−1.85)	(−1.86)	(−1.63)	(−0.63)
Lagged income squared	0.000	0.000	0.000	0.000	0.002*	0.000
	(0.10)	(0.16)	(1.16)	(1.15)	(1.65)	(0.02)
Number of observations	23,066	23,066	20,530	20,530	10,174	10,365
Pseudo *R*-squared	0.03	0.03	0.01	0.01	0.02	0.01

Note: *, **, and *** represent significance levels of 10, 5, and 1 per cent; robust *t*-statistics, which allow for correlation of errors within household, are

government has recently been shifting its focus from the more developed coastal areas to the poor inland areas, introducing a series of preferential policies in favour of the latter; such as a wider range of fiscal subsidies, lower tax rates, and cheaper loans. The government is also shifting its focus from the fast developing industries to the sluggish agricultural sector, which employs most of China's poor. Recently, it has started to remove all agricultural taxes nationwide. While it remains to be seen how well these policies are implemented and how effective they are, the government is moving in the right direction in fighting inequality. As suggested by our results, income redistribution will improve the health of the population in regions where significant inequality prevails.

Notes

We would like to thank the Carolina Population Center for kindly supplying the data and the World Institute for Development Economics Research for an award. We are very grateful to Julan Du, Kai Yuen Tsui, Guanghua Wan and an anonymous referee for very helpful comments.

1. For a systematic review of previous empirical work, see Deaton (2003) and Lynch *et al.* (2004).
2. For example, Osler *et al.* (2002), Shibuya, Hashimoto and Yano (2002) and Gerdtham and Johannesson (2004) employ data from Denmark, Japan and Sweden, respectively.
3. Gerdtham and Johannesson (2004) test both hypotheses, but their measure of relative income is a simple one.
4. See the review by Feinstein (1993) and a more recent discussion by Smith (1999).
5. We also control for income squared to capture the nonlinear relationship between income and health.
6. Kawachi and Kennedy (1999) summarize three plausible mechanisms linking income inequality to health: disinvestment in human capital, the erosion of social capital, and stressful social comparisons.
7. Using a new data set, Deaton (2003) shows a recent version of the Preston curve and suggests that income redistribution from rich to poor countries will, in principle, increase average health worldwide.
8. The rank extends the concept of relative income, as it can be measured by socioeconomic factors other than income, such as occupation and education.
9. Some research on monkeys and primates (for example, Cohen *et al.* 1997; Shively, Laber-Laird and Anton 1997) provides biological evidence of how relative status may affect health.
10. Deaton (2003) takes the case of local housing in a town: the richest people are able to get the hilltop plots with fine views while the poorest are left with the plots downward of the smokestacks. This is an example of 'where it is not money itself that is important, but rank, here determined by money'.
11. The definition of relative deprivation is originally proposed by Runciman (1966), who argues that one is deprived if others in the group possess

something that one does not have. Yitzhaki (1979) develops the definition by viewing income as personal possessions, and shows the link between relative deprivation and income inequality.

12 A detailed description of the data and quality control procedures can be obtained from http://www.cpc.unc.edu/projects/china/

13 Liaoning was replaced by Heilongjiang in the round of 1997 and returned to the survey in 2000.

14 As a community is defined as being either a sub-unit of a city (urban) or a county (rural), constructing the income inequality and relative income at the community level avoids the situation where rural and urban households are pooled in the same reference group. Thus, in our analysis we highlight the within-community inequality rather than the substantial urban–rural gap.

15 In the survey, the interviewees were asked the question: 'Right now, how would you describe your health compared to that of other people of your age?'

16 In the survey, SRHS is a categorical variable coded on a scale of 1 (excellent) to 4 (poor).

17 Kawachi and Kennedy (1997) show that the six inequality measures (including the Gini coefficient and the Theil index) used in their study are highly correlated with each other, and the choice of inequality indicators does not change the relationship between income inequality and mortality. We also use another inequality index, the Theil index, to test the robustness of our results; the use of a different measure of inequality does not change our results qualitatively.

18 The household income used here has taken account of production costs. We also calculate the gross income by not subtracting production costs, and generate similar estimates (not shown, but available upon request).

19 On average, each community has 18 households and 75 individuals in the sample (Table 6.2).

20 The distance to medical facilities is obtained from the CHNS community survey and measures the availability of public health services to the community. We use the average distance, if more than one facility is frequently used.

21 We use the consumer price index provided in the CHNS data to adjust per capita income to prices in urban areas in the province of Liaoning.

22 The statistics that are reported here, as in all of the regressions in this chapter, allow for the correlation of errors within the household.

23 This is consistent with the findings of LeClere and Soobade (2000) who use US data.

24 To save space, we only report two PF measures here, and two ADL measures in Table 6.5. The estimates for other PF and ADL variables are compiled in Table 6.6.

25 An alternative test is to control for health behaviour in health outcome regressions to see whether these controls attenuate the effect of income inequality. We present the estimates for SRHS (male sample only) in Table 6.8, which shows that adding health behaviour does not change the estimates of income inequality significantly. These results suggest that there may exist some other mechanisms through which income inequality influences health, but exploration of these mechanisms is beyond the scope of this study.

26 This is in line with our previous finding that the weak version of the income inequality hypothesis cannot be confirmed by the sample (Table 6.3). As discussed in the section 'Hypotheses and previous research', the relative income hypothesis is a similar argument to the weak version of the income inequality hypothesis.

27 The effect remains significant after we control for lagged health behaviour in Table 6.8 (columns 4 to 6).

28 We also tried some fixed effects estimations to control for time-invariant unobservable characteristics using four waves of the CHNS data in 1991, 1993, 1997 and 2000. Due to the changes in survey questions, the only available health measures across all rounds are SRHS, blood pressure and health behaviour. As shown in Table 6.11, the lagged inequality continues to have a significant effect on SRHS. However, neither current inequality nor lagged inequality has a significant effect on other dependent variables. We may not give too much weight to these fixed effects' estimates because the health measures do not have much variation over time. For example, less than 15 per cent of the individuals changed SRHS across waves, even fewer for objective measures.

References

Aghion, P., Caroli, E. and Garcia-Penalosa, C. (1999) 'Inequality and Economic Growth: The Perspective of the New Growth Theories', *Journal of Economic Literature*, 37: 1615–60.

Alesina, A. and Perotti, R. (1996) 'Income distribution, political instability, and investment', *European Economic Review*, 40: 1203–28.

Ben-Shlomo, Y., White, I.R. and Marmot, M. (1996) 'Does the Variation in Socioeconomic Characteristics of an Area Affect Mortality?', *British Medical Journal*, 312, 20: 1013–14.

Benjamin, D., Brandt, L. and Giles, J. (2006) 'Inequality and Growth in Rural China: Does Higher Inequality Impede Growth?', Mimeo, Michigan State University.

Blakely, T.A., Kennedy, B.P. and Kawachi, I. (2001) 'Socioeconomic Inequality in Voting Participation and Self-rated Health', *American Journal of Public Health*, 91, 1: 99–104.

Blakely, T.A., Lochner, K. and Kawachi, I. (2002) 'Metropolitan Area Income Inequality and Self-rated Health – A Multilevel Study', *Social Science and Medicine*, 54: 65–77.

Bramall, C. (2001) 'The Quality of China's Household Income Surveys', *China Quarterly*, 167: 689–705.

Cohen, S., Line, S., Manuck, S., Rabin, B., Heise, E. and Kaplan, J. (1997) 'Chronic Social Stress, Social Status, and Susceptibility to Upper Respiratory Infections in Nonhuman Primates', *Psychosomatic Medicine*, 59, 3: 213–21.

Daly, M.C., Duncan, G.J., Kaplan, G.A. and Lynch, J.W. (1998) 'Macro-to-micro Links in the Relation between Income Inequality and Mortality', *Milbank Quarterly*, 76, 3: 315–39.

Deaton, A. (2001) 'Relative Deprivation, Inequality, and Mortality', Working Paper 8099 (Cambridge, MA: NBER).

Deaton, A. (2003) 'Health, Inequality, and Economic Development', *Journal of Economic Literature*, 41: 113–58.
Deaton, A. and Paxson, C. (1998) 'Aging and Inequality in Income and Health', *American Economic Review*, 88, 2: 248–53.
Eibner, C.E. and Evans, W.N. (2005) 'Relative Deprivation, Poor Health Habits, and Mortality', *Journal of Human Resources*, 40, 3: 591–620.
Feinstein, J.S. (1993) 'The Relationship between Socioeconomic Status and Health: A Review of the Literature', *Milbank Quarterly*, 71: 279–322.
Fiscella, K. and Franks, P. (1997) 'Poverty or Income Inequality as Predictor of Mortality: Longitudinal Cohort Study', *British Medical Journal*, 314: 1724–28.
Fiscella, K. and Franks, P. (2000) 'Individual Income, Income Inequality, Health and Mortality: What are the Relationships?', *Health Services Research*, 35, 1: 307–18.
Gerdtham, U.-G. and Johannesson, M. (2004) 'Absolute Income, Relative Income, Income Inequality, and Mortality', *Journal of Human Resources*, 39, 1: 228–48.
Gravelle, H. (1998) 'How Much of the Relation between Population Mortality and Unequal Distribution of Income is a Statistical Artefact?', *British Medical Journal*, 316: 382–85.
Grossman, M. (1972) 'On the Concept of Health Capital and the Demand for Health', *Journal of Political Economy*, 80, 2: 223–55.
Gustafsson, B. and Li, S. (2002) 'Income Inequality Within and Across Counties in Rural China, 1988 and 1995', *Journal of Development Economics*, 69: 179–204.
Hsieh, C.-C. and Pugh, M.D. (1993) 'Poverty, Inequality, and Violent Crime: A Meta-analysis of Recent Aggregate Data Studies', *Criminal Justice Review*, 18: 182–202.
Idler, E.L. and Benyamini, Y. (1997) 'Self-rated Health and Mortality: A Review of Twenty-seven Community Studies', *Journal of Health and Social Behavior*, 38: 21–37.
Kaplan, G.A., Pamuk, E.R., Lynch, J.W., Cohen, R.D. and Balfour, J.L. (1996) 'Inequality in Income and Mortality in the United States: Analysis of Mortality and Potential Pathways', *British Medical Journal*, 312: 999–1003.
Kawachi, I. and Kennedy, B.P. (1997) 'The Relationship of Income Inequality to Mortality: Does the Choice of Indicator Matter?', *Social Science and Medicine*, 45, 7: 1121–7.
Kawachi, I. and Kennedy, B.P. (1999) 'Income Inequality and Health: Pathways and Mechanisms', *Health Services Research*, 34, 1: 215–27.
Kawachi, I., Kennedy, B.P. and Prothrow-Stith, D. (1997) 'Social Capital, Income Inequality and Mortality', *American Journal of Public Health*, 87, 9: 1491–8.
Kennedy, B.P., Kawachi, I., Glass, R. and Prothrow-Stith, D. (1998a) 'Income Distribution, Socioeconomic Status, and Self-rated Health in the United States', *British Medical Journal*, 317: 917–21.
Kennedy, B.P., Kawachi, I., Glass, R., Prothrow-Stith, D., Lochner, K. and Gupta, V. (1998b) 'Social Capital, Income Inequality, and Firearm Violent Crimes', *Social Science and Medicine*, 47, 1: 7–17.
Kennedy, B.P., Kawachi, I., Prothrow-Stith, D. (1996) 'Income Distribution and Mortality: Cross-sectional Ecological Study of the Robin Hood Index in the United States', *British Medical Journal*, 312: 1004–7.
LeClere, F.B. and Soobader, M.-J. (2000) 'The Effect of Income Inequality on the Health of Selected US Demographic Groups', *American Journal of Public Health*, 90: 1892–7.

Li, W. (1997) 'The Impact of Economic Reform on the Performance of Chinese State Enterprises (1980–1989)', *Journal of Political Economy*, 105, 5: 1080–106.

Lin, J. (1992) 'Rural Reforms and Agricultural Growth in China', *American Economic Review*, 82, 1: 34–51.

Lynch, J., Davey Smith, G., Harper, S., Hillemeier, M, Ross, N., Kaplan, G.A. and Wolfson, M. (2004) 'Is Income Inequality a Determinant of Population Health? Part 1. A Systematic Review', *Milbank Quarterly*, 82, 1: 5–99.

Lynch, J.W., Kaplan, G.A., Pamuk, E.R., Cohen, R.D., Heck, K.E., Balfour, J.L. and Yen, I.H. (1998) 'Income Inequality and Mortality in Metropolitan Areas of the United States', *American Journal of Public Health*, 88, 7: 1074–80.

Marmot, M.G. (1997) 'Inequality, Deprivation and Alcohol Use', *Addiction* 92 (Suppl. 1), s13.

Marmot, M.G., Davey-Smith, G. *et al.* (1991) 'Health Inequalities among British Civil Servants: The Whitehall II Study', *Lancet*, 337, 8754: 1387–93.

Marmot, M.G., Shipley, M. and Rose, G. (1984) 'Inequalities in Death-specific Explanations of a General Pattern', *Lancet*, 323, 8384: 1003–6.

Meara, E. (1999) 'Inequality and Infant Health', Manuscript, Harvard Medical School.

Mellor, J.M. and Milyo, J. (2002) 'Income Inequality and Health Status in the United States: Evidence from the Current Population Survey', *Journal of Human Resources*, 37: 510–39.

Osler, M., Prescott, E., Gronbaek, M., Christensen, U., Due, P. and Engholm, G. (2002) 'Income Inequality, Individual Income, and Mortality in Danish Adults: Analysis of Pooled Data from Two Cohort Studies', *British Medical Journal*, 324: 13–16.

Preston, S.H. (1975) 'The Changing Relation between Mortality and Level of Development', *Population Studies*, 29: 231–48.

Qian, Y. and Weingast, B. (1997) 'Federalism as a Commitment to Reserving Market Incentives', *Journal of Economic Perspectives*, 11, 4: 83–92.

Robert, Stephanie A. (1998) 'Community-level Socioeconomic Status Effects on Adult Health', *Journal of Health and Social Behavior*, 39: 18–37.

Runciman, W.G. (1966) *Relative Deprivation and Social Justice* (London: Routledge and Kegan Paul).

Shibuya, K., Hashimoto, H. and Yano, E. (2002) 'Individual Income, Income Distribution, and Self-rated Health in Japan: Cross-sectional Analysis of Nationally Representative Sample', *British Medical Journal*, 324: 16–19.

Shively, C.A., Laber-Laird, K. and Anton, R.F. (1997) 'Behavior and Physiology of Social Stress and Depression in Female Cynomolgus Monkeys', *Biological Psychiatry*, 41: 871–82.

Smith, J.P. (1999) 'Healthy Bodies and Thick Wallets: The Dual Relation between Health and Economic Status', *Journal of Economic Perspectives*, 13: 145–66.

Soobader, M.-J. and LeClere, F. (1999) 'Aggregation and the Measurement of Income Inequality: Effects on Morbidity', *Social Science and Medicine*, 48, 6: 733–44.

Waldmann, R.J. (1992) 'Income Distribution and Infant Mortality', *Quarterly Journal of Economics*, 107, 4: 1283–302.

Wennemo, I. (1993) 'Infant Mortality, Public Policy, and Inequality – A Comparison of 18 Industrialized Countries (1950–1985)', *Sociology of Health and Illness*, 15, 4: 429–46.

Wilkinson, R.G. (1992) 'Income Distribution and Life-expectancy', *British Medical Journal*, 304: 165–8.
Wilkinson, R.G. (1996) *Unhealthy Societies: The Affliction of Inequality* (London: Routledge).
Wilkinson, R.G. (1997) 'Health Inequalities: Relative or Absolute Material Standards?', *British Medical Journal*, 314: 591–5.
Yitzhaki, S. (1979) 'Relative Deprivation and the Gini Coefficient', *Quarterly Journal of Economics*, 93, 2: 321–4.

7

Social Benefits in Urban China: Determinants and Impact on Income Inequality in 1988 and 2002

*Qin Gao**

Introduction

The growing income inequality in China since the economic reforms has attracted considerable attention. Official statistics show that China's Gini coefficient rose from 0.33 in 1980 to 0.40 in 1994 and to 0.46 in 2000 (Chang 2002). Using the largest national household survey data conducted by the National Bureau of Statistics (NBS), Wu and Perloff (2004) find that the Gini coefficient of income increased from 0.31 in 1985 to 0.42 in 2001. This seems to conform with the Kuznets curve, in that economic growth and development are initially associated with increasing inequality.[1]

There have always, however, been two sides to the overall story of China – urban and rural China – resulting from the rural–urban division which was formally established in 1955 as the household registration system. Although both urban and rural income inequalities have increased substantially since the mid-1980s, urban inequality was lower than rural inequality, but has grown faster (Wu and Perloff 2004; Wu and Treiman 2004). Meanwhile, relative urban poverty increased from 2 per cent in 1988 to 10 per cent in 2002.[2] This transition has happened along with two major changes. First, economic reforms have enlarged the market income gap in urban areas that had been kept minimal under the old 'iron bowl' system. Some of the less advantaged have been left behind by the market economy and have become the 'new urban poor'. Second, a series of social benefit reforms has been carried out since the early 1980s and have resulted in significant reduction in the share of social benefits in urban families' total economic resources, mainly post-tax post-transfer household income (Gao 2006).

One of the major objectives of a nation's social benefit system is to reduce income inequality (Barr 2001; Garfinkel 1996). Although a large volume of literature exists on the income inequality trend in urban China, little prior work has explored the role of social benefits in affecting this trend. This study represents one of the first attempts to examine the impact of social benefits on income inequality in urban China in 1988 and 2002, using the China Household Income Project (CHIP) survey data.

Specifically, this chapter intends to address two closely related questions. First, at the micro level, how did pre-tax pre-transfer market income and other household characteristics affect the level of social benefits received by urban households in 1988 and 2002? Second, at the aggregate level, did the social benefits change the income distribution and affect overall urban income inequality during the same timeframe?

The next section reviews the literature on China's urban income inequality since the economic reforms, and is followed by discussion of data and methods used in this study. The subsequent section presents descriptive statistics of household demographics according to their pre-tax pre-transfer income distribution in 1988 and 2002. To address the first question, we then present cross-tabulations and regression models, both intending to explain the level of social benefits in relation to household pre-tax pre-transfer market income and other demographic characteristics. The second question is then answered by exploration of the impact of social benefits on the overall income redistribution and inequality. The chapter closes with a discussion of our findings and their policy implications.

Recent income inequality trend in urban China

Urban income inequality has been rising steadily during the post-reform period, particularly since the early 1990s. Table 7.1 summarizes the Gini coefficients for urban China as reported in the recent literature. Official NBS estimates indicate that the Gini coefficient increased constantly from 0.23 in 1990 to 0.32 in 2001, with only one period showing a decrease, from 0.30 in 1994 to 0.28 in 1995 (Li 2003). The World Bank estimates show a similar trend: the Gini coefficient increased from 0.17 in 1987 to 0.25 in 1991 and 0.33 in 2001 (Chen, Datt and Ravallion 2004). A set of different studies using the NBS household survey data and the CHIP data confirm this trend. These studies show that income inequality increased from 0.23 in 1988 to 0.32 in 2002 (Khan and Riskin 1998, 2004; Gustafsson and Li 2001; Chang 2002; Meng 2003; Li and Yue 2004).

The studies mentioned above are based on per capita disposable household income, which includes cash income from social benefits but

Table 7.1 Comparison of Gini coefficient estimates for urban China in the literature

Year	Sources (details below)					
	(1)	(2)	(3)	(4)	(5)	(6)
1981		0.18				
1985		0.17	0.191			
1986			0.189			
1987		0.17	0.194			
1988			0.201	0.230		0.233
1989			0.198			
1990	0.23		0.198			
1991	0.24	0.25	0.184	0.230		
1992	0.25	0.24	0.200		0.244	
1993	0.27	0.28	0.219			
1994	0.30	0.29	0.229		0.300	
1995	0.28	0.28	0.221	0.280	0.302	0.332
1996	0.28	0.29	0.221	0.280	0.298	
1997	0.29	0.29	0.232	0.290	0.303	
1998	0.30	0.30	0.239	0.297	0.312	
1999	0.30	0.32	0.246	0.302		
2000	0.32		0.258	0.314		
2001	0.32	0.33	0.269	0.323		
2002				0.319		0.318

Note: All studies defined income by per capita household disposable income.

Sources:		Dataset:
Column (1)	NBS official estimates (Li 2003)	NBS survey data
Column (2)	Chen, Datt and Ravallion (2004)	NBS survey data
Column (3)	Wu and Perloff (2004)	NBS summary statistics by income interval
Column (4)	Chang (2002); Li and Yue (2004)	NBS survey data
Column (5)	Fang, Zhang and Fan (2002)	NBS survey data
Column (6)	Khan and Riskin (1998; 2004)	CHIP survey data

ignores major in-kind or reimbursed benefits such as health, education, housing and other in-kind benefits originated from work units. Further, simply lumping together market income and cash transfers cannot provide a clear picture on the contribution of government social benefits to inequality. This chapter addresses these weaknesses.

Data, measures and methods

Data

The data are from the China Household Income Project (CHIP) 1988 and 2002 surveys, collectively designed by a group of Chinese and western economists and conducted by the Institute of Economics, Chinese Academy of Social Sciences (CASS) (Griffin and Zhao 1993; Li and Knight 2004). The surveys were conducted in 1989 and 2003, each collecting data for the previous year. Although welfare reforms were initiated in the early 1980s, the most significant changes occurred only in the late 1980s. Thus, our data sets allow examination of social benefits of the urban regions before and after reform. The CHIP surveys were drawn from larger samples of the National Bureau of Statistics (NBS) using a multi-stage stratified probability sampling method. Sampling units – province, city, county, township, village and household – were ranked according to average per capita income at each level. A random starting point was then selected and a fixed interval was used so that the pre-determined number of units was covered. Appendix Table 7.A1 presents the sample design of the two waves of data. More details can be found in Eichen and Zhang (1993).

To make the analytical results compatible over years, this study limits the sample to the ten provinces sampled in both years, and these are grouped into three regions: eastern (Beijing, Liaoning, Jiangsu and Guangdong), central (Shanxi, Anhui, Henan and Hubei) and western regions (Yunnan and Gansu). There are 8,996 households and 31,775 individuals in the 1988 sample and 5,969 households and 18,109 individuals in the 2002 sample.

Measures

Household income

The household post-tax post-transfer income is measured in both 1988 and 2002 as the sum of pre-tax pre-transfer market income, social benefits and private transfers minus taxes and fees paid. This study aggregates the incomes at household level, but keeps the analysis at the individual level. For this analysis, economic resources are assumed to be equally shared among household members, regardless of age, gender and employment status. That is, we simply use per capita household income throughout this chapter.[3] Individuals or families reporting no income from extra sources, or those to whom certain income types did not apply, were imputed zero income for these sources. All other missing values (very few) are imputed using multiple regression models controlling for individual and household socio-demographic characteristics. Health benefits in 1988 and education benefits in both years are the exception and are imputed using administrative data.

The pre-tax pre-transfer market income in both survey years consisted of four elements: (i) market earnings from working for an employer;

(ii) market income from own private enterprise or self-employment; (iii) property income; and (iv) rental value of owner-occupied housing. Market earnings made up the largest proportion of market income. These covered salary (including bonuses) from working for an employer, wages from secondary jobs and other income from compensation (*peichang*),[4] fees paid by relatives or friends who regularly ate in and in-kind income received from others. Each individual in the household was asked about their income from each source. The individual incomes were summed at the household level and divided by household size to yield household per capita values.

Those who had private enterprises or were self-employed were asked about their income from such activities, minus taxes and paid fees.[5] Property income included income from interest on savings accounts and bonds, dividends, subletting housing and other properties. Rental value of owner-occupied housing is measured by subtracting the amount of the debt or loan on the housing from its estimated market rent. In 1988, the market value of rent was not directly collected in the survey and, thus, is estimated by a formula adopted by the CHIP Research Team (1993), accounting for both provincial construction costs at the time and sanitary facilities of the house as reported by the survey participants.[6] In 2002, families were asked to estimate the market rental value of their housing: the rental value of owner-occupied housing is imputed by subtracting the self-reported housing debt or loans from the estimated market rental value. The rental value of owner-occupied housing accounted for 8 per cent of the household's pre-tax pre-transfer market income in 1988 and 5 per cent in 2002.

Private transfer incomes were directly obtained from the survey questions and in both years these included alimony, elderly support, gifts and other transfers from family, friends or relatives.

Information on taxes and fees paid by households was collected in both waves, but in different manners. The 1988 survey recorded taxes and fees paid by individual private enterprises, but did not specify personal income taxes or compulsory social insurance contributions (including pension, housing account, health and unemployment insurance contributions), while the 2002 survey did exactly the opposite. This may lead to an underestimation of taxes and fees in both years. It is true that personal income taxes and social security contributions were insignificant in 1988, and that taxes in 2002 from individual private enterprises might also be small, given that only a small proportion of the labour force was engaged in the private sector. However, it is difficult to know the exact magnitude of each and, thus, difficult to gauge which year's underestimation is greater.

Using these self-reported taxes and fees is not the optimal option. The best approach is to conduct a balance budget tax simulation in order to obtain a full evaluation of the social benefits. However, two aspects hinder such an exercise: first, one major financing source of the Chinese government (after individual or household taxes) has been firm or enterprise taxes, especially so before economic reforms. Theoretically, firm taxes are de facto taxes from employees and should, therefore, be calculated as part of their pre-tax pre-transfer market income and then subtracted as part of taxes paid. However, there is no clear ruling on what proportion of social benefits is being financed by firm taxes and individual taxes, or which could be used for taxation simulation.

Second, even though the taxation schemes for urban and rural areas are different, it is very likely that the Chinese government pools the resources for reallocation across the urban–rural division. Thus, it is incorrect to assume balanced budget taxation within urban or rural areas. Moreover, there is no clear information on what proportions or types of rural/urban taxes are used to finance social benefits, and this makes it extremely difficult to simulate taxes across the urban–rural division line.

Therefore, the complex taxation issue is beyond the scope of this study and the self-reported taxes and fees offer the best information. Future work might make detailed investigation of the financing scheme of China's social benefits in order to develop better measures of taxation at the micro level.

Social benefits

Benefits provided by both government and by employers are considered to constitute social benefits. In pre-reform China, most work units were public institutions, or state-owned or collective enterprises. Even though many employment related benefits were directly financed through the operational expenses of each work unit, ultimate responsibility was borne by the government because the work unit was considered an appendage of the state and, thus, not responsible for its profits and losses (Saunders and Shang 2001; Leung 2003). More than half of all urban employees still work in such institutions or enterprises. Given the socialist nature of these work units, the benefits provided should be counted as social benefits.

We also consider the benefits that are received by the minority of the workforce employed in private institutions or enterprises as social benefits because they serve the same function as public benefits in supporting families. Therefore, from the viewpoint of the household, these private benefits are the same as social benefits. This, however, might be a weakness. Future research could address this issue by either separating benefits provided by private enterprises or dropping such benefits from the total package.

Cash transfers

Cash transfer benefits are grouped into three categories: (i) social insurance; (ii) supplementary income; and (iii) public assistance. The value of all cash transfers was directly identified in the survey, summed at the household level and then divided by household size to calculate per capita values. In the 1988 survey, social insurance was composed of a pension and retirement subsidies for retirees. Supplementary income included the one-child subsidy and living subsidies for heating, water and electricity, books and newspapers, bathing and haircuts, transportation and rational fuel supply. The hardship allowance was the only type of public assistance that families received in 1988.

In 2002, retirement subsidies were eliminated and social insurance was made up of only the pension. Supplementary income included price and regional subsidies. In addition to the hardship allowance, public assistance in 2002 covered a living subsidy for those who had been laid off and the Minimum Living Standard Assurance subsidy.

Health

Health benefits were obtained differently in 1988 and 2002. As health benefits were not directly identified in the 1988 survey, they are imputed with provincial level administrative data on public expenditure per capita on employee healthcare, including both government and employer contributions. The administrative data differentiate public health expenditures for three types of employer (state, collective and other enterprises) and retirees.[7] Public institutions are treated as state enterprises.

Provincial health expenditure per capita for current employees is obtained by dividing the total provincial health spending (NSB and Ministry of Labour 1989) by the number of employees (*China Labor Yearbook 1991*) according to employer type. Provincial health expenditure per capita for retirees is calculated in a similar manner based on data from *China Labor and Wage Statistical Yearbook 1989* (NSB and Ministry of Labour 1989). These are then imputed to individuals according to their employment status and type.[8] Appendix Table 7.A2 presents the administrative data on provincial per capita health expenditures in 1988.

The 2002 survey directly recorded the amounts paid either by the government or the employer for individual health care fees, as well as the cash value of in-kind health benefits provided by the employer. These values are summed at the household level and divided by household size to obtain the per capita health benefit. Using these data, the household health benefit per capita is CNY 594 (CNY 587 if in-kind health benefits provided by the work unit are not counted).

The inconsistency in constructing health benefit data across the two years may affect analytical results. As a sensitivity test, administrative data are used to estimate individual level health benefits in 2002, so as to be compatible with the 1988 data. Per capita public health expenditure in 2002 is obtained by dividing total contributions to provincial health expenditure from the government, employers and individuals by the total number of contributors (including both employees and retirees). We then use two approaches to impute micro-level data. One approach is to assign the provincial per capita health expenditure to individuals who contributed to a health insurance plan. This results in a per capita health benefit of CNY 118. Another method is to estimate the provincial proportion of contributors out of the total number of employees and retirees, and then impute provincial per capita health expenditure for all employees and retirees adjusted by the proportion. For example, administrative data show that in Beijing 43 per cent of employees and 62 per cent of retirees contributed to health insurance in 2002. The health benefit for each employed Beijing resident is therefore imputed at CNY 491 (43 per cent of the aggregate per capita health expense of CNY 1,135) and for each retiree CNY 703 (62 per cent of CNY 1,135). The imputed individual level benefits are then summed at the household level and divided by the household size to obtain the per capita measure. This approach yields a per capita health benefit of CNY 174. Both approaches of the sensitivity test result in a much lower level of health benefits than the self-reported value.

The difference between the 2002 survey data and administrative data is somewhat worrisome. There is no clear evidence indicating the source of the inconsistency. However, there is no reason to question the quality of the self-reported survey data. Thus, the survey data are considered to be more reliable and will be adopted for this study. The inconsistency, however, should still be borne in mind and will be further explored in future endeavours.

Education

Education benefits are imputed using administrative data on the provincial per capita education expenditure by educational levels in both years. Data on the provincial education expenditure per capita are derived from the *China Education Expenditure Statistical Yearbook* (CEESY) (2003) and *China Provincial Education Expenditure Annual Development Report 1989*

(Ministry of Education 1989). The 1988 data do not distinguish urban and rural expenditures. Therefore, the national average education expenditure is imputed for each enrolled student according to his/her school type (elementary or junior high school). The 2003 data differentiate between expenditures for elementary and junior high school for urban and rural areas. However, they only provide the overall per capita expenditure at the provincial level as well as that for rural areas. To estimate the per capita education expenditure for elementary and junior high school students in urban communities, the following formula is used:

$$E_{urban} = \frac{E_{all}N_{all} - E_{rural}N_{rural}}{N_{urban}}$$

where, E denotes the per capita education expenditure, N denotes the total number of students enrolled, *all* denotes the whole province, *urban* denotes urban areas within a province, and *rural* denotes rural areas within a province.

The number of enrolled students is taken from the *China Statistical Yearbook* (NBS 2003), based on three geographic classifications: urban areas (*chengshi*), counties and towns (*xianzhen*) and rural areas (*nongcun*).[9] There is no formal documentation on the rules classifying the three areas. Because the majority of enrolled students in the 'county and town' schools are actually from villages and because the county-and-town per capita expenditures are closer to those in the rural areas, this study assumes that the counties and towns form part of the rural areas.[10] Appendix Table 7.A3 presents administrative data on provincial per capita public education expenditures in 1988 and 2002.

This measure does not capture other important education benefits in the Chinese context: (i) early childhood education and care (ECEC) benefits; (ii) higher education benefits; and (iii) other cash or in-kind education benefits provided by employers. First, the ECEC benefit was identified in the 1988 survey only and not in the 2002 survey, and the lack of administrative data on ECEC in China prevents imputation. Second, administrative data on higher education (technology or vocational, normal school and college or university) are available in both years. However, students in these institutions often lived on campus in dorms and, thus, were most probably not covered in the household surveys. Third, some employers – particularly public institutions and state and collective enterprises – often provided employees with other cash or in-kind education benefits (such as advanced training and educational materials), especially before and during the early stages of the reforms. The 2002 survey recorded these educational benefits; however, similar questions were not included in the 1988 survey. For consistency, this study does not include this type of education benefit.

Housing

Information on both in-kind and cash housing benefits were collected in both surveys. In 1988, families were asked whether they were living in public housing. If so, the rental value of their housing is imputed based on the same formula as used for estimating the rental value of owner-occupied housing (CHIP Research Team 1993). In 2002, families living in public housing were also asked to evaluate the market rental value of their accommodation. The in-kind public housing benefit is, thus, calculated as the rental value of housing minus self-paid rent, if any. In addition, both surveys asked about any additional cash or in-kind housing benefits received from the employer. All housing benefits are summarized at the household level and then divided by household size to yield per capita housing benefits.

Food assistance

Information in the 1988 survey on food assistance included family reports on income from price subsidies for non-staple foods received by both working and non-working members, food ration coupon subsidies and values of in-kind food items received as 'welfare goods'. Food benefits had been considerably reduced as a result of policy changes and, in the 2002 survey, families were asked only about the values of any in-kind food items from work units.

Other in-kind benefits

Other in-kind benefits in 1988 included consumables and durables received as 'welfare goods' from the government and other in-kind items from the workplace. Note that many other in-kind benefits – such as the free supply of water, an employer-paid home phone service and even baths taken at the workplace bathhouse – were also recorded in the 1988 survey, but their values were difficult to impute. Thus, they are not considered in this study. This, however, may lead to underestimation of the 1988 public benefits, mostly from employers. In 2002, families were asked to report the values of clothing, home equipment or services, communication and transportation and other miscellaneous goods or services (other than health, education, housing and food) provided by employers.

Comparing 1988 and 2002

To compare the levels of income and benefits across the two years, the consumer price index (CPI) is used to convert the 1988 values to constant 2002 values. Accordingly, all 1988 nominal values are divided by 39.7 and multiplied by 100 for conversion to 2002 constant values (NBS 1996, 2004).

Demographic characteristics

The demographic characteristics of the household head can be important in determining the level of household income and social benefits. The head of the household was self-identified in the surveys, conventionally – but not always – by referring to the most educated working member of the household. The household head's age, ethnicity (minority or Han), marital status, gender, Chinese Communist Party (CCP) membership, education level and employment status and type are recorded.

Age is measured as a continuous variable. Ethnicity and CCP membership are dichotomous variables, taking the value of 1 when the household head is of ethnic minority or a CCP member. Household heads are classified in three categories according to their marital status and gender: (i) married; (ii) unmarried female head; and (iii) unmarried male head. Level of education is measured in five categories: primary school or less, junior high school, senior high school or equivalent secondary technology school, two-year college (*dazhuan*) and college education or above. Employment status is categorized into four groups: employed by a public institution, state-owned or collective enterprise; employed at other types of institutions or enterprises (mainly private); retired; and unemployed.

At the household level, household size and region of residency are identified. In addition, we also calculate the numbers of children (less than 18 years old), elders (older than 60 years) and other adults (aged between 18 and 60 years) in each family. The three regions are: eastern (including Beijing, Liaoning, Jiangsu and Guangdong provinces); central (Shanxi, Anhui, Henan and Hubei); and western (Yunnan and Gansu).

Income distribution and inequality

The pre-tax pre-transfer income deciles reflect the relative position of a household in the distribution of market income. It is an important determinant of the social benefit received by households, particularly with regard to means tested benefits. The pre-tax pre-transfer income decile itself is usually the outcome of various demographic characteristics such as age, gender, ethnicity, marital status, education and employment status.

Income inequality is measured with two broad approaches. The first is to compare the income shares held by each pre-tax pre-transfer income decile (comprising 10 per cent of the total population). The more income shares accumulating to the top income deciles or the fewer income shares in the bottom income deciles, the higher the overall income inequality.

The second approach is to estimate income inequality indices, including the p90/p10 decile dispersion ratio, the Gini coefficient and the Atkinson index. The p90/p10 decile dispersion ratio reflects the gap between society's richest and poorest income groups. However, it only takes two data points along the income distribution – the 10th and 90th percentiles – and ignores others. The Gini coefficient is the most widely used inequality measure because of its independence from income mean and population size, and its sensitivity to income transfers between population groups. The Atkinson index is one of the few inequality measures that explicitly incorporate normative judgements on social welfare. Its parameter *e* reflects the strength of society's preference for equality. Typically used values of *e* include 0.5, 1 and 2. As *e* rises, society attaches more weight to income transfers at the lower end of the distribution and less weight to transfers at the top (Atkinson 1970; Kawachi 2000).

Methods

Determinants of social benefits

The first research question in this chapter concerns the relationship between the social benefits received by households and the pre-tax pre-transfer market income, as well as other demographic characteristics. The dependent variable covers cash transfers, health, education, housing, food and other in-kind benefits. Three sets of independent variables – household head demographics, household characteristics and pre-tax pre-transfer income decile dummies – are considered.

Two steps are taken to find the answer to this question. First, the average level of social benefits is summarized according to the pre-tax pre-transfer income deciles and other demographic groups to identify the patterns of association between the two sets of variables. Second, Ordinary Least Squares (OLS) regression models are used to detect significant determinants of social benefit levels.[11] The particular purpose of this analysis is to understand the effects of household demographic characteristics on levels of social benefits, controlling for pre-tax pre-transfer market income deciles.

The impact of social benefits on income inequality

As shown by the results of an earlier study (Gao 2006), the difference between pre- and post-transfer income is mostly due to the reallocation of government and employer social benefits.[12] Therefore, the change in income inequality from the pre- to post-transfer level is considered to constitute the impact of social benefits. It is important to note that behavioural effects of the social benefits are beyond the scope of this study and are thus ignored in the current analysis. Empirical evidence suggests that more generous cash social benefits often lead to decreased labour supply, while withdrawing benefits can result in increased market work. On the other hand, the effects of education and health are likely to increase effective labour supply.

Using the first approach of measuring income inequality – that is, comparing income shares across pre-tax pre-transfer income deciles – this chapter examines the gaps in the income share of each pre-tax pre-transfer income decile – particularly the bottom and top deciles – before and after social benefit transfers. Compared to the second approach – which uses summary indices – this approach shows in greater detail the redistributional dynamics of social benefits along the income distribution.

In the second approach – that is, adopting the three income inequality indices – this chapter also estimates two differences: a value change, calculated as the difference between the pre- and post-transfer income inequality levels, and a percentage change, which is equal to the value change as a percentage of the pre-tax pre-transfer income inequality level. The larger the percentage change in 1988 or 2002, the greater the redistributive role of social benefits in that year, given that the percentage change, rather than the value change, measures the impact conditional on the pre-tax pre-transfer income inequality level (Gao 2006).

Descriptive statistics of demographic characteristics by pre-tax pre-transfer income decile

Household head demographics

Table 7.2 presents the demographics of household heads by pre-tax pre-transfer income deciles. Overall, the average age of household heads was 44 years in 1988, and 48 years in 2002. The four-year increase in the age of the household head reflects the increasing postponement of marriage and having children. The bottom deciles tended to have older household heads (average age 48 years in 1988, and 62 years in 2002) than in other deciles. The household heads of the bottom two deciles in 2002 in particular

Table 7.2 Demographics of household heads according to pre-tax pre-transfer

Decile	Age	Married	Unmarried		Minority	CCP
			Female	Male		
1988						
1st	48.01	0.81	0.10	0.09	0.04	0.28
2nd	42.80	0.90	0.04	0.06	0.04	0.33
3rd	43.32	0.94	0.03	0.03	0.04	0.38
4th	42.60	0.95	0.03	0.02	0.05	0.41
5th	42.38	0.95	0.04	0.01	0.04	0.40
6th	42.07	0.95	0.02	0.03	0.03	0.40
7th	43.16	0.96	0.02	0.02	0.04	0.44
8th	43.06	0.95	0.02	0.03	0.03	0.44
9th	45.06	0.94	0.03	0.03	0.05	0.44
10th	46.39	0.93	0.04	0.04	0.04	0.41
All	43.88	0.93	0.04	0.04	0.04	0.39
2002						
1st	62.22	0.94	0.05	0.02	0.05	0.40
2nd	51.86	0.93	0.05	0.02	0.04	0.30
3rd	47.04	0.95	0.03	0.01	0.06	0.30
4th	46.86	0.95	0.04	0.01	0.05	0.33
5th	45.69	0.95	0.03	0.01	0.05	0.34
6th	45.13	0.97	0.02	0.01	0.04	0.34
7th	44.85	0.96	0.03	0.00	0.04	0.40
8th	43.73	0.96	0.03	0.01	0.04	0.42
9th	44.65	0.98	0.02	0.00	0.04	0.46
10th	45.33	0.97	0.02	0.01	0.05	0.52
All	47.74	0.96	0.03	0.01	0.05	0.38

*E = Elementary.
**UE = Unemployed.
Source: Author's calculations using the CHIP data.

were older than those in 1988 and other decile groups in 2002, corresponding to China's incremental ageing trend, particularly in urban areas.[13]

There were more unmarried household heads in 1988 than in 2002, and they were more likely to be in the bottom pre-tax pre-transfer income deciles, particularly in 1988. The proportion of ethnic minorities did not change much across the two years and seemed not to be related to pre-tax pre-transfer income distribution in either year. In 1988, CCP membership was clearly and positively related to the pre-tax pre-transfer income level. A similar pattern was largely maintained in 2002, except that the bottom income decile had a more-than-average proportion (40 per cent relative to the average of 38 per cent) of CCP members.

income deciles in urban China: 1988 and 2002

	Education (level of schooling)				Employment status/type			
≤ E*	Junior high	Senior high	Two-year college	College+	Public	Private	Retired	UE**
0.29	0.36	0.26	0.05	0.04	0.64	0.02	0.34	0.00
0.19	0.39	0.30	0.06	0.05	0.90	0.02	0.09	0.00
0.17	0.34	0.33	0.07	0.09	0.94	0.01	0.05	0.00
0.18	0.33	0.32	0.08	0.09	0.95	0.02	0.03	0.00
0.15	0.39	0.28	0.08	0.09	0.96	0.02	0.02	0.00
0.15	0.37	0.31	0.08	0.09	0.98	0.01	0.02	0.00
0.14	0.34	0.31	0.10	0.12	0.96	0.01	0.03	0.00
0.09	0.35	0.35	0.09	0.10	0.97	0.01	0.02	0.00
0.16	0.35	0.27	0.09	0.13	0.94	0.03	0.04	0.00
0.17	0.36	0.29	0.06	0.11	0.91	0.05	0.04	0.00
0.17	0.36	0.30	0.08	0.09	0.92	0.02	0.07	0.00
0.20	0.39	0.28	0.07	0.06	0.06	0.05	0.83	0.06
0.16	0.41	0.35	0.06	0.02	0.27	0.21	0.41	0.12
0.09	0.39	0.38	0.10	0.03	0.40	0.27	0.27	0.07
0.10	0.33	0.36	0.17	0.03	0.48	0.25	0.23	0.04
0.05	0.32	0.41	0.17	0.06	0.53	0.22	0.20	0.04
0.02	0.29	0.42	0.21	0.06	0.61	0.21	0.14	0.04
0.04	0.24	0.41	0.21	0.10	0.64	0.20	0.13	0.02
0.03	0.20	0.40	0.25	0.13	0.65	0.22	0.12	0.02
0.02	0.17	0.37	0.28	0.16	0.73	0.16	0.10	0.02
0.01	0.11	0.34	0.31	0.23	0.70	0.21	0.08	0.01
0.07	0.29	0.37	0.18	0.09	0.51	0.20	0.25	0.04

Household education levels appeared to be positively related to market income levels to a much greater degree in 2002 than in 1988. In both years, there was a disproportionate number of households whose heads had elementary school education or less at the bottom of the pre-tax pre-transfer income distribution. Consistently, household heads with more than senior high school education – particularly those with college education or above – were concentrated at the higher end of the income distribution, more so in 2002 than in 1988. Such a phenomenon corresponds to the widely observed trend that education, rather than family background, has played an increasingly significant role in upward mobility and socioeconomic achievement since the economic reforms.

In 1988, the vast majority of household heads (92 per cent) were employed in public institutions or state-owned or collective enterprises. Only 2 per cent were employed by private institutions and 7 per cent retired. None of the household heads was unemployed in 1988, reflecting the pre-reform policy of 'full employment', which was largely in existence even in the beginning stages of reform. By 2002, only half of the household heads were employed by public institutions or enterprises,[14] while the share of those employed by private institutions had increased to 20 per cent. The retirees accounted for a quarter of all household heads in 2002, partly due to increasing ageing and partly because of the new application of forced 'early retirement' from state-owned or collective enterprises at a younger age (usually 55 years for males and 50 years for females). Four per cent of household heads were unemployed in 2002. In both years, households with retirees as heads dominated the bottom deciles. In 2002, the bottom three deciles, in particular the second, had disproportionately more unemployed household heads.

Household characteristics

Table 7.3 presents household size, the number of household members in the different age groups and the region of residency according to pre-tax pre-transfer income deciles in both years. Overall, household size dropped from 3.84 in 1988 to 3.24 in 2002, with the number of children nearly halved (from 1.05 to 0.59) and the number of elders increasing (from 0.27 to 0.36). Households with more children appeared to have less market income in both years, with the exception of the bottom decile in 2002. In contrast, households at the lower end of income distribution had disproportionately more elderly members. This was most noticeable in the bottom decile in 2002 and may explain why the bottom decile in 2002 had fewer children than other groups. Consistently, the bottom decile also had significantly fewer other adults in 2002 compared to 1988. These facts confirm that the presence of elders in the household largely determines the lag in market income in both years, particularly in 2002.

Consistent with the literature, households living in the eastern region were concentrated at the higher end of income distribution, while those in the other two regions were more likely to be at the lower end in both years. Strikingly, this trend was more predominant in 1988 than in 2002, indicating that the economic reforms may have benefited the central and western regions more than the eastern region.

Table 7.3 Household characteristics according to pre-tax pre-transfer income deciles in urban China: 1988 and 2002

Decile	Household size	No. of members by age group			Region		
		Children (<18 yrs)	Elders (>60 yrs)	Other adults (18–60 yrs)	Eastern	Central	Western
1988							
1st	4.08	1.19	0.68	2.22	0.21	0.57	0.22
2nd	4.28	1.36	0.42	2.50	0.22	0.59	0.18
3rd	4.10	1.26	0.29	2.55	0.28	0.52	0.20
4th	3.98	1.20	0.25	2.54	0.32	0.49	0.19
5th	3.85	1.11	0.21	2.53	0.36	0.47	0.17
6th	3.75	1.06	0.17	2.51	0.42	0.40	0.18
7th	3.64	0.92	0.17	2.55	0.42	0.41	0.17
8th	3.60	0.90	0.15	2.55	0.46	0.36	0.17
9th	3.61	0.83	0.18	2.60	0.54	0.31	0.15
10th	3.48	0.68	0.23	2.58	0.66	0.20	0.14
All	3.84	1.05	0.27	2.51	0.39	0.43	0.18
2002							
1st	2.98	0.40	1.31	1.27	0.30	0.51	0.19
2nd	3.66	0.67	0.69	2.30	0.33	0.51	0.16
3rd	3.52	0.71	0.42	2.39	0.31	0.51	0.18
4th	3.41	0.66	0.31	2.44	0.32	0.51	0.18
5th	3.29	0.64	0.26	2.40	0.34	0.49	0.17
6th	3.28	0.64	0.18	2.46	0.41	0.44	0.16
7th	3.19	0.62	0.15	2.43	0.41	0.40	0.19
8th	3.13	0.63	0.15	2.36	0.45	0.35	0.20
9th	3.03	0.54	0.11	2.38	0.55	0.27	0.18
10th	2.89	0.44	0.06	2.39	0.74	0.17	0.09
All	3.24	0.59	0.36	2.28	0.42	0.41	0.17

Source: Author's calculations using the CHIP data.

Associations between social benefit levels and pre-tax pre-transfer market income and demographics

This section examines the association between the level of social benefit received by households and their pre-tax pre-transfer market income and demographic characteristics.

Social benefit levels by pre-tax pre-transfer income decile

Table 7.4 presents the average social benefit levels and household post-tax post-transfer income by pre-tax pre-transfer income deciles in 1988 and 2002. Column 1 shows the distribution of total social benefits by pre-tax pre-transfer income decile. The bottom deciles, being heavily targeted, received more social benefits in both years than other income groups. The magnitude of the total social benefits received by the bottom deciles indicate that social benefits, however, reallocated more resources to the bottom decile in 2002 (a surprisingly high CNY 7,474 relative to the overall average of CNY 2,743, 2.5 times greater) than in 1988 (only CNY 2,478 relative to the overall average of CNY 2,077). This can be explained by the higher concentration rate of elders – who received

Table 7.4 Mean social benefit levels by pre-tax pre-transfer income decile in urban China: 1988 and 2002

	Total social benefits	Social benefits by domain						PPTI
		Cash transfers	Health	Education	Housing	Food	Other in-kind	
1988								
1st	2,478	973	197	75	807	425	1	3,454
2nd	1,875	465	163	80	709	455	3	3,377
3rd	1,811	372	161	85	726	463	4	3,588
4th	1,849	331	167	83	752	513	3	3,836
5th	1,887	339	177	81	769	517	3	4,082
6th	1,904	310	179	81	811	517	5	4,308
7th	2,008	377	192	71	815	547	5	4,668
8th	2,059	363	200	71	854	562	9	5,063
9th	2,183	367	217	67	966	555	11	5,725
10th	2,721	441	245	61	1,414	543	18	8,468
All	2,077	434	190	75	862	510	6	4,656
2002								
1st	7,474	5,543	1,573	90	251	15	2	8,426
2nd	2,886	2,136	315	202	210	19	4	5,306
3rd	1,994	1,409	127	236	197	22	4	5,344
4th	2,535	1,251	789	227	233	28	8	6,836
5th	1,936	1,088	327	242	234	32	13	7,060
6th	2,100	1,044	526	248	229	41	11	8,095
7th	1,731	858	295	278	246	42	13	8,783
8th	1,804	917	311	286	223	51	17	10,125
9th	2,689	797	1,045	310	452	69	16	12,963
10th	2,272	779	636	333	344	148	32	19,380
All	2,743	1,583	594	245	262	47	12	9,231

PPTI = Post-tax post-transfer income.
Source: Author's calculations using the CHIP data.

little market income but more pension income – in this income group in 2002 than in 1988. As shown in Table 7.2, the average age of household heads in the bottom decile was 62 years in 2002 compared to only 48 in 1988 (which was still older than in other decile groups). Regression analysis would be able to verify this association.

Figure 7.1 demonstrates that the redistributional pattern of social benefits differs between 1988 and 2002. Excluding the bottom decile, social benefits were distributed regressively across income groups in 1988, with the top decile gaining a substantial bulk. In 2002, by contrast, leaving the bottom decile aside, the distribution of social benefits fluctuated by moving from the lower to the higher end of the income distribution, but without a clear pattern.

In terms of the different social benefit domains, *cash transfers* were heavily targeted at the bottom two deciles, in particular the very bottom decile, especially in 2002. Similarly, this might also be due to the high proportion of pensioners at the bottom of the income distribution. Another factor might be the growing number of unemployed in 2002, which increased the possibility of public assistance being received by those in the bottom decile.

Given the important contributions of cash transfers to total social benefits, which were apparent in both years but far more significant in

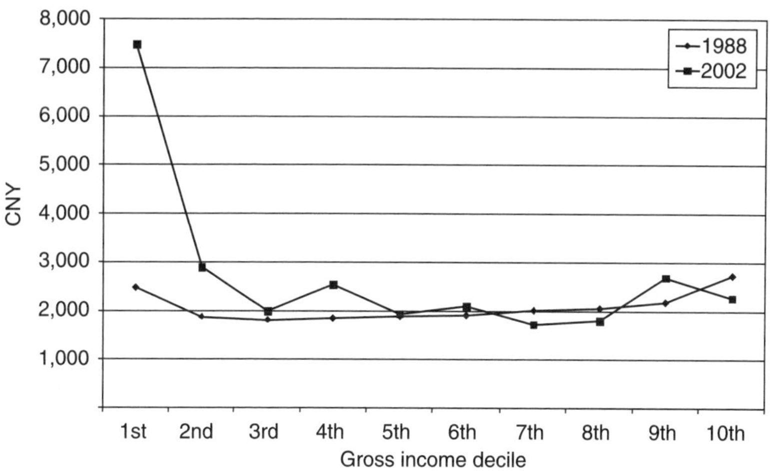

Figure 7.1 Total social benefits by pre-tax pre-transfer income deciles in urban China
Source: Author's calculations using the CHIP data.

2002, Table 7.5 disaggregates cash transfers into three sub-categories: social insurance, supplementary income and public assistance, as described earlier. It is clear that social insurance, mainly pensions, made up the vast majority of cash transfers in both years, particularly in 2002. They also dominated the distributional pattern of total cash transfers, heavily targeting the bottom deciles. Public assistance was minimal in 1988, but became more important in 2002 for those at the lower end of the income distribution. Supplementary income, which was mainly provided by state-owned or collective enterprises, shrank during this period along with the market and social benefit reforms, but maintained its regressive nature of favouring the richer rather than the poorer.

Table 7.5 Mean levels of cash transfers by pre-tax pre-transfer income decile in urban China: 1988 and 2002

Decile	Total cash transfers	Social insurance	Supplementary income	Public assistance
1988				
1st	973	913	59	1
2nd	465	363	102	1
3rd	372	239	131	1
4th	331	172	159	0
5th	339	176	162	0
6th	310	139	170	1
7th	377	199	178	0
8th	363	170	191	1
9th	367	181	186	0
10th	441	252	188	1
All	434	281	153	1
2002				
1st	5,543	5,436	38	70
2nd	2,136	2,000	40	96
3rd	1,409	1,309	49	51
4th	1,251	1,155	56	40
5th	1,088	967	78	43
6th	1,044	926	79	40
7th	858	708	112	37
8th	917	751	147	19
9th	797	680	91	26
10th	779	614	142	23
All	1,583	1,455	83	45

Source: Author's calculations using the CHIP data.

Health benefits were somewhat more evenly reallocated across pre-tax pre-transfer income deciles in 1988 than in 2002, as shown in Table 7.4, although, in both years, the bottom decile and the top two deciles received more health benefits than other income groups. The bottom decile was likely to receive more health benefits because they had a greater number of elderly members (especially in 2002) who usually incur higher health costs than other age groups. The top income groups received more health benefits, possibly because of their higher employment status, which was strongly linked to a more generous provision of health benefits by employers. However, the distribution of health benefits across pre-tax pre-transfer income deciles in 2002 is still puzzling. The benefit level of the 4th decile was higher than the average and its neighbouring deciles; the 9th decile received unusually high health benefits.

Education benefits were skewed towards the lower pre-tax pre-transfer income groups in 1988, but were distributed regressively in 2002, with higher income groups at an advantage. Three factors may have contributed to this trend. First, primary and secondary school enrolment was low in the late 1980s,[15] particularly among low-income families, because many children of these families dropped out of school to take jobs offered by the newly emerging market economy. Because low-income families tended to have more children than higher-income families, their low enrolment rate partly equalized the per capita education benefits across the rich and the poor. Second, pre-tax pre-transfer market income and education levels became more positively related in 2002 than in 1988. Under the pre-reform 'iron bowl' system, which was still broadly in place in 1988, jobs and associated wage levels were largely determined by parental work status rather than self-achievement. By 2002, education had become the major upward channel for mobility and a more significant predictor of market income. Therefore, parents wanted to send their children to better quality schools, and education benefits as a whole increased. Third, educational reform in the late 1980s decentralized responsibility for financing education from central to local governments. Thus, government educational expenditure became closely related to the economic development and capacity of the locality. Because more affluent families tended to live in more developed provinces and districts, they appeared to enjoy more education benefits in 2002.

Housing benefits were largely distributed regressively along the pre-tax pre-transfer income distribution in both years, despite the fact that they somewhat targeted the bottom decile. In both years, the bottom deciles received more housing benefits, most probably because of the high portion of elders in this group and their access to housing benefits originating from prior employment. For other groups, housing had been the benefit most closely linked with employment status and, thus, increased as income groups moved towards the top, particularly in 1988 before public housing reforms. Similarly, in both surveys, *food assistance* and *other in-kind benefits* originated mostly from employers and these benefits favoured those at the higher end of the income distribution.

After social benefit transfers, the distribution of post-tax post-transfer household income was different in the two years, as shown in Figure 7.2. The 1988 post-tax post-transfer income distribution by pre-tax pre-transfer income deciles was largely upward-sloped, with most decile groups maintaining the same relative position (with only the bottom and 2nd deciles changing positions, but with small differences in their mean post-tax post-transfer income). In 2002, the bottom decile received such high social benefits that their post-tax post-transfer household income jumped to the 6th decile, while there was no change in the relative position of other income groups. In both years, the top decile had strikingly higher post-tax post-transfer income than other deciles (1.8 times the average in 1988 and more than twice the average in 2002), indicating that the income gap between the rich and the poor was enlarged by the social benefit transfers in both years and that it had also expanded over time.

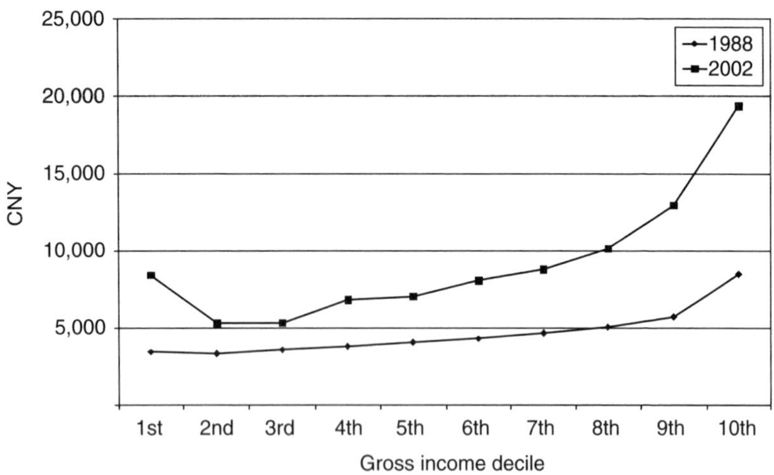

Figure 7.2 Post-tax post-transfer income by pre-tax pre-transfer income decile in urban China
Source: Author's calculations using the CHIP data.

Social benefit levels by demographic characteristics

Tables 7.6 and 7.7 present the mean social benefit levels according to household head demographics and household characteristics in 1988 and 2002. Households headed by older members (>60 yrs) enjoyed more total social benefits in both years, as expected. This is due in particular to the cash transfers geared towards the elderly in the form of pensions, especially in 2002. This group also received more health and housing benefits than households with younger heads in 1988, while in 2002 households with middle-aged heads (40–59 yrs) enjoyed more health and housing benefits.

In both years, households whose heads were unmarried received more total social benefits than households with married heads, while unmarried male-headed households received more total social benefits than female-headed households. Unmarried households benefited mostly from cash transfers, but less from education benefits. In 1988, households headed by married spouses enjoyed less health benefits, but more housing benefits. Interestingly, unmarried female-headed households in 2002 received more housing and food assistance than other groups.

Compared to the Han people, ethnic minorities appeared to receive slightly more cash transfers and food assistance in 1988 and more cash transfers, health and education benefits in 2002. CCP members received more housing benefits in 1988 and more cash transfers in 2002 than non-CCP members. Education at primary school level or lower was associated with more cash transfers in both years. Education was strongly positively related to housing benefits in 1988, but positively associated with health and education benefits in 2002.

With regard to employment status and type, social benefits were targeted more towards households headed by retirees than those headed by the employed or unemployed (in 2002). Households headed by retirees also received more health and housing benefits in 1988 but not in 2002. Households whose heads were employed by government public institutions or state-owned and collective enterprises profited from more food assistance in 1988 and more health benefits in 2002 than other households. Families with unemployed heads in 2002 were more disadvantaged with regard to all types of in-kind benefits than other households.

In both years, fewer social benefits were afforded to a greater number of children was associated, with the exception of education. In contrast, the presence of more elder members increased the total social benefits of a household. Excluding children and elderly, the number of other adults (aged 18–59 yrs) had no association with social benefits, except in the case of households with only one other adult – usually a single parent – to

Table 7.6 Mean social benefit levels by demographic groups in urban China: 1988

Demographics	Total social benefits	Social benefits by domain						Post-tax post-transfer income
		Cash transfers	Health	Education	Housing	Food	Other in-kind	
Household head demographics								
Age								
21–29	2,240	734	239	6	764	493	3	4,556
30–39	1,802	266	169	66	807	486	8	4,361
40–49	1,793	189	152	123	812	510	7	4,357
50–59	2,311	502	217	60	973	553	6	5,108
60+	3,502	1,643	304	26	1,042	486	1	5,765
Marital status								
Married	2,041	397	185	77	866	509	6	4,631
Unwed, female	2,420	768	225	59	845	517	5	4,921
Unwed, male	2,671	1,049	278	42	781	511	11	5,072
Ethnic minority								
No	2,079	433	190	75	869	507	6	4,661
Yes	2,081	484	200	86	719	582	10	4,619
CCP member								
No	1,996	451	193	70	772	504	6	4,519
Yes	2,207	408	186	84	1,003	519	6	4,878
Education								
Primary school	2,084	555	207	68	729	514	11	4,530
Junior high school	1,950	398	184	77	770	514	6	4,527
Senior high school	2,121	425	190	71	923	507	6	4,721

Partial college	2,080	381	188	80	927	499	6	4,688
4 years college+	2,421	419	188	93	1,209	510	3	5,199
Employment status/type								
Govt/SOE/collective	1,962	322	180	79	856	518	7	4,581
Private enterprise	2,107	769	214	46	744	333	2	5,586
Retired	3,716	1,922	331	31	973	457	2	5,483
Household characteristics								
No. of children <18 yrs								
0	2,888	946	281	20	1,059	576	7	5,811
1	1,925	332	180	69	827	510	6	4,569
2	1,668	167	128	137	773	456	7	3,850
3+	1,360	128	95	164	587	384	2	3,073
No. of elders >60 yrs								
0	1,939	287	176	83	866	519	7	4,593
1	2,376	770	219	53	843	487	4	4,793
2+	3,141	1,510	301	27	855	447	1	5,140
No. of other adults 18–59 yrs								
0	4,375	2,263	366	22	1,219	505	0	6,099
1	3,206	1,365	263	52	1,029	491	7	5,736
2	1,936	309	171	84	862	504	7	4,516
3	2,111	418	197	83	884	520	8	4,775
4	1,959	394	200	57	775	528	5	4,601
5+	1,859	412	206	37	695	505	4	4,376
Region								
Eastern	2,556	527	250	80	1,133	559	6	5,633
Central	1,621	371	145	65	602	434	4	3,837
Western	2,141	384	168	90	901	585	13	4,512

Source: Author's calculations using the CHIP data.

Table 7.7 Mean social benefit levels by demographic groups in urban China: 2002

Demographics	Total social benefits	Social benefits by domain						Post-tax post-transfer income
		Cash transfers	Health	Education	Housing	Food	Other in-kind	
Household head demographics								
Age								
21–29	1,472	938	139	40	152	168	35	8,982
30–39	1,293	345	167	308	189	53	13	8,426
40–49	1,668	452	201	404	301	44	11	9,025
50–59	2,962	1,989	203	68	308	44	14	9,787
60+	7,115	5,394	87	98	225	31	7	10,075
Marital status								
Married	2,706	1,544	176	247	254	44	12	9,220
Unwed, female	3,471	2,294	144	239	501	125	23	9,460
Unwed, male	3,753	2,848	158	142	236	58	12	9,474
Ethnic minority								
No	2,705	1,571	171	243	262	48	12	9,202
Yes	3,510	1,815	237	296	263	26	11	9,858
CCP member								
No	2,501	1,321	162	265	278	44	11	8,558
Yes	3,138	2,008	195	214	235	51	14	10,333
Education								
Primary school	3,196	2,416	88	169	175	18	8	6,761
Junior high school	2,745	1,683	150	193	272	37	9	7,747
Senior high school	2,614	1,475	179	287	285	54	13	9,101

Partial college	2,613	1,215	212	263	220	51	15	11,020
4 years college+	3,154	1,767	227	264	283	63	12	12,873
Employment status/type								
Govt/SOE/collective	1,647	619	213	295	275	50	13	9,492
Private enterprise	1,771	612	157	310	251	57	13	8,576
Retired	6,043	4,506	122	88	254	36	10	9,850
Unemployed	1,456	804	106	276	194	27	4	5,752
Household characteristics								
No. of children <18 yrs								
0	3,950	2,550	195	71	340	51	12	10,614
1	1,790	812	165	369	209	44	12	8,285
2+	1,308	523	69	606	70	33	7	5,913
No. of elders >60 yrs								
0	1,707	720	194	280	273	51	13	9,074
1	4,019	2,921	139	160	232	37	10	8,721
2+	8,036	5,707	88	110	218	32	7	10,770
No. of other adults 18–59 yrs								
0	11,783	8,534	67	43	321	30	6	13,537
1	6,238	4,480	124	201	343	91	19	10,472
2	1,891	893	179	342	237	48	12	8,911
3	2,412	1,262	199	149	308	42	12	9,342
4+	1,586	1,147	140	60	144	34	5	6,988
Region								
Eastern	3,681	1,845	935	324	484	75	18	11,592
Central	2,039	1,364	365	157	111	34	8	7,333
Western	2,205	1,478	219	281	90	11	6	8,204

Source: Author's calculations using the CHIP data.

whom more social benefits would be targeted. This is consistent with earlier findings that unmarried households tend to be favoured with more social benefits.

The determinants of social benefits

Tables 7.8 and 7.9 present the OLS regression results on the determinants of social benefit levels in 1988 and 2002, respectively. The results are broadly consistent with early findings based on cross-tabulations. In 1988, even after controlling for demographics, the greatest total social benefit accrued to the top income decile (with a regression coefficient of 31, though statistically insignificant), followed by the bottom decile (the omitted group whose regression coefficient is 0), while all other groups in the middle range of the pre-tax pre-transfer income distribution received less (with negative regression coefficients). Lower-income groups received more cash transfers, while housing benefits were skewed towards the richest (10th) income group. In 2002, the bottom decile profited from significantly higher social benefits (the omitted group with a regression coefficient of 0) than all other income groups (regression coefficients all negative and the absolute values close to or more than 1,500 in seven of the remaining nine groups). This is net of the effects of demographic characteristics, age and the retirement status of household heads in particular. Pre-tax pre-transfer income distribution was negatively related to cash transfers, but positively related to education and food benefits.

A household being headed by an elder member (60 years or older in 1988) or a retiree (in both years) was positively related to total social benefits, mainly cash transfers. However, regression results differ from early findings regarding the effects of some demographic variables.

Based on the cross-tabulations, households with unmarried male heads were related to more total social benefits in 1988; in particular, cash transfers, health and education. However, after controlling for the effects of the pre-tax pre-transfer market income, unmarried households in 2002 were negatively related to cash transfers (statistically significant) and total social benefits (statistically insignificant).

Referring to Tables 7.8 and 7.9, ethnic minorities tended to receive less total social benefits in 1988 than the Han people, which was mainly driven by the negative housing benefits. Minorities, in comparison to the Han people, were somewhat more likely to receive cash transfers, health benefits and food assistance. In 2002, minority status became a strong positive predictor of total social benefits as well as cash transfers, health, education and housing benefits. CCP membership in 1988 was

Table 7.8 OLS regression of demographics and pre-tax pre-transfer income decile on social benefits in urban China in 1988 (N = 30,968)

	(1) Total social benefits	(2) Cash transfers	(3) Health	(4) Education	(5) Housing	(6) Food	(7) Other in-kind
Household head characteristics							
Age (21–29 yrs omitted)							
30–39	−200**	−226**	−33**	36**	24	−4	4*
	(31)	(12)	(2)	(2)	(25)	(10)	(2)
40–49	−17	−195**	−33**	85**	72**	50**	3
	(32)	(13)	(2)	(2)	(26)	(11)	(2)
50–59	315**	−39**	−7**	66**	226**	68**	0
	(33)	(13)	(2)	(2)	(27)	(11)	(2)
60+	477**	28	−13**	58**	305**	102**	−3
	(49)	(20)	(4)	(3)	(40)	(16)	(3)
Marital status (married omitted)							
Unmarried female	−8	16	9**	13**	−66*	19	0
	(38)	(15)	(3)	(3)	(31)	(13)	(2)
Unmarried male	313**	293**	40**	24**	−58+	6	7**
	(38)	(15)	(3)	(3)	(31)	(13)	(2)
Ethnic minority	−61+	68**	15**	3	−196**	47**	1
	(34)	(14)	(2)	(2)	(28)	(11)	(2)
CCP	228**	37**	2*	5**	184**	−1	0
	(14)	(6)	(1)	(1)	(12)	(5)	(1)
Education (elementary school or less omitted)							
Junior high school	138**	63**	−3*	9**	79**	−1	−8**
	(20)	(8)	(1)	(1)	(17)	(7)	(1)

(*Continued*)

Table 7.8 continued

	(1) Total social benefits	(2) Cash transfers	(3) Health	(4) Education	(5) Housing	(6) Food	(7) Other in-kind
Senior high school	290**	84**	1	5**	222**	−13+	−8**
	(21)	(9)	(2)	(1)	(17)	(7)	(1)
2 years college	267**	71**	3	11**	207**	−19+	−7**
	(30)	(12)	(2)	(2)	(24)	(10)	(2)
4 years college or above	516**	99**	−3+	17**	443**	−29**	−11**
	(28)	(11)	(2)	(2)	(23)	(9)	(2)
Employment status/type (employed at public institutions or state-owned or collective enterprises omitted)							
Private enterprises	−217**	217**	−11**	−14**	−184**	−216**	−8**
	(49)	(19)	(3)	(3)	(39)	(16)	(3)
Retired	935**	978**	101**	−12**	−15	−115**	−1
	(38)	(15)	(3)	(3)	(31)	(13)	(2)
Household characteristics							
No. of children <18 yrs	−401**	−226**	−47**	47**	−108**	−66**	0
	(11)	(4)	(1)	(1)	(9)	(4)	(1)
No. of elders 60+ yrs	−28+	198**	17**	−19**	−169**	−53**	−1
	(15)	(6)	(1)	(1)	(12)	(5)	(1)
No. of other adults 18–59 yrs	−266**	−107**	−7**	−6**	−123**	−22**	−0
	(8)	(3)	(1)	(1)	(7)	(3)	(0)
Region (eastern omitted)							
Central	−876**	−137**	−90**	−29**	−504**	−116**	0
	(15)	(6)	(1)	(1)	(12)	(5)	(1)

Western	−335**	−94**	−64**	−10**	−209**	34**	9**
	(20)	(8)	(1)	(1)	(16)	(6)	(1)
Pre-tax pre-transfer income deciles (1st decile omitted)							
2nd	−149**	−104**	8**	−10**	−67**	24*	1
	(30)	(12)	(2)	(2)	(25)	(10)	(2)
3rd	−291**	−151**	4	−6**	−146**	6	3
	(31)	(12)	(2)	(2)	(25)	(10)	(2)
4th	−287**	−185**	6**	−8**	−148**	46**	1
	(31)	(12)	(2)	(2)	(25)	(10)	(2)
5th	−289**	−173**	12**	−7**	−162**	39**	2
	(32)	(13)	(2)	(2)	(26)	(11)	(2)
6th	−352**	−212**	7**	−7**	−172**	28**	4*
	(32)	(13)	(2)	(2)	(26)	(11)	(2)
7th	−346**	−203**	14**	−11**	−201**	51**	4*
	(32)	(13)	(2)	(2)	(26)	(11)	(2)
8th	−346**	−218**	16**	−12**	−197**	56**	9**
	(32)	(13)	(2)	(2)	(26)	(11)	(2)
9th	−331**	−275**	19**	−16**	−109**	41**	11**
	(32)	(13)	(2)	(2)	(26)	(11)	(2)
10th	31	−276**	27**	−18**	274**	5	19**
	(33)	(13)	(2)	(2)	(27)	(11)	(2)
Constant	3,445**	1,121**	308**	5	1,363**	643**	5+
	(50)	(20)	(4)	(4)	(41)	(17)	(3)
R-squared	0.31	0.53	0.47	0.29	0.13	0.06	0.01

Note: Regression coefficients presented with standard errors in parentheses; + $p < 0.10$; * $p < 0.05$; ** $p < 0.01$.
Source: Author's calculations using the CHIP data.

positively related to total social benefits, mainly from housing benefits and cash transfers, but in 2002 turned to be negatively associated with total social benefits as well as health, education and housing benefits.

A positive relation between the educational level of the household head and total social benefits was found in both years. However, the source of benefits differed across the two years. In 1988, the positive relationship was mainly due to housing benefits, followed by cash transfers. In 2002, however, it was mainly due to cash transfers, followed by health and housing benefits. This reflects the shrinking of employment based housing benefits and the trend that the better educated were more likely to contribute to health insurance and thus received more health benefits after the health policy reforms.

The results with regard to employment status and type provided strong evidence that retired members in both years brought in more social benefits than employed individuals, mainly from pensions (as part of cash transfers), followed by health benefits. One interesting change is that individuals employed in 1988 in private enterprises received fewer social benefits than those in public institutions or enterprises, due to fewer housing and food assistance benefits being provided by employers. However, they received more total social benefits in 2002, mainly accruing from health benefits (which were based on self-contribution, though statistically insignificant) and cash transfers.

Consistent with the findings from cross-tabulations, households with more children received fewer social benefits in total and in each domain, with the exception of education. This might be because these households were partially excluded from the system or penalized for their violation of China's policy of 'one child' per family unit. The presence of more adults aged 18 to 59 was also negatively related to total social benefits and to almost all benefit domains, perhaps because fewer members on average received benefits provided by employers and there were more economically dependent members in these large households. Residents from both the central and western regions received fewer social benefits than those in the eastern region. However, in 1988 residents in the central region received even fewer benefits than those in the western region; however, this pattern did not hold in 2002.

The impact of social benefits on income inequality

This section examines the impact of social benefits on income inequality using two approaches: a comparison of the income shares of pre-tax pre-transfer income deciles before and after social benefit transfers and a

Table 7.9 OLS regression of demographics and pre-tax pre-transfer income decile on social benefits in urban China in 2002 (N = 17,654)

	(1) Total social benefits	(2) Cash transfers	(3) Health	(4) Education	(5) Housing	(6) Food	(7) Other in-kind
Household head characteristics							
Age (21–29 yrs omitted)							
30–39	−48	−594**	411	175**	91+	−110**	−22**
	(452)	(100)	(429)	(14)	(54)	(21)	(5)
40–49	294	−501**	428	376**	143**	−126**	−25**
	(445)	(99)	(422)	(14)	(53)	(21)	(5)
50–59	1,044*	560**	301	191**	139*	−126**	−21**
	(464)	(103)	(440)	(15)	(55)	(22)	(5)
60+	−31	285*	−458	193**	120+	−138**	−31**
	(549)	(122)	(520)	(17)	(65)	(25)	(6)
Marital status (married omitted)							
Unmarried female	−387	−392**	−354	40**	224**	84**	11**
	(356)	(79)	(337)	(11)	(42)	(16)	(4)
Unmarried male	−531	−263+	−313	4	40	3	−1
	(623)	(138)	(590)	(20)	(74)	(29)	(7)
Ethnic minority	1,435**	486**	811**	35**	103**	−4	2
	(299)	(66)	(284)	(9)	(36)	(14)	(3)
CCP	−256+	53+	−244+	−14**	−60**	7	2
	(139)	(31)	(132)	(4)	(17)	(6)	(1)
Education (elementary school or less omitted)							
Junior high school	1,017**	650**	322	−17*	56+	9	−2
	(268)	(59)	(254)	(8)	(32)	(12)	(3)

(Continued)

Table 7.9 continued

	(1) Total social benefits	(2) Cash transfers	(3) Health	(4) Education	(5) Housing	(6) Food	(7) Other in-kind
Senior high school	1,609**	1,066**	414	16+	98**	15	−1
	(271)	(60)	(257)	(9)	(32)	(13)	(3)
2 years college	2,336**	1,318**	960**	−14	77*	−2	−2
	(304)	(67)	(288)	(10)	(36)	(14)	(3)
4 years college or above	2,644**	1,712**	823*	−17	136**	−2	−8*
	(345)	(76)	(327)	(11)	(41)	(16)	(4)
Employment status/type (employed at public institutions or state-owned or collective enterprises omitted)							
Employed at private enterprises	285+	129**	210	−16**	−47*	8	0
	(169)	(37)	(160)	(5)	(20)	(8)	(2)
Retired	2,120**	1,740**	432*	−37**	−34	13	5*
	(223)	(49)	(212)	(7)	(27)	(10)	(2)
Unemployed	−471	−160*	−215	12	−106**	0	−3
	(320)	(71)	(303)	(10)	(38)	(15)	(3)
Household characteristics							
No. of children <18 yrs	−1,373**	−984**	−539**	280**	−122**	−8	0
	(127)	(28)	(121)	(4)	(15)	(6)	(1)
No. of elders 60+ yrs	1,363**	760**	762**	−54**	−105**	−0	1
	(161)	(36)	(153)	(5)	(19)	(7)	(2)
No. of other adults 18–59 yrs	−1,239**	−839**	−243**	−52**	−88**	−13**	−4**
	(95)	(21)	(90)	(3)	(11)	(4)	(1)

Region (eastern omitted)							
Central	−1,719**	−593**	−521**	−197**	−381**	−22**	−5**
	(145)	(32)	(137)	(5)	(17)	(7)	(2)
Western	−1,710**	−512**	−640**	−73**	−425**	−51**	−10**
	(187)	(41)	(177)	(6)	(22)	(9)	(2)
Pre-tax pre-transfer income deciles (1st decile omitted)							
2nd	−1,436**	−820**	−627*	7	−13	12	4
	(298)	(66)	(282)	(9)	(35)	(14)	(3)
3rd	−1,689**	−932**	−737*	4	−45	16	5
	(309)	(68)	(293)	(10)	(37)	(14)	(3)
4th	−973**	−996**	7	6	−22	24	9**
	(312)	(69)	(296)	(10)	(37)	(14)	(3)
5th	−1,668**	−1,183**	−492+	14	−45	24	14**
	(314)	(70)	(298)	(10)	(37)	(15)	(3)
6th	−1,478**	−1,126**	−313	−1	−87*	35*	13**
	(321)	(71)	(304)	(10)	(38)	(15)	(3)
7th	−1,835**	−1,302**	−533+	26*	−76*	35*	14**
	(323)	(71)	(306)	(10)	(38)	(15)	(3)
8th	−1,967**	−1,338**	−589+	29**	−128**	42**	18**
	(325)	(72)	(308)	(10)	(39)	(15)	(3)
9th	−1,362**	−1,609**	74	52**	46	60**	17**
	(331)	(73)	(313)	(10)	(39)	(15)	(4)
10th	−2,355**	−1,870**	−547+	65**	−168**	134**	32**
	(341)	(75)	(323)	(11)	(40)	(16)	(4)
Constant	5,978**	3,941**	1,089+	63**	687**	163**	35**
	(625)	(138)	(592)	(20)	(74)	(29)	(7)
R-squared	0.10	0.59	0.01	0.43	0.05	0.02	0.01

Notes: Regression coefficients presented with standard errors in parentheses; + p < 0.10; * p < 0.05; ** p < 0.01.
Source: Author's calculations using the CHIP data.

comparison of a set of inequality indices based on pre- and post-transfer incomes.

Table 7.10 presents the pre- and post-transfer income shares by income deciles. Clearly, the distribution of pre-tax pre-transfer incomes was quite unequal in both years. The bottom decile accounted for only 3 per cent of urban society's total market income in 1988; this share decreased to 1 per cent in 2002. In contrast, the top decile enjoyed 23 per cent in 1988, increasing their share of the total urban market income to 27 per cent in 2002. From 1988 to 2002, the market income shares of the lower deciles (2nd to 4th deciles) diminished while those of the higher groups (7th to 9th deciles) increased.

In both years, social benefit transfers reduced income inequality. As a result, post-transfer incomes were more fairly distributed than pre-tax pre-transfer incomes. The income shares at the lower end of income distribution increased, while those at the higher end dropped in both years. For example, in 1988 the bottom decile increased its income share from 3 to 7 per cent (an increase of 4 percentage points) and, in 2002, from 1 to 9 per cent (an increase of 8 percentage points). Similarly, the income share of the top decile dropped 4 and percentage points, respectively, in 1988 and 2002, suggesting that social benefits redistributed resources and reduced income inequality to a greater extent in 2002 than in 1988.

Table 7.11 presents estimates of inequality indices. Overall, the pre-tax pre-transfer income inequality based only on market income increased dramatically from 1988 to 2002. Although social benefit transfers in both years did help to reduce the gap somewhat, post-transfer income inequality levels in 2002 were still higher than in 1988, indicating that the increase in social benefits was not sufficient to close the gap caused by increasing market income inequality during the period.

The pre-tax pre-transfer p90/p10 dispersion ratio in 1988 was 3.10 and jumped to 7.37 in 2002, indicating a substantial increase in the gap between the rich and the poor. Social benefit transfers helped to reduce the income gap in both years – by 0.58 (a reduction of 19 percentage points) in 1988 and 3.26 (a reduction of 44 percentage points) in 2002, suggesting that the social benefits had a greater redistributional effect in 2002 than in 1988. This is consistent with the results in Table 7.10. However, the post-transfer income dispersion ratio was still greater in 2002 (4.11) than in 1988 (2.52).

Results from the Gini coefficient and Atkinson indices present a slightly different story. It is obvious that social benefits reduced income inequality in both years. The Gini coefficient decreased from 0.27 to 0.22 in 1988 and from 0.38 to 0.33 in 2002. Meanwhile, the Atkinson

Table 7.10 Pre- and post-transfer income shares by pre-tax pre-transfer income deciles in urban China: 1988 and 2002

Decile	Pre-transfer	Post-transfer	Δ (post–pre)
1988			
1st	3%	7%	4%
2nd	6%	7%	2%
3rd	7%	8%	1%
4th	8%	8%	1%
5th	9%	9%	0%
6th	9%	9%	0%
7th	10%	10%	0%
8th	12%	11%	−1%
9th	14%	12%	−1%
10th	23%	18%	−4%
All	100%	100%	0%
2002			
1st	1%	9%	8%
2nd	3%	6%	2%
3rd	5%	6%	1%
4th	6%	7%	1%
5th	8%	8%	0%
6th	9%	9%	0%
7th	11%	10%	−1%
8th	13%	11%	−2%
9th	16%	14%	−2%
10th	27%	21%	−6%
All	100%	100%	0%

Source: Author's calculations using the CHIP data.

indices decreased by 0.03, 0.06 and 0.24 in 1988 and by 0.04, 0.11 and 0.40 in 2002, depending on the value of *e*. It appears that social benefits reduced income inequality to a greater degree in 1988 than in 2002, as the Gini coefficient decreased by 18 per cent in 1988 but only 14 per cent in 2002. With regard to the Atkinson indices, as one attaches more weight to income transfers at the lower end of the income distribution (that is, the value of *e* changing from 0.5 to 1 to 2), the effect of the social benefit transfers on the reduction of income inequality increased in both years and, again, the role of social benefits in alleviating income inequality was stronger in 1988 (that is, larger percentage changes) than in 2002 using the percentage change measures.

Table 7.11 The impact of social benefits on income inequality indices in urban China: 1988 and 2002

	Pre-transfer	Post-transfer	Value change (=post–pre)	Change % (=change/pre)
1988				
p90/p10	3.10	2.52	−0.58	−0.19
Gini	0.27	0.22	−0.05	−0.18
A(*e* = 0.5)	0.07	0.04	−0.03	−0.38
A(*e* = 1)	0.13	0.08	−0.06	−0.42
A(*e* = 2)	0.38	0.14	−0.24	−0.62
2002				
p90/p10	7.37	4.11	−3.26	−0.44
Gini	0.38	0.33	−0.05	−0.14
A(*e* = 0.5)	0.13	0.09	−0.04	−0.31
A(*e* = 1)	0.28	0.17	−0.11	−0.39
A(*e* = 2)	0.70	0.29	−0.40	−0.58

Source: Author's calculations using the CHIP data.

Conclusion

This chapter analyses the determinants of social benefits and their impact on income inequality in urban China. The results show that even after controlling for various demographic characteristics, total urban social benefits strongly targeted the bottom income deciles, particularly in 2002. The top income decile in 1988 also gained substantially from total social benefits, mainly from housing benefits. Cash transfers were negatively associated with pre-tax pre-transfer income distribution in both years, while important in-kind benefits – namely, health and food in 1988 and education in 2002 – were positively related to pre-tax pre-transfer income levels.

Household head being an elder (>60 yrs) or retiree was strongly associated with higher levels of total social benefits, mainly reflecting their pension income. The educational level of a household head was positively related to total social benefits to a much greater extent in 2002 than in 1988. The economic and welfare reforms during this period directly reduced the social benefits of those employed in public institutions or state-owned or collective enterprises. Larger households, including those with more children and more adults aged 18 to 59, were disadvantaged in both years with regard to receiving social benefits. Residents in the central and western regions almost consistently received fewer social benefits of all types than those in the eastern region in both years.

Results also show that social benefits played a significant role in reducing income inequality in urban China in 1988 and 2002. However, they were insufficient to close the rising income gap driven by growing market income inequality during the period. Consequently, the level of the post-tax post-transfer income inequality was still greater in 2002 than in 1988. In addition, social benefits – particularly cash transfers – became more targeted towards the bottom segments of income distribution in 2002 than in 1988. This is very probably an outcome of two combined driving forces: the rapid ageing trend in China (which yields more pension benefits) and the beginnings of the government's effort to provide a basic safety net to the newly emerged urban poor since the mid-to-late 1990s, mainly through the minimum living standard assurance programme and unemployment living subsidy. As a result, the post-tax post-transfer income of the bottom deciles was raised considerably and those who were left behind by both market income and social benefits were the 2nd and 3rd income deciles, or the working poor.

The findings of this chapter have important policy implications. Noticeably, certain vulnerable groups are less targeted by social benefits and, thus, are left behind by both the market and public support. For example, families headed by persons who are single, with low education (elementary school or less), unemployed, and those with more children or residing in a less developed region (western or central) all tend to receive fewer social benefits than their more advantageous peers. Being an explicit redistributive mechanism, the basic goal and functions of social benefits are to reallocate resources (typically after allocations of resources through the market) and improve the wellbeing of disadvantaged groups, as well as overall social justice. As the economic reforms move forward, social benefits need to play a larger redistributional role to support these vulnerable groups. At the aggregate level, even though absolute levels of social benefits have increased since the reforms, their contribution to alleviating income inequality have declined compared to the increase in market income and, thus, needs to be strengthened.

As the government continues to increase public assistance to the bottom level of income distribution, the working poor – that is, the near-bottom income groups – have not only fared poorly in market competition but have also been left behind with respect to social benefits. As a result, their post-tax post-transfer incomes have been much lower than those who earned less through market work. It is important to recognize that this group needs the greatest intervention through social policies. More generous social benefits, including cash assistance and in-kind benefits such as health, education and housing, need to be redistributed towards this group.

This study has several limitations that need to be addressed in future research. First, the growing numbers of rural migrants are missing from this analysis because of unavailability of data.[16] The income inequality level would presumably be higher had the rural migrants been included. Given that social benefits on the part of rural migrants are in most cases trivial, the redistributional role of social benefits could, in fact, be weaker than indicated in this chapter. Furthermore, since the migrant population was much greater in 2002 than in 1988, the cutback of social benefits during the period could be even more predominant in comparison to the results presented in this chapter.

Second, this study measures income on a per capita basis but ignores the specific benefits to particular population subgroups, as well as income sharing patterns within the household. For example, health benefits are often specific to individuals with health problems; education benefits can in most cases only be enjoyed by enrolled children; cash transfers, especially pension income, may be allocated differently among children, elders and other adults. Future research should take these factors into account by using suitable measuring or imputation methods and equivalent scales.

Notes

*I am grateful to Carl Riskin and Li Shi for allowing me to use the China Household Income Project (CHIP) 2002 dataset for this study; to Irwin Garfinkel, Stephan Haggard, Sheila Kamerman, Andrew Nathan, Carl Riskin, Michael Sherraden, Jane Waldfogel and Fuhua Zhai for valuable comments; and to Ding Yanqing, Gao Yan, Emily Hannum, Mun C. Tsang, Wang Rong, Wallace L. Wang and Wen Dongmao for helping gather and clarify administrative data on education. I am also thankful for the financial support from the V.K. Wellington Koo Fellowship awarded through the Columbia University Weatherhead East Asian Institute and the Columbia University Public Policy Consortium Fellowship. The Asian Development Bank, the Ford Foundation and the Swedish International Development Agency financed the surveys that provide data for this research.

1 Some argue that, in contrast to the prediction of the Kuznets curve, income inequality in China will still rise for an extended period, even though economic growth has levelled off somewhat (Riskin 2005; Wu and Perloff 2004).

2 This is based on the author's calculation using the CHIP data with a poverty line defined as 50 per cent of the median income of urban areas. Income is

measured as per capita household post-tax post-transfer income, including market earnings, social benefits and private transfers, less taxes and fees.

3 Different equivalent scales have been proposed and adopted in existing literature, mostly in conjunction with the study of western industrialized nations. Some scales are proposed for studying developing countries, but there seems no particular fit for urban Chinese households.

4 'Income from compensation' was not clearly defined in the surveys, so they were based on the individual interpretation of the survey participant.

5 In 1988, taxes and fees paid for private enterprises or self-employment were recorded separately, and then subtracted from the total reported pre-tax pre-transfer income for this type of employment. In 2002, families were asked to report directly the net income from private enterprises or self-employment. Thus, the two years' data are compatible in this regard, but it was impossible to know the amount of taxes and fees paid for private enterprises or self-employment in 2002.

6 The formula is: rental value of public housing = 0.08**C**(total living area square metre + auxiliary area square metre)*(1 + *s*), where *C* is provincial construction cost per square metre and *s* is an index for sanitary facilities in housing ($s = -0.33$ if a house lacks sanitary facilities; $s = -0.25$ if a house shares sanitary facilities; $s = -0.15$ if a house has a toilet but lacks a bath; and $s = -0.10$ if a house has both a toilet and a bath). This study adopts the values of *C* and *s* from a CHIP 1988 SAS programme for computing income available at the Interuniversity Consortium for Political and Social Research (ICPSR).

7 Administrative data on public health expenditures for retirees of different types of employer do exist. However, the survey data do not contain information on the type of the retirees' employer. Therefore, provincial public health expenditure per capita for retirees is computed by dividing the total public health expenditure on retirees across employment types by the total number of retirees.

8 For example, suppose there is a family from Beijing with four members: a middle-aged couple, a retired elderly person who is one of the couple's parents and the couple's teenager studying at school. Suppose one of the spouses works in a state enterprise and the other in a collective enterprise, they are assigned the values of CNY 186.46 and CNY 111.57, respectively, as their health benefits. The retiree is assigned an imputed value of CNY 394.32 for health benefits and the student zero. The health benefits are then pooled, yielding a total of CNY 692.35 and divided by household size to obtain the household per capita health benefit of CNY 173.09.

9 CEESY (2003) provides data on the total number of students enrolled in junior and senior high schools, as well as the number of students only attending senior high school at each of the three areas. The number of senior high school students is subtracted from the total to obtain the number of junior high school students enrolled.

10 This analysis also tried treating 'counties and towns' as part of the urban areas, with no major difference apparent in the final results.

11 Regression models are not run on whether families receive certain social benefits because most families receive all of these benefits, and the sample sizes of non-recipients were often quite small.

12 The values of private transfers and taxes and fees paid are both quite small.

13 According to official national data, the proportion of the elderly aged 65 or over increased from 5.57 per cent in 1990 to 8.16 per cent in 2002 (NBS 2004).
14 The 2002 data show that households headed by individuals who work in public institutions received more benefits than those in state-owned or collective enterprises. However, as the data for 1988 could not distinguish between the two, this study combines them in both years to render the data comparable across the two waves.
15 The national enrolment rate of children of school age (6–14 yrs) has increased steadily since 1978. It rose from 95.5 per cent in 1978 to 97.8 per cent in 1990, 98.5 per cent in 1995, and 99.1 per cent in 2000, but dropped slightly to 98.6 in 2002 (NBS 2004: 175).
16 See Gao (2006) for further discussion of this issue.

References

Atkinson, A.B. (1970) 'On the Measurement of Inequality', *Journal of Economic Theory*, 2: 244–63.

Barr, N. (2001) 'Introduction', in N. Barr (ed.), *Economic Theory and the Welfare State*, Volume I (Northampton, MA: Edward Elgar).

CEESY (2003) *China Education Expenditure Statistical Yearbook* (Beijing: China Statistics Press for the Ministry of Education and National Bureau of Statistics, Department of Social Science and Technology Statistics).

Chang, G.H. (2002) 'The Cause and Cure of China's Widening Income Disparity', *China Economic Review*, 13: 335–40.

Chen, S., Datt, G. and Ravallion, M. (2004) 'POVCAL: A Program for Calculating Poverty and Measures from Grouped Data' (Washington, DC: Poverty and Human Resources Division, Policy Research Department, World Bank).

China Labor Yearbook Editorial Group (1991) *China Labor Yearbook 1988–1989*. (Beijing: China Labor Press (Zhongguo Laodong Chubanshe)).

CHIP Research Team (1993) 'The Chinese Household Income Project (1988) Extended Definition of Income' (Ann Arbor, MI: Inter-university Consortium for Political and Social Research (ICPSR 9836)).

Eichen, M. and Zhang, M. (1993) 'Annex: The 1988 Household Sample Survey – Data Description and Availability', in K. Griffin and R. Zhao (eds), *The Distribution of Income in China* (New York, NY: St. Martin's Press).

Fang, C., Zhang, X. and Fan, S. (2002) 'Emergence of Urban Poverty and Inequality in China: Evidence from Household Survey', *China Economic Review*, 13 (4): 430–43.

Gao, Q. (2006) 'The Social Benefit System in Urban China: Reforms and Trends from 1988 to 2002', *Journal of East Asian Studies*, 6, 1: 31–67.

Garfinkel, I. (1996) 'Economic Security for Children: From Means Testing and Bifurcation to Universality', in I. Garfinkel, J.L. Hochschild and S.S. McLanahan (eds), *Social Policies for Children* (Washington, DC: Brookings Institution).

Griffin, K. and Zhao, R. (1993) 'Chinese Household Income Project, 1988', Computer file (Ann Arbor, MI: Inter-university Consortium for Political and Social Research distributor).

Gustafsson, B. and Li, S. (2001) 'A More Unequal China? Aspects of Inequality in the Distribution of Equivalent Income', in C. Riskin, R. Zhao and S. Li (eds),

China's Retreat from Equality: Income Distribution and Economic Transition (Armonk, NY: M.E. Sharpe).
Kawachi, I. (2000) 'Income Inequality', in *Notebook on the Social and Physical Environment*, available at www.macses.ucsf.edu/Research/Social%20Environment/notebook/inequality.html (accessed 16 May) (San Francisco: University of California San Francisco).
Khan, A.R. and Riskin, C. (1998) 'Income and Inequality in China: Composition, Distribution and Growth of Household Income, 1988 to 1995', *China Quarterly*, 154, June: 221–53.
Khan, A.R., and Riskin, C. (2004) 'Growth and Distribution of Household Income in China between 1995 and 2002', Unpublished manuscript, University of California, Riverside.
Leung, J.C. (2003) 'Social Security Reforms in China: Issues and Prospects', *International Journal of Social Welfare*, 12, 2: 73–85.
Li, S. (2003) 'New Trends in Income Distribution in China and Related Policy Changes' (Beijing: Institute of Economics, China Academy of Social Science).
Li, S. and Knight, J. (2004) 'China Household Income Project 2002' (Beijing: Chinese Academy of Social Sciences (CASS) Institute of Economics).
Li, S. and Yue. X. (2004) 'The Latest Changes of Individual Income Inequality in China' (Beijing: China Academy of Social Science, Institute of Economics): available at: www.cass.net.cn/jingjisuo/
Meng, X. (2003) 'Economic Restructuring and Income Inequality in Urban China'. Canberra: Australian National University, Unpublished manuscript.
Ministry of Education (1989) *China Provincial Education Expenditure Annual Development Report 1989* (Beijing: China Higher Education Press for the Ministry of Education).
NBS (National Bureau of Statistics) (1996) *China Statistical Yearbook 1996* (Beijing: China Statistics Press (Zhongguo Tongji Chubanshe)).
NBS (National Bureau of Statistics) (2003) *China Statistical Yearbook 2003* (Beijing: China Statistics Press (Zhongguo Tongji Chubanshe)).
NBS (National Bureau of Statistics) (2004) *China Statistical Abstract and Yearbook 2004* (Beijing: China Statistics Press (Zhongguo Tongji Chubanshe)).
NSB (National Statistical Bureau) and Ministry of Labour (1989) *China Labor and Wage Statistical Yearbook 1989* (Beijing: Labor and Personnel Press (Laodong Renshi Chubanshe)).
Riskin, C. (2005) 'Income Inequality in China and the Kuznets Hypothesis', Unpublished manuscript, Columbia University, New York.
Riskin, C., Zhao, R. and Li, S. (2001) 'Introduction: The Retreat from Equality: Highlights of the Findings', in C. Riskin, R. Zhao and S. Li (eds), *China's Retreat from Equality: Income Distribution and Economic Transition* (Armonk, NY: M.E. Sharpe).
Saunders, P. and Shang, X. (2001) 'Social Security Reform in China's Transition to a Market Economy', *Social Policy and Administration*, 35, 3: 274–89.
Wu, X. and Perloff, J.M. (2004) 'China's Income Distribution over Time: Reasons for Rising Inequality', CUDARE Working Paper 977, Berkeley: Department of Agricultural and Resource Economics, University of California at Berkeley: available at: www//repositories.cdlib.org/are_ucb/977
Wu, X. and Treiman, D.J. (2004) 'The Household Registration System and Social Stratification in China: 1955–1996', *Demography*, 41, 2: 363–84.

Appendix

Table 7.A1 China Household Income Project (CHIP) sample designs

		1988	2002
Urban			
Households		9,009	6,835
Individuals		31,827	20,632
Provinces:	Total	10	12
	Common to both waves	10	10
Cities:	Total	60	70
	Common to both waves	60	60
Rural			
Households		10,258	9,200
Individuals		51,352	37,968
Provinces:	Total	28	21
	Common to all three waves	19	19

Source: Riskin, Zhao and Li (2001: 5).

Table 7.A2 Administrative data on provincial per capita public health expenditures in 1988 (in 2002 CNY)

Province	Employees by enterprise type			Retirees
	State	Collective	Other	
Beijing	470	281	125	993
Shanxi	181	92	259	377
Liaoning	327	169	344	684
Jiangsu	295	180	312	578
Anhui	205	117	175	380
Henan	223	107	807	568
Hubei	271	125	313	553
Guangdong	420	209	212	751
Yunnan	289	150	332	590
Gansu	250	105	671	441

Source: Author's calculation based on NSB and Ministry of Labour (1989) and *China Labour Yearbook* (1991).

Table 7.A3 Administrative data on provincial per capita public education expenditures in 1988 and 2002 (in 2002 CNY)

Province	**1988**		**2002**		
	Senior and junior high school	**Elementary school**	**Senior high school**	**Junior high school**	**Elementary school**
Beijing	1,466	620	4,996	3,835	2,904
Shanxi	529	239	1,335	1,060	744
Liaoning	675	320	1,603	1,635	1,202
Jiangsu	496	252	1,942	2,234	1,740
Anhui	373	151	1,190	1,007	935
Henan	398	123	912	1,178	915
Hubei	471	116	1,109	1,096	868
Guangdong	632	302	3,055	3,523	2,098
Yunnan	625	275	2,131	2,293	1,600
Gansu	471	259	1,560	1,448	1,223

Source: Author's calculation based on Ministry of Education (1989), CEESY (2003) and NBS (2003).

8

China's Urban Poverty and its Contributing Factors, 1986–2000

Xin Meng, Robert Gregory and Guanghua Wan

Introduction

Food price increases and the introduction of radical social welfare and enterprise reforms during the 1990s generated significant changes in the lives of urban households in China. During this period, urban poverty increased considerably. This chapter uses household level data from 1986 to 2000 to examine what determines whether households fall below the poverty line over this period and investigates how the impact of these determinants has changed through time. We find that large households and households with more non-working members are more likely to be poor, suggesting that perhaps the change from the old implicit price subsidies, based on household size, to an explicit income subsidy, based on employment, has worsened the position of large families. Further investigation into regional poverty variation indicates that over the 1986–93 period food price increases were also a major contributing factor. Between 1994 and 2000, the worsening of the economic situation of state sector employees contributed to the poverty increase.

Although income increases in urban China pushed the average household to higher living standards, economic circumstances among poor households may not have improved in the 1990s. For example, Gustafsson and Wei (2000), Khan and Riskin (2001), Xue and Wei (2003) and Meng, Gregory and Wang (2005) find that urban poverty increased considerably during this period.[1] There were many reasons for this. First, in the early 1990s price reform led to a significant increase in food prices, which play an important role in determining living standards of the poor. Second, acceleration of social welfare reform – which switched government provision of medical care, old age pensions, and highly subsidized education and housing to more reliance on individual provision – also put significant economic strains on low income groups. Third, poor households were particularly affected by enterprise restructuring, which increased the urban unemployment rate from 6 per cent in 1993 to 12 per cent in 2000 (Giles, Park and Zhang 2005; Knight and Xue 2004).

Within this environment of rapid economic change, a range of questions naturally arises as to who are the urban poor? What are their important demographic, family and labour market characteristics? Has the impact of these characteristics on poverty changed over time and can the change of the impact be linked to the broad macro structural changes described above? This chapter uses 1986 to 2000 urban household data from 15 provinces to address these questions.

The next section discusses factors that may have contributed to increased poverty. We go on to describe the data and poverty measures, search for the determinants of poverty and explore how they changed during the 1990s, and close the chapter with our conclusions.

Economic restructuring and social welfare reform in the 1990s

The 1990s saw the most radical economic restructuring in China since gradualist economic reform began in 1978. Three important reform measures may have contributed to the growth of poverty: food price, social welfare and enterprise reforms.

Before reform, food prices in urban China were highly subsidized through a coupon ration system, whereby coupons were distributed according to the number of family members and their ages. In the late 1970s and early 1980s, market orientated reforms in the agriculture sector led to significant increases in production and to the introduction of an urban two-tier food price system, in that urban households received subsidized food coupons but were also free to purchase better and more varieties of food in the market place. Gradually, however, the government increased subsidized food prices so that the two-tier prices were almost equal to each other (Tang 1998). When the government finally abolished food coupons in 1993, workers were compensated by an explicit wage subsidy at a universal rate. Households with more non-working members, however, were disadvantaged because food coupons had been distributed according to the number of household members and their ages, while the explicit wage subsidies were distributed only to household working members. In addition, financial help for transportation, rent and many other consumption items was switched from implicit price subsidies to explicit income subsidies. All these changes would have had an adverse impact on living conditions of large households with fewer working members, who are more likely to have lower per capita income. Indeed, Meng, Gong and Wang (2007) find that, after the food price increase in 1993, low income households had a reduction of calorie availability and, at the same time, a reduction in the proportion of calorie from protein.

Social welfare reform also began in the late 1980s and early 1990s. By the mid-1990s, reform had gradually removed most of the public provision of subsidized low rent housing, free education and free medical services. According to the Urban Income and Expenditure Survey conducted by the National Statistical Bureau, medical, education and housing expenditure as a share of total expenditure more than doubled between 1986 and 2000 for both average and poor (bottom 20 percentile income) households alike (see Figure 8.1). Furthermore, the government-provided pension scheme was changed to a three pillar system, and individual contributions would eventually play the most important role. These

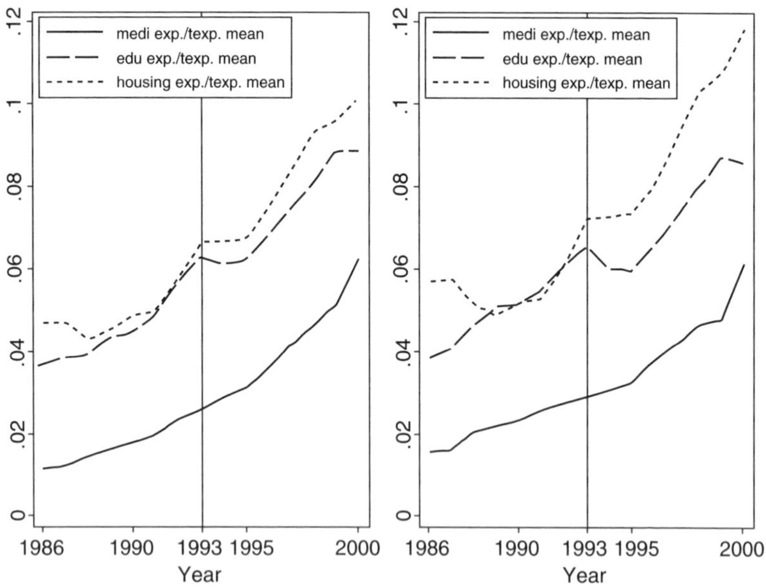

Figure 8.1 Medical, education and housing expenditure shares of total expenditure

reforms reduced 'real' disposable incomes as households were increasingly faced with the need to provide for pensions and to pay higher prices for many services that had been previously provided free or almost free. Figure 8.2 presents real per capita income and expenditure over the period by different income groups. It can be seen that real income/expenditure for the bottom 10 percentile income group hardly increased over the period. Based on this condition, the increased need to spend on medical, housing, education and pension contributions would have further reduced the real disposable income of low income groups, and increased their probability of living in poverty.

The third important reform involved state sector restructuring. State enterprises often made losses, and received substantial subsidies, but by the mid-1990s these losses quickly increased due to intensified competition from the non-state sector. In response, a reform policy of 'keeping the large state enterprises and letting go the medium and small ones' was introduced and subsidies became more difficult to obtain. Many small and medium-size state enterprises were bankrupted and those that survived began to take efficiency measures seriously. These two forces

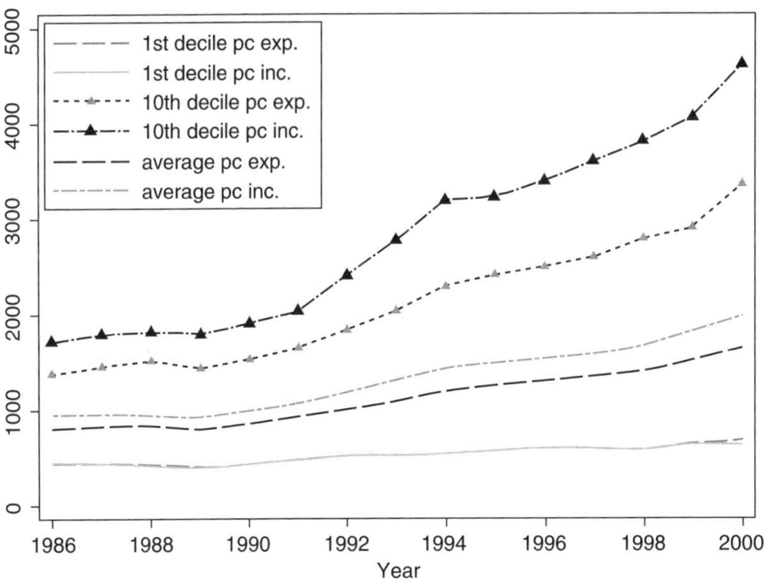

Figure 8.2 Real per capita income and expenditure by income group

led to large-scale retrenchments. Between 1995 and 2001, around 43 million workers were laid off (Ministry of Labour and Social Security 2002) and the urban unemployment rate doubled (Giles, Park and Zhang 2005; Knight and Xue 2004). The poverty impact of increased unemployment is straightforward. However, there was an additional poverty effect which appeared in the form of arrears in wages, pensions and medical reimbursements from loss making or bankrupted state enterprises. Based on a survey of five large cities (China Urban Labour Survey), Giles, Park and Cai (2006) estimated that, in 2000, among employed workers aged 16 to 60, 11 per cent experienced wage arrears and 22 per cent experienced health insurance arrears. For retired workers, 11 per cent had been subject to pension arrears and 30 per cent had been subject to health insurance arrears.

To help offset increasing rates of urban poverty, the government introduced the Urban 'Di Bao' programme (the minimum living allowance) towards the end of the period (1997–2000). Di Bao guaranteed a minimum income defined with respect to a local poverty line for individuals with urban registration (O'Keefe 2004). The programme was initially piloted in Shanghai in 1993. Later, when it was introduced to other regions, it was not effectively enforced at the beginning and the degree of enforcement differed from region to region. It became national policy during 1997–99, and from 1999 it was fully implemented nationwide.

Data and poverty measure

We use the Urban Household Income and Expenditure Survey (UHIES) 1986–2000 to examine factors associated with household poverty. The UHIES began in 1956 and was resumed in 1980 after its suspension during the Cultural Revolution 1966–76 (Fang, Zhang and Fan 2002). The survey samples households with Urban Household Registration for every province in the nation (29 provinces before 1990 and 30 after 1990 due to the newly established province of Hainan in 1990).[2] The sample is based on several stratifications at the regional, provincial, county, city, town and neighbourhood community levels. The intention is randomly to select households within each chosen neighbourhood community; these households are expected to keep a diary of all expenditures (disaggregated for hundreds of product categories) for each day for a full year. Enumerators visit sample households once or twice each month to review the records, assist the household with their questions, and to collect the household records for data entry in the local Statistical Bureau office (Han, Wailes and Cramer 1995; Fang, Zhang and Fan 2002;

Gibson, Huang and Rozelle 2003). The earliest electronic data available is from 1986. Gibson and Rozelle (2003) argue that in recent years, in some regions, some households have been reluctant to participate in the surveys due to the falling value of the payment. This may make the sampling procedure less random, but the UHIES is still the most nationally representative urban household survey in China. We use data from 15 of the 29 provinces: Beijing, Shanxi, Liaoning, Heilongjiang, Shanghai, Jiangsu, Anhui, Jiangxi, Shandong, Henan, Hubei, Guangdong, Sichuan, Yunnan, and Gansu. The total number of households ranges from 8,100 to 10,250.[3]

The poverty lines used in this study are calculated using various applications of the 'cost-of-basic-needs' (CBN) method proposed by Ravallion (1994). The usual CBN poverty line used in the literature is to allow the CBN bundle in one year to differ by region and to keep each regional CBN bundle fixed through time, adjusting it by a regional CPI deflator (see, for example, Ravallion and Chen 2004). This approach is often supported by the argument that it is desirable to keep a fixed bundle of goods through time to measure absolute poverty. But the exceptional circumstances associated with Chinese economic reforms over this period lead us to adopt different approaches.[4]

One of the approaches adopted is to apply the CBN method to calculate a poverty line *for each province and each year* over the data period (labelled as the 'varying weight CBN poverty line'). The implications of these poverty line calculations are twofold: first, we allow the poor in each region, over time, to change the pattern of food consumption in response to changes in food availability and prices. Second, we allow the poor to change their allocation between non-food necessities and food in response to reforms that significantly lifted prices of many non-food necessities; such as education, healthcare and housing. Poverty lines calculated in this manner are not based on a fixed basket of goods.

The other approach is to use a 'chained weight CBN poverty line'. For each region, we calculate the food poverty line (cost of 2100 calories for the lowest 20 per cent income group) and a non-food poverty line (as used in the normal CBN poverty line calculation) at the beginning of the period and adjust them, within a four-year period, by the grain price index (for food poverty line) and the CPI (for non-food poverty line). For the fifth year, we recalculate the food and non-food poverty lines and perform the same deflating adjustment for the next four years and so on. This procedure can be thought of as being similar to a Chained Laspeyres index. This poverty line allows the poor to change their pattern of food consumption and to substitute between food and non-food every five years.[5,6]

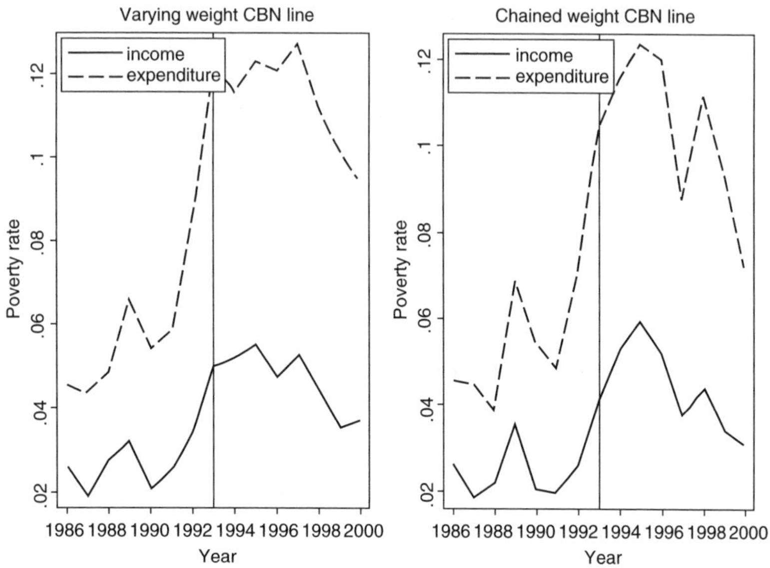

Figure 8.3 Poverty headcount index

Once the poverty lines are estimated we calculate the proportion of sample population with per capita income or expenditure under the poverty lines for each province and each year (a headcount index). This index is calculated in two ways: an income measure, those with per capita income less than the poverty line, and an expenditure measure, those with per capita expenditure less than the poverty line. We present these indices in Figure 8.3. They show that while the poverty rate, as measured by expenditure, is lower than the poverty line as measured by income, the changes over time are very similar. Poverty increased from 1990, reached a peak in 1993, and then remained at a high level for most of the 1990s. Poverty began falling from 1998, coinciding with the national implementation of the Di Bao programme. The results are similar if we adopt the 'chained weight CBN poverty line', with the exception that it peaks at 1995 rather than 1993. However, 1992–93 still exhibits the highest one-year poverty increment.

We also examine the severity of poverty at each point in time using the 'varying weight CBN line' only.[7] Panel 1 of Figure 8.4 shows the estimated mean poverty line and mean total expenditure of those below the poverty line. The gap between the two lines seems to have widened. Panel 2 of Figure 8.4 presents the squared poverty gap,[8] which illustrates

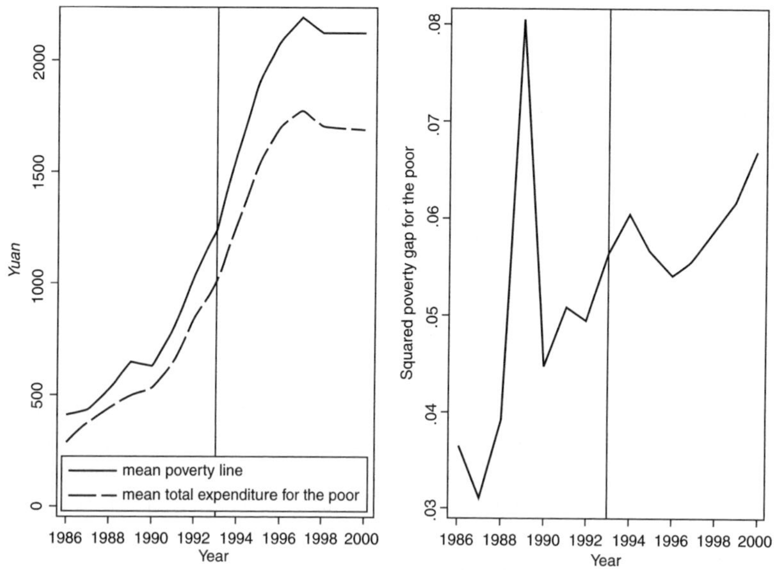

Figure 8.4 Severity of poverty

even more clearly that the severity of poverty has increased more or less continuously since 1988, with the exception of 1989–90. On average, the squared poverty gap for the poor is much higher for the 1990s than for the 1980s, and it is higher for the late 1990s than for the early 1990s.

Summary statistics by poverty status for each of the 15 years are presented in Table 8.A1 in the Appendix. We find that poor households are, on average, larger, less educated, have fewer members working, more members working as labourers, significantly fewer members working as professionals or government/enterprise officials, more children aged 15 and below, and more elderly female members.

Methodology and empirical results

We examine two questions: what determines whether a household falls below the poverty line; and has the importance of these determinants changed over time? Initially we proceed in two ways. One way is to estimate the following probit model for each survey year:

$$P_{ij} = X'\beta + v_j + \varepsilon_i \qquad (8.1)$$

where P_{ij} indicates whether per capita expenditure of household i in province j is below the poverty line for the province and survey year. X is a vector of observable characteristics which may be related to household income or other factors affecting poverty, υ is a vector of provincial fixed effects, and ε is a standard normal error term.

The other way is to follow Datt and Jolliffe (2005) and Gibson and Rozelle (2003) and utilize the consumption variable directly.[9] Their approach may be summarized as follows:

$$\ln\left(\frac{c_{ij}}{z_j}\right) = X'\beta + \upsilon_j + \varepsilon_i \tag{8.2}$$

where the dependent variable is log nominal per capita consumption expenditure of household i in province j, deflated by provincial specific poverty lines, z_j. Normalizing household per capita consumption by the poverty line indicates that any household whose $\ln(c_{ij}/z_j) < 0$ is living below the poverty line and the probability of the household being poor can be derived from the following equation:

$$prob\left[\ln\left(\frac{c_{ij}}{z_j}\right) < 0\right] = \Phi\left[\frac{(-X'\hat{\beta})}{\hat{\sigma}}\right] \tag{8.3}$$

where Φ [•] is the standard normal cumulative density function, and $\hat{\sigma}$ is the standard error of the regression. Using estimated results from equation (8.2), we can simulate the marginal effect of one unit change in X on the change in the probability of being poor.

We find no significant difference in the estimated results from the two methods presented above. So, after discussing the results, attention is focused on equation (8.1) because it leads naturally to a probit decomposition procedure proposed by Doiron and Riddell (1994) to quantify the changing impact of different variables over time. Their decomposition of the difference in the probabilities of falling below the poverty line between any two years can be written as:

$$\Phi_t(\tilde{X}_t^k \hat{\beta}_t^k) - \Phi_{t+n}(\tilde{X}_{t+n}^k\ \hat{\beta}_{t+n}^k) \simeq \frac{\partial \Phi(\varphi)}{\partial \varphi}(\tilde{X}_l^k \hat{\beta}_t^k - \tilde{X}_{t+n}^k\ \hat{\beta}_{t+n}^k) \tag{8.4}$$

where subscript t indicates the year of the survey and k is the number of variables included in the probit estimation. The first term on the right hand side of equation (8.4) is the normal probability density function evaluated at point φ, while the second term is a linear function of characteristics and coefficients.

The X vector used in this study includes household size, age and gender of the household head, years of schooling of household head and spouse, the proportion of household members who are working and their occupational distributions. Household composition variables, such as the proportion of household members who are male and household members' age and gender distributions, are also included. Finally, as income and price variations across different regions in China have always been high and persistent, fixed provincial effects are included. We loosely group our variables into economic reform (household size and proportion of household members who are working), human capital and regional dispersion effects.

Determinants of poverty at the household level

The estimated results from equations (8.1) and (8.2) using the 'varying weight CBN line' measured poverty as the dependent variable, are reported in Tables 8.1 and 8.2, respectively. Table 8.1 gives the marginal effects obtained from the probit estimation of whether a household has a per capita expenditure below the poverty line, while Table 8.2 reports the OLS coefficients from the log per capita expenditure equation. The results from the two tables are very consistent but, because of the different dependent variables used, the signs are opposite and the magnitudes are different. All standard errors are adjusted for the clustered nature of the sample. We also estimate the two equations using the 'chained weight CBN line' measured poverty as the dependent variable and the results are also very similar to those presented here.[10]

The marginal effects for a group of selected important variables from equation (8.1) are presented in the first panel of Figure 8.5.[11] The second panel of Figure 8.5 shows the simulated marginal effects for the same set of variables using estimated results form equation (8.2).[12] The trend of the change in the marginal effect for all the variables is remarkably similar across the two estimation procedures. The magnitude difference at each point in time is mainly due to the difference in the estimation procedure, the evaluating point and the difference in the choice of the marginal effect as indicated in endnote 12.

Since both estimation procedures provide consistent trends and the results from Table 8.1 are more intuitive, the discussion will focus on Table 8.1. The model (probit estimation of equation (8.1)) performs fairly well, considering the low variation in the dependent variable, with pseudo R^2 being around 0.20 for each of the 15 years.[13]

Table 8.1 Selected results of estimated equation (8.1) dependent variable:

	1986	1987	1988	1989	1990	1991	1992
Household size	0.002	0.007	0.008	0.010	0.011	0.017	0.027
	(0.000)***	(0.001)***	(0.001)***	(0.002)***	(0.002)***	(0.003)***	(0.004)***
HH age	−0.001	−0.004	−0.004	−0.002	−0.004	−0.009	−0.013
	(0.000)***	(0.001)***	(0.001)***	(0.002)	(0.001)***	(0.002)***	(0.003)***
HH gender	0.002	0.004	0.005	0.005	0.001	0.006	0.014
	(0.001)***	(0.002)*	(0.002)***	(0.003)**	(0.002)	(0.002)**	(0.005)***
HH years of schooling	−0.001	−0.001	−0.002	−0.001	−0.003	−0.003	−0.004
	(0.000)***	(0.000)	(0.001)***	(0.001)*	(0.001)***	(0.001)***	(0.001)***
Spouse years of schooling	0.000	−0.001	−0.001	−0.002	−0.001	−0.002	−0.003
	(0.000)**	(0.000)**	(0.000)***	(0.000)***	(0.000)***	(0.000)***	(0.001)***
Members working (%)	−0.013	−0.043	−0.053	−0.079	−0.044	−0.080	−0.090
	(0.002)***	(0.006)***	(0.008)***	(0.013)***	(0.007)***	(0.011)***	(0.013)***
Managerial (%)	−0.001	−0.009	−0.007	−0.020	−0.008	−0.014	−0.032
	(0.002)	(0.006)	(0.007)	(0.009)**	(0.007)	(0.010)	(0.013)**
Clerks (%)	0.000	0.004	0.001	−0.004	0.005	0.004	0.014
	(0.001)	(0.004)	(0.004)	(0.005)	(0.004)	(0.006)	(0.009)
Retail/wholesale trade (%)	0.007	0.019	0.022	0.014	0.021	0.021	0.036
	(0.002)***	(0.004)***	(0.005)***	(0.006)**	(0.004)***	(0.007)***	(0.009)***
Service workers (%)	0.005	0.027	0.015	0.018	0.008	0.007	0.024
	(0.002)***	(0.005)***	(0.005)***	(0.007)**	(0.006)	(0.011)	(0.009)**
Production workers (%)	0.002	0.008	0.007	0.009	0.014	0.008	0.017
	(0.001)**	(0.003)**	(0.004)*	(0.004)**	(0.004)***	(0.005)	(0.008)**
Other labourer (%)	0.007	0.011	0.028	0.028	0.030	0.043	0.034
	(0.003)***	(0.008)	(0.006)***	(0.009)***	(0.007)***	(0.010)***	(0.017)**
Male members (%)	−0.002	−0.003	−0.001	−0.006	0.015	0.013	0.004
	(0.002)	(0.005)	(0.005)	(0.007)	(0.005)***	(0.009)	(0.013)
Children 0–5 years (%)	0.001	0.005	0.053	0.093	0.035	0.054	0.083
	(0.004)	(0.010)	(0.010)***	(0.018)***	(0.011)***	(0.015)***	(0.023)***
Children 6–10 years (%)	0.009	0.003	0.034	0.051	0.028	0.033	0.053
	(0.003)***	(0.007)	(0.008)***	(0.013)***	(0.009)***	(0.014)**	(0.020)***
Children 11–15 years (%)	0.004	0.010	0.032	0.053	0.024	0.038	0.027
	(0.002)*	(0.006)*	(0.007)***	(0.012)***	(0.007)***	(0.012)***	(0.016)
Female 16–20 years (%)	0.001	−0.006	0.038	0.046	0.024	0.023	0.039
	(0.004)	(0.009)	(0.011)***	(0.015)***	(0.009)***	(0.016)	(0.020)*
Male 16–20 years (%)	−0.004	−0.018	0.025	0.071	0.025	0.034	0.073
	(0.004)	(0.011)	(0.010)***	(0.016)***	(0.009)***	(0.014)**	(0.021)***
Male >65 years (%)	−0.002	0.003	0.010	−0.033	−0.022	−0.007	−0.002
	(0.003)	(0.009)	(0.013)	(0.017)**	(0.013)*	(0.018)	(0.033)
Female >65 years (%)	0.007	0.011	0.029	0.027	0.023	0.037	0.050
	(0.003)**	(0.007)	(0.008)***	(0.014)*	(0.011)**	(0.014)***	(0.019)***
Regional	Yes	Yes	Yes	Yes	Yes	Yes	Yes
Observations	8084	7698	7948	6948	7581	7692	9341
Adjusted R^2	0.26	0.24	0.27	0.26	0.28	0.23	0.22

Notes: Cluster adjusted and robust standard errors in parentheses; * significant at 10 per cent,

dummy for being poor

1993	1994	1995	1996	1997	1998	1999	2000
0.043	0.038	0.049	0.048	0.051	0.046	0.041	0.034
(0.006)***	(0.005)***	(0.006)***	(0.005)***	(0.005)***	(0.005)***	(0.004)***	(0.004)***
−0.025	−0.014	−0.022	−0.022	−0.015	−0.018	−0.017	−0.013
(0.005)***	(0.004)***	(0.005)***	(0.003)***	(0.004)***	(0.003)***	(0.003)***	(0.003)***
0.037	0.027	0.027	0.021	0.033	0.026	0.028	0.021
(0.008)***	(0.005)***	(0.008)***	(0.006)***	(0.006)***	(0.005)***	(0.005)***	(0.005)***
−0.007	−0.010	−0.012	−0.011	−0.008	−0.011	−0.010	−0.008
(0.001)***	(0.002)***	(0.002)***	(0.002)***	(0.002)***	(0.002)***	(0.001)***	(0.001)***
−0.006	−0.005	−0.006	−0.006	−0.008	−0.005	−0.004	−0.004
(0.001)***	(0.001)***	(0.001)***	(0.001)***	(0.001)***	(0.001)***	(0.001)***	(0.001)***
−0.142	−0.106	−0.147	−0.137	−0.125	−0.106	−0.070	−0.067
(0.019)***	(0.014)***	(0.021)***	(0.015)***	(0.017)***	(0.016)***	(0.015)***	(0.012)***
−0.047	−0.027	−0.024	−0.019	−0.034	−0.031	−0.045	−0.036
(0.019)**	(0.014)*	(0.018)	(0.016)	(0.019)*	(0.018)*	(0.012)***	(0.014)**
0.018	0.030	0.027	0.021	0.019	0.013	0.004	−0.008
(0.012)	(0.012)**	(0.013)**	(0.013)*	(0.014)	(0.010)	(0.007)	(0.010)
0.088	0.067	0.085	0.071	0.086	0.060	0.053	0.055
(0.016)***	(0.011)***	(0.014)***	(0.016)***	(0.017)***	(0.012)***	(0.010)***	(0.009)***
0.023	0.043	0.062	0.068	0.052	0.042	0.050	0.045
(0.017)	(0.011)***	(0.019)***	(0.018)***	(0.015)***	(0.012)***	(0.011)***	(0.010)***
0.031	0.034	0.046	0.041	0.040	0.025	0.031	0.024
(0.012)**	(0.008)***	(0.011)***	(0.009)***	(0.011)***	(0.010)***	(0.008)***	(0.007)***
0.108	0.051	0.103	0.093	0.092	0.053	0.065	0.066
(0.032)***	(0.014)***	(0.026)***	(0.029)***	(0.032)***	(0.025)**	(0.015)***	(0.021)***
0.014	0.007	−0.003	0.004	0.024	−0.005	0.001	0.025
(0.014)	(0.016)	(0.017)	(0.014)	(0.016)	(0.013)	(0.011)	(0.013)*
0.116	0.100	0.095	0.142	0.141	0.084	0.061	0.074
(0.028)***	(0.026)***	(0.032)***	(0.033)***	(0.033)***	(0.027)***	(0.028)**	(0.030)**
0.104	0.098	0.050	0.081	0.111	0.071	0.036	0.043
(0.029)***	(0.023)***	(0.028)*	(0.027)***	(0.028)***	(0.024)***	(0.019)*	(0.024)*
0.048	0.038	0.036	−0.004	0.042	0.016	0.024	0.046
(0.022)**	(0.020)**	(0.023)	(0.021)	(0.023)*	(0.020)	(0.018)	(0.019)**
0.075	0.071	0.056	0.073	0.057	0.053	−0.004	0.056
(0.035)**	(0.022)***	(0.033)*	(0.032)**	(0.029)**	(0.028)*	(0.024)	(0.022)**
0.076	0.108	0.051	0.069	0.066	0.031	0.032	0.009
(0.032)**	(0.026)***	(0.034)	(0.025)***	(0.030)**	(0.024)	(0.023)	(0.026)
0.047	−0.037	−0.024	−0.087	−0.105	−0.072	−0.066	−0.050
(0.031)	(0.028)	(0.026)	(0.039)**	(0.031)***	(0.028)***	(0.022)***	(0.024)**
0.084	0.045	0.029	0.086	0.070	0.090	0.060	0.020
(0.041)**	(0.022)**	(0.028)	(0.032)***	(0.037)*	(0.033)***	(0.023)***	(0.023)
Yes	Yes	Yes	Yes	Yes	Yes	Yes	Yes
9824	9991	9999	10000	9999	10000	10000	9999
0.19	0.22	0.19	0.17	0.18	0.19	0.21	0.20

** significant at 5 per cent, *** significant at 1 per cent.

Table 8.2 Selected results of estimated equation (8.2) dependent variable: log

	1986	1987	1988	1989	1990	1991	1992
Household size	−0.078	−0.089	−0.110	−0.116	−0.129	−0.139	−0.126
	(0.008)***	(0.008)***	(0.006)***	(0.007)***	(0.006)***	(0.008)***	(0.010)***
HH age	0.063	0.068	0.039	0.029	0.044	0.057	0.050
	(0.007)***	(0.008)***	(0.007)***	(0.008)***	(0.008)***	(0.009)***	(0.008)***
HH gender	−0.053	−0.060	−0.051	−0.029	−0.046	−0.024	−0.047
	(0.010)***	(0.011)***	(0.010)***	(0.013)**	(0.012)***	(0.010)**	(0.010)***
HH years of schooling	0.017	0.018	0.015	0.014	0.018	0.014	0.018
	(0.002)***	(0.002)***	(0.002)***	(0.002)***	(0.002)***	(0.002)***	(0.002)***
Spouse years of schooling	0.000	0.000	0.013	0.009	0.013	0.012	0.009
	(0.001)	(0.002)	(0.001)***	(0.002)***	(0.002)***	(0.001)***	(0.001)***
Members working (%)	0.235	0.229	0.495	0.429	0.372	0.360	0.319
	(0.029)***	(0.029)***	(0.030)***	(0.036)***	(0.024)***	(0.029)***	(0.027)***
Managerial (%)	0.108	0.108	0.050	0.070	0.061	0.062	0.055
	(0.021)***	(0.022)***	(0.025)**	(0.028)**	(0.020)***	(0.019)***	(0.026)**
Clerks (%)	−0.022	−0.019	−0.051	−0.043	−0.076	−0.062	−0.072
	(0.017)	(0.018)	(0.018)***	0.024*	(0.019)***	(0.019)***	(0.018)***
Retail/wholesale trade (%)	−0.160	−0.142	−0.184	−0.138	−0.196	−0.205	−0.212
	(0.032)***	(0.032)***	(0.028)***	(0.036)***	(0.029)***	(0.026)***	(0.027)***
Service workers (%)	−0.112	−0.149	−0.126	−0.087	−0.101	−0.106	−0.144
	(0.025)***	(0.032)***	(0.033)***	(0.039)**	(0.036)***	(0.035)***	(0.029)***
Production workers (%)	−0.064	−0.046	−0.098	−0.090	−0.086	−0.069	−0.112
	(0.017)***	(0.020)**	(0.018)***	(0.022)***	(0.018)***	(0.017)***	(0.018)***
Other labourer (%)	−0.143	−0.089	−0.362	−0.284	−0.200	−0.270	−0.210
	(0.035)***	(0.045)**	(0.044)***	(0.044)***	(0.055)***	(0.059)***	(0.060)***
Male members (%)	0.033	0.058	−0.010	0.017	−0.049	−0.056	−0.041
	(0.023)	(0.036)	(0.027)	(0.028)	(0.028)*	(0.025)**	(0.024)*
Children 0–5 years (%)	−0.175	−0.062	−0.654	−0.604	−0.414	−0.456	−0.507
	(0.054)***	(0.085)	(0.054)***	(0.064)***	(0.061)***	(0.059)***	(0.054)***
Children 6–10 years (%)	−0.424	−0.341	−0.436	−0.454	−0.386	−0.364	−0.366
	(0.046)***	(0.051)***	(0.049)***	(0.056)***	(0.054)***	(0.051)***	(0.039)***
Children 11–15 years (%)	−0.377	−0.340	−0.477	−0.436	−0.342	−0.322	−0.318
	(0.046)***	(0.051)***	(0.039)***	(0.045)***	(0.043)***	(0.045)***	(0.039)***
Female 16–20 years (%)	−0.124	−0.002	−0.403	−0.361	−0.284	−0.371	−0.346
	(0.061)**	(0.061)	(0.057)***	(0.055)***	(0.059)***	(0.052)***	(0.053)***
Male 16–20 years (%)	−0.079	−0.040	−0.439	−0.493	−0.396	−0.387	−0.375
	(0.066)	(0.055)	(0.054)***	(0.055)***	(0.057)***	(0.055)***	(0.047)***
Male >65 years (%)	−0.151	−0.117	−0.079	−0.074	−0.031	−0.053	−0.048
	(0.052)***	(0.058)**	(0.068)	(0.061)	(0.057)	(0.060)	(0.071)
Female >65 years (%)	−0.348	−0.280	−0.288	−0.218	−0.200	−0.287	−0.252
	(0.043)***	(0.050)***	(0.059)***	(0.053)***	(0.055)***	(0.051)***	(0.040)***
Regional effects	Yes	Yes	Yes	Yes	Yes	Yes	Yes
Observations	8078	7698	7946	7147	7580	7692	9991
R^2	0.37	0.3	0.36	0.36	0.32	0.34	0.46

Notes: Cluster adjusted robust standard errors in parentheses; * significant at 10 per cent,

per capita expenditure deflated by poverty line

1993	1994	1995	1996	1997	1998	1999	2000
−0.139	−0.147	−0.143	−0.143	−0.142	−0.149	−0.163	−0.162
(0.013)***	(0.013)***	(0.014)***	(0.014)***	(0.010)***	(0.013)***	(0.014)***	(0.011)***
0.063	0.059	0.050	0.054	0.043	0.053	0.060	0.066
(0.012)***	(0.010)***	(0.009)***	(0.008)***	(0.008)***	(0.008)***	(0.009)***	(0.010)***
−0.075	−0.074	−0.056	−0.058	−0.073	−0.099	−0.095	−0.099
(0.014)***	(0.013)***	(0.013)***	(0.011)***	(0.012)***	(0.012)***	(0.012)***	(0.016)***
0.024	0.026	0.028	0.027	0.026	0.032	0.034	0.038
(0.003)***	(0.003)***	(0.002)***	(0.002)***	(0.003)***	(0.002)***	(0.003)***	(0.003)***
0.013	0.015	0.014	0.015	0.016	0.016	0.015	0.019
(0.002)***	(0.002)***	(0.002)***	(0.002)***	(0.002)***	(0.002)***	(0.002)***	(0.002)***
0.309	0.362	0.368	0.310	0.259	0.262	0.313	0.336
(0.027)***	(0.031)***	(0.026)***	(0.027)***	(0.030)***	(0.026)***	(0.034)***	(0.033)***
0.070	0.098	0.061	0.062	0.092	0.104	0.107	0.115
(0.025)***	(0.022)***	(0.027)**	(0.024)**	(0.030)***	(0.027)***	(0.034)***	(0.032)***
−0.072	−0.091	−0.083	−0.071	−0.072	−0.063	−0.051	−0.055
(0.019)***	(0.022)***	(0.019)***	(0.020)***	(0.017)***	(0.019)***	(0.025)**	(0.028)*
−0.207	−0.277	−0.256	−0.233	−0.254	−0.254	−0.274	−0.288
(0.028)***	(0.031)***	(0.035)***	(0.031)***	(0.035)***	(0.027)***	(0.029)***	(0.034)***
−0.082	−0.164	−0.215	−0.167	−0.175	−0.175	−0.202	−0.238
(0.028)***	(0.029)***	(0.030)***	(0.034)***	(0.020)***	(0.028)***	(0.035)***	(0.032)***
−0.101	−0.164	−0.155	−0.122	−0.137	−0.150	−0.179	−0.177
(0.021)***	(0.019)***	(0.020)***	(0.016)***	(0.020)***	(0.023)***	(0.029)***	(0.024)***
−0.299	−0.227	−0.193	−0.190	−0.179	−0.184	−0.236	−0.287
(0.081)***	(0.046)***	(0.065)***	(0.054)***	(0.054)***	(0.059)***	(0.049)***	(0.081)***
−0.045	−0.043	−0.035	−0.014	−0.002	−0.044	−0.020	−0.091
(0.027)	(0.026)	(0.026)	(0.025)	(0.026)	(0.028)	(0.029)	(0.037)**
−0.364	−0.354	−0.401	−0.407	−0.475	−0.402	−0.323	−0.333
(0.055)***	(0.061)***	(0.061)***	(0.066)***	(0.063)***	(0.063)***	(0.057)***	(0.069)***
−0.388	−0.295	−0.310	−0.292	−0.358	−0.327	−0.261	−0.243
(0.056)***	(0.060)***	(0.039)***	(0.047)***	(0.054)***	(0.053)***	(0.053)***	(0.053)***
−0.241	−0.182	−0.191	−0.137	−0.231	−0.205	−0.207	−0.170
(0.046)***	(0.055)***	(0.040)***	(0.040)***	(0.044)***	(0.041)***	(0.044)***	(0.054)***
−0.279	−0.260	−0.247	−0.235	−0.258	−0.278	−0.166	−0.212
(0.057)***	(0.053)***	(0.061)***	(0.055)***	(0.055)***	(0.055)***	(0.051)***	(0.057)***
−0.318	−0.295	−0.268	−0.196	−0.274	−0.141	−0.238	−0.050
(0.062)***	(0.053)***	(0.065)***	(0.055)***	(0.068)***	(0.055)**	(0.053)***	(0.067)
−0.078	−0.034	0.013	0.028	0.028	0.016	0.055	0.047
(0.057)	(0.042)	(0.040)	(0.061)	(0.058)	(0.049)	(0.042)	(0.047)
−0.242	−0.167	−0.220	−0.172	−0.201	−0.219	−0.127	−0.057
(0.057)***	(0.060)***	(0.052)***	(0.064)***	(0.054)***	(0.054)***	(0.059)**	(0.056)
Yes	Yes	Yes	Yes	Yes	Yes	Yes	Yes
9824	9991	9999	10000	9999	10000	10000	9999
0.32	0.39	0.3	0.27	0.26	0.28	0.27	0.3

** significant at 5 per cent, *** significant at 1 per cent.

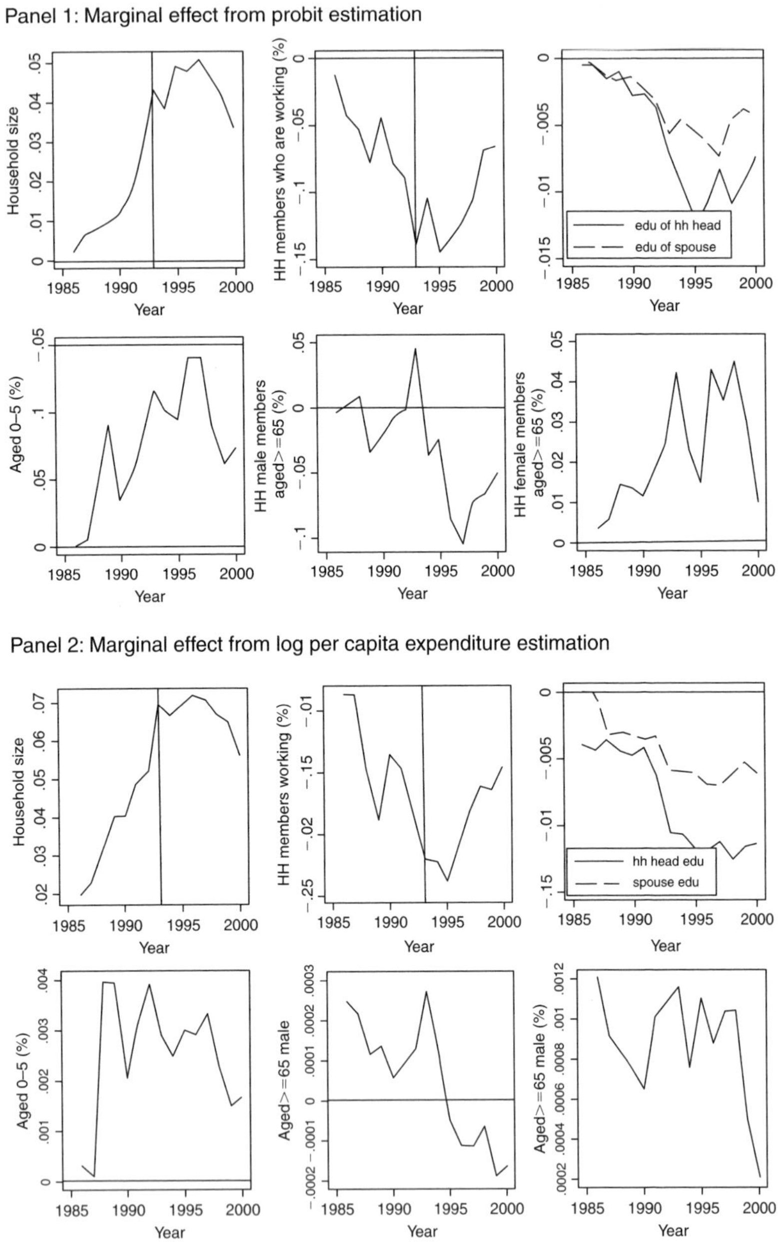

Figure 8.5 Change in poverty determinants
Panel 1: Marginal effect from probit estimation
Panel 2: Marginal effects from log per capita expenditure estimation

First, we consider the effects of the changing influence of household composition characteristics. One important finding is that household size has a strong positive effect on the probability of a household being poor. The effect increases dramatically from 0.2 per cent in 1986 to 4.3 per cent in 1993, further increases to 5.1 per cent in 1997, and then reduces to 3.4 per cent in 2000.[14] The year-by-year increment is highest during 1992 to 1993, when food coupons were abolished. The increasing household size effect continued slowly until 1998 when the Di Bao (Minimum Living Allowance) programme was implemented. After this, the household size effect began to decline. We also observe that the proportion of household members who are working is associated with poverty reduction and this effect increased the most in 1993. The effects of household size and proportion of household members working are related, and the changing pattern in the effect of these two variables may be associated with macro-economic policy changes during this period. As we know, food coupons were distributed according to the number of household members and their age but, after the abolition of food coupons, compensation was only provided to the working population via a wage increase. Thus, households with proportionally less employed members might be worse off.[15]

A similar effect to the food coupon compensation applies to many non-food products, such as transportation, rental and medical care. In the 1980s, when price subsidies were in place, larger households received more of these subsidies. But, once again, compensation for the price reforms was paid through the wage system and available only to those employed. This is probably why the effects on poverty of household size and the percentage of working members continue throughout the mid- to late 1990s as price and social welfare reforms proceeded. We also find that households with a higher proportion of children are more likely to be poor, suggesting that households with more children were disproportionately hit by the switch from the price subsidy system to wage adjustments. More elderly male members reduce poverty (mostly in the last four years of our data) while more elderly male females increase poverty, perhaps because elderly males are more likely to have worked and currently enjoy a state pension while elderly females are less likely to have a pension.

Next, we turn to human capital effects. We find that more human capital (years of schooling of the household heads and their spouses) reduces poverty, and this effect increases over time. This, to a large extent, reflects the increasing labour market returns to education. Zhang *et al.* (2005) find a considerable increase in return to education for the same period. There is, however, a slight trend reversal towards the end of the period, mainly since 1998. Another important finding related to labour market returns is that, relative to having more professionals, households with more production or service workers are increasingly more likely to be poor, suggesting that the earnings gap between high and low paid occupations has increased over time.

Finally, the effects of regional variation seems to have increased over time, and we discuss this result in a later section (Figure 8.6 plots the coefficients for regional dummy variables for each of the 15 years).

Change of poverty determinants over time

In this sub-section we combine changes in coefficients and household characteristics to put into perspective the changing significance of poverty determinants over time. From Figure 8.5 it is apparent that the data period can be divided into two, with the division year being 1993. Thus, we employ equation (8.4) to decompose the poverty change between 1986–93, and 1993–2000. During the first period, the proportion of households who lived under the poverty line increased significantly from 3 to 11 per cent, while in the second period it reduced slightly from 11 to 8 per cent.[16]

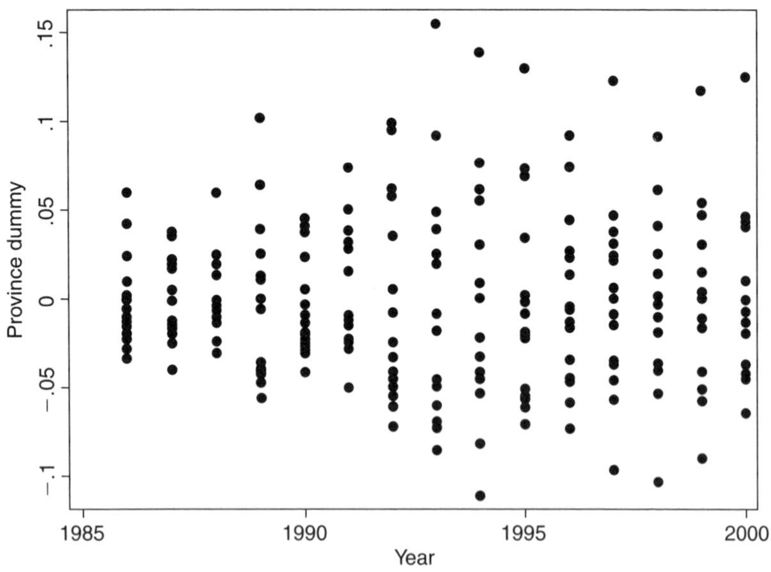

Figure 8.6 Regional variation in poverty determination

To implement a decomposition using equation (8.4), we need to choose the endowments of a representative household at each of the two points in time and an evaluation point φ on the density function. Due to the non-liner nature of the probit model, and the low probability of being poor, the representative households are not sample means; hence, the following adjustment is taken to adjust the sample mean to the endowments for the representative households:

$$\tilde{X}_t^k = \overline{X_j^k}\left[\frac{\Phi^{-1}(\overline{\widehat{\Pr}})}{\overline{X}_j^k \hat{\beta}_t^k}\right] \tag{8.5}$$

where $\overline{\widehat{\Pr}}$ is the mean predicated probability. The linearization is performed around the point φ, which is defined as: $\varphi = (N_t \tilde{X}_t^k \hat{\beta}_t^k + N_{t+n} \tilde{X}_{t+n}^k \hat{\beta}_{t+n}^k)/(N_t + N_{t+n})$.[17]

The results are presented in Table 8.3 where negative and positive values indicate the decreasing or increasing effect on poverty over the period.[18] At this point, we would like to emphasize that the change in the poverty impact presented in Table 8.3 is obtained from combining the change in estimated coefficients and the change in endowments. The factors are grouped into three. The first group is those variables that proxy the direct reform impact on households. These reforms include food and non-food price reform, social welfare reform (which moved from direct price subsidies to households to wage compensation to those employed) and enterprise reform (which generated an increase in unemployment in the mid-to late 1990s). The household variables that reflect these reforms include family size; the proportion of household members who are working; and household composition, including the age of the household head, the proportion of household members who are male, and the proportion of household members who are in each of the gender and age categories. The second group of variables reflecting labour market changes in human capital variables measured by years of schooling of the household head and spouse, and the proportion of household members in different occupational classifications. The third group of variables measuring changing regional effects are variations in regional income, price, income inequality and varying degrees of enterprise reform. Regional effects include the constant term as it embodies the omitted regional dummy variable.

During the first period, 1986–93, the poverty rate increased significantly from 3.1 to 11.0 per cent, an increase of 7.9 percentage points. Reform impact on households and regional variables contributed to this

Table 8.3 Decomposition results for probit estimations

	Poverty change 1986–93		Poverty change 1993–2000	
	Decomposition of components	**As % of total actual changes**	**Decomposition of components**	**As % of total actual changes**
Total actual change	0.079	100.00	−0.029	100.00
Household effects	0.069	87.85	0.056	192.47
Of which: Household size	0.044	55.43	0.002	8.02
Proportion of household members working	0.019	24.14	0.037	126.80
Household composition	0.007	8.55	0.017	58.19
Human capital	−0.049	−61.86	−0.049	−168.51
Region	0.060	76.39	−0.036	−123.73
Total approx. change	0.081	103.11	−0.029	99.81
Approximation error	−0.002	−3.11	0.000	0.19

increased poverty by similar amounts. Among the reform variables, the changing impact of household size is the most important, accounting for 4.4 percentage points of the increased poverty incidence. The changing effect of the average proportion of household members who are working also increased poverty by 1.9 percentage points. But this is mainly the result of the reduction in the proportion of household working members over the period (change in endowments) rather than the result of changes in coefficients. Human capital variables are also an important force for poverty reduction. Increased average years of schooling and increased return to schooling both contributed.

In the second period, 1993 to 2000, poverty headcount indices reduced from 11.0 per cent to 8.1 per cent, a reduction of 2.9 percentage points. The contrast between the two periods is noticeable. The impact of household characteristics contributes much the same percentage point to an increase in poverty in both periods, but the effect is now primarily caused by the reduction in the proportion of household working members rather than household size, which now makes little contribution to the change.

The increased contribution to poverty reduction from human capital is also the same in both periods, indicating the continuous growing interactions between poverty and labour market outcomes.

The large change between the two periods, however, is the impact of the regional/constant terms, which have changed from a powerful force increasing poverty in the first period to a force for poverty reduction in the second. However, the regional effects and the constant term cannot be separately identified.

Further understanding of the regional effects

China has significant spatial variation in economic development, income levels, income inequality and output prices (see, for example, Chen and Fleisher 1996; Khan and Riskin 2001), which is reflected in regional poverty patterns. In this sub-section, we look more closely at these patterns.

Following Bryk and Raudenbush (1992), we adopt the hierarchical linear modelling approach to investigate this variation. The approach involves two sequential stages. First, equation (8.1) is estimated using a fixed effects linear probability model. Second, the fixed provincial effects (υ) from regressions for each of the survey years are retrieved and then used as a dependent variable in the following regression analysis:

$$\upsilon_{jt} = Z'_{jt}\delta + \varepsilon_{jt} \tag{8.6}$$

where Z is a vector of variables that may be associated with regional poverty, including provincial average income levels, Gini coefficients, share of state sector employment and provincial level unit food and non-food values for each survey year. The food and non-food unit values are calculated from the UHIES, where both quantity and expenditure data are available at the household level. We calculate the unit calorie value for grain products, as it is the major food item for the poor. For non-food basic necessities, we include three major components: rent, medical expenses and education.[19] As the three non-food prices changed in the same direction, and at a similar rate through time and across regions, we solve the problem of multicollinearity by using a principal component method to generate a single non-food 'price'.[20]

We estimate equation (8.6) for the total sample, as well as separately for the periods 1986–93 and 1994–2000. The results are presented in Table 8.4. For the total sample, we observe that the income variable has a significant and negative coefficient, indicating that provinces with higher average income levels have lower poverty. With regard to the basic necessities, a higher food price is associated with higher poverty. In addition, income inequality also reduces poverty. Other variables do not appear to be significant.

When the sample is split into the 1986–93 and 1994–2000 periods, different pictures are revealed, apart from a similar effect of higher average income on poverty reduction. First, after controlling for average income levels, income inequality within a province is negatively related

Table 8.4 Determinants of regional variations on poverty (fixed-effects)

	Total sample	**1986–93**	**1994–2000**
Income/1000	–0.018	–0.025	–0.013
	(0.004)***	(0.011)**	(0.004)***
Grain unit price	0.547	1.107	0.354
	(0.094)***	(0.178)***	(0.108)***
Non-food price	–0.01	–0.055	–0.009
	(0.008)	(0.039)	(0.009)
Proportion of state employment	0.044	–0.112	0.239
	(0.047)	(0.057)*	(0.070)***
Gini coefficient	–0.203	–0.547	0.133
	(0.110)*	(0.140)***	(0.161)
Constant	–0.018	0.087	–0.209
	(0.047)	(0.084)	(0.073)***
Number of observations	225	120	105
R^2	0.33	0.33	0.48

Notes: Standard errors in parentheses; * significant at 10 per cent, ** significant at 5 per cent, *** significant at 1 per cent.

to poverty in the first period, but has no impact on poverty in the second period. The reason that regions with the largest inequality tend to have less poverty in the first period may be related to the fact that increases in inequality in the first period were primarily generated by greater income increases at the top of the income distribution rather than income falls at the bottom. In the second period, inequality increases were generated by changes in both ends of the income distribution, increased income at the top and reduced income at the bottom (Meng 2004).

Second, provinces with a high level of state sector employment have lower poverty in the first period and higher poverty in the second period. The sign reversal is probably the result of enterprise reform measures introduced in the mid-to late 1990s. The increase in unemployment in the second half of the 1990s is mainly a state sector phenomenon and, in addition to job loss, those who remain employed in the state sector suffered from significant wage, pension and medical reimbursement arrears.

Finally, the relative changes in the price of basic necessities are important. Provinces with higher food prices have a higher poverty rate, but the effect is much larger in the first period when the coupons were phased out than in the second period. This is consistent with the timing of the food price reform and the conjecture presented earlier that food price reform is one of the major contributing factors for poverty increases in the early 1990s.

Robustness check

The dependent variables used in equations (8.1) and (8.2) are not equivalence scale adjusted. Since our story places a significant weight on household composition, it is important to ensure that these results would not significantly change if the dependent variables were equivalence scale adjusted. To do this, we adopt two commonly used equivalence scales – the 'old' OECD scale (assigning the first adult a weight of one, every additional adult a weight of 0.7, and each child a weight of 0.5) and the OECD modified scale (the weight for an additional adult is 0.5 and for a child is 0.3). Detailed results are available upon request from the authors. In Figure 8.A2 in the marginal effects from equation (8.1) are presented for a group of selected variables using the two equivalence scale adjusted independent variables. Comparing Figure 8.A2 with Figure 8.5, it is clear that the trend of the change in the marginal effect for the important selected variables (such as family size, proportion of household members working and education variables) is almost the same as those obtained from the unadjusted data, except that the magnitudes are different. The variables especially related to scale adjustments (such as proportion of household members in different age groups) differ significantly in magnitudes. This is the result of the equivalence scale adjustment.

Conclusion

This chapter identifies factors associated with urban poverty and how they changed over the 1986–2000 period. During this period, the poverty head count index increased between 1986 and 1993, stayed at a high level after 1993 for five years, and started to fall after 1998. By 2000, the poverty rate had fallen from its peak of 12 per cent (1993) to 8 per cent.

There appear to be three sets of factors associated with the changing pattern of household poverty. The most important factors are related to the demographic structure and labour market involvement of households. The fact that poverty increased most in larger households and households with fewer working members suggests that the move from implicit price subsidies for basic necessities to an explicit wage subsidy to compensate families when removal of the subsidies worsened the position of larger households with fewer working members.

The second set of factors relates to human capital variables which impact on poverty in the ways that might be expected. Households with more educated heads/spouses, and more workers employed in higher paying occupations have a lower probability of being poor.

The third set of factors relates to important regional effects. Households in regions with higher average income levels, relative to the poverty line, were less likely to be poor. In the period of 1994–2000, households in regions with more state sector employees fared worst, as state sector reform impacted adversely on many households. In addition, the changing impact of income inequality within regions is interesting. Regions with the largest inequality in the early period tended to have less poverty, partly because higher inequality was primarily generated by higher incomes at the top of the income distribution. In the second period, this effect disappeared.

Notes

1 The findings of Ravallion and Chen (2004), however, differ. They find extremely low poverty rates in urban China in the 1990s (the highest was in 1990 at 2.6 per cent and the lowest was in 2000 at 0.54 per cent).

2 The UHIES excludes rural migrants in cities. As rural migrants disproportionately constitute the lower end of the income distribution, excluding them will result in an underestimate of urban poverty. This should be borne in mind when interpreting the results.

3 The UHIES questionnaire changed three times during the data period (1988, 1992 and 1997) with the introduction of more detailed food categories in 1992 being the most relevant change for this study. Before 1992, 39 food items were included in the expenditure questions. Since 1992, the number was increased to 112. Consequently, some discontinuity in the data series may occur.

4 For detailed discussion of this issue, see Meng, Gregory and Wang (2005).

5 There are a number of important issues that should be borne in mind when applying the CBN method. For example, we use unit values for food prices faced by the poor to calculate the cost of buying 2100 calories. The use of unit values as price proxies may produce biases caused by quality variations and measurement errors (see for example, Deaton 1988; 1990). In addition, Capéau and Dercon (2006) and Gibson and Rozelle (2005) show that for poor rural villages in Ethiopia and Papua New Guinea unit values may overstate prices faced by the rural poor and suggest that rural poverty may be overstated by as much as 20 per cent. The extent to which this problem in rural data collections applies to urban China, where the data have been collected by a year long continuous diary (checked each month by authorities from the statistical bureau), is unknown. The unit values used in this section are calculated for the bottom 20 per cent of households in the expenditure distribution. We later explore regional variations in poverty and uses average unit values for each province.

6 There might be a concern that if real incomes of the low income group increased significantly over the period, our choice of poverty lines may allow the poor to obtain calories from higher quality food and, at the same time, allow them to spend an increasing proportion on non-food items. However, as indicated in Figure 8.2, real per capita income and expenditure for the lowest 10 percentile households hardly increased at all, especially over the period of the mid-to late 1990s. In addition, as indicated in Meng, Gong and Wang (2007), for the low income group not only has their per capita calorie availability reduced since 1993, the proportion of calories obtained from protein has also reduced. These facts seem to suggest that the above mentioned concern should not be a serious problem.

7 The results using the 'chained weight CBN line' are similar and are available upon request from the authors.

8 Note that the squared poverty gap (SPG) calculated here is for households under poverty only. The formula for the calculation is $SPG = \frac{\sum_{i-1}^{Q}[(Z-Y_i)/Z]^2}{Q}$ where Q is the total number of households whose per capita total expenditure is under the poverty line Z.

9 Ravallion (1996) has criticized using a dichotomous variable (whether a household's per capita expenditure is below the poverty line) to analyze poverty determinants when the underlying continuous variable (expenditure) is available. His criticism is mainly related to the inefficiency of suppressing information on the degree to which households living standards are above or below the poverty line. He is also concerned with the use of a nonlinear probit model estimation that requires more assumptions than the OLS estimation of the underlying consumption variable. Datt and Jolliffe (2005) and Gibson and Rozelle (2003) have followed Ravallion (1996) and developed this empirical approach.

10 These results are not presented here but are available upon request from the authors. We do, however, present the plots of some of the important coefficients in Figure 8.A1 in the Appendix. There is a close similarity between Figure 8.A1 and Figure 8.5.

11 Note that most of the marginal effects presented in Figure 8.5 are statistically significant.

12 Practically, we first estimate the predicted baseline average probability of being poor from equation (8.3). Second, we recalculate the same predicted average probability of being poor with a one unit increment for one of the explanatory variables. (Note that the unit chosen is arbitrary. The increment for all the percentage variables in Figure 8.4 are chosen to be a 30 per cent increase.) Finally, we take the difference between the baseline average poverty rate and the poverty rate with the additional increase in a particular variable, and this gives us the simulated marginal effects.

13 F-tests are conducted to test whether these regressions can be pooled. The test results reject the null hypothesis in most cases. Furthermore, most coefficients for the early years are statistically significantly different from coefficients at the middle and end of the 1990s.

14 The coefficient differences between the late 1980s and 1993 and any year after 1993 are statistically significant at the 5 per cent level.

15 This effect could be best understood by as example. Imagine two households both with five members. Household A has one working member who earns Y500 a month and Household B has five working members each of whom earns Y100 a month. With food coupons, both households were equally well off but when the wage compensation is introduced (say, at the rate of Y10 per worker per month) household A's income increases to Y510, while household B's income increases to Y550. Household A is now more likely to be poor than household B, relative to the coupon environment.

16 These poverty rates refer to households. Those in Figure 8.3 are headcount indices (calculated for individuals).

17 Even with these adjustments, a slight approximation error still exists wher conducting the decomposition exercise.

18 The decomposition results calculated from the linear probability model are consistent with the calculations presented here and are available upon request from the authors.

19 The rent price is rent per square metre, for medical expenses we use per capita expenditure, while for tuition fees we calculate per student per semester cost.

20 The correlation coefficients among the three non-food prices are:

	Rent	Medical	Education
Rent	1.00		
Medical	0.63	1.00	
Education	0.86	0.78	1.00

References

Bryk, A.S. and Raudenbush, S.W. (1992) *Hierarchical Linear Models: Applications and Data Analysis Methods* (Newbury Park: Sage).

Capéau, B. and Dercon, S. (2006) 'Prices, Unit Values, and Local Measurement in Rural Surveys: An Econometric Approach with an Application to Poverty Measurement in Ethiopia', *Journal of African Economies*, 15, 2: 181–211.
Chen, J. and Fleisher, B.M. (1996) 'Regional Income Inequality and Economic Growth in China', *Journal of Comparative Economics*, 22, 2: 141–64.
Chinese Academy of Preventive Medicine (2001) *Recommended Nutrition Intake for Chinese Households* (in Chinese) (Beijing: Publishing House of the Chinese Light Industry).
China Urban Poverty Research Group (2003) *Urban Poverty: New Challenge for China's Development* (Beijing: Chinese Economics Press).
Datt, G. and Jolliffe, D. (2005) 'Poverty in Egypt: Modeling and Policy Simulations', *Economic Development and Cultural Change*, 53, 2: 327–46.
Deaton, A. (1988) 'Quality, Quantity, and Spatial Variation of Price', *American Economic Review*, 78, 3: 418–30.
Deaton, A. (1990) 'Price Elasticities from Survey Data: Extensions and Indonesian Results', *Journal of Econometrics*, 44, 3: 281–309.
Doiron, D. and Riddell, W.C. (1994) 'The Impact of Unionization on Male–Female Earnings Differences in Canada', *Journal of Human Resources*, 29, 2: 504–34.
Fang, C., Zhang X. and Fan, S. (2002) 'Emergence of Urban Poverty and Inequality in China: Evidence from Household Survey', *China Economic Review*, 13: 430–43.
Gibson, J., Huang J. and Rozelle, S. (2003) 'Improving Estimates of Inequality and Poverty from Urban China's Household Income and Expenditure Survey', *Review of Income and Wealth*, 49 1: 53–68.
Gibson, J. and Rozelle, S. (2003) 'Poverty and Access to Roads in Papua New Guinea', *Economic Development and Cultural Change*, 52, 1: 159–85.
Gibson, J. and Rozelle, S. (2005) 'Prices and Unit Values in Poverty Measurement and Tax Reform Analysis', *World Bank Economic* Review (Washington, DC: World Bank).
Giles, J., Park, A. and Cai, F. (2006) 'How Has Economic Restructuring Affected China's Urban Workers?', *China Quarterly*, 185: 61–95.
Giles, J., Park, A. and Zhang, J. (2005) 'What Is China's True Unemployment?', *Chinese Economic Review*, 16, 2: 149–70.
Gustafsson, B. and Wei, Z. (2000) 'How and Why Has Poverty in China Changed? A Study Based on Microdata for 1988 and 1995', *China Quarterly*, 164: 983–1006.
Han, T., Wailes, E.J. and Cramer, G.L. (1995) 'Rural and Urban Data Collection in the People's Republic of China', in the *China Market Data and Information Systems, Proceedings of WCC-101 Symposium*, Washington, DC.
Khan, A.R. and Riskin, C. (2001) *Inequality and Poverty in China in the Age of Globalization* (Oxford and New York: Oxford University Press).
Knight, J. and Xue, J. (2004) 'How High Urban Unemployment in China?', Mineo.
Meng, X. (2004) 'Economic Restructuring and Income Inequality in Urban China', Review of Income and Wealth, 50, 3: 357–79.
Meng, X., Gong, X. and Wang, Y. (2007) 'Impact of Income Growth and Economic Reform on Nutrition Availability in Urban China: 1986–2000', Unpublished manuscript, Australian National University.
Meng, X., Gregory, R.G. and Wang, Y. (2005) 'Poverty, Inequality, and Growth in Urban China, 1986–2000', *Journal of Comparative Economics*, 33, 4: 710–29.
Ministry of Labour and Social Security (2002) *China Labour and Social Security Yearbook* (Beijing: Ministry of Labour and Social Security).

O'Keefe, P. (2004) 'Social Assistance in China: An Evolving System', Paper presented at the Poverty Inequality, Labour Market and Welfare Reform in China Conference, Canberra, August.
Ravallion, M. (1994) *Poverty Comparisons* (Chur, Switzerland: Harwood Academic Publishers).
Ravallion, M. (1996) 'Issues in Measuring and Modelling Poverty', *Economic Journal*, 106, 438: 1328–43.
Ravallion, M. and Chen, S. (2004) 'China's (Uneven) Progress against Poverty', Paper presented at the Poverty, Inequality, Labour Market and Welfare Reform in China Conference, Canberra, August.
Tang, Y. (1998) *Choices: the Chinese Reform since 1978* (Beijing: Economics Daily Publishing House).
Xue, J. and Wei, Z. (2003) 'Unemployment, Poverty and Income Disparity in Urban China', *Asian Economic Journal*, 17, 4: 383–405.
Zhang, J., Zhao, Y., Park, A. and Song, X (2005) 'Economic Returns to Schooling in Urban China, 1988–2001', *Journal of Comparative Economics*, 33: 730–52.

Appendix

Table 8.A1 Summary statistics for poor and non-poor households

Poor	1986	1987	1988	1989	1990	1991	1992	1993	1994	1995	1996	1997	1998	1999	2000
Log(per capita expend/Z)	−0.19	−0.16	−0.18	−0.30	−0.19	−0.22	−0.21	−0.22	−0.23	−0.22	−0.21	−0.22	−0.23	−0.23	−0.24
HH size	5.50	4.55	4.33	4.08	4.38	4.05	3.84	3.65	3.73	3.69	3.66	3.66	3.65	3.64	3.63
HH head age	43.17	44.81	44.10	43.95	45.86	43.90	43.51	43.45	44.98	44.81	44.61	45.26	45.67	45.05	46.27
HH head gender	0.70	0.70	0.70	0.72	0.67	0.74	0.77	0.78	0.75	0.72	0.70	0.73	0.71	0.73	0.75
HH head years of education	11.12	11.29	11.06	11.64	10.86	11.67	12.09	12.24	11.95	12.02	12.15	12.22	12.17	12.24	12.15
Spouse years of education	8.62	8.86	8.57	9.65	8.86	9.80	10.50	10.83	10.55	10.74	10.79	10.61	10.84	11.11	10.52
HH members working (%)	0.50	0.48	0.42	0.45	0.47	0.46	0.52	0.52	0.52	0.51	0.52	0.52	0.51	0.52	0.48
HH members as professionals (%)	0.13	0.16	0.16	0.20	0.11	0.17	0.17	0.20	0.17	0.17	0.18	0.17	0.18	0.15	0.18
HH members as managerial (%)	0.05	0.04	0.03	0.04	0.03	0.03	0.03	0.03	0.03	0.03	0.03	0.03	0.03	0.02	0.02
HH members as clerk (%)	0.12	0.15	0.13	0.14	0.14	0.17	0.17	0.18	0.17	0.17	0.17	0.16	0.17	0.16	0.13
HH members as trades (%)	0.13	0.12	0.14	0.09	0.11	0.11	0.10	0.11	0.11	0.11	0.10	0.11	0.11	0.12	0.14
HH members as service worker (%)	0.10	0.13	0.07	0.05	0.04	0.05	0.06	0.04	0.05	0.06	0.06	0.07	0.08	0.09	0.10
HH members as labourer (%)	0.44	0.39	0.42	0.43	0.52	0.43	0.45	0.42	0.45	0.45	0.44	0.44	0.42	0.44	0.42
HH members as other worker (%)	0.03	0.02	0.05	0.05	0.06	0.05	0.02	0.02	0.02	0.01	0.01	0.02	0.02	0.02	0.02
HH members are men (%)	0.46	0.47	0.46	0.48	0.49	0.49	0.49	0.49	0.49	0.49	0.49	0.49	0.48	0.49	0.49

(*Continued*)

Table 8.A1 continued

	1986	1987	1988	1989	1990	1991	1992	1993	1994	1995	1996	1997	1998	1999	2000
HH members aged 0–5 years (%)	0.03	0.03	0.09	0.08	0.06	0.08	0.08	0.06	0.06	0.06	0.06	0.05	0.05	0.05	0.06
HH members aged 6–10 years (%)	0.09	0.05	0.08	0.07	0.07	0.08	0.08	0.09	0.08	0.08	0.08	0.08	0.08	0.07	0.06
HH members aged 11–15 years (%)	0.12	0.13	0.12	0.11	0.12	0.11	0.08	0.09	0.08	0.08	0.07	0.08	0.08	0.08	0.09
HH members male 16–20 years (%)	0.04	0.05	0.06	0.05	0.05	0.04	0.03	0.03	0.03	0.04	0.03	0.03	0.03	0.03	0.03
HH members female 16–20 years (%)	0.03	0.03	0.05	0.06	0.06	0.04	0.04	0.03	0.04	0.03	0.03	0.03	0.03	0.04	0.03
HH male aged >65 (%)	0.03	0.04	0.03	0.02	0.02	0.02	0.03	0.03	0.03	0.03	0.03	0.03	0.03	0.03	0.03
HH female aged >66 (%)	0.06	0.06	0.05	0.04	0.04	0.05	0.04	0.04	0.04	0.04	0.04	0.04	0.04	0.04	0.04
Observations	251	273	323	397	326	374	706	1087	1015	1081	1057	1108	964	874	818
Non-poor	**1986**	**1987**	**1988**	**1989**	**1990**	**1991**	**1992**	**1993**	**1994**	**1995**	**1996**	**1997**	**1998**	**1999**	**2000**
Log (per capita expend/Z)	0.75	0.76	0.79	0.75	0.75	0.72	0.67	0.65	0.72	0.66	0.64	0.65	0.70	0.77	0.84
HH size	3.62	3.67	3.53	3.48	3.41	3.32	3.25	3.19	3.16	3.13	3.12	3.11	3.08	3.05	3.05
HH head age	42.53	43.16	43.60	43.80	44.89	43.69	44.92	45.61	45.57	45.82	46.05	46.01	46.41	46.62	47.41
HH head gender	0.60	0.59	0.65	0.66	0.66	0.69	0.70	0.67	0.66	0.64	0.63	0.64	0.62	0.61	0.66
HH head years of education	12.10	12.21	12.22	12.30	12.43	12.60	12.86	12.90	12.97	13.06	13.07	13.07	13.15	13.21	13.18
Spouse years of education	10.62	10.71	10.91	11.11	11.18	11.44	11.66	11.73	11.82	11.92	12.01	11.99	12.05	12.14	11.96
HH members working (%)	0.72	0.72	0.59	0.59	0.59	0.59	0.60	0.59	0.58	0.58	0.58	0.58	0.57	0.57	0.54

HH members as professionals (%)	0.20	0.21	0.22	0.23	0.25	0.27	0.27	0.29	0.32	0.31	0.31	0.30	0.30	0.29	0.31
HH members as managerial (%)	0.09	0.09	0.08	0.08	0.08	0.07	0.08	0.08	0.08	0.07	0.07	0.07	0.07	0.07	0.07
HH members as clerk (%)	0.19	0.21	0.20	0.20	0.20	0.20	0.20	0.20	0.19	0.20	0.20	0.19	0.21	0.22	0.20
HH members as trades (%)	0.06	0.06	0.07	0.07	0.06	0.06	0.06	0.06	0.06	0.06	0.06	0.06	0.06	0.06	0.06
HH members as service worker (%)	0.05	0.05	0.05	0.04	0.04	0.04	0.04	0.04	0.04	0.04	0.04	0.05	0.05	0.06	0.06
HH members as labourer (%)	0.38	0.36	0.37	0.36	0.35	0.34	0.34	0.32	0.31	0.32	0.32	0.32	0.31	0.29	0.29
HH members as other worker (%)	0.02	0.02	0.02	0.02	0.02	0.02	0.01	0.01	0.01	0.01	0.01	0.01	0.01	0.01	0.01
HH members are men (%)	0.49	0.49	0.50	0.50	0.50	0.50	0.50	0.50	0.50	0.50	0.50	0.49	0.49	0.49	0.49
HH members aged 0–5 years (%)	0.02	0.02	0.06	0.05	0.05	0.06	0.05	0.04	0.05	0.04	0.03	0.03	0.03	0.03	0.03
HH members aged 6–10 years (%)	0.04	0.03	0.08	0.08	0.08	0.08	0.08	0.07	0.06	0.06	0.06	0.06	0.05	0.05	0.05
HH member aged 11–15 years (%)	0.06	0.06	0.08	0.08	0.08	0.08	0.08	0.08	0.08	0.08	0.08	0.08	0.08	0.07	0.07
HH members aged 16–20 years (%)	0.02	0.02	0.03	0.03	0.03	0.03	0.03	0.03	0.02	0.02	0.02	0.03	0.03	0.03	0.03
HH members aged 16–20 years (%)	0.02	0.03	0.04	0.04	0.03	0.03	0.03	0.03	0.02	0.03	0.03	0.03	0.03	0.03	0.03
HH male aged >65 (%)	0.02	0.02	0.02	0.02	0.03	0.02	0.03	0.03	0.04	0.04	0.04	0.04	0.04	0.04	0.05
HH male aged >66 (%)	0.03	0.03	0.02	0.02	0.03	0.03	0.03	0.03	0.03	0.03	0.03	0.03	0.03	0.03	0.04
Observations	7833	7425	7625	6551	7255	7318	8635	8737	8976	8918	8943	8891	9036	9126	9181

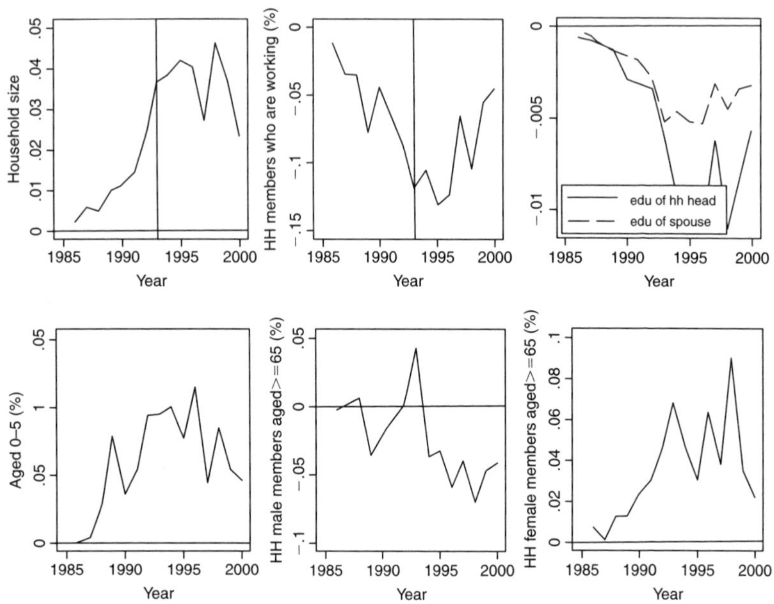

Figure 8.A1 Selected coefficients using 'chained weight CBN poverty line' generated poverty as the dependent variable

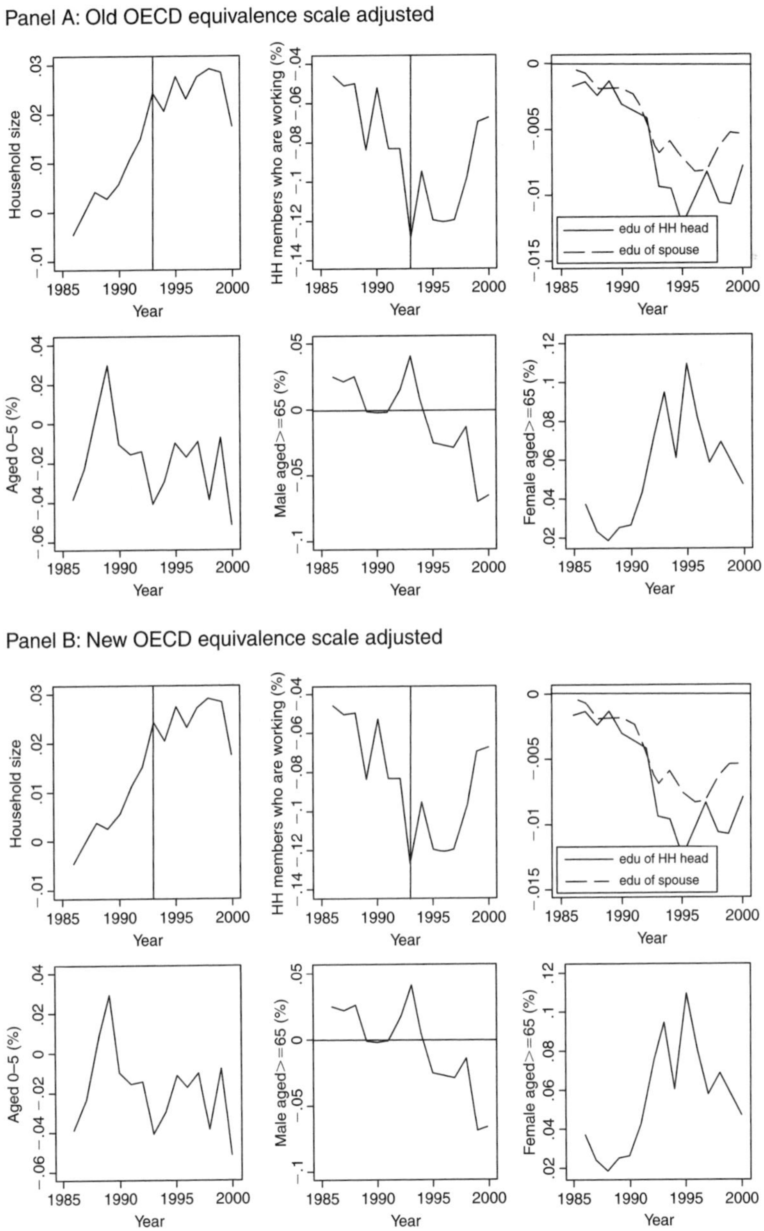

Figure 8.A2 Change in poverty determinants (equivalence scale adjusted): probit estimation
Panel A: Old OECD equivalence scale adjusted
Panel B: New OECD equivalence scale adjusted

9

Poverty, Pro-Poor Growth and Mobility: A Decomposition Framework with Application to China

Yin Zhang and Guanghua Wan

Introduction

In reviewing the current status of poverty research, Thorbecke (2004) noted that most unresolved issues in poverty analysis are related to the dynamics of poverty. One approach to understanding the dynamics of poverty is to decompose the changes of poverty over time, captured by changes in a particular poverty measure, into their two proximate contributing factors: the growth of average income and shifts in the distribution of income (Datt and Ravallion 1992).[1] While a change in the poverty measure represents the total gains (or losses) to the poor, the distributional component of the decomposition can be interpreted as an indication of whether and to what extent aggregate income growth has been 'pro-poor'. If the distributional component is negative (that is, poverty reducing), the poor are said to have benefited more than proportionately from income growth and, as a result, increased their share of total income.

A drawback of the Datt–Ravallion decomposition, and other schemes of poverty decomposition in the same vein, is that only cross-sectional changes in income distribution are considered. The heterogeneity among households implies that not only are their incomes affected by individual shocks, but also that even common shocks to income may have diverse impacts. Therefore, the relative position of a household in income distribution rarely stays the same over time. This means the composition of the poor households is also constantly changing. In any period of time, there will be non-poor households falling into poverty and poor households climbing out of poverty. Even when households are persistently poor, their positions relative to the other poor may move up and down. The growth–distribution decomposition, essentially comparing the cross-sectional features of two income distributions, is innately unable to convey such longitudinal dynamics.

Purely cross-sectional data are, of course, uninformative of longitudinal dynamics of poverty. When panel data are available, however, distinguishing the effects on poverty of the income growth of the poor from those of the changes in the composition of the poor is of practical interest for at least two reasons. First, cross-sectional and longitudinal dynamics do not necessarily coincide in timing or intensity. As found in studies on income mobility, substantial movements up and down the income ladder can occur alongside little change in the cross-sectional distribution of income (Jenkins 2000). Taking a longitudinal perspective can thus help interpret and assess observed poverty trends. Second, various provisions and services of the social security system differ in their effectiveness in facilitating the escape from poverty and in protecting the vulnerable group from falling into poverty. When resources are limited, prioritization is necessary. This, in turn, requires the tracking of income changes in individual households through time and identifying whether promoting pro-poor income growth or providing insurance against downward mobility is of more pressing concern.

The longitudinal dimension of poverty dynamics have been analyzed in different ways. For instance, Bane and Ellwood (1986) study the duration of spells of poverty, Stevens (1994) examines the rates of exit from and entry into poverty, and Jalan and Ravallion (1998) differentiate between transitory and chronic poverty. In this chapter, we take the approach of decomposing poverty trends as summarized by an appropriate poverty index. Despite the growing recognition of the multidimensional nature of poverty, the use of a single poverty index is still of wide practical appeal. It provides a succinct way of evaluating progress and communicating it to the general public. The poverty index to be used is the Sen–Shorrocks–Thon (SST) index. The SST index measures the intensity of poverty. Unlike the more commonly used headcount ratio and poverty gap index, the SST index satisfies the monotonicity and transfer axioms, and has a geometrical representation analogous to the Lorenz curve (Shorrocks 1995). Moreover, as demonstrated by Osberg and Xu (2000), percentage changes in the SST index can be decomposed into three poverty measures that are intuitively interpretable.

In the next section, the SST is decomposed using the intertemporal joint distribution of income. We show that a change of the SST index over time is the sum of two components – a measure of pro-poor growth and an indicator of downward mobility reflecting changes in the composition of the poor. Jenkins and Van Kerm (2003) have examined inequality trends along a similar line. The derived decomposition scheme is then applied to appraising recent poverty developments in China, a country that was exceptionally successful, and yet one that has since the 1990s experienced significant slowdown in poverty reduction. Our analysis focuses on the period between 1988 and 1996, making use of the longitudinal income data from the China Nutrition and Health Survey (CNHS). Concluding remarks close the chapter.

Decomposing poverty dynamics: growth, distribution and mobility

In trying to understand poverty changes over time, one of the leading concerns is the relationship between poverty reduction and income growth. Since equal sharing in the gains from growth among different income groups is an empirical impossibility, the question always arises as to how pro-poor growth is. The common theme of various decomposition schemes attempting to disentangle the effects of growth from those of other concurrent factors is to posit a hypothetical income distribution where the other factors are held constant.[2]

Suppose the poverty index P takes the following form (Sen 1976):

$$P(\mathbf{y};z) = \sum_{i=1}^{q} \theta(z,\mathbf{y},y_i) \tag{9.1}$$

where z is the poverty line, $\mathbf{y}$ is the income vector of the community sorted in ascending order, y_i is the income of the i-th poorest person, and q is the number of individuals with incomes less than z. Note that θ is a function of both y_i and $\mathbf{y}$, implying that the perception of deprivation does not depends on the level of one's income alone, but is also affected by how one's income compares with that of the others in the community.[3]

The growth–distribution decomposition, first proposed by Datt and Ravallion (1992), later improved upon by Shorrocks (1999), exploits the fact that an income distribution can be completely described by its mean income μ and Lorenz curve L. Hence, for a given poverty line, the poverty index can always be expressed as a function of μ and L; that is, $P(\mathbf{y};z) = P(\mu,L;z)$. The changes in P can then be decomposed into a growth component due to changes in μ and a distribution component attributable to changes in L. The Shapley values of the growth component G and the distribution component D can be written as (Shorrocks 1999):

$$\begin{aligned} G &\equiv 0.5\times[P(\mu^1,L^0)-P(\mu^0,L^0)+P(\mu^1,L^1)-P(\mu^0,L^1)] \\ D &\equiv 0.5\times[P(\mu^0,L^1)-P(\mu^0,L^0)+P(\mu^1,L^1)-P(\mu^1,L^0)] \end{aligned} \tag{9.2}$$

where the superscripts index time periods and

$$\Delta P = P^1 - P^0 = P(\mu^1, L^1) - P(\mu^0, L^0) = G + D \tag{9.3}$$

The growth component G represents the reduction in poverty that would have been achieved in the absence of distributional changes. The distribution component D shows whether distributional changes have helped (if D is negative) or hindered (if D is positive) poverty reduction. The poverty reduction observed in reality is a result of the confluence of the growth of mean income and distributional changes. Ravallion and Chen (2003) thus suggest using the mean growth rate of the poor as a measure of pro-poor growth rate (PPG). This PPG rate can be considered as the growth of mean income adjusted for distributional changes embodied in D (Ravallion 2004).

To carry out the decomposition in expression (9.2), it suffices to know the marginal distributions of $\mathbf{y}$. This constitutes a convenience when only cross-sectional data are available. What is not reflected in the growth–distribution decomposition is that the instances of y_i used to calculate P in period 0 may be associated with different individuals than those in period 1 (see expression (9.1)). It follows that the PPG rate obtained as per Ravallion and Chen (2003) may not equal the real gains to those who are poor in period 0. Also neglected in expression (9.2) is the possibility that the relative position of y_i in $\mathbf{y}$ may have changed between the two periods even if both μ and L stay the same. Examining such changes in the composition of the poor requires the knowledge of the joint distribution of the incomes of the two periods. When panel data are available, a different view of poverty dynamics, complementary to that of the growth–distribution decomposition, ensues. To fix ideas, we use the SST index below to show that the same changes in poverty trends can be decomposed into a component measuring the 'pro-poorness' of real income gains to the group who are originally poor, and a component indicating the degree of downward mobility experienced by those who end up poor.

As demonstrated by Osberg and Xu (2002), the SST index is a composite of the headcount ratio of poverty, the average poverty gap ratio among the poor and the Gini coefficient of the poverty gap ratio over the entire population. It also has the desirable theoretical property of satisfying the entire set of Sen's (1976) axioms for poverty measures. The SST index is given by (Shorrocks 1995):

$$SST = P(\mathbf{y}; z) = \frac{1}{n^2} \sum_{y_i < z} [2n - 2r(y_i) + 1] \frac{z - y_i}{z} \tag{9.4}$$

where n is the size of the population, and $r(y_i)$ denotes the rank of y_i in the income distribution. Let $\mathbf{y}^0$ and $\mathbf{y}^1$ be the income vectors of periods 0 and 1 respectively. The difference between the values of the SST index for these two periods SST^1 and SST^0 result from changes in the incomes of three groups of individuals: those who are poor in both periods (that is, $y_i^0 < z$ and $y_i^1 < z$), those who are poor in period 0 only (that is, $y_i^0 < z$ and $y_i^1 \geqslant z$), and those who fall into poverty in period 1 (that is, $y_i^0 \geqslant z$ and $y_i^1 < z$).[4] It can be shown that this difference is the sum of the following two components:

$$PG \equiv -\frac{1}{n^2}\left\{\sum_{y_i^0<z,y_i^1\geq z}[2n-2r(y_i^0)+1]\frac{z-y_i^0}{z} + \sum_{y_i^0<z,y_i^1<z}[2n-2r(y_i^0)+1]\frac{y_i^1-y_i^0}{z}\right\} \quad (9.5)$$

$$DM \equiv \frac{1}{n^2}\sum_{y_i^0\geq z,y_i^1<z}[2n-2r(y_i^1)+1]\frac{z-y_i^1}{z} - \frac{2}{n^2}\sum_{y_i^0<z,y_i^1<z}[r(y_i^1)-r(y_i^0)]\frac{z-y_i^1}{z} \quad (9.6)$$

We name the first component, defined by expression (9.5) the *pro-poor growth* (*PG*) component. It is a weighted average of the absolute income changes of those who are initially poor. For an individual, the maximum income change is the poverty gap $z - y_i^0$, which is attained when the individual escapes poverty in period 1. The weights attached to individual incomes are a decreasing function of their ranks in period 0. Thus, for individuals who are poor in period 0, the lower they are down the income ladder, the greater the marginal impact on the SST index of their income changes in period 1. The income changes of initially non-poor individuals do not affect *PG*. If income growth of the poor occurs mostly among individuals at the very bottom of the income spectrum, *PG* will be negative (that is, poverty reducing). By contrast, if positive growth is concentrated in the poor whose incomes are close to the poverty line, *PG* tends to be positive (that is, poverty increasing). The magnitude and sign of *PG*, therefore, reflect the 'regressivity' of income growth among the poor. This measure of pro-poor growth is close in spirit to the Ravallion–Chen (2003) PPG rate if the PPG rate is calculated over individuals who are poor in the initial period. Both summarize the absolute gains to the poor.[5] Unlike the PPG rate which weights the absolute income changes by the reciprocal of the period-0 income, our weights are rank dependent. This reflects Sen's view that the social value of individual welfare is a relative concept and should depend crucially on the welfare levels of others.

Directly associated with this 'relativist' view of poverty, the terms on the right-hand side of expression (9.6) summarize changes in the income ranking positions of individuals who are poor in the terminal period. This could be made more manifest if the initial ranks of the new additions to the poor group are set to $n + 1/2$.[6] This component is then the weighted average shift of individual income ranks, with the weights given by the poverty gaps in period 1. The poorer an individual is in period 1, the greater is the weight assigned to the change in his income ranks. Since the individuals who end up in the bottom income stratum are more likely to have experienced downward movement in the order of income – that is, $r(y_i^1) < r(y_i^0)$ – the component reflects the extent of downward mobility between period 0 and period 1. We thus call it the *downward mobility* (*DM*) component. If there is no newly impoverished individual in period 1 and the income ranking of those who fail to escape poverty remains the same, the *DM* component will be zero. Otherwise, it is always positive, signifying a change in the composition of the poor.[7]

The decomposition represented by expressions (9.5) and (9.6) reveals a different aspect of poverty dynamics than that presented by the growth–distribution decomposition in expression (9.2). We now use three growth scenarios to show how the assessment of poverty dynamics differs between the two decomposition procedures. These scenarios are detailed in Table 9.1. Assume that individuals A, B and C are associated

Table 9.1 Decompositions of poverty trends in hypothetical income distributions

Scenario	Incomes in Period 1	SST[1]	ΔSST	Growth–distribution decomposition		Longitudinal decomposition	
				Growth	Distribution	PG	DM
1	(2, 3, 4)	0.11	−0.29	−0.20	−0.09	−0.29	0.00
2	(1, 3, 2)	0.40	0.00	0.00	0.00	−0.07	0.07
3	(2, 1, 3)	0.40	0.00	0.00	0.00	−0.09	0.09

Notes:
1 The base period income vector is (1, 2, 3).
2 The poverty line is set at 2.5. (c) $SST^0 = 0.40$.
Source: Authors' calculations.

with an income vector of (1, 2, 3) in period 0. The first scenario is where the income of every individual increases by one unit. The income vector in period 1 is thus (2, 3, 4). With the poverty line fixed at 2.5, this would lead to a fall in the SST index from 0.40 to 0.11, signifying a reduction in the intensity of poverty. The growth–distribution decomposition would characterize this as a situation with positive overall income growth ($G = -0.2$) and favourable distributional changes ($D = -0.09$), while the longitudinal decomposition would show that there is pro-poor growth ($PG = -0.29$) and there is no downward mobility ($DM = 0$).

In the second scenario, one poor individual switches position with one rich individual in period 1. The income vector in period 1 changes to (1, 3, 2). Using the growth–distribution decomposition, one would conclude that there is no change in the wellbeing of the poor since the SST index stays the same and the growth and distribution components are all equal to zero. However, the *PG* component of the longitudinal decomposition is negative in this case, suggesting an increase in the welfare of those who were originally poor (the income of individual B increases from 2 to 3). Meanwhile, the *DM* component would be positive and of the same absolute value as the *PG* component, suggesting a welfare loss to society due to the existence of downward mobility (individual C falls into poverty).

The last scenario is where two poor individuals A and B switch positions in period 1. The growth–distribution decomposition, again, would not identify any welfare changes. The longitudinal decomposition would show that the growth pattern is still pro-poor (since the income change of the poorer is given a higher weight), but there is also a welfare loss in the form of downward mobility which balances out the welfare gain.

The above three examples show that the proposed decomposition in expressions (9.5) and (9.6) can convey information contained in the growth–distribution decomposition consistently (as for scenario 1). Its added value, however, lies in its ability to throw light on occasions where cross-sectional stability exists alongside large intra-distribution movements. As in the last two scenarios, such movements are much less visible via the growth–distribution decomposition. It is not difficult to conjure up real-life situations where this type of zero-sum scenario might be played out. For example, when a firm moves its operation from one city to another city in the same province, the relocation might reduce poverty in the local community of the new site at the cost of increased poverty in the old site, while leaving total poverty in the province largely unchanged. Or when, in an effort to alleviate poverty in certain parts of the country, the central government grants tax concessions to new investments in the those areas: this policy may reduce poverty in the targeted areas but inadvertently increase poverty in some other parts of the country. In these cases, although the headline poverty index may not change, society is unlikely to be indifferent to the outcomes. Ignoring the changes in the composition of the poor can thus lead to erroneous evaluation of poverty reduction policy.

Decomposition of poverty trends in China

In this section, we apply the longitudinal decomposition to poverty trends in China from the late 1980s to the mid-1990s. A quick review of China's record of growth, poverty reduction and economic reform suggests that this might be a period of longitudinal flux. While significant progress against poverty accompanied rapid economic growth in the earlier years, poverty reduction nearly halted in the late 1980s and early 1990s, and only recovered in the mid-1990s, even though growth remained robust throughout (Ravallion and Chen 2004). In the meantime, the economy underwent profound structural changes, resulting in changing fortunes for different regions, industries and social groups.[8] Might the balancing effect of large numbers of entries into and exits from poverty, as well as 'seat-switching' among the poor, partly explain the weak responsiveness of poverty reduction to growth in this period?

Data

That the longitudinal decomposition requires individual/household level panel data severely limits the choices of data for carrying out such analysis. The rural and urban household surveys administered by China's National Bureau of Statistics (NBS) have been the most important data source for research about poverty and income inequality issues concerning China. However, the NBS surveys have only been published in highly aggregated format, rendering them unusable for the purpose of this study. The data we use come from the China Health and Nutrition Survey (CHNS), a joint project run by the Carolina Population Centre at the University of North Carolina, the National Institute of Nutrition and Food Safety, and the Chinese Centre for Disease Control and Prevention. The survey was first conducted in 1989, and repeated in 1991, 1993, 1997 and 2000. The data from the 2000 round were pending cleaning up at the time of writing. In addition, there are significant differences in reported household sizes between the 1991 round and the 1989 and 1993 rounds, casting doubts on the reliability of the 1991 data. Thus, only data from the 1989, 1993 and 1997 rounds are used. As the income data are traceable through different rounds at the household level but not at the individual level, a balanced panel of 2664 households is formed. Of these, 740 are urban households and 1924 are rural households.[9]

Several deficiencies in the NBS survey design are avoided in the CHNS. These include the incomplete and inconsistent coverage of non-monetary incomes in the NBS urban household survey, the undervaluation of self-consumed production in the NBS rural household survey, and the failure in both the urban and the rural surveys to include imputed rents for owner-occupied housing. Furthermore, the CHNS collects local price information alongside income data so that spatial variations in the cost of living can be accounted for when comparing incomes across localities.[10] The nominal income figures in our panel have been converted to their 1988 values using the CHNS cost-of-living indices.[11]

Despite the above advantages over the NBS surveys, the CHNS has a rather limited sampling frame. The assembled panel covers seven provinces:[12] Jiangsu and Shandong in the booming coastal region, Guangxi and Guizhou from the southwest, and Henan, Hubei and Hunan in central China. While the sample is reflective of a large proportion of China's economic geography, there remains the question whether poverty developments in these provinces can be generalized to the national level. To assess the likelihood and direction of bias entailed by such generalization, it is useful to compare average income growth rates and Gini indices based on the NBS surveys with those based on the CHNS. This is done in Table 9.2.

As shown on the left side of Table 9.2, both sets of growth rates indicate rapid increase of per capita income during the 1988–96 period in urban as well as rural areas, though urban incomes were growing faster than rural incomes. Both also pick up a slowdown in urban income growth in the second half of the period. However, a major difference exists in rural income growth rates concerning the 1988–92 period, with the estimate based on the CHNS panel more than twice the size of that based on the NBS national average rural income. On the right-hand side of Table 9.2, the NBS Gini coefficients are taken from Ravallion and Chen (2004) who managed to gain access to household level NBS survey data. It is easily seen that the two sets of Gini estimates agree on a number of points. Most noticeable of these is that, unlike in most developing economies, income distribution in China is less equal among rural households than it is among urban households. However, urban income distribution worsened significantly during the period, with the 1996 Gini coefficient 35–40 per cent higher than its 1988 level. Changes in inequality were much less pronounced in rural areas. The Gini estimates

Table 9.2 Comparison of income growth and inequality

Period	Income growth				Year	Gini coefficient			
	NBS		CHNS			NBS		CHNS	
	Rural	Urban	Rural	Urban		Rural	Urban	Rural	Urban
1988–92	3.17	8.13	6.69	7.37	1988	29.71	21.08	40.31	26.10
1992–96	5.46	6.46	4.15	4.55	1992	32.03	24.18	40.54	34.71
1988–96	4.48	7.18	5.42	5.96	1996	32.98	28.52	39.47	36.32

Notes:
1 Income growth is calculated as annual exponential growth rate of average per capita income.
2 Growth rates listed in columns under 'NBS' are based on real per capita income indices reported in *Statistical Yearbook of China 2003*.
3 Gini coefficients listed in columns under 'NBS' are taken from Ravallion and Chen (2004).
4 Figures listed in columns under 'CHNS' are based on the panel compiled from the 1989, 1993 and 1997 rounds of the CHNS.
5 All figures are expressed in percentage points.
Sources: *Statistical Yearbook of China 2003*, Ravallion and Chen (2004) and authors' calculations.

based on the CHNS panel actually indicate a slight decrease in inequality, especially during 1992–96. While the inequality trends based on the two datasets seem to be largely in accord, there are substantial differences regarding inequality levels. The CHNS Gini coefficients are much higher, sometimes more than 10 percentage points above the NBS estimates. Since we are essentially concerned with the shifts in income distribution, however, this result should cause less unease than if there were large discrepancies in the changes of the Gini coefficients.

The preceding discussion shows that on account of the two main aspects of income distribution dynamics – mean income growth and changes in overall inequality – the CHNS urban sample appears to match up well with the NBS urban household sample. This suggests that, despite its limited scale and geographical coverage, the CHNS urban sample can serve as a window on nationwide urban poverty developments.

The comparison between the CHNS and NBS rural samples is not as reassuring. The large gaps between the estimated growth rates signal systematic differences between the two samples. Such differences might stem from the fact that the CHNS rural sample has a rather high proportion of suburban households. Indeed, 397 out of the 1924 (or just over one fifth of) households in the CHNS rural sample reside in suburbs. The incomes of suburban households are likely to be highly correlated with those of their urban neighbours. They are also likely to be higher than the incomes of villagers living far away from cities. If true, this would explain the similar rural and urban growth patterns in the CHNS panel (see Table 9.2) and, to the extent that the proportion of suburban households in the NBS sample is smaller, also lead to the higher level of rural inequality in the CHNS panel. To gauge how much this feature of the CHNS survey design can account for the differences between the two samples, we excluded suburban households from the CHNS rural panel and recalculated growth rates and Gini coefficients based on the smaller sample. As it turns out, the average per capita incomes of the smaller sample are 110–170 *yuan* lower than those of the full rural sample. However, excluding suburban households only marginally reduces the growth rate for 1988–92 and the Gini coefficients. As far as income distribution changes are concerned, therefore, the inclusion of a high proportion of suburban households does not seem to have introduced serious sampling bias into the CHNS rural sample.

Another possible explanation for the differences is that the sampling frame of the CHNS is simply too small to be representative of China's vast and diverse countryside. An analysis of the household-level NBS data should be able to verify whether that is the case. Without access to such data and because the NBS survey is not without its own problems, one should probably work with the imperfect CHNS data while bearing in mind that the results regarding rural poverty pertain to the particular CHNS sample in question and may or may not be representative of the nation at large.

Poverty intensity trends and decomposition

Mindful of the above qualifications, we now turn to the SST index estimates based on the CHNS panel. For the lack of a better alternative, the US$1-a-day threshold is adopted as our principle poverty line. Its 1988 PPP value stands at RMB 391.7 per year.[13] Osberg and Xu (2006) argue for China to use relative poverty lines on the grounds that rapid income growth is increasingly rendering extreme poverty[14] irrelevant and pushing relative deprivation to the forefront. To assess the sensitivity of poverty trends to the choice of poverty line, we also calculated the SST index using one half of the median income as the poverty line. Table 9.3 presents the results for the entire CHNS panel and for the rural and urban sub-samples separately.

The estimated values of the SST index in the left panel of Table 9.3 show that until the mid-1990s the intensity of extreme poverty was several times higher among rural households than it was among urban households. This gaping difference is corroborated by the figures in the middle panel, where the poverty line for each year is half the median per

Table 9.3 Estimates of the SST index with different poverty lines

Year	PPP US$1 per day		Half median income (combined)		Half median income	
	SST	SE	SST	SE	SST	SE
1988	136.00	6.32	156.64	6.13		
1992	90.25	5.07	139.05	6.57		
1996	65.37	4.46	143.18	6.41		
Rural						
1988	175.07	8.80	200.33	8.05	159.82	7.69
1992	107.12	6.99	163.00	7.53	137.08	7.30
1996	73.98	5.59	164.44	7.33	132.40	6.87
Urban						
1988	26.77	5.26	33.13	5.77	61.04	7.35
1992	45.11	7.75	73.96	8.83	127.10	10.90
1996	42.63	7.37	85.27	10.23	128.46	11.92

Notes:
1 The poverty line is alternatively defined as: for the left panel, the 1988 PPP value of US$1 per day; for the middle panel, one half of the median income of the combined rural and urban sample; and for the right panel, one half of the median income of the rural sample and one half of the median income of the urban sample.
2 There are altogether 2,664 households in the panel, of which 1,924 are rural households and 740 are urban households.
3 The standard errors are calculated from 500 bootstrap iterations.
4 The figures reported in the table are the estimated values multiplied by 1,000.
Source: Authors' calculations.

capita income for that year of all households in the panel. Here, again, the value of the rural SST index is found to be at least twice as great as that of the urban SST index. This comes, of course, as little surprise. Given the large and widening urban–rural income gap,[15] applying the same poverty line to rural and urban households alike will show higher poverty intensity in rural areas. A comparison of the rural and urban Gini coefficients in Table 9.2 suggests, however, that poor rural households may be further disadvantaged by higher levels of income inequality in rural China. In obtaining the results in the right panel, one half of the median rural per capita income of each year is used as the rural poverty line. Similarly, the urban poverty line is one half of the median urban per capita income of the corresponding year. As can be seen, this leads to higher estimated poverty intensity than using the US$1-a-day poverty line for both rural and urban samples in nearly all years. The only exception is the 1988 estimate of the rural SST index. If the CHNS panel is nationally representative, this would indicate that, even for rural poverty assessment, the US$1-a-day threshold has become a more stringent poverty line than one half of the median income. There is, hence, even less justification for using poverty lines lower than US$1 a day.[16]

The three sets of SST index estimates also appear to be in agreement over poverty trends. The period 1988–92 saw a relatively large reduction in rural poverty intensity (in the range of 15–40 per cent of the 1988 level), and a sharp rise in urban poverty intensity (the SST index more than doubled in the two cases using a relative poverty line). During 1992–96, poverty reduction in rural areas either slowed down or stagnated, while the worsening of urban poverty was halted, but far from being reversed. Poverty trends in the combined rural and urban panel are expectedly driven by developments in the rural sample, since rural households make up over 70 per cent of the combined sample and the magnitude of absolute changes of the rural SST index is several times greater than that of the urban SST index.

Poverty trends expressed as changes in the SST index can be translated into more familiar terms. Osberg and Xu (2002) note that the percentage change in the SST index is approximately the sum of the percentage changes in the headcount ratio and average poverty gap ratio among the poor.[17] Our results from this exercise show that changes in both rural and urban SST indices during the sample period were mostly due to changes in the respective headcount ratios. More specifically, over four fifths of the drop of the rural SST index in 1988–92 and nearly all that during 1992–96 consisted in reductions of the rural headcount ratio.[18] As for the urban SST index, increase of the urban headcount ratio constituted 70 per cent of its rise between 1988 and 1992. The 1996 urban SST index would have been lower, at 40.25 rather than 42.63 (see Table 9.3), if the decrease of the headcount ratio has not been half offset by an increase in the average poverty gap.[19]

Based on the above evidence, poverty developments during the late 1980s and early 1990s among households in the CHNS panel can be summarized as follows: there was sustained reduction in rural poverty, and the reduction was chiefly manifested in a substantially lower incidence of extreme poverty in 1996 as compared to that in 1988. By comparison, urban poverty increased. Although the average poverty gap ratio was creeping up (that is, the poor became poorer on average) over the entire period, increased intensity in urban poverty was primarily the result of a rise in poverty incidence in the late 1980s.

The developments in rural and urban poverty stand in obvious contrast to each other, especially in view of the higher growth rates of average urban per capita income. The Gini coefficients in Table 9.2 might lead one to conclude that the key to the differential poverty performances is the different inequality trends in the rural and urban samples. That the rural Gini coefficient was stable, and even decreased slightly, indicates, it might be argued, that the incomes of the rural poor were growing in proportion to, if not faster than, the incomes of other rural households. Similarly, the constantly rising urban Gini coefficient is a sign that the urban poor were getting an increasingly small proportion of total urban income, and hence the increases in both the headcount ratio and the average poverty gap ratio despite rapid growth of average urban income. This reasoning is not so much wrong as incomplete, for it fails to take into account two important aspects of the relationship between an aggregate inequality index and the distribution of relative income.

The first of the two aspects is that there is no exact mapping between the value of an aggregate inequality index and the Lorenz curve. In other words, the Gini coefficients of two distinct income distributions may have the same value if their Lorenz curves intersect. This implies that for the CHNS rural sample, for example, distributional changes unfavourable to the poor may have been offset by inequality reducing changes in the middle and/or high income ranges, so as to leave the aggregate Gini little altered. To gauge the contribution by distributional shifts to poverty trends, the Lorenz curve itself has to be involved. This is what the growth–distribution decomposition does.

As the decomposition results in Table 9.4 show, income growth was the dominant factor for the reduction of rural poverty. Changes in rural relative income distribution were small but indeed advantageous to the poor. Even without these changes, the record of rural poverty reduction would still be quite impressive. Note that between 1988 and 1992, distributional changes helped reduce rural poverty: the distribution component of the decomposition is negative in value. This is an example of the nonlinear relationship between the Gini coefficient and the Lorenz curve, since the rural Gini coefficient for 1992 was not smaller; if anything, it was greater than the 1988 Gini coefficient (see Table 9.2). For the urban sample, the distributional changes were adverse to the poor throughout the period and stymied progress in urban poverty reduction. Distributional changes in the late 1980s were particularly detrimental. According to the decomposition results, if urban income growth had been distribution neutral in 1988–92, urban poverty would have been eliminated by 1996.

The second of the two aspects is that changes in aggregate inequality measures by definition do not capture the re-ranking of income units in the income pecking order. Should rank switching be a concern for poverty analysis? Perhaps not in all circumstances. However, one suspects

Table 9.4 Decomposition of poverty trends in China

Year	SST	SE	Period	ΔSST	Growth-distribution decomposition		Longitudinal decomposition	
					Growth	Distribution	PG	DM
1988	136.00	6.32	1988–92	−45.75	−51.30	5.55	−74.51	28.76
1992	90.25	5.07	1992–96	−24.88	−22.66	−2.22	−43.95	19.07
1996	65.37	4.46	1988–96	−70.63	−71.58	0.95	−89.84	19.20
Rural								
1988	175.07	8.80	1988–92	−67.95	−59.05	−8.90	−103.80	35.85
1992	107.12	6.99	1992–96	−33.14	−25.56	−7.58	−55.97	22.83
1996	73.98	5.59	1988–96	−101.09	−83.76	−17.33	−123.45	22.37
Urban								
1988	26.77	5.26	1988–92	18.34	−24.48	42.82	2.31	16.03
1992	45.11	7.75	1992–96	−2.48	−13.24	10.76	−13.48	11.00
1996	42.63	7.37	1988–96	15.86	−30.79	46.65	2.96	12.91

Notes:
1 The poverty line used is the 1988 PPP value of US$1 per day.
2 There are altogether 2,664 households in the panel, of which 1,924 are rural households and 740 are urban households.
3 The standard errors are calculated from 500 bootstrap iterations.
4 The figures reported in the table are the estimated values multiplied by 1,000.
Source: Authors' calculations.

that policy makers seeking effective targeted intervention for poverty reduction would not be indifferent to whether those poor households at the conclusion of a poverty alleviation programme were the same ones that had started out poor. As the illustrative example in Table 9.1 shows, intra-distribution movements do not show up as shifts in the Lorenz curve. This excludes the use of growth–distribution decomposition excluding for examining re-ranking dynamics. Rather, the longitudinal decomposition in expressions (9.5) and (9.6) should be used. The results from applying it to the CHNS panel are tabulated in the last two columns of Table 9.4.

As can be seen, the *PG* component of rural poverty trends is negative for both 1988–92 and 1992–96, indicating that, throughout the period under study, it was the poorer households of the rural poor that tended to experience larger increases in their incomes. As a result of 'pro-poor' growth, 80 per cent of the rural households that were poor in 1988 had escaped poverty by 1996. Of those remaining in poverty in 1996, half were earning more than they did in 1988. The magnitude of the *DM* component suggests that there was considerable re-ranking in action. Recall that the *DM* component sums up two types of intra-distribution movements: rank switching among the income units that are poor in both the beginning and the terminal years of a period, and movements down the income pecking order of the income units that fall into poverty during the period. A comparison of the contributions by the two to the *DM* component of rural poverty trends reveals the latter to be the dominant factor. About 60–70 per cent of the rural households who were poor in the terminal year of each period had incomes above the poverty line in the beginning year of the same period.

Movements into and out of poverty are also very visible in the urban sample. In fact, the *DM* component of urban poverty trends almost solely reflects changes in the income rankings of the newly impoverished, as they constitute 82–94 per cent of the poor households in any year. Unlike the rural sample, however, the poverty-increasing effects of the *DM* component are not dominated by those of a poverty-reducing *PG* component. The *PG* component for 1988–92 is even positive, suggesting that negative income growth suffered by some poor households outweighed the positive income growth of the other households; the 1988 poor households, as a whole, did not see their incomes rise between 1988 and 1992. A look at the underlying income data shows that positive income growth in this period mostly happened to those households whose incomes were not far below the poverty line. The growth pattern changed during 1992–96, so that on the whole growth became pro-poor (as the negative *PG* component for this period demonstrates).

The evidence in Table 9.4 allows the following summary account of the distribution dynamics underlying the rural and urban poverty trends in the CHNS panel. The distribution of rural relative income (that is, the rural Lorenz curve) did not seem to have undergone much change during the period under review. This ensured that the full potential for poverty reduction created by rapid rural income growth was realized. Contemporaneous with the stability of the cross-section distribution were active intra-distribution movements. Hence, although rural income growth was 'pro-poor' (in the sense that poorer households tended to experience positive and larger income changes) and in each period the majority of the poor moved out of poverty, the constant new entries into poverty and the ever-changing positions of the poor in the income pecking order meant that rural poverty was not eliminated: similar intra-distribution dynamics were also exhibited by the urban income panel. Unlike the rural panel, however, there were also shifts in the cross-section distribution of urban relative income, which increased urban inequality in general and disadvantaged the urban poor in particular. As a result, urban income growth was not always pro-poor. Though still less severe than rural poverty, urban poverty persisted and may have even worsened, notwithstanding rapid growth of the average urban income.

Conclusion

A widely used device for analyzing poverty dynamics is decomposing poverty trends into a growth component and a distributional component. While the growth–distribution decomposition provides information on the relative importance of average income growth versus distributional changes for poverty reduction, it cannot reflect changes in the composition of the poor. Such changes are worthy of examination because they shed light on the intra-distribution dynamics that partly underlie changes (or lack thereof) in the cross-section distribution of income. The longitudinal poverty decomposition proposed in this chapter offers a framework for incorporating the intra-distribution movements of income units into the analysis of poverty dynamics. It is shown that changes in the SST index over time can be decomposed into two components: one component reflects the 'regressivity' of income growth among the original poor, the other measures the extent of downward mobility experienced by the incumbent poor.

The longitudinal decomposition scheme, along with the growth–distribution decomposition, has been applied to appraising poverty developments in China between 1988 and 1996, using a panel assembled from the CHNS data. It is found that the sustained decline in rural poverty as measured by the SST index was primarily the result of robust rural income growth. The cross-section distribution of rural income was stable over the entire period. Thus, despite a high level of income inequality (with the Gini coefficient at around 40 per cent), rural income growth in this period appeared to be broad-based. A number of forces could be at work for this to have taken place. A major factor, however, seems to be that the increases in farming incomes contributed half of the total addition to rural income during those years.[20] Since the land tenure system at the time essentially enforced egalitarian access to land, the gains were shared fairly equally among rural households. This raises doubts about the sustainability of the distribution-neutral growth pattern. The importance of farming as a rural income source is set to decline and, as revealed by the large value of the rural Gini coefficient, the distribution of incomes from non-farm activities is highly unequal. Unless action is taken to improve the distribution of incomes from non-farm activities, there will come a time when rural income growth becomes disequalizing.

In contrast to the significant reduction in rural poverty, no progress was made against urban poverty, even though urban income inequality was lower at the start of the period and urban average income growth higher during the period. The decomposition results attribute that outcome entirely to adverse changes in the cross-section distribution of urban income. More worryingly, the deterioration of the position of the poor in urban income distribution appeared to reflect a long-term trend rather than being cyclical. A most probable cause for the deterioration was rising urban unemployment, which in turn was mainly caused by the ongoing restructuring of state-owned and collective enterprises during the period.

The longitudinal decomposition results indicate high poverty entry and exit rates for both rural and urban samples. This suggests that a large proportion of poverty observed in cross-section data might be transient poverty. Based only on three non-consecutive years of data, however, this result must be considered preliminary and need to be corroborated by data from the more recent CHNS rounds.

Notes

1 The Datt–Ravallion decomposition is not exact, in that it contains an interaction term of income growth and distributional shifts. The Shapley value decomposition proposed in Shorrocks (1999) overcomes the problem.
2 The type of poverty decomposition under discussion here does not include decomposition by population subgroup or factor component. Nor does it include the decomposition proposed by Osberg and Xu (2000).
3 This is not the case for the Atkinson (1987) class of additively separable poverty measures where only the level of individual income matters.
4 As the SST index satisfies the focus axiom, it is not affected by changes in the incomes of individuals who are not poor in either period.
5 Incidentally, our pro-poor growth measure also satisfies the focus, monotonicity and transfer axioms.
6 Intuitively, this arrangement could be justified as follows: if poverty is considered strictly inferior to being non-poor, descending into poverty must represent a downward movement of one's welfare status in the society. No matter how high the new poor rank currently, their initial income ranks should still be higher and, thus, must be given the maximum rank possible.
7 Although the *PG* and *DM* components can both be redefined in the Shapley value fashion, we feel expressions (9.5) and (9.6) better suit our intention of designating these two components as, respectively, a measure of pro-poor income changes and a measure of downward mobility.
8 For example, many opportunities opened up in the coastal region and the export industries, whereas lay-offs and unemployment increased in some historically well off inland provinces and heavy industries.
9 More details are available on the CHNS website at www.cpc.unc.edu/projects/china.

10 The NBS also compiles and publishes provincial price indices. The indices trace price changes within each province, but cannot by themselves be used to compare price levels across provinces.
11 The reference period of the income information collected in each round is the year immediately before the survey year. Hence, our panel contains annual household incomes for 1988, 1992 and 1996.
12 Two other provinces, Liaoning and Heilongjiang, were included in some but not all of the survey rounds.
13 The US$1-a-day poverty line has been criticized for the many inaccuracies and uncertainties involved in estimating PPP. For instance, the basket of goods and services used to calculate the PPP can diverge greatly from the spending patterns of the poor. A number of calculation methods exist, and they sometimes produce quite different estimates. The PPP can also be affected by the choice of benchmark year.
14 Extreme poverty is usually defined as living on less than US$1 a day per person. We use this term loosely to refer to earning less than US$1 a day per person.
15 In the CHNS panel, the average per capita income of the urban households is 30–40 per cent higher than that of the rural households.
16 The official rural poverty line in 2006 is 680 *yuan*, which, if using the 2003 PPP *yuan*/dollar rate, is below the US$1-a-day threshold.
17 The SST index is the product of three terms: the headcount ratio, the average poverty gap ratio among the poor, and 1 plus the Gini coefficient of the poverty gap ratio over the entire population. According to Osberg and Xu (2002), changes in the last term are empirically small, and hence should have negligible effects on the SST index. Our calculations show that, for the CHNS data, their observation describes urban poverty well. Changes in the last term, which essentially reflect changes in inequality among the poor, contribute less than 1 per cent of the total changes in the urban SST index. For rural poverty, the contribution by changes in inequality among the poor is discernible but small, in the range of 3–6 per cent of the total change in the rural SST index.
18 The rural headcount ratios of extreme poverty and average poverty gap ratios are, respectively: 24.6 per cent and 38.7 per cent for 1988, 16.0 per cent and 35.2 per cent for 1992, and 10.8 per cent and 35.6 per cent for 1996.
19 The urban headcount ratios for 1988, 1992 and 1996 are, respectively: 4.6 per cent, 6.6 per cent, and 5.9 per cent. The urban average poverty gap ratios for the three years are, respectively: 29.6 per cent, 34.8 per cent, and 36.6 per cent.
20 This was estimated by the authors based on statistics reported in *Statistical Yearbook of China 1996 and 1997.*

References

Atkinson, A.B. (1987) 'On the Measurement of Poverty', *Econometrica*, 55: 749–64.

Bane, M.J. and Ellwood, D. (1986) 'Slipping Into and Out of Poverty: The Dynamics of Spells', *Journal of Human Resources*, 21: 1–23.

Datt, G. and Ravallion, M. (1992) 'Growth and Redistribution Components of Changes in Poverty Measures: A Decomposition With Applications to Brazil and India in the 1980s', *Journal of Development Economics*, 38: 275–95.

Jalan, J. and Ravallion, M. (1998) 'Transient Poverty in Post-Reform Rural China', *Journal of Comparative Economics*, 26: 338–57.
Jenkins, S.P. (2000) 'Modelling Household Income Dynamics', *Journal of Population Economics*, 13: 529–67.
Jenkins, S.P. and Van Kerm, P. (2003) 'Trends in Income Inequality, Pro-Poor Income Growth and Income Mobility', IZA Discussion Papers 904 (Bonn: Institute for the Study of Labour).
Osberg, L. and Xu, K. (2000) 'International Comparisons of Poverty Intensity: Index Decomposition and Bootstrap Inference', *Journal of Human Resources*, 35: 51–81.
Osberg, L. and Xu, K. (2002) 'The Social Welfare Implications, Decomposability, and Geometry of the Sen Family of Poverty Indices', *Canadian Journal of Economics*, 35, 1: 138–52.
Osberg, L. and Xu, K. (2006) 'How Should We Measure Global Poverty in a Changing World?', WIDER Research Paper RP2006/64 (Helsinki: UNU-WIDER).
Ravallion, M. (2004) 'Pro-Poor Growth: A Primer', Policy Research Working Paper 3242 (Washington, DC: World Bank).
Ravallion, M. and Chen, S. (2003) 'Measuring Pro-Poor Growth', *Economics Letters*, 78: 93–9.
Ravallion, M. and Chen, S. (2004) 'China's (Uneven) Progress Against Poverty', Policy Research Working Paper 3408 (Washington DC: World Bank).
Sen, A. (1976) 'Poverty: An Ordinal Approach to Measurement', *Econometrica*, 44: 219–31.
Shorrocks, A.F. (1995) 'Revisiting the Sen Poverty Index', *Econometrica*, 63: 1225–30.
Shorrocks, A.F. (1999) 'Decomposition Procedures for Distributional Analysis: A Unified Framework Based on the Shapley Value', Mimeo, University of Essex.
Statistical Yearbook of China (2003) (Beijing: State Statistical Press).
Stevens, A.H. (1994) 'Persistence in Poverty and Welfare: The Dynamics of Poverty Spells: Updating Bane and Ellwood', *American Economic Review*, 84: 34–7.
Thorbecke, E. (2004) 'Conceptual and Measurement Issues in Poverty Analysis', Discussion Paper 2004/04 (Helsinki: UNU-WIDER).

Index

Notes: f = figure; n = note; t = table; **bold** = extended discussion or heading emphasized in the main text.